International Time Zones

The Earth rotates through 360° in 24 hours, and so moves 15° every hour. The World is divided into 24 standard time zones, each centred on lines of longitude at 15° intervals.

The Greenwich meridian lies on the centre of the first zone. All places to the west of Greenwich are one hour behind for every 15° of longitude; places to the east are ahead by one hour for every 15°.

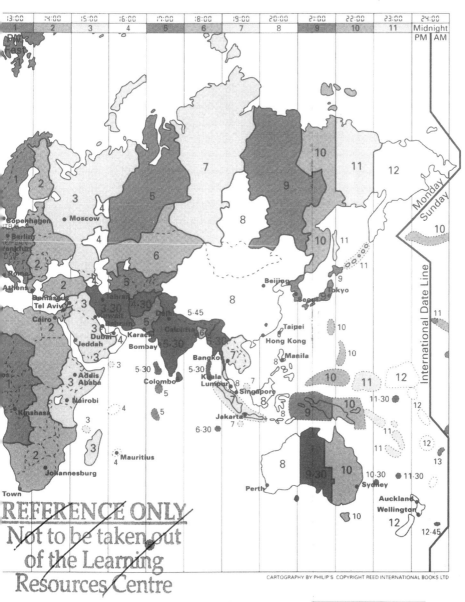

CARTOGRAPHY BY PHILIP'S COPYRIGHT REED INTERNATIONAL BOOKS LTD

Zones using Greenwich Mean Time

Half hour zones

Zones fast of Greenwich Mean Time

Equatorial scale 1:160 000 000

- - - - - International boundaries

——— Time zone boundaries

━━━ International date line

Noon   1   2

Actual Solar Time when noon at Greenwich is shown along the top of the map.

Note: Certain of the time zones are affected by the incidence of "Summer Time" in countries where it is adopted.

B47687

Dictionary of Travel, Tourism and Hospitality

By the same author

Britain – Workshop or Service Centre to the World?
The British Hotel and Catering Industry
The Business of Hotels (with H. Ingram)
Europeans on Holiday
Higher Education and Research in Tourism in Western Europe
Historical Development of Tourism (with A.J. Burkart)
Holiday Surveys Examined
The Management of Tourism (with A.J. Burkart eds)
Managing Tourism (ed.)
A Manual of Hotel Reception (with J.R.S. Beavis)
Paying Guests
Profile of the Hotel and Catering Industry (with D.W. Airey)
Tourism and Hospitality in the 21st Century (with A. Lockwood eds)
Tourism and Productivity
Tourism Council of the South Pacific Corporate Plan
Tourism Employment in Wales
Tourism: Past, Present and Future (with A.J. Burkart)
Trends in Tourism: World Experience and England's Prospects
Trends in World Tourism
Understanding Tourism
Your Manpower (with J. Denton)

Dictionary of Travel, Tourism and Hospitality

S. Medlik

Third edition

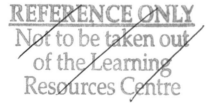

OXFORD AMSTERDAM BOSTON LONDON NEW YORK PARIS
SAN DIEGO SAN FRANCISCO SINGAPORE SYDNEY TOKYO

Butterworth-Heinemann
An imprint of Elsevier Science
Linacre House, Jordan Hill, Oxford OX2 8DP
200 Wheeler Road, Burlington MA 01803

First published 1993
Reprinted (with amendments) 1994
Second edition 1996
Third edition 2003

British Library Cataloguing in Publication Data
A catalogue record for this book is available from the British Library

Library of Congress Cataloguing in Publication Data
A catalogue record for this book is available from the Library of Congress

ISBN 0 7506 5650 6

For information on all Butterworth-Heinemann publications
visit our website at www.bh.com

Printed and bound in Great Britain by Biddles Ltd
www.biddles.co.uk
Composition by Scribe Design, Gillingham, Kent, UK

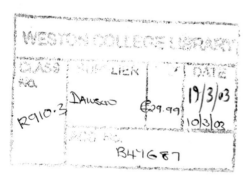

Contents

Preface   vii

Part 1
Dictionary of Terms   1

Part 2
International Organizations   187

Part 3
National Organizations   201
   Australia and New Zealand   203
   North America   206
   United Kingdom and Ireland   210

Part 4
Biographical Dictionary: Who Was Who   221

Part 5
Abbreviations   231

Part 6
Countries of the World   255

Part 7
Bibliography   267

Comments on earlier editions

'An authoritative new resource ... deserving a place on many bookshelves.'
Travel & Tourism Programme News

'... this important contribution to the literature of the world's biggest industry.'
Tourism Management

'His dictionary will, I predict, be an essential reference book on the shelves of all tourism teaching academics, and for many of their students it will be that invaluable support at critical moments of confusion and uncertainty. Professor Medlik's unique Dictionary is very simply a good buy ...'
Tourism, The Bulletin of the Tourism Society

'... it will become a very useful source of reference for the industry for years to come.'
Hotel, Catering & Institutional Management Association

'Excellent compendium for all tourism students.'
Swansea Institute of Higher Education

'... it will provide a real service for the industry.'
University of Nevada, Las Vegas

'This book is recommended to those in the fields of travel, tourism and hospitality throughout the world, including those who perceive dictionaries as dull things. This one is certainly not.'
Annals of Tourism Research

'... an exceptional dictionary of current terms used in travel, tourism and hospitality ... besides being an excellent authority on tourism terms today, browsing this dictionary is a treat.'
Journal of Travel Research

'Easy to read, well expressed, extensive, accurate.'
British Hospitality Association

'It fills a real need ... we will certainly recommend it to students on our business and operational management programmes.'
Hotel & Catering Training Company

Preface

'When *I* use a word', Humpty Dumpty said in a rather scornful tone, 'it means just what I choose it to mean – neither more nor less.'

'The question is', said Alice, 'whether you *can* make words mean different things.'

'The question is', said Humpty Dumpty, 'which is to be the master – that's all.'

Lewis Carroll, *Alice in Wonderland*

Of the three broad related fields covered by this volume, *travel* is the most common activity for most people. It includes any journey from one place to another, over short or long distances; to, from and as part of one's work, during leisure and for any purpose; using any mode of transport by air, land or sea. Those who travel are tourists, but also commuters, diplomats, migrants, nomads, refugees, as well as other travellers. All tourism includes some travel but not all travel is tourism.

For most people *tourism* has a connotation of leisure travel and tends to be synonymous with holidays (vacations). This is also reflected in dictionaries, which commonly refer to tourism as travel for pleasure. By contrast, tourist boards and others concerned with the development, marketing and coordination of tourism in their countries tend to take a broader view; for them tourism means travel for most purposes, with such exceptions as travel to work, to migrate and as part of local and neighbourhood activities. Between these ends of the spectrum lies business usage, the language of those who earn their living from serving the tourists; most of them see tourism in terms of the products they sell and the markets they serve. Academics are not a homogenous breed, and between them probably cover the whole spectrum.

Travel for pleasure with an overnight stay appears to be the lowest common denominator of most perceptions of this activity. However, the final test of any definition cannot be its apparent harmony with its usage in everyday speech or, for that matter, that the definition is confined to what nobody would exclude. Moreover, most accepted definitions go beyond the concept of tourism as a leisure or holiday activity. According to the World Tourism Organization (WTO), tourism comprises 'the activities of persons travelling to and staying in places outside their usual environment ... for leisure, business and other purposes'. The view taken in this Dictionary is that conceptually tourism denotes a temporary short-term movement of people to destinations outside their normal environment and their activities; within this broad concept 'technical' definitions are formulated for particular purposes, to include or exclude particular trips and visits, mainly by reference to purpose, time and distance criteria.

Hospitality, too, is used by different people in different ways. Common usage of the term is reflected in dictionaries as, for example, 'the act or practice of being hospitable; the reception and entertainment of guests or strangers with liberality and goodwill' [*The Shorter Oxford English Dictionary*]. In more recent years a particular use of the term has become evident, which denotes hospitality that is the concern of the hospitality industry, also sometimes referred to as 'commercial' or 'professional' hospitality: the provision of accommodation, food and drink for people away from home for reward. This is broadly in line with the concept and practice of travel and tourism in this volume, which indicates the scope of the book in this direction.

This book was conceived in the early 1990s to provide first and foremost clear explanations of the meaning of the commonly used words and phrases in travel, tourism and hospitality for those concerned with these fields in one way or another. This aim seemed to be reinforced by an increasing need for a common language in which, as in other walks of life, the same words mean the same things when the accuracy of expression matters, as well as by the apparent need to promote a greater understanding of what travel, tourism and hospitality are about.

This revised and expanded edition includes more than 4000 entries. The major part explains terms, acronyms and abbreviations. Other sections describe some 300 international and national organizations, profile 100 outstanding individuals connected in some way with travel, tourism and hospitality, and give key data for well over 200 countries.

What is included in the Dictionary of Terms was selected from words used in the study of these fields, by those who work in them and by those who take part in them as consumers. The selection process reflects for whom the book is intended. First, it is for academics, who are the main propagators and communicators of definitions, and for students, their principal audiences; as lecturers appear to follow increasingly their own paths rather than particular texts, this volume may also be used by students as a flexible textbook. Second, it is for those employed in a wide range of travel, tourism and hospitality businesses and organizations who may need a ready source of reference in their work. Third, it should also be of interest to a still wider audience – the travellers, tourists and guests – who are the focus and the *raison d'être* of it all – and who may be excused for finding it sometimes difficult to understand some of the language to which they are exposed.

For the most part the Dictionary consists of terms of three main types. First, terms drawn from economics, geography and other disciplines, mainly social sciences. Second, many terms stem from particular industries and occupations, especially passenger transport, hotel and catering services, tour operations and travel agencies. Third, the study and practice of travel, tourism and hospitality comprises planning and development, marketing and organization, each with its own terminology.

The Dictionary includes many business terms, which cover various arrangements between parties, documents and techniques, but generally stops short of basic accounting, computing and statistical terminology, with which users may be expected to be familiar or which they may need to seek elsewhere. Common words in ordinary everyday use are included only if they have a specialized or more specific meaning in travel, tourism and hospitality than elsewhere, or if it was thought that it might be helpful to have them explained

for other reasons. Dictionary entries extend beyond basic definitions to include further explanations, when considered appropriate, and extensive cross-referencing (indicated in bold type).

Where the lexicographer's task is the impartial recording of usage, however illogical it may be, the province of a technical dictionary is the selection and definition of terms with such ends in view as contributing to more effective communication and promoting greater uniformity in terminology. This, especially when combined with explanations beyond basic definitions, also offers an opportunity of enhancing the understanding of the subject area.

Various types of organizations ranging from tourist boards to trade unions are explained in the Dictionary of Terms and international and national organizations are listed with concise descriptions in the separate sections that follow; the latter cover Australia and New Zealand, North America, United Kingdom and Ireland. For other national bodies readers are referred to sources in particular countries. Individuals connected with travel, tourism and hospitality represent a new section in this edition, and the biographies offered are confined to those no longer alive. Country entries show areas, populations, capitals and currencies, as well as country and currency codes and political status.

The bibliography lists sources used and other known dictionaries, which provided ideas on the approach adopted in this volume, and their contribution is gratefully acknowledged. But generally, the definitions, explanations and descriptions are the author's and his contributors'. Hence, when information is reproduced from the only source of that information, the source is given, but not when it is available from a number of sources.

Several approaches are employed throughout to cross-referencing. First, terms represented by separate entries, when referred to elsewhere, are printed in **bold type**, the main exceptions being such frequently used terms as travel, tourism and hospitality. Second, at the end of many entries, the words 'see' and 'see also' indicate clarifying or complementary entries included elsewhere. Third, in order to facilitate locating related terms, certain generic words are used as headings for a list of terms; thus, for example, an entry headed **airport terms** gives cross-references to all entries concerned with airports. A complete list of these generic terms is given on page 2.

An early idea to produce a book of this kind came from a friend and former colleague at the University of Surrey, John Burkart, after some joint authorship in the 1970s, and this book owes much to that stimulus and association. A particular appreciation is due to a number of people who supplied information, commented on drafts of entries in their fields of expertise, suggested additional entries or contributed definitions of their own. Those who influenced this or earlier editions in one or more ways included:

David Airey, Professor of Tourism Management, University of Surrey; Thomas Bauer, Senior Lecturer, Victoria University of Technology, Melbourne; Lester Borley, lecturer and consultant; Nicola Burrows, Assistant Publisher, OAG Worldwide; the late Terry Coppock, Professor Emeritus, University of Edinburgh; Catherine Doran, Market Research and Planning, Irish Tourist Board; Douglas Frechtling, Professor of Tourism Studies,

George Washington University; Rebecca Hawkins, author and consultant; David Jeffries, author and consultant; Brian King, Professor, Victoria University of Technology, Melbourne; Elaine Leek, freelance editor; Victor Middleton, Consultant and Visiting Professor; Philip Ogilvie, George Washington University; Ivan Polunin, Research Fellow, Nanyang Technological University, Singapore; Trevor Ward, Managing Director, TRI Hospitality Consulting, London; Stephen Wheatcroft, Director, Aviation and Tourism International, London; John Yacoumis, consultant; more than 50 users of earlier editions.

The end product owes again much to Margie Ward, whose word processor produced the final copy and the disk from which the book was typeset.

It is hoped that this volume will serve the needs of its users as well as earlier editions appear to have done. Suggestions for additions and other improvements for future editions are welcome and should be addressed to the author, care of the publishers.

S. Medlik
Guildford 2002

1

Dictionary
of Terms

List of generic terms

	page
airport terms	10
awards	17
baggage	18
bed types/descriptions	21
bonding schemes (UK)	24
competition	40
conventions and treaties	44
employment	61
environmental issues	63
food	71
geographical names	77
holidays (vacations) forms, terms, types	85
hotel tariff terms	87
hotel types	88
instruments	93
measures	112
measures of tourism distribution and impact	112
named trains	118
nautical terms	120
occupations	123
pricing	133
rail passes	138
religions of the world	141
restaurant types	142
roads	143
room types/descriptions	144
table service	160
taxes	160
travel/tourism forms/terms/types	171
travel-related illnesses	171

à la carte menu A menu providing a choice of items, each of which is priced separately. See also **bill of fare**; **table d'hôte menu**.

Abacus One of the main **computer reservation systems (CRS)** serving the Asian and Pacific **region**, established 1987 to include All Nippon Airways, Cathay Pacific, China Airlines, Malaysia Airlines, Philippine Airlines, Royal Brunei and Singapore Airlines as principal shareholders, with a **partnership** agreement with the **Amadeus** and **Worldspan** systems. See also **Fantasia**.

abaft A nautical term denoting **stern** half of ship.

ABC Islands Term used to describe the islands of Aruba, Bonaire and Curacao off the north coast of South America.

abeam A nautical term denoting on a line at right-angles to the ship's or **aircraft's** length, i.e., at right-angles to the direction of travel.

aboard On, in or into ship, train, **aircraft** or another vehicle.

abonnement Rail ticket available on the **Continent** of Europe, which allows unlimited travel within a specified area for a specific period of time. See also **rail passes**.

aborigine/aboriginal One of the original inhabitants of an area or a descendant of one, term used to describe, e.g., a member of the indigenous race of Australia as opposed to a colonist. *Abo* is a derogatory abbreviation.

abort To cancel an **aircraft** take off in progress.

above-the-line advertising Term used to describe **advertising** for which a **commission** is normally payable by the **media** to **advertising agencies** operating on behalf of **clients**.

The media included are the press, television, radio, cinema and posters. Thus, broadly speaking, above-the-line advertising expenditure is usually the responsibility of the agency. Sometimes called *media advertising*. See also **below-the-line advertising**.

aboyeur French term for *kitchen clerk* who calls out orders from waiters to **chefs** and keeps the waiters' written orders arranged by tables.

absorption Term used particularly in air transport in connection with joint fares when a **carrier** accepts (i.e., absorbs) for its part of a joint **fare** the difference between a regular fare and a lower fare as a result of computing a joint fare.

ABTA Bonding Scheme Bonding scheme operated by the UK **Association of British Travel Agents (ABTA)**, which requires all **firms** to put up a bond as a condition of membership. The scheme covers products and services provided by ABTA members. For example, in the case of ABTA **tour operator** failure, while on **holiday (vacation)** the holidaymaker will be rescued; if the holiday has not been started, any money held by the ABTA tour operator or **travel agent** will be returned. See **bonding schemes (UK)** for other schemes.

ABTOT Bonding Scheme Bonding scheme of the Association of Bonded Travel Organisers' Trust Ltd operated by Travel and General Insurance Company, which covers all money paid to travel organizers by holidaymakers in the UK. See **bonding schemes (UK)** for other schemes.

Acapulco Document Outcome of a meeting convened in 1982 by the **World Tourism Organization** in Acapulco, Mexico, to implement the aims agreed by the **Manila Declaration**.

DICTIONARY OF TRAVEL, TOURISM AND HOSPITALITY

accessibility The ease of approach of a location from other locations, one of the prime factors which, together with its attractions and amenities (the three As), determine how important an area may be as a **tourism destination**. In tourism, accessibility is a function of distance from centres of population, which constitute tourist **markets**, and of external transport, which enables a destination to be reached. It is measured in terms of distance travelled, the time taken or the cost involved.

acclimatization The process by which living organisms, including human beings, become accustomed to a new **climate**, i.e., one different from their normal **environment**. **Tourists** vary in their ability to acclimatize, according, i.a., to their age, gender, body build and **ethnic** origin.

accommodation
(a) See **tourism accommodation**
(b) See **acculturation**

accommodation address Address used for receiving mail and messages, which is not the real address where a person lives or a business is located.

accommodation classification (Australia) Prepared by the Australian Bureau of Statistics (ABS), *Standard Classification of Visitor Accommodation (SCOVA)* defines the full range of accommodation types, largely for the purpose of statistical measurement.

accompanied/unaccompanied baggage Accompanied **baggage** is carried in the same vehicle as the passenger (and may be **checked** or **unchecked baggage**); unaccompanied baggage is carried separately as cargo. In order to avoid **excess baggage** rates, it is sometimes cheaper for passengers to send some of their baggage as unaccompanied baggage. For example, airlines normally carry such baggage at 50 per cent of cargo rates, which is often less than half the rate charged for excess baggage, but this is subject to particular airline and **customs** regulations.

accompaniment Small helping of food served with a dish, e.g., chutney with curry, horseradish sauce with roast beef, red currant jelly with venison.

accompanying person A person who accompanies a registered delegate to a **conference**, who does not normally attend the business programme but may attend the social programme or a special programme for accompanying persons.

accreditation
(a) Appointment or authorization to act as, e.g., a **hotel representative** by a hotel **company**, or a **travel agent** by a **tour operator** or by a shipping **conference**. See also **agency appointment**.
(b) Acknowledgement of competence or level of training received by individuals, **firms** and **establishments** or institutions.

acculturation A sociological term used to describe the process and the results of interaction between different cultures. The process may involve direct contact or, e.g., exposure through **mass media**. As a result, one or both cultures are affected by assimilating new ways, as occurs, e.g., between **visitors** and resident **host communities** through travel and tourism. Acculturation is also sometimes described as *accommodation* or *assimilation*, particularly when referring to interaction between and integration of immigrant or **ethnic** groups into receiving resident communities.

acid rain Rain contaminated by chemicals, mainly sulphur and nitrogen oxides, released into the **atmosphere** by burning fossil fuels, especially from coal-burning industrial plants and power stations. Acid rain is the cause of such environmental problems as degeneration of coniferous forest, the **pollution** of rivers and lakes and a destruction of fish and other wildlife, and damage to monuments and exteriors of buildings. Many affected areas to be found in various parts of Europe and in the north-eastern United States are of tourism significance.

ACORN Acronym for *A Classification of Residential Neighbourhoods*, a socio-economic **segmentation** system by type of residential area in which **consumers** live based on **Census of Population** data. It is of particular value in **market** and opinion surveys and **target marketing**. Also known as a *geo-demographic segmentation* (population type by location).

ACP States African, Caribbean, Pacific independent countries, which were signatories to the **Lomé Conventions** and eligible for assistance from the **European Community (EC)**. There were 77 ACP States in June 2000, which signed the **Cotonou Agreement**, successor to the Lomé Conventions.

acre (a) A British unit of area measurement, formerly denoting as much land as could be ploughed in a day by a team of oxen, later defined by statute as 4840 square **yards** (0.4 **hectare**). One square **mile** equals 640 acres.

acronym A word formed from the first letters of other words. See, e.g., **tip** = To Insure Promptitude; **UNESCO = United Nations Educational, Scientific and Cultural Organization**.

acrophobia Morbid fear of heights.

act of God An event resulting from natural causes that is not preventable by reasonable foresight or care, such as an earthquake or flood. See also **force majeure**.

activities host(ess) American term for an entertainment organizer in a **hotel**, **resort** or on board a **cruise** ship; the latter is also called *cruise director*. See also **animator**.

activity holidays (vacations) A generic term for **holidays (vacations)** based on a particular sport, hobby or other interest, which enable participants to pursue it as a form of active **recreation**, which may but need not be undertaken with a view to improving their standards of performance. See also **adventure holidays (vacations)**; **special interest holidays (vacations)**.

activity rate The proportion of the population of working age who are employed or unemployed but seek work. In recent years in the UK this has been above 70 per cent overall, made up of over 80 per cent for men and over 60 per cent for women. See also **participation rate**.

actual demand See **demand for tourism**

ad hoc charter See **charter**

ad valorem 'According to value', term used as an adjective in conjunction with **taxes**, duties and similar payments, denoting that they are levied in proportion to the value as, e.g., is value added tax (VAT), and not as a fixed amount as, e.g., is normally a **departure tax**.

adaptation In sociology, term used to describe the process of psychological reaction whereby individuals or groups accept and adjust themselves to fit into novel or unfamiliar **environments**, as occurs, e.g., between **tourists** and host communities.

additional holiday (vacation) Term used in some **holiday (vacation)** surveys, e.g., **British National Travel Survey (BNTS)**, to distinguish between **main holiday (vacation)** and others, when more than one holiday (vacation) is taken by respondents during the year, an important trend in most **developed countries**. See also **holiday (vacation) frequency**; **holiday (vacation) propensity, gross**.

add-on Extra, that for which an additional charge is made as, e.g.: (a) an optional item, which may but need not be bought by the **customer**, such as **sightseeing** as part of an **inclusive tour** (see also **option**); (b) an item not included in the advertised price, which must be bought by the customer, such as **travel insurance** specified by the **tour operator**.

add-on fare Additional air **fare** to construct a **through** fare when, e.g., fare to/from a particular point is not published or when a domestic fare is combined with an international fare.

adjoining rooms Rooms in a **hotel** or another building adjacent to each other without direct access between them. See also **connecting rooms**.

admission The ticket price charged for entrance by a facility such as a **tourist/visitor attraction**.

admissions
(a) The number of people entering a **tourist/visitor attraction** or facility over a given period of time.
(b) The amount of entry fees to a **tourist/visitor attraction** or facility over a given period of time.

Adult and Continuing Education Term covering a broad spectrum of educational activities, in the UK ranging from non-vocational courses of general interest, through courses to acquire special vocational skills needed in **industry** and commerce, to study for a degree of the Open University. See also **Further Education; Higher Education**.

Advance Booking Charter (ABC) A **charter** that requires a minimum advance booking period, designed to protect **scheduled carriers** from revenue dilution.

Advance Purchase Excursion (APEX) Special return air **fare** offered by airlines on **scheduled** flights, subject to various restrictions, including minimum advance booking period and minimum/maximum stay requirement. Must be bought and paid for at the time of booking and cannot be altered or cancelled without charge. See also **British National Rail Apex; Public Excursion (PEX); Seat Sale**.

advance timetable A timetable issued by a transport operator for planning purposes of passengers and the **travel industry** in advance of the period to which it is to apply, often in summary form; it may be changed subsequently.

Advanced Passenger Train (APT) A high-speed train of British Railways, designed to operate on ordinary tracks using a special tilting mechanism. After several years' experiments in the early 1980s, the train was introduced into service in 1984 but withdrawn because of technical problems in 1985. See also **Bullet Train; Train à Grande Vitesse (TGV)**.

Advantage Travel Centre Brand name of agencies of members of the UK **National Association of Independent Travel Agents (NAITA)**.

adventure holidays (vacations) Activity **holidays (vacations)** that contain an element of personal challenge, through controlled risk, daring and/or excitement, often in an inaccessible (wilderness) **environment**. Examples include **caving**, hang gliding, rock climbing, **safaris**, white water rafting.

advertised tour Term often used loosely to refer to any tour included in a brochure or other **media**. However, in the USA an advertised tour has a more precise meaning: it denotes an approved tour, which includes air transport and meets specific airline require-

ments, to which an **IT (inclusive tour)** number has been assigned, and which allows **travel agents** to receive **overriding commission** in respect of the air transport element of the tour.

advertising Use of paid space in publications, posters and **outdoor advertising**, or of time on radio or on cinema and television screens, intended to influence people to take a particular course of action or to form a particular attitude or point of view. This focus on the buying of space or time in various **media** differentiates advertising from **publicity** on the one hand and from **sales promotion** and **merchandising** on the other hand. See also **above-the-line advertising; below-the-line advertising**.

advertising agency Organization employed by advertisers to manage their **advertising**. It is remunerated by **commissions** from the **media** on the rates charged for **media** space or time, charges for materials and services used in the preparation of advertisements, and fees charged for non-commissionable services, such as **market** surveys.

aero- Prefix used in combination with nouns usually relating to air and **aircraft**. Hence, e.g., *aerodrome, aeroplane, aerospace*; the physics of air motion and its effects is *aerodynamics*; the science and practice of aircraft design, construction and operation is *aeronautics*.

aerodrome/airdrome See **airport**

aerospace industry Firms and establishments engaged in the manufacture of **aircraft**, spacecraft, missiles and related electronic equipment.

affinity charter The **charter** of an aircraft by an **affinity group**.

affinity group Members of an organization formed for purposes other than travel, such as a school, **firm** or club, who get together to travel as a group and are then eligible for special group air fares. Such groups must not solicit members publicly and members must be of not less than six months' standing before the date of travel. See also **affinity group fares**.

affinity group fares Air **fares** restricted to bona fide **affinity groups**. See also **air fare rebates (groups)**.

Afghani (Af) Unit of **currency** of Afghanistan.

aft Originally a nautical term, now denoting rear of a ship or **aircraft**. See also **abaft**; **(a)midship(s)**; **astern**; **bow**; **forward**.

afternoon tea A light snack served in late afternoon, normally comprising sandwiches, cakes, pastries and tea. See also **high tea**; **cream tea**.

after-sales service Normally related to articles, the term covers the provision of repairs and maintenance, and the supply of advice and spares, by the vendor or the vendor's **agent** once the sale has been completed. When used in the context of travel, tourism and hospitality, after-sales service normally refers to the provision of advice and information to **visitors** or guests after arrival at their destination and/or keeping in touch with them after their stay or visit.

agency agreement A contract between an **agent** (such as **travel agent**) and **principal** (such as **hotel**, transport or **tour operator**) setting out the terms and conditions for the transaction of business by the agent with and on behalf of the principal.

agency appointment Authorization of a **travel agent** by a **principal** or by a **conference** to represent them and sell their services. A fully fledged agency would normally hold a number of appointments of individual **companies**, as well as appointments such as by the **International Air Transport Association (IATA)**; the latter enables the agency to hold international air ticket stocks of IATA members and a **validation** stamp, and receive a **commission** on sales. See also **accreditation**.

agency code An identifying code provided by a **principal** to a retail **travel agent** when granted **accreditation**.

agency coupon The part of an airline ticket retained by an agency.

agency tour American term for a **familiarization trip**.

AGENDA 21 See **Earth Summit**

agent Person with express or implied authority to act for or represent another (**principal**). See also **travel agent**.

agoraphobia Fear of open spaces.

agritourism, agricultural tourism, agrotourism See **farm tourism**

AIDA A mnemonic for Attention, Interest, Desire, Action, attributed to American **marketing** academic E.K. Strong, and describing the sequence in the **customer** reaction to marketing stimulus: to be effective, it has to move through a logical sequence based on attracting attention, arousing interest, creating desire and enabling action.

AIDS An **acronym** from *Acquired Immune Deficiency Syndrome*, a condition caused by a virus known as *HIV (Human Immuno-Deficiency Virus)*, which attacks the body's immune system, making it unable to fight off infections. The virus can be passed on by contaminated blood or body fluids, e.g., through infected medical equipment or through sexual contact. The risk exists worldwide and people infected with HIV remain infected and infectious all their lives; there is no vaccine or cure.

air carrier
(a) An **aircraft** carrying passengers, mail or cargo.
(b) A firm engaged in air transportation of passengers, mail or cargo.

air corridor See **corridor**

air fare rebates (groups) The following main parties are entitled to discounts off normal First, Club and Economy air **fares**, the size of the reductions varying between **regions** and according to other criteria: common interest groups, **convention** groups, families, IATA passenger sale **agents** on **familiarization trips**, incentive tours, school parties, **visitors** to trade fairs. Some similar reductions also apply in **bus** and **coach**, rail and sea transport. See also **air fare rebates (individuals)**.

air fare rebates (individuals) The following main categories of passenger are entitled to discounts off normal First, Club and Economy air **fares**, the size of the reductions varying between **regions** and according to other criteria: infants (under 2 years), children (over 2, under 12 years), youth (over 12, under 22), students (over 12, under 28), seamen/ships' crews, airline staff, IATA passenger sales agents (also accompanying spouse). Some similar reductions also apply in **bus** and **coach**, rail and sea transport. See also **air fare rebates (groups)**.

air fare types Main **scheduled** air **fare** types are: Supersonic (available only on Air France and British Airways Concorde flights); First; Business (not available on all flights and names differ between airlines, e.g., Club, Clipper); Economy. The above are known as *normal air fares* and have few or no conditions or restrictions attached. See separate entries for those below known as *promotional air fares*: **Advance Purchase Excursion (APEX); Eurobudget; Excursion; Public Excursion (PEX); Seat Sale; Special Group Inclusive Tour fare**. See also **air fare rebates; tour-basing fare**.

air hostess See **flight attendant**

air mile See **mile**

Air Miles A promotional scheme operated by British Airways of awarding points when purchasing certain goods and **services** which may be exchanged in full or in part for free flights and some other products.

Air Passenger Duty (UK) Charge payable on tickets for flights departing from UK **airports** introduced in 1995 and amended from April 2001 and again November 2002. It varies between flights within and outside Europe and also between economy and higher class flights. The amount is included in the price of ticket or **holiday (vacation)** by the operator and accounted for to the Treasury.

air quality A subjective concept indicative of the level of air **pollution** and varying inversely with that level. Although it can be assessed by reference to medical, biological or material damage, air quality also varies with wind speed, **humidity** and other meteorological parameters. It also varies culturally in that different societies have different views on what constitutes bad air quality. Of increasing concern in **developed countries** are levels of pollution in **cities** arising from level of motor traffic. See also **comfort index**.

air/sea An arrangement using both air and sea transportation, normally booked at the same time or as a **package** at an inclusive price. This is, e.g., available during the summer months on the North Atlantic as a flight on the onward journey and a return sea crossing, or vice versa.

air services agreement An agreement between two (**bilateral**) or more (**multilateral**) states, regulating air services between them. See also **Bermuda Agreement; freedoms of the air**.

air steward(ess) See **flight attendant**

air taxi A small **aircraft** operating within a limited radius for private hire; in the USA, an aircraft carrying up to 19 passengers and operating within 250 miles of its home base, used particularly by business travellers.

air terminal A building in the town from which passengers travel by **bus** or train to the airport. Also known as **city terminal**. See also **airport terminal**.

air traffic control A system of controlling **aircraft** movements in and out of **airports**. In the UK it is the responsibility of the **Civil Aviation Authority (CAA)**, in the USA of the **Federal Aviation Administration (FAA)**.

air travel organizer A person who makes 'available, as a **principal** or an **agent**, accommodation for the carriage of persons or cargo in any part of the world' requiring a **licence** to operate by the UK **Civil Aviation Authority (CAA)** (Civil Aviation Act 1971). This is a wider term than **tour operator** and includes, for example, air brokers acting as agents for airlines. The licence is the **Air Travel Organiser's Licence (ATOL)**. The licence shows that the organizer of **charter** flights has lodged a bond with CAA to safeguard the holidaymakers' money in case of the **company** failure.

Air Travel Organiser's Licence (ATOL) Licence issued by the UK **Civil Aviation Authority (CAA)** to operators organizing **holidays (vacations)** by air from the UK.

airborne An aviation term denoting the period of flight between lifting off the earth's surface and landing, i.e., the time when the **aircraft** is actually in the air.

airbridge Corridor attached to **aircraft** doors to enable people to enter from or leave the aircraft for the **airport terminal**.

Airbus Wide body jet (see **aircraft types**) with the cruising speed of up to 600 miles per hour and a large passenger capacity, designed mainly for **short haul** flights on high density **routes**, as between large **cities**.

aircraft Any machine used for flying which is heavier than air with on-board means of propulsion. See also **airship** and several entries for **aircraft types**.

aircraft grounding Voluntary or mandatory restriction or prohibition on flying an **aircraft** by an airline itself, aircraft manufacturers, aviation or other authorities, for such reasons as adverse weather conditions, industrial disputes and mechanical faults.

aircraft leasing Lease or hire of **aircraft** for a pre-determined period of time on specified conditions. A *dry lease* denotes the provision of aircraft only. A *wet lease* includes the provision of crew and supporting services, e.g., fuel. *Operational lease* describes a short-term lease which need not be included in the airline balance sheet. See also **dry/wet lease**; **bareboat charter**; **provisioned charter**.

aircraft stacking Term used for **aircraft** flying in large circles at two or more levels at busy **airports** awaiting permission to land.

aircraft types: bodies
(a) *Regular/narrow body aircraft* – jet aircraft with a fuselage diameter less than 200 in. and propulsion by turbine engines of less than 30 000 pounds per engine, e.g., Boeing 707 or 727.
(b) *Wide body aircraft* – jet aircraft with a fuselage diameter exceeding 200 in. and propulsion greater than 30 000 pounds per engine, e.g. Boeing 747 or 767, commonly also described as *jumbo jet*.
See also other **aircraft types** entries.

aircraft types: codes One-letter standard designators specified by the **International Air Transport Association (IATA)** for use in timetables and other communications and publications: J = Pure Jet, T = Prop Jet, P = Propeller, H = Helicopter, A = Amphibian/Seaplane. See also other **aircraft types** entries.

aircraft types: speed A *supersonic transport* (SST) aircraft is capable of a normal cruising speed greater than the speed of sound (741 miles or 1190 km per hour) at sea level; *subsonic* denotes speed slower than the speed of sound. Concorde is the first and still (in 2002) the only supersonic passenger aircraft, brought into regular service between London/Paris and New York in 1977. See also other **aircraft types** entries.

aircraft types: take-off and landing *Vertical take-off and landing* (VTOL) aircraft (including *helicopters*) can take off and land vertically; *short take-off and landing* (STOL) aircraft can take off and land within a short horizontal distance; other aircraft types require various horizontal distances for take-off and landing. See also other **aircraft types** entries.

aircraft types: wings A *fixed wing aircraft* has wings fixed to the **fuselage** and may be propelled by either piston (internal combustion) engines or gas turbine (jet) engines. A *helicopter* derives lift from revolving wings or blades (rotors) driven by an engine on a vertical axis; it can hover and take off or land vertically. See also other **aircraft types** entries.

airfield See **airport**

airline alliances Airline groupings in which two or more airlines collaborate, without necessarily forming a separate independent organization, with a view to achieving one or more common strategic objectives. See also **Oneworld**; **Star Alliance**; **Qualiflyer Group**; **Skyteam**; **Wings**.

airline codes Two-letter airline designators, assigned and published by the **International Civil Aviation Organization (ICAO)**, for use in reservations, timetables and ticketing, as well as other inter- and intra-industry applications. Thus, e.g., BA = British Airways, DL = Delta Airlines, QF = QANTAS. See *OAG Flight Atlas* for a full list. See also **code sharing**.

airline clubs Special clubs created by most major airlines for frequent **travellers**, offering various privileges and services, such as the use of special **airport** lounges. Membership of clubs run by US airlines is usually open to anyone prepared to pay a fixed annual membership fee. Membership of clubs run by other airlines is often free but admission is restricted to those considered valuable enough

customers. See also **frequent flyer programmes (FFPs)**.

airpasses Airline tickets for extensive travel within large countries or areas, normally available only to **visitors**, who have to buy them in their countries of residence. Some airpasses are valid for unlimited travel in a given period; others cover a set number of flights; yet others offer discounts rather than free travel. Seats are subject to availability; some airlines offer booking confirmed seats, others **standby** only. Airpasses are offered by most large US and Canadian airlines, some covering both countries; several cover Australia, New Zealand and the Pacific islands, and combinations of these countries.

airport An area used for the landing and take off of **aircraft** and including any related buildings and facilities. *Aerodrome* (US *airdrome*) is synonymous with airport but now little used. *Airfield* usually denotes a military airport or a small airport with limited facilities.

airport apron Airport hard surface area off the runways, used for **aircraft** loading, unloading, servicing and other handling purposes.

airport art Pejorative term for souvenirs offered for sale at **airports**.

airport capacity Airport capacity is made up of the capacities of:
(a) the **terminal** (the number of passengers per hour moving through such parts of the terminal building as security, immigration and **customs**);
(b) the **apron** (the number of **aircraft** handled per hour, which depends on the number of parking stands and the aircraft servicing capability);
(c) the aircraft movements (the number of movements per hour that can be supported by the **airport**).

airport codes See **city/airport codes**

airport maintenance tax A charge levied on airline passengers in some countries, e.g., China, for the construction or maintenance of the **airport** and its facilities.

airport service charge Charge levied at certain **airports** on departing passengers, and

payable either at **check-in time** or included with the price of the ticket. See also **departure tax**.

airport terminal An **airport** building used by arriving and departing airline passengers. See also **air terminal**.

airport terms

See **aerodrome**	**airstrip**
air traffic control	**alternate airport**
airbridge	**city/airport codes**
airfield	**heliport**
airport	**holding bay**
airport apron	**international**
airport art	**airport**
airport capacity	**landing fee**
airport codes	**landside**
airport maintenance tax	**runway**
airport service charge	**slot**
airport terminal	**tarmac**
airside	**time slot**
airspace	**wayports**

airship A dirigible motor-driven balloon, usually cigar-shaped, lighter than air.

airsickness Motion sickness caused by the motions of the **aircraft** or **altitude**, manifesting itself by nausea and vertigo.

airside Airport terminal area beyond the **passport** and security checks, used by departing passengers and also transit passengers (see **passenger designations)** waiting for **connecting flights** where **duty-free** shops are located. See also **landside**.

airspace The space above the land and sea territory of a state and subject to its exclusive jurisdiction. See also **freedoms of the air**.

airstrip Short strip of rough land used by **aircraft** for take off and landing.

airworthiness See **certificate of airworthiness**

AITO Trust Bonding Scheme Bonding scheme of the **Association of Independent Tour Operators (AITO)**, which covers **inclusive tour (IT) holidays (vacations)** from the UK operated by AITO Trust bonded **companies**. See **bonding schemes (UK)** for other schemes.

Al Andalus Express Named train service in Spain linking three major cities: Seville, Granada and Cordoba.

Alaskan Standard Time A US time zone based on the 135th meridian. Time equals GMT –9.

albergo Italian term for **hotel**.

alfresco In the open air, hence *alfresco dining*, eating out of doors, as in a rooftop **restaurant**.

alien A person who is not a **citizen** of the country of his/her residence. **Tourists** are normally classified for statistical purposes by the country of residence rather than by **nationality**. Resident aliens are, therefore, treated in statistics of **domestic** and **international travel/tourism** as **residents** of the country. See also **expatriate**; **migration**; **national**; **nomad**; **refugee**.

alienation In sociology, term used to describe the estrangement of individuals from themselves and others, suffering from the feeling of isolation, placelessness, powerlessness and meaninglessness. Tourism is seen by some as providing the opportunity to escape, however temporarily, from the condition.

all found Employment term denoting remuneration which includes accommodation, food and other amenities in addition to wages, an arrangement particularly common in the **hospitality industry**. See also **fringe benefits**.

all space hold Situation in which all function space in a facility such as a **hotel** or exhibition centre is reserved for a single user.

all-expense tour See **all-in**

all-in Term for inclusive arrangements, such as **American Plan/en pension** terms/**full board** for **hotel** stays, or **inclusive tours** including transportation, **accommodation** and possibly other specified items for an inclusive price, the latter also described in North America as *all-expense tour*.

all-suite hotel Hotel with all units arranged as **suites**.

Allemansrätt Traditional Swedish law (meaning 'every man's right'), which guaran-

tees public access to the countryside by allowing **visitors** to hike, ride, cycle, picnic, as well as camp overnight on private land.

allocation See **allotment**

allocentric/psychocentric Terms to describe types of **tourist**, attributed to tourism researcher Stanley Plog. An *allocentric* is a **traveller** with a preference for exploration and inquisitiveness, continually seeking new destinations. A *psychocentric* is unadventurous, wants security, seeks the familiar and a 'tried and tested' destination. In between these extremes is the *midcentric* who has some of both characteristics and makes up the bulk of the **market**.

allotment Allocation of a specific number of **hotel** rooms or transport seats to a **tour operator** or another travel organizer to sell until a given date, when the unsold rooms or seats are 'released back' to the hotel or **carrier** without payment.

alphanumeric Combination of letters and numbers as, e.g., used in the UK and Canadian postcodes to aid computerized sorting of mail. Other countries use a purely numeric code for the same purpose, such as the **Zip code** in the USA.

Alpine Of the Alps or other high **mountains**; thus, e.g., Alpine **climate**, Alpine vegetation, Alpine tourism.

alternate airport An **airport** to which a flight is diverted when a landing at the **scheduled** airport is not possible, e.g., because of adverse weather conditions.

alternative technology See **appropriate technology**

alternative tourism Term generally used to refer to forms of tourism that seek to avoid adverse and enhance positive social, cultural and environmental impacts and perceived as alternative to **mass tourism**. Usually characterized by small scale; individual, independent or small group activity; slow, controlled and regulated development; as well as an emphasis on travel as experience of host cultures and on maintenance of traditional values and societies. Also referred to variously as *appropriate, green, responsible* or *soft tourism*. See also **sustainable tourism**.

altimeter An instrument for measuring **altitude** in **aircraft** and on the ground, using the relationship between the change in atmospheric pressure and height above sea level. See also **barometer**.

altitude The height of a point on the earth's surface above its base, normally measured vertically from the mean sea level as a zero base. See also **datum level/line**.

altitude sickness A feeling of nausea accompanied by sickness, which afflicts at high **altitudes** those unaccustomed to them, caused by breathing air deficient in oxygen. Also known as *mountain sickness*.

Amadeus One of two main European **computer reservation systems (CRS)**, established in 1987 by a **consortium** led by Air France, Iberia, Lufthansa and SAS, and including several smaller airlines, with US **System One** supplying the software. Now owned in equal shares by Air France Group, Iberia, Lufthansa and Sabena, with **partnership** agreements with **Abacus** and **Worldspan**.

Amazonia Name used to describe the Amazon Basin, an area of the size of Australia, between the Atlantic coast of Brazil and the Andes **mountains** in Peru. The area is mainly covered by tropical rain forests, which absorb large quantities of carbon dioxide and give out large amounts of oxygen. The large-scale destruction of the forests with mining, ranching and other development (*deforestation*) has become a global political issue, as less carbon dioxide absorbed from the atmosphere contributes to **global warming**.

American breakfast A term used especially outside North America to describe a breakfast that includes such small dishes as cereals, eggs, corned beef hash, pastries and waffles, to differentiate it from, e.g., **Asian breakfast**.

American Plan (AP) En **pension** or full-board **hotel tariff**, which includes room and three meals per day (breakfast, lunch, dinner). Also referred to in the USA as *bed and board*.

American service Style of **restaurant** table service, in which food is portioned and plated in the kitchen before being served to **customers**. Also described as *plate service*. See

also **English service; family-style service; French service; Russian service**.

American ton See **ton (tonne)**

Americas Collective term for North, Central and South America.

(a)midship(s) A nautical term denoting middle part of a ship. See also **abaft; aft; astern; bow; forward**.

amoebiasis A recurrent dysentery, which contains blood and mucus, and can cause liver abscesses and peritonitis. It is spread by infected carriers in unsanitary conditions in all tropical areas. Strict personal hygiene is the main precaution.

Amsterdam Treaty See **Treaty of Amsterdam**.

Amtrak Name used by the US *National Railroad Passenger Corporation* created by the Rail Passenger Service Act 1970 as a semi-public body with the responsibility for **marketing** and operating US intercity passenger trains. Although a few private passenger trains continue to operate, the great majority of US rail services other than **commuter** trains are operated by Amtrak.

Amtrak California Rail Passes Rail Passes issued by **Amtrak** which offer 7 days' travel within 21 days statewide or 5 days' travel within 7 days in Northern or Southern California.

Amtrak North America Rail Pass Rail Pass issued by **Amtrak** available for 30 consecutive days of travel in both the USA and Canada to permanent **residents** of other countries.

Amtrak USA Rail Passes Rail Passes issued by **Amtrak** for six different US **regions** and available to permanent **residents** of countries other than the USA and Canada, normally valid for 15 or 30 days with unlimited stopovers.

anchorage A place where a boat or ship may lie at anchor.

anemometer An instrument for measuring and recording the strength and direction of wind, which is mainly influenced by the gradient between high- and low-pressure areas, by the earth's rotation, and by **topography**.

animator Term of French origin (*animateur*) to describe a person employed to organize social and other activities for guests in a **hotel**, **holiday (vacation)** centre or another location. Often described as *social* or *cruise director* or *officer* on board a **cruise** ship and as *entertainments director* or *officer* in a **resort**. See also **activities host(ess)**.

anomie A social condition characterized by breakdown of social interaction, which is seen by sociologists as a push-factor in tourism, providing **motivation** for people lacking interpersonal contacts in the home **environment**.

Antarctic The area within the Antarctic Circle (66°32' South), opposite to the **Arctic**; also as an adjective, of that area; thus, e.g., *Antarctic landscape*. The **region** has a more limited tourism potential than the Arctic, except for summer **cruises**. *Antarctica* is the term used to describe the continental area around the South Pole. See also **overflights of Antarctica**.

Antarctic tourism **Trips** and visits to destinations within the Antarctic Circle, most by sea. See also **Antarctic**; **Arctic tourism**; **overflights of Antarctica**.

Antipodean Day Day 'gained' by crossing the **International Date Line** in the eastern (American) direction. Also called *Meridian Day*.

antipodes Places on earth's surface diametrically opposite each other, e.g., Australia and New Zealand in relation to the **British Isles**.

antiquities A general term, descriptive of ancient historical monuments (particularly Greek and Roman) and archaeological features, often in the care of a public body and frequently important attractions for tourists, e.g., the Coliseum in Rome, the Parthenon in Athens, the Pyramids in Egypt and the Great Wall of China. They are particularly numerous in Europe and Asia. What constitutes antiquities varies with history; e.g., in the United States the antiquities legislation has been applied to pueblo dwellings of a fifteenth-century Indian community.

antitrust laws US legislation designed to promote competition and prevent unfair practices that may lead to **monopolies** or suppression of competition.

apartment hotel An **establishment** combining the features of an apartment building and a **hotel**, i.e., providing furnished accommodation with cooking facilities without service, and also offering such optional facilities as maid service or a **restaurant**, catering commonly but not exclusively for longer-stay residents. Also known as *apartotel*.

apéritif Alcoholic appetizer, commonly sherry, gin and tonic, dry and sweet martini, whisky.

Apollo US **computer reservation system (CRS)** originally owned 50 per cent by United Airlines and operated by the Covia Corporation. Following the merger of **Apollo** and **Galileo** in 1992 with United Airlines as major shareholder in **Galileo International**, the Apollo brand name is now used by Galileo International in the USA, Mexico and Japan.

appellation d'origine contrôlée (AOC) French wine classification which shows the area from which the wine comes and that it is of certain quality.

Apple Isle A term used for Tasmania, off the south coast of Australia, where large amounts of apples are grown.

appropriate technology Technology suitable for an area in view of its stage of technical development. When intended to be used in **developing countries**, typical requirements are that it should be easy to use by the unskilled, have no parts difficult to obtain and be easily repaired. Also called *alternative* and *intermediate technology*.

appropriate tourism The type and scale of tourism which is considered suitable for an area in view of its economic, social, environmental and other conditions. The term is also used as a synonym for **alternative tourism**.

après-ski Activities which take place in the evening after **skiing** at the **hotel** or another place of stay.

apron
(a) An **airport tarmac** area on which **aircraft** are parked.
(b) The part of a theatre stage in front of the main curtain.

aquatic sports Sports conducted in or on water, such as swimming, **scuba diving**, water polo.

archipelago Term originally applied to the Aegean Sea between Greece and Asia Minor, then to any sea or expanse of water studded (like the Aegean) with many islands. Nowadays the term is applied only to a group of islands as, for example, the Alexander Archipelago in the Gulf of Alaska.

architecture styles See **Baroque; Gothic; Neoclassical; Rococo; Romanesque**

Arctic The area within the Arctic Circle (66°32' North), opposite the **Antarctic**; also as an adjective, of that area; thus, e.g., *Arctic climate*. The region is undeveloped as a **tourism destination** and is currently visited mainly by scientists, students and trekkers. But especially northern Canada and northern **Scandinavia** are attractive for those in search of wilderness and may receive more **visitors** in the future for **adventure holidays (vacations)** and summer **cruises**.

Arctic tourism Trips and visits to **destinations** within the Arctic Circle, already significant in Canada and **Scandinavia** where road access is possible. See also **Antarctic; Antarctic tourism; Arctic**.

Area Tourism Companies (ATC) Area framework of three bodies covering South and West, Mid and North Wales, with **local authority** and **tourism industry** participation and operating under contract with the **Wales Tourist Board (WTB)** to develop, promote and coordinate tourism in their respective areas of the Principality.

Area Tourist Boards (ATBs) Network of voluntary bodies with **local authorities**, **tourism industry** and **Scottish Tourist Board (STB)** or **Highlands and Islands Enterprise** participation and funding, created under the terms of the Local Government and Planning (Scotland) Act 1982, which transferred responsibility for tourism from regional to local level based on islands and districts. In the mid 1990s, following a major reorganization, the network of 32 boards was reduced to a total of 14.

Area(s) of Outstanding Natural Beauty (AONBs) Conservation areas in England, Wales and Northern Ireland designated on account of their scenic beauty and not large enough or wild enough to be designated as **National Parks**, subject to strict planning control over development. Designation is made by the **Countryside Agency**, Countryside Council for Wales and Department of the Environment for Northern Ireland. There were 42 AONBs in England and Wales and nine in Northern Ireland in mid 2000. See **countryside conservation designation schemes** for other schemes.

arrival/departure card Document completed by **international travellers** at borders, **ports** and **airports** as an instrument of government controls. Information included often provides a basis for statistics of **international tourism**.

Asian breakfast A term used especially in the **region** to describe a breakfast which includes Asian dishes, such as cougee (rice porridge), noodles and dim sum (different small dishes), to differentiate it from, e.g., **American breakfast**.

assimilation See **acculturation**

astern At/in/to the **stern**, a nautical term denoting rear of a ship. See also **abaft; aft; (a)midship(s); bow; forward**.

astronaut One who travels in space, outside the earth's **atmosphere**. Also referred to as *cosmonaut*, especially in countries of Eastern Europe and the former Soviet Union.

Athens Convention An international agreement made in 1974 which limits the liability of shipping **companies** for loss of or damage to luggage and injury to or death of passengers on international services by sea.

Atlantic Standard Time A Canadian **time zone** based on the standard of the 60th **meridian**, also called *Provincial Standard Time*. Time equals GMT −4.

atmosphere
(a) The layer of gases (carbon dioxide, nitrogen, oxygen and others) that envelopes the earth.

(b) The air in any particular place as affected by heat or cold or other influences.

(c) Mental, moral or other non-physical **environment**.

ATOL Bonding Scheme Bonding scheme of the **Civil Aviation Authority (CAA)** in the UK, which requires any person selling **holidays (vacations)** by air or seats using **charter** flights to the public, to hold an **Air Travel Organiser's Licence (ATOL)**. It covers **package** holidays including charter-type arrangements on **scheduled** flights. See **bonding schemes (UK)** for other schemes.

atoll A low coral island consisting of a ring-shaped reef enclosing a **lagoon**, common in the Pacific Ocean.

atrium Enclosed covered pedestrian space often forming the lobby or an interior court-yard of large buildings, including **hotels**.

attendance factor A rough measure of the effectiveness of a **leisure** facility or service, calculated by dividing total attendances by the population within its perceived **catchment area**. This may be compared with a national norm derived from such sources as the **General Household Survey** in **Great Britain**.

attractions See **tourist/visitor attractions**.

attribution theory An approach to under-standing how people explain negative experi-ences or problematic events. In tourism, the theory may help, e.g., with tourists' complaints.

auberge See **brasserie**

audience Of the several uses of the term, probably the most relevant in the travel, tourism and hospitality context is the meaning attached to it for promotional purposes, i.e., group of people exposed to particular promo-tional **media**, usually cinema, radio or tele-vision. Data relating to the size of audiences and the composition, usually expressed in demographic, psychographic or socio-economic terms, are of particular significance to advertisers of goods and **services**, including travel, tourism and hospitality products.

audioconferencing See **teleconferencing**

audit coupon Normally the top coupon of a **carrier's** ticket which is returned to the carrier with the **travel agent's** sales return.

aurora See **Northern Lights**

Australasia Term used to denote (a) Australia and New Zealand, or (b) the **region** consisting of Australia, New Zealand and the islands of the Pacific east of Indonesia and the Philippines. The latter comprise *Melanesia* (Fiji, New Caledonia, Papua New Guinea, Solomon Islands, Vanuatu); *Micronesia* (Federated States of Micronesia, Guam, Kiribati, Mariana Islands, Marshall Islands, Nauru, Palau/ Belau); *Polynesia* (American Samoa, Cook Islands, French Polynesia, Niue, Tokelau, Tonga, Tuvalu, Wallis and Futuna, Samoa). See also **Oceania**.

Australia New Zealand Closer Economic Relations Trade Agreement (ANZCERTA) A treaty to establish a free trade area, which came into effect on 1 January 1983, replacing the earlier agreement of 1 January 1966. A review of the 1983 Agreement in 1988 broadened it to include **services** and deepened it in other areas. Because of its emphasis on trade in goods and the absence of barriers to the expansion of tourism, the Agreement has had little direct effect on tourism between the two countries. However, the Agreement has stimulated an increase in business traffic and moves to a single aviation **market**, representing a significant liberaliza-tion of air transport between and beyond the two countries.

Australian Dollar ($A) Unit of **currency** of Australia, Kiribati, Nauru, Norfolk Island, Tuvalu.

Australian tourism statistics
(a) Movements and activities of **international visitors** to Australia are recorded by *International Visitor Survey* from interviews conducted with outgoing passengers and published annually by the Australian **Bureau of Tourism Research (BTR)**.
(b) Movements and activities of **domestic tourists** within Australia are recorded by *Domestic Tourism Monitor* from household interviews and are published annually by the Australian Bureau of Tourism Research (BTR).

authenticity The quality of being genuine, real or true, as opposed to simulated, contrived or fake. Applied in tourism in particular to **heritage** sites and to **event attractions**, when referring, e.g., to buildings and objects of art or to ceremonies and performances.

auto rental American synonym for *car hire*.

autobahn A German **motorway**, the first of their kind being built in the early 1930s. See also **autopista**; **autoroute**; **autostrada**; **expressway**.

automated immigration lane Computer-controlled immigration procedure operated first as an international experiment in a number of locations, such as **airports** and also the US–Mexico border, which uses **biometrics** and identifies people from the characteristics of their hands. If the experiment is successful, it is envisaged that the technology might ultimately replace **passports**. See also **INSPASS**.

automated reservation systems See **computer reservation systems (CRS)**

automated teller machines (ATMs) Also known as *cash points* or *cash dispensers*, facilities offered by banks and building societies to current account holders to obtain cash up to an agreed amount and such other services as the balance of one's account by inserting a service card in the machine and keying a PIN number.

automated ticket and boarding pass (ATB2) Electronic ticket used by some airlines, which contains information about the passenger and the reservation on a magnetic strip. The ticket enables travellers carrying hand **baggage** only to **check in** for a flight by swiping the card against a magnetic reader and **board**, without other **check-in** procedures.

automatic vending Retailing of products, including, e.g., food, beverages and cigarettes, through vending machines.

automobile club Individual membership organization providing roadside and other services to motorists, such as the *Automobile Association (AA)* in **Great Britain**, or the *American Automobile Association (AAA)*. See also **motoring organization**.

autopista A Spanish **motorway**. See also **autobahn**; **autoroute**; **autostrada**; **expressway**.

autoroute A French **motorway**. See also **autobahn**; **autopista**; **autostrada**; **expressway**.

autostrada An Italian **motorway**, the first motorway to be built in Europe in the 1920s. See also **autobahn**; **autopista**, **autoroute**; **expressway**.

available seat kilometres (ASK) A transport measure calculated as the product of the number of **aircraft** seats available for sale and the **kilometres** flown.

available seat miles (ASM) A transport measure calculated as the product of the number of **aircraft** seats available for sale and the **miles** flown.

available tonne-kilometres (ATK) See **capacity tonne-kilometres**

avalanche The rapid descent down steep slopes of masses of snow, ice or rock, usually without warning. The term is commonly applied to snow, when it may be triggered by heavy falls in winter or by sudden spells of warm weather in spring. Most avalanches follow regular avalanche tracks and to that extent are predictable in terms of location; but avalanches may occur from time to time unexpectedly in other areas. Avalanches are a particular hazard to climbers and skiers, especially those **skiing** off piste.

average room rate (ARR) The average daily rate paid by guests in **hotels and similar establishments**. The *average room rate* is calculated by dividing room sales by the total number of occupied rooms, the *average rate per guest* by dividing room sales by the total number of guests. The figures of room sales used are net of any **taxes** and **service charges** paid to employees. The average rates and **occupancy** are key operating ratios and measures of performance.

avoirdupois The original British system of weights still used in English-speaking countries for goods except precious metals and stones and medicines:

16 drams	= 1 ounce (oz)
16 ounces	= 1 pound (lb)

14 pounds	= 1 stone
28 pounds	= 1 quarter (qr)
112 pounds	= 1 hundredweight (cwt)
20 hundredweight	= 1 ton*

*American ton = 2000 lb (20 cwt of 100 lb), also called **short ton**.

awards

See **Best Practice Forum**
Blue Flag
Blue Riband of the Atlantic
BS 5750
BS EN ISO 9000
European Prize for Tourism and the Environment
Excellence Through People
Hales Trophy
Hospitality Assured
Investors in People
Queen's Awards
Seaside Awards

awning Roof made of canvas or other material above the **deck** of a ship to provide shade from the sun, nowadays also used for a similar structure elsewhere, e.g., a shop or **restaurant**.

Axess A **computer reservation system (CRS)** owned by Japan Air Lines and Korean Airlines with a cooperation agreement with **Sabre**.

B

baby boomers Those born in the USA during the 'baby boom' years of 1946–64. In the year 2000 this group occupied the 36–54 age group, which shows higher **propensities** to travel and tourism than other age groups, and the increased numbers, therefore, provided a boost to demand for travel, tourism and hospitality **services**.

baby-listening service Service offered by some **hotels** to enable parents when out of the room or a member of staff to hear the baby cry by means of a microphone placed in the room.

baby-sitting service Service offered by some **hotels** to look after a baby when the parents are out of the room.

bach A **beach** or lakeside **holiday (vacation)** home in North Island, New Zealand, called a **crib** in South Island.

back load See **return load**

back of house The operational areas and staff, e.g., all parts of a **hotel**, **motel** or **restaurant**, not normally in direct contact with the **customer**, such as kitchens, stores and administrative offices. See also **front of house**.

back-to-back A sequence of group arrivals and departures arranged so as to maximize the utilization of the means of transport or **accommodation**. For example, a **charter aircraft** transports a group of passengers to a destination on its outward flight and returns with another group, or **hotel** rooms vacated by a group of departing guests are occupied the same day by another group arriving. See also **empty leg**.

back-to-back ticketing The practice (against **IATA** regulations) of buying multiple return tickets to avoid regulations requiring Saturday night stay at the destination in order to qualify for a reduced fare. Thus, e.g., to visit Paris from London twice in two weeks (flying out one weekday and returning the next each time) could be covered by buying two return tickets (both over Saturday nights) one London–Paris and the other Paris–London, and 'mixing' the tickets.

backpacking Informal **recreation**, particularly in mountainous and wilderness areas, by those carrying their gear and food supplies, generally in rucksacks, and relying on sleeping bags, tents or huts for **accommodation**. Hence, *backpacker*, a traveller engaged in backpacking who tends to be usually young and on a low **budget**. See also **hiking**.

backward pricing Setting prices by reference to such criteria as competitors' prices and **customers'** attitudes, wants and preferences, and adjusting the costs and levels of service to the predetermined prices.

baggage Packed possessions taken by a **traveller** on a journey. Usual term in the USA, *luggage* is more usual in the **UK**, but *baggage* is in common use among **carriers** worldwide. See **accompanied/unaccompanied baggage**
  baggage allowance
  baggage check
  baggage claim area
  baggage master
  baggage room
  baggage tag
  Bagtrack
  cabin baggage
  carry-on baggage
  checked/unchecked baggage
  excess baggage
  hold baggage

baggage allowance Amount of **baggage** per passenger, determined by weight, number of pieces and/or dimensions, transported by a **carrier** 'free'. For example, under the weight system used by many airlines, this is normally 30 kg (66 lb) for first-class and 20 kg (44 lb) for

DICTIONARY OF TRAVEL, TOURISM AND HOSPITALITY

each economy passenger. See also **excess baggage**.

baggage check Receipt issued by a **carrier** to a passenger for **accompanied checked baggage**, establishing the passengers' right to compensation. See also **Property Irregularity Report (PIR)**; **Warsaw Convention**.

baggage claim area An area of a transportation **terminal** where **accompanied checked baggage** is claimed by passengers on arrival at the destination. See also **baggage check**; **baggage tag**.

baggage master The person who controls **baggage** handling on a ship.

baggage room
(a) An area of a ship where **baggage** is stored, which is available to passengers at certain times during the voyage, as distinct from **hold baggage**, stored in the ship's **hold** and not available.
(b) A room in a **hotel** where luggage is stored on arrival before it is taken to the guest's room or after vacating the room before departure.

baggage tag A personal identification attached to a piece of luggage.

Bagtrack A worldwide computerized system used by most major airlines for tracing lost air passengers' **baggage**, based on matching details of baggage reported missing against details of unclaimed baggage.

Baht Unit of **currency** of Thailand.

bait and switch See **switch selling**

balance of payments An account of a country's transactions with the rest of the world, i.e., with other countries and international institutions. The main divisions are the current account and the capital account. The current account is sub-divided into visible items (balance of trade, i.e., exports and imports of goods) and **invisibles** (**services**, return on investments, private transfers and government transactions). The capital account includes money flows for investment, grants and loans. **International travel** spending in the countries visited is shown as a separate invisi-ble item; other transactions due to travel and tourism are submerged with other items.

balance of trade See **balance of payments**

Balboa (B) Unit of **currency** of Panama. The US Dollar is also used.

Balkans The **peninsula** of south-east Europe, bounded by the Adriatic, the Aegean, the Mediterranean, the Sea of Marmara and the Black Sea, comprising Albania, Bulgaria, Greece, Romania, countries of the former Yugoslavia and Turkey in Europe. All countries of the **region** have substantial tourism resources but their recent tourism development has been uneven. Greece and Turkey have shown fast growth; that of the former Yugoslav territories has been arrested by civil wars; Bulgaria and Romania experienced a decline in the 1990s.

balneology Scientific study of bathing and mineral springs and the healing effects of their waters. The treatment of disease by baths or medicinal springs is *balneotherapy*, a significant aspect of **health tourism**.

balneotherapy See **balneology**

Baltic States Term given to the countries on the eastern side of the Baltic Sea – Lithuania, Latvia, Estonia – which were independent between the two World Wars, annexed by the Soviet Union in 1940, and have been independent again since 1991. The Baltic States have many attractions but many facilities are still to be developed for **international tourism**.

bank buying rate The **rate of exchange** at which a bank will buy a foreign **currency** or **traveller's cheques (traveler's checks)**. See also **bank selling rate**.

bank(er's) draft A **cheque (check)** drawn by a bank, as distinct from a cheque drawn by a bank's **customer**. Banker's drafts are used at the request of a customer when a creditor is not willing to accept a personal cheque in payment. The drawer's account is debited when the draft is drawn and the draft is regarded as cash, since it cannot be returned unpaid. Used in travel, tourism and hospitality in transactions between **firms** and other organizations rather than by individuals. See also **bill of exchange**; **letter of credit**.

bank guarantee A guarantee by a bank that it will pay in the event of default, so that no enquiries regarding the solvency of an individual need be made.

Bank Holidays Days on which banks in the UK are legally closed, also usually kept as **public holidays**. Bank Holidays in England, Wales, Northern Ireland and the Channel Islands are: New Year's Day, Good Friday, Easter Monday, Early May Holiday (first Monday in May), Spring Holiday (late May/early June), Late Summer Holiday (last Monday in August), Christmas Day, Boxing Day. In Scotland the public holidays fall on the same days as in England, except that 2 January is substituted for Easter Monday and August Bank Holiday is taken on the first Monday instead of the Late Summer Holiday. In Northern Ireland 17 March (St Patrick's Day), and in the Channel Islands 9 May (Liberation Day), are also public holidays.

bank selling rate The **rate of exchange** at which a bank will sell a foreign **currency** or **traveller's cheques (traveler's checks)**. See also **bank buying rate**.

Bank Settlement Plan (BSP) A system of settlement of travel agency accounts with airlines based on uniform documentation for all airlines, in which payments are made through a bank and not directly to **carriers**. Under the system **agents** report airline sales and their bank accounts are debited with the amounts owed.

bar code *Universal Product Code (UPC)*, system of printed lines on a product, which gives a price when read by a computer.

bareboat charter An arrangement whereby a yacht or another vessel is hired without a crew or supplies for a specified period. Evidence of competence is usually required by the charterer and seashore facilities are usually available to provide fuel and other supplies. This is a highly developed approach in principal sailing areas, such as the Caribbean and is also common in Queensland, Australia; it is to be distinguished from **crewed charter** and **provisioned charter**. See also **flotilla cruising**.

barge A wide flat-bottomed boat used mainly on rivers and in **harbours**.

barometer An instrument for measuring atmospheric pressure, also used in estimating **altitude** and in weather forecasting. See also **altimeter**.

Baroque Architectural style of the seventeenth and early eighteenth centuries in Europe characterized by ornate decoration, complex spatial arrangement and grand vistas. The term is also applied to the painting of the period.

barrage A structure built across a river to hold back water for such purposes as irrigation, storage and also for flood control, as, e.g., the *Thames Barrier* in London, which has become a major **tourist/visitor attraction**. Sometimes a distinction is drawn between a barrage and a **dam**, the latter but not the former being used for power generation.

barrel A unit of capacity used in the brewing **industry** equal to 36 Imperial **gallons**.

barrier island A low sandy ridge running parallel to a coastline, from which it is separated by a **lagoon**, so that it acts as a barrier between the lagoon and the open sea. Well-known examples are to be found along the eastern seaboard of the USA, north coast of continental Europe and the coast of east Africa. See also **barrier reef**.

barrier reef A **coral reef** running parallel to a coastline, from which it is often separated by a **lagoon**, so that it acts as a barrier between the lagoon and the open sea. A well-known example is the *Great Barrier Reef*, extending for over 2000 kilometres (1200 miles) off the coast of Queensland, which is one of Australia's chief **tourist/visitor attractions**. See also **barrier island**.

barter Exchange of goods or **services** without the exchange of money, to be found in primitive communities, but see also **black economy**.

base fare The **fare** excluding taxes and other **surcharges**.

basing fares See **basing point**

basing point A location to and from which air **fares** are established, and which is used in the absence of published fares for a given **itinerary** to construct **through** fares between the point of origin and the final destination. The component part fares are known as *basing fares*.

Bathing Water Directive European Community Council Directive of 1975 laying down minimum or 'mandatory' and stricter 'guideline' water quality standards for **beaches** in member states. At the end of each bathing season member states have to present the results of weekly testing to the EC, which publishes the season's results in an annual report *Quality of Bathing Water*, available from public libraries and European Documentation Centres. See also **Blue Flag**; **Seaside Awards**.

Bay Express New Zealand rail service linking Wellington and Napier in the North Island.

bazaar
(a) An Oriental **market** place, usually consisting of a large number of shops or stalls, such as the Istanbul bazaar, one of the city's major **tourist/visitor attractions**.
(b) A fair for the sale of articles, commonly with a charitable objective, attended mainly by **residents** of a locality, but sometimes also by **visitors**.

beach An area of sand or shingle on the shore of a lake or of the sea; when the latter, primarily between low and high water mark, but often extending above highwater and backed by cliffs, dunes and vegetated land. On a rocky coastline, in bays between headlands, beaches are characteristically arcuate in shape and less than a mile in length, but on soft coasts they can be much longer and straighter, e.g., Ninety Mile Beach in New Zealand. Beaches are a major **tourist/visitor attraction**, both in their own right and for water-based activities. While beaches are, within the tidal range, to a large extent self-cleansing, they, and the offshore waters in densely settled areas, have been greatly affected by **pollution**, by litter deposited by users, by refuse dumped offshore, by urban sewage, and by oil spills; the **European Union** is attempting to promote clean beaches by a system of evaluation and the award of **Blue Flags** for those that achieve the required standard.

beam A nautical term denoting the breadth of a ship at its widest point.

Beaufort scale A numerical scale of wind force, ranging from 0 (calm) to 12 (hurricane, above 120 km per hour).

bed and board See **American Plan (AP)**

bed and breakfast
(a) An **establishment** providing sleeping accommodation with breakfast, usually operated by private households and particularly common in the **British Isles**. Often referred to as a 'B & B'.
(b) **Accommodation** tariff which includes sleeping accommodation and **Continental** or **English breakfast**, offered by private households as well as commercial establishments. See also **Bermuda Plan (BP)**; **Continental Plan (CP)**; **European Plan (EP)**.

bed tax Tax levied by **central** or **local government** or another agency on staying **visitors** collected at the place of stay, as a means of raising revenue; sometimes the proceeds are applied to tourism purposes. May be also called *hotel*, or *room tax*. See also **resort tax**; **tourist tax**.

bed types/descriptions
See **berth** / **bunk** / **double** / **double double** / **Hollywood** / **king (size)** / **Murphy** / **queen (size)** / **rollaway bed** / **single** / **sofa bed** / **studio bed** / **twin** / **'Z' bed**

beehive-style hotel A Japanese-style soundproof, airconditioned cubicle with bed, table, television, telephone and small bathroom.

bell boy American term for page boy in a **hotel**.

bell captain American term for **hotel** head porter. See also **concierge**.

bell hop American term for **hotel** porter, also called *bellman*.

bellman See **bell hop**

below-the-line advertising Term often used to describe any form of **advertising** and promotional activity other than in the **commission**-paying **media**, and including, e.g., **direct**

mail and **merchandising**. See also **above-the-line advertising**.

beltway An American road round a town or city providing an alternative **route** for **through** traffic, called **bypass** in the UK.

Ben Gaelic term for mountain peak in Scotland and Ireland, e.g., Ben Nevis (the highest **mountain** in the **British Isles**).

benchmark Something that serves as the standard by which similar items can be compared or measured. Hence *benchmarking* in business involves comparing the performance of different businesses and identifying the best practice, with a view to improving the performance of one's own organization. See also **competitor analysis**.

Benelux Group of countries consisting of Belgium, the Netherlands and Luxembourg, which in 1948 set up a **customs** union, abolishing internal tariffs, reducing import quotas and adopting a common external tariff. This, together with a free movement of labour and capital within the union, preceded the three countries' joining the **European Economic Community (EEC)** in 1958, to be followed by increasing integration of their fiscal and monetary systems. With a combined population of more than 26 million (2000) and a high **standard of living**, the Benelux countries are significant generators of **international travel/tourism**. See also **Low Countries**.

Benelux Tourrail Pass Unlimited travel first or second class rail ticket for any five days in a month within Belgium, the Netherlands and Luxembourg available from railway stations in those countries or **agents** elsewhere. See also **rail passes**.

Bermuda Agreement A **bilateral air services agreement** made in 1946 between the United Kingdom and the USA regarding air services between the two countries (renegotiated as Bermuda 2 in 1977), which established a model for other similar bilateral agreements, hence described as Bermuda-type agreements. See also **Chicago Convention; freedoms of the air; traffic rights**.

Bermuda Plan (BP) Hotel tariff which includes room and **English breakfast**. See also **Continental Plan (CP); European Plan (EP)**.

Bermuda triangle A triangular area south of Bermuda known for unexplained disappearances of ships and **aircraft**.

Berne Convention An international agreement made in 1961 and amended in 1966 for the regulation of transport by rail in Europe.

berth
(a) Place where a boat or ship may lie when at anchor, at a **wharf** or in a **marina**.
(b) A sleeping place on a ship or train, often folding and attached to a wall.

best available Term used in reservation requests and/or confirmations to seek and/or promise the best room available in the **hotel**, for the required period, normally implying an undertaking on the part of the guest to pay the appropriate price.

Best Practice Forum (BPF) British Government-backed initiative launched in September 2001 by six leading **trade associations** in the tourism, hospitality and **leisure** sectors to set best practice standards. See also **Excellence Through People (ETP); Hospitality Assured (HA); Investors in People (IIP)**.

beverage cycle The sequence of stages in the beverage operation of a **hotel** or **restaurant**, usually seen for control purposes as comprising purchasing, receiving, storing and issuing, preparing, selling.

biannual Half-yearly, twice a year, e.g., a biannual meeting. See also **biennial**.

biennial Every two years, e.g., a biennial **festival**. See also **biannual**.

Big Apple A term used for New York.

Big Orange A term used for the state of California, adapted from New York's **Big Apple**.

bilateral Concerning relationship between two sides or parties as, for example, in *bilateral agreements* between countries, in which two countries agree reciprocal privileges not extended to others. Aspects of travel and tourism covered by bilateral agreements include, i.a., **passport** and **visa** requirements and **scheduled** air services between countries.

However, compared with international trade in goods, there is less regulation of **international travel** and **tourism**; much that exists is **multilateral** rather than bilateral.

bilharziasis Also known as *schistosomiasis*, a parasitic disease caused by a worm which penetrates the skin and can cause damage to the intestines, the liver and the urinary tract. The risk is present in many tropical and subtropical areas, especially in waterways in Africa. There is no vaccine but the disease can be treated. The main precaution is avoiding bathing and water/sports in streams, rivers and lakes in affected areas.

bilingual Fluent in two languages.

bill of exchange 'An unconditional order in writing addressed by one person to another, signed by the person giving it, requiring the person to whom it is addressed to pay on demand, or at a fixed or determinable future time, a sum certain in money, to or to the order of a specified person or to bearer' (Bills of Exchange Act 1882). The bill becomes valid once the recipient has 'accepted' it and like a **cheque (check)** it can be endorsed to bearer or to a named person. It is mainly used in international transactions but is of declining importance. See also **bank(er's) draft**; **letter of credit**.

bill of fare Literally list of dishes served in a **restaurant**, synonymous with menu.

billabong An Australian term for a branch of a river that flows away from the main stream and comes to a dead end.

billion In Europe, one million million; in the USA, one thousand million. American usage is now common worldwide.

biometrics A process that identifies people by their physical characteristics. The best-known forms are finger-printing, retina scans, hand geometry, voice recognition and digitized photography. See **automated immigration lane** and **INSPASS** for the application of biometrics in travel and tourism.

Biosphere Reserves Conservation areas of land and coast with significant 'biomass' (i.e., important wildlife species) designated by the **United Nations Educational, Scientific and Cultural Organization (UNESCO)**. See **countryside conservation designation schemes** for other schemes.

Birr (EB) Unit of **currency** of Ethiopia.

bistro A small informal **restaurant** serving light meals and refreshments. See also **bodega**; **brasserie**.

black box See **flight recorder**

black economy Economic activities not declared to the authorities for taxation purposes and hence not included in national accounts and other official statistics. Also described as *hidden*, *informal* or *parallel economy*. Guesstimates of the size of the black economy in the UK have ranged from 2 or 3 to 15 per cent of the **gross domestic product (GDP)**. Much of it appears to be undertaken on a cash or **barter** basis and to be particularly significant among small businesses and the **self-employed**, both prominent in tourism and hospitality activities. See also **black market**; **ghosting**; **moonlighting**.

black market Illegal transactions in scarce commodities, officially controlled goods or **currencies**. When currencies are to a significant extent bought and sold in the black market in the course of **international travel/tourism**, it is difficult to arrive at reliable estimates of **international tourism receipts** and **expenditures**; this is particularly the case when the estimates are based on such indirect methods as bank reporting rather than **visitor** surveys. See also **black economy**.

black tie Term used in invitations to social occasions to indicate that formal dress is to be worn. *Black tie optional* denotes that formal dress is preferred but a dark suit is also acceptable. See also **business attire**; **casual attire**.

block spacing An allocation by one airline to another of a number of seats on some of its flights, which the airline sells to the travelling public through its own marketing and distribution system. A block spacing agreement is used when the allocating airline has spare capacity and the airline to whom the seats are allocated is for some reason unable to serve an **airport**. For example, under an agreement between Delta Airlines and Virgin Atlantic in mid 1990s, Delta bought between 50 and 100 seats on every Virgin flight between London and a number of US **cities**, thereby gaining access indirectly to London Heathrow, as well as boosting Virgin's **load factor**. Among European airlines the approach is particularly favoured by Finnair, Swiss, SAS, CSA and LOT Polish Airlines.

Blue Flag Originally a pan-European award for **beaches** and **marinas** meeting the stricter 'guideline' water quality standards and environmental management of the **EC Bathing Water Directive** and offering good on-shore facilities, now extending also outside Europe. A list of European Blue Flag beaches is available from the Foundation for Environmental Education [www.fee-international.org]. See also **Seaside Awards**.

Blue Riband of the Atlantic Common term for the *Hales Trophy* awarded to a passenger vessel holding the speed record for crossing the Atlantic. The current holder is the UK Hoverspeed **catamaran** *Great Britain*, which succeeded *SS United States* in 1990.

Blue Train Luxury train service linking Pretoria, Johannesburg and Cape Town, a major tourist attraction in South Africa.

blue-collar An American term used to describe manual workers, especially skilled manual workers, nowadays also widely used elsewhere. See also **class**; **socio-economic group**; **white-collar**.

board
(a) To go on to a ship, train, **aircraft** or another vehicle.
(b) Meals provided to a guest or lodger. See **bed and board**.

boarding house Establishment common in the **British Isles** and other English-speaking countries, providing **accommodation** and meals to residents. Generally a small owner-managed establishment, which often has the character of an extended household, the boarding house has declined in popularity and is now a minority provider of **holiday (vacation)** accommodation. See also **bed and breakfast**; **guest house**; **pension**.

boarding pass A card given to airline passengers on completion of **check-in** procedures prior to boarding an **aircraft**, showing the passenger's name, flight number, section of aircraft and seat number. The analogous pass used in ships is called an *embarkation card*.

boat and breakfast Overnight accommodation on a boat with full **American breakfast** included in the price.

boatel See **botel**

bodega A Spanish term for a wineshop, wine bar or cellar, also in use elsewhere. See also **bistro**; **brasserie**.

Bolivar (B) Unit of **currency** of Venezuela.

Boliviano (B) Unit of **currency** of Bolivia.

Bonded Coach Holidays Bonding scheme operated by the UK **Confederation of Passenger Transport (CPT)** for **coach holiday (vacation)** operators who subscribe to it on a voluntary basis. The scheme covers coaching holidays in the UK and on the Continent of Europe. Around 100 coach holiday operators belong to it (2000). See **bonding schemes (UK)** for other schemes.

bonding Purchase of a guarantee of financial protection for a premium from a bonding or insurance company. Often employees handling cash require to be bonded as a condition of employment. Bonding is also a requirement for retail **travel agents** and **tour operators** in the UK and USA, as well as a number of other countries, to protect **principals** and/or **consumers** against default and/or failure. For bonding schemes in operation in the UK see **bonding schemes (UK)**.

bonding schemes (UK)
See **ABTA Bonding Scheme**
ABTOT Bonding Scheme
AITO Trust Bonding Scheme
ATOL Bonding Scheme
Bonded Coach Holidays
FTO Bonding Scheme
IATA Bonding Scheme
PSA Bonding Scheme

boom A major increase in activity as, e.g., *economic boom* or *baby boom*. In the economic boom, demand, prices and wages rise, while unemployment falls.

botel Two main uses of the term are evident: (a) an **establishment** providing customary **hotel** facilities and services on a permanently anchored ship; (b) more generally, a **hotel** or **motel** adjacent to a **marina** and serving wholly or mainly boat users. Also referred to as *boatel*.

bothie/bothy Scottish term for one-room building originally used for accommodating workmen, nowadays also describing such basic shelter without facilities to accommodate walkers, as in the Scottish Highlands.

bottom line Colloquial term for net profit or net loss, i.e., the amount shown in the last line of a profit-and-loss statement.

boutique Small specialized shop normally selling fashion clothing and similar items, sometimes a section of a department store or located in a **hotel**.

boutique hotel A relatively new designation of **hotel** accommodation, usually small in scale, privately owned and managed, with the emphasis on high quality personal service, comfort, decor and design, often operated in a distinctive restored building. See also **country house hotel**.

bow A nautical term denoting front of a ship or boat, also called **forward**; opposite end to **abaft**, **aft** or **stern**. See also **(a)midship(s)**.

brand An established product name, which readily identifies and differentiates a product from others in the minds of buyers. Avis, Hilton and Thomas Cook are prominent examples in travel, tourism and hospitality. *Brand awareness* denotes the extent to which potential buyers recognize a brand and its characteristics. *Brand image* refers to the impression people have of a product with a brand name. The extent to which **customers** continue to purchase a particular brand rather than competitive products is known as *brand loyalty*, in contrast to *brand switching*.

Brandt Commission *Independent Commission on International Development* set up in 1977 at the suggestion of the President of the **World Bank** under the chairmanship of Willy Brandt, German statesman and Nobel Peace Prize winner, to study global issues arising from economic and social disparities of the world community and to suggest ways of promoting solutions. The report of the Commission under the title *North–South: A Programme for Survival*, known as the *Brandt Report*, was published in 1980.

brasserie An **establishment** of French origin serving simple quick meals at most hours of the day, whilst **restaurants** (some called *auberges* or *relais*) tend to be more formal and open at traditional meal times. See also **bodega**; **bistro**.

breakbone fever See **dengue**

bridging loan A short-term loan to bridge the gap between the purchase of an asset and the sale of another, commonly used in the property and housing **market**.

bridlepath/bridleway A path suitable for use by pedestrians and horses but not vehicles, which may also be a **right of way** for pedestrians and riders on horseback in English law.

brig Scottish term for a bridge.

Bring Your Own (BYO) Term used for **restaurants** and other food outlets in Australia which allow **customers** to bring and consume their own beverages on the premises for a small charge (**corkage**). They are particularly common in Australia's second largest city, Melbourne. See also **brown bagging**.

Britain England, Wales and Scotland, more accurately called **Great Britain**, both to be distinguished both from **British Isles** and **United Kingdom (UK)**.

British Conference Market Survey (GB) Annual survey of **conferences** conducted by the **British Tourist Authority** since 1993 and giving data on volume of activity, types of conference, revenues, conference size and length.

British Home Tourism Survey (BHTS) See **British Tourism Survey (BTS)**

British Isles **United Kingdom** and the Republic of Ireland, to be distinguished from **Britain** and **Great Britain**.

British National Travel Survey (BNTS) An annual sample enquiry carried out by personal interviews intermittently in the 1950s and then each year since 1960 by a **market research company** for the **British Tourist Authority (BTA)** to establish the extent of **holidays (vacations)** away from home by British **residents** and information about the holidays they take in **Britain** and abroad. For a time (1985–8) also referred to as **British Tourism Survey** Yearly (BTS-Y). Summary results appear in the *Digest of Tourist Statistics* published by the British Tourist Authority. To be distinguished from **National Travel Survey**.

British National Rail Apex A return ticket following airline concept and terminology and available on InterCity trains from particular stations in **Great Britain** with fixed allocation of seats, offering a significant saving on normal **fare** plus free seat reservation. Must be booked at least seven days in advance and return date confirmed at the same time; travel must be on the train nominated on the ticket; there is a cancellation fee. See also **British National Rail Saver**; **British National Rail Supersaver**.

British National Rail Saver A return rail ticket offered in **Great Britain** without advance purchase requirement at a higher price than **British Rail Supersaver** but available on any day and with fewer restrictions. See also **British National Rail Apex**.

British National Rail Supersaver A return rail ticket available on most InterCity trains in **Great Britain** on most days of the week without advance purchase requirement, giving a major reduction off normal fare. See also **British National Rail Apex**; **British National Rail Saver**.

British railcards Discount cards for rail travel in **Britain**, which enable card holders to buy discounted tickets for use at certain times during the week; most discounts apply nationally. There are four types available, all valid for 12 months, with varying benefits and restrictions:

Senior Railcard	to anyone aged 60 and over
Young Persons Railcard	to those between 16 and 25 years of age and full-time students over 25
Family Railcard	for adults travelling with children
Disabled Railcard	to people registered as disabled and certain other categories

There are also *Network Cards* (for use in London and South-East England only) and *Forces Cards* (issued directly through military units).

British Summer Time (BST) Local **daylight saving time** one hour in advance of **Greenwich Mean Time (GMT)** observed in the UK between late March and late October, in order to extend the period of daylight at the end of a normal working day. See also **standard time**.

British Tourism Survey (BTS) Name given to two separate sample surveys of British **residents'** tourism between 1985 and 1988: (a) an annual **holiday (vacation)** survey in late autumn, known as British Tourism Survey Yearly (BTS-Y), but until 1984 and again since 1989 as **British National Travel Survey (BNTS)**; and (b) a monthly survey of tourism for all purposes, known as British Tourism Survey Monthly (BTS-M), but formerly called British Home Tourism Survey (BHTS) and in 1989 replaced by **United Kingdom Tourism Survey (UKTS)**.

Britrail Pass An unlimited travel ticket for periods up to one month over **British rail** network only sold overseas to **visitors** to **Great Britain** and intended for the independent traveller who spends a number of days touring outside London. See also **rail passes**.

broad/Broadlands/The Broads *Broad* is used in **East Anglia** for shallow fresh water lakes formed by the widening of a river where peat was extracted for fuel in mediaeval times. *Broadlands* or the *Broads* is the area on Norfolk/Suffolk border of major **conservation** and tourism interest popular for angling, **power boating**, sailing and nature study. Designated as a **National Park** in 2002.

brochures Printed material used to communicate with existing or potential **travellers** in **tourism destination** promotion and in the promotion of tourism-related facilities and **services** such as **hotels**, **cruises** and **inclusive tours**.

brown bagging American term for the practice of bringing one's own alcoholic drinks into a **restaurant** not licensed to sell them. See also **Bring Your Own (BYO)**.

brunch A meal served between normal breakfast and lunch times and replacing breakfast and lunch. An American concept, which has met with success when introduced in private households as well as **hotels** elsewhere in recent years.

Brundtland Report See **sustainable tourism**

Brussels Convention An international agreement made in 1961 for the regulation of sea transport by stipulating the obligations of the **carrier** and the conditions of the carrier's responsibility, to be distinguished from **International Convention on the Travel Contract**, also adopted in Brussels.

BS 5750 A series of guidelines to **companies** on what is required of a quality system (see **total quality management**) was first provided by the British Standards Institution in BS 5750, ISO 9000 being the international equivalent of BS 5750. Subsequently BS 5750 was renamed BS EN ISO 9000 as part of a revision of the Standard, in order to remove confusion caused by the existence of both the British BS 5750 and the international ISO 9000.

BS EN ISO 9000 See **BS 5750**

bubble car See **dome car**

bucket shop A slang term for a retail outlet selling cut-price wares, e.g., a travel agency which deals in unofficially discounted airline tickets, also known as *discount ticket agency*. The practice of discounting arises because on many **routes** the supply of seats exceeds demand. It is usually not an offence to buy discounted tickets but, as airlines agree with governments that they will not sell their tickets at discounted rates, in a number of countries including UK, they and also **travel agents** render themselves liable to prosecution.

buckshee Slang term for something extra or free.

Buddha Day See **Wesak**

Buddhism The Asian religious system founded by Buddha, a religious teacher in North India in the sixth and fifth centuries BC.

budget
(a) Estimate of future income and expenditure.
(b) Term used to describe inexpensive facilities and **services**, e.g., *budget hotels, budget fares, budget travel*.

buffer zone The **zone** extending 225 miles north and south of the US border with Canada and Mexico subject to special tax arrangements.

buffet
(a) A self-service meal consisting of a selection of dishes displayed on a table or counter. Hence, e.g., cold or hot buffet; buffet breakfast, lunch or dinner.
(b) An outlet serving food and refreshments at **airports**, other transport **terminals**, and similar locations.

building conservation schemes Conservation schemes for buildings, ancient monuments and built-up areas considered worthy of protection. For schemes in the UK see **Listed Buildings**; **Scheduled Ancient Monuments**; **Conservation Areas**. See also **countryside conservation designation schemes**.

built attractions See **tourist/visitor attractions**

bulk fare American term for the **fare** charged by transport operators, normally to **tour operators**, for a minimum number of booked seats.

bulkhead An interior wall separating areas in a ship or **aircraft**. Hence *bulkhead seats*, i.e., the seats immediately behind a partition wall.

Bullet Train Japanese high-speed train introduced in 1964; until 1981 when the French TGV came into service, the bullet trains were the fastest trains in the world. See also **Advanced Passenger Train (APT)**; **Train à Grande Vitesse (TGV)**.

bumboat A boat engaged in selling stores alongside ships in a harbour. Hence *bumboatman*, a person selling stores from a bumboat.

bumping Refusing to transport a passenger or accommodate a guest with a reservation, in favour of another, as in case of **overbooking**. A common airline practice is for passengers to

27

be 'bumped' according to the order in which they **check in**, with those checking in last most likely to lose their seats. However, an increasing number of airlines tend to follow the US approach, where airlines must ask for passengers who want to volunteer to be bumped for a payment. The Council of **European Community** Transport Ministers agreed minimum levels of compensation to airline passengers from April 1991. See also **denied boarding compensation**.

bungee-jumping A significant adventure tourism activity whose modern version originated in New Zealand, but claimed to have its origins in the land diving still staged on the island of Pentecost in Vanuatu. There it is performed by men diving head first from a 70 ft tower with vines attached to their ankles to break the fall.

bunk Two-tier bed, common in youth **hostels**, and ships; hence *bunkhouse*, a facility providing such accommodation, sometimes as a part of a larger facility, such as a **hotel** or **restaurant** offering additional **services**, including meals and refreshments, to bunkhouse users, found, e.g., in Scotland.

bureau-de-change An office dealing in foreign **currencies** and **traveller's cheques (traveler's checks)**.

bus
(a) In the UK, a road passenger motor vehicle operating short **scheduled** stage services, to be distinguished from vehicles operating long distance services or tours and described as **coaches**.
(b) In North America, a road passenger motor vehicle operating **scheduled** or **charter** services irrespective of distance.
(c) Also American term for clearing **restaurant** tables, hence **busboy** or **busgirl**, or **busser**, an employee responsible for the task.

busboy/busgirl/busser American term for assistant waiter or waitress, who pours water, clears away plates and cutlery but does not take orders or serve the food.

bush Term applied to uncleared or uncultivated areas in former British colonies, especially Africa and Australia, and hence to the country as opposed to the town. See also **outback**.

business attire Semi-formal dress of business suit or jacket with shirt and tie for men and day dress or suit for women. See also **black tie**; **casual attire**.

business centre
(a) Commercial centre of a town or **city** where the main banks and shops are located (see **central business district**).
(b) Facility providing services such as photocopying, **facsimile transmission (fax)** and secretarial services, to business users when travelling, and located, e.g., in a **hotel**, **airport** or conference centre.

Business Class A **class** of transport, usually airline, service between first and economy class, i.e., less expensive than the former and more comfortable than the latter, with various special amenities. Also known as *Club Class* on some airlines.

business cycle Type of fluctuation in economic activity around the longer-term trend observed in **industrialized countries**, consisting of general expansion followed by similarly general **recession**. Reflected in the level of national income, employment and other aggregates, the fluctuation is recurrent but the span from peak to peak or trough to trough of the cycle varies, typically around five years or more. The general cycle influences the demand for travel, tourism and hospitality **services**, and *vice versa*, although different forms differ in the extent and also in the time lag of the influence.

business house agency A retail agency catering principally for the travel needs of commercial and industrial **firms** as **clients** rather than the general public.

business mix Term used to describe the combination of **market** segments for which a business caters or plans to cater. Thus a **visitor attraction** may cater to local residents; day visitors from within, say, three hours' driving distance from home; **visitors** on **holiday (vacation)** staying within, say, an hour's drive; these groups may be subdivided into individuals, schools and other groups. A **hotel** business mix may consist of **leisure** and business guests, subdivided between individuals and groups. Also referred to as *customer mix*. See also **sales mix**.

business travel department
(a) Department or section of a travel agency handling **business travel**.
(b) **In-house** travel agency in a **firm** or organization, which makes travel arrangements for their employees and not the general public. In the USA, also called *in-plant agency*.

See also **implant**.

business travel/tourism Trips and visits made by employees and others in the course of their work, including attending meetings, **conferences** and exhibitions.

buyers' market A **market** for goods or **services** in which buyers are in a strong negotiating position, usually as a consequence of an excess of supply over demand, characterized by falling prices. In travel, tourism and hospitality, a buyers' market exists when there is, e.g., overcapacity of airline seats or **hotel** rooms. See also **sellers' market**.

bylaw/by-law/byelaw Regulation made by a **local authority** or another public body, such as a railway **company** (not by **central government**). Many are directed, e.g., at **visitors** to **beaches**, parks and users of travel facilities with a view to preventing damage, offence or nuisance.

bypass
(a) Road round a town providing an alternative **route** for **through** traffic. Called a **beltway** in the USA.
(b) In the USA, selling by transport and **tour operators** direct to **customer** without the use of **travel agents**, known as **direct selling** in the UK.

cab Abbreviation of *cabriolet*, a two-wheeled one-horse carriage with a large hood, but nowadays used more widely for a vehicle for hire by the general public with a driver and a meter for registering the fare, as a synonym for *taxi*.

cabana A room or structure on the **beach** or by the swimming pool separated from the main **hotel** building, which may but need not be furnished with beds. See also **cabin**.

cabin
(a) Small simple dwelling, often a **second home**.
(b) Simple room or structure on the **beach** or by the swimming pool. See also **cabana**.
(c) Enclosed lift (elevator).
(d) Sleeping room on a ship.
(e) Passenger interior of an **aircraft**.
Hence, e.g., *cabin steward* (a member of ship's crew); *cabin attendant* (a member of aircraft crew); *cabin crew* (staff responsible for on-board safety and comfort of passengers of an aircraft).

cabin baggage See **checked/unchecked baggage**

cabin cruiser A power-driven vessel with one or more **cabins** providing living and sleeping **accommodation** and sometimes also cooking facilities, and used for **leisure** purposes.

cabin lift American term for **cable car**.

cable car
(a) A means of transport up the **mountain** used mainly for **sightseeing** and **skiing**, moved by an endless cable. In North America, called *cabin lift*.
(b) A tram car drawn by a cable set in the road in San Francisco, USA.

cabotage In *shipping*, coastal trade or transport between **ports** of the same country. In *civil aviation*, travel and transport on domestic **routes** or between territories of a sovereign state, including its colonies and dependencies. Thus, e.g., not only London–Glasgow and New York–Los Angeles, but also London–Gibraltar and Los Angeles–Honolulu are *cabotage routes*. International agreements do not extend to cabotage routes. Hence, **residents** of a country may be eligible for special reduced **fares**, known as *cabotage fares*. *Cabotage rights* refer to the right of the country's **carrier** to carry passengers between two points in another country.

café Establishment providing food and refreshments for consumption on the premises to the general public. Commonly a small unit with a limited menu and no alcoholic liquor available, sometimes open only during the day but not in the evening. See also **bistro**; **bodega**; **brasserie**; **restaurant**.

café complet A mid-morning or afternoon snack with coffee, sometimes also used to describe **Continental breakfast**.

cafeteria Self-service **restaurant** often located in a factory, office block or another place of employment for the use of staff or in an educational **establishment** for the use of students and staff.

cairn A mound of stones piled up as a **route** marker, landmark or monument.

campaign As used in **marketing**, the term describes any organized programme of action in the promotion of goods or **services** to achieve specific objectives. Each campaign is normally planned over a specified period of time and has a common theme or message. Although the term has been traditionally most often used in relation to **advertising**, it is equally applicable to other promotional aspects of the **marketing mix**, and several of them are typically combined in a single campaign. Well-known marketing campaigns in travel, tourism and hospitality have included 'World's biggest offer' (British Airways); 'We try harder' (AVIS); 'I love New York' (New York State).

camper See **caravan**; **recreation(al) vehicle (RV)**

campground Synonym for **camping site**.

camping site
(a) In Europe, an area used for camping in own tents and/or in static tents, which may be rented.
(b) In North America, an area used for tents as well as **trailer** and motor **caravans**. Such combined facilities are usually described in Europe as *camping and caravan sites.*

campus holidays (vacations) Holidays based on student **accommodation** on a university campus during **vacations**, often **activity holidays** or what may be regarded as **special interest holidays (vacations)**.

canal An artificial watercourse constructed to link rivers, lakes and other waterways for (a) inland navigation, or (b) water supply and irrigation. Major examples of the former include the Panama Canal and the Suez Canal; numerous canals in south-west USA and in Pakistan exemplify the latter. Long narrow boats with living accommodation used on canals are known as *canal boats.*

cancellation Making void something that has been agreed or planned. Hence *cancellation charge* (charge to be paid when a booking is cancelled); *cancellation clause* (clause in a contract giving terms on which the contract may be cancelled); *cancellation rate* (proportion of all bookings cancelled).

Canine Corps Dogs belonging to US **customs** and the Department of Agriculture used to sniff out drugs and other **contraband** items at international **airports**.

canyon A Spanish term describing a deep, steep-sided valley, with a river flowing at the bottom, characteristic of plateau country under arid and semi-arid **climates**. A well-known example and a major **tourist/visitor attraction** is Grand Canyon in Arizona, USA, a **National Park**, where **tourist** pressures and erosion pose serious management problems; flights by **aircraft** and rafting on the Colorado River add to them.

capacity limitation agreement An agreement between **carriers**, commonly airlines, stipulating the maximum capacity to be offered by each carrier on a particular **route**.

capacity tonne-miles A measure of transport output calculated as the product of **aircraft payload** (measured in short **tons** of 2000 lb) and the miles flown.

capacity tonne-kilometres A measure of transport output calculated as the product of **aircraft payload** (measured in metric **tonnes**) and the kilometres flown. Also known as *available tonne-kilometres (ATK)*. See also **load tonne-kilometres**.

capital *Inter alia*, main town or **city** in a country, state, province or another geographical entity. In some countries the administrative capital and the business capital are separate as, e.g., in the Netherlands (The Hague and Amsterdam), Scotland (Edinburgh and Glasgow) or Tanzania (Dodoma and Dar-es-Salaam).

capital gearing The relationship between loans and owners' funds in the capital structure of a **firm**, in the USA called *leverage*. Various approaches are used in the calculation of the ratio, but essentially high gearing denotes a high proportion and low gearing a low proportion of fixed interest capital in relation to **equity** capital. Gearing influences the respective risks of owners and lenders.

capital-intensive An economic activity is capital-intensive when capital represents a high proportion of resources used in production compared with labour. Although tourism and hospitality **services** are generally considered to be **labour-intensive**, such **tourism-related industries** as transport are highly capital-intensive. See also **productivity**.

captain's table Dining room table on a ship, which passengers are invited to share with the captain during the voyage.

captive Term commonly used in relation to (a) an **audience** that cannot avoid exposure to a communication (e.g., cinema-goers to screen **advertising**) or (b) a **market**, i.e., potential purchasers who have to buy a particular product in the absence of alternatives (e.g., meals and refreshments from the only **restaurant** in an isolated **resort**).

car hire UK synonym for *auto rental*.

car hop An American term for an employee
(a) who parks cars of arriving guests and returns them on departure; the practice is known as *valet parking*;
(b) who serves **customers** in their cars in a **drive-in restaurant**.

car occupancy The number of people per car visiting a **tourist/visitor attraction** or facility; an important statistic with implications for the provision of car parking.

caravan
(a) A group of merchants, pilgrims or others travelling together through deserts and other 'empty' areas in the East and in northern Africa. See also **caravanserai**.
(b) Accommodation vehicle for permanent, seasonal or temporary occupation, which meets requirements for construction and use of road vehicles. Basic distinctions are between *trailer* (towed) and *motor* (self-propelled) caravans, also called *campers* and in the USA *motor homes*. Caravan *sites* or *parks* are divided according to their use into *permanent, static* and *touring sites*, providing permanent places of residence and **second homes** on the one hand and temporary short-term facilities for **holiday (vacation)** use on the other hand. See also **recreation(al) vehicle (RV)**.

caravanserai An Eastern **inn** consisting of a quadrangular building enclosing a large court where **caravans** put up.

cardinal points The four main points of the **compass**: north, south, east, west.

Caribbean tourism statistics Statistics of individual countries as well as for the **region** as a whole are published in an annual report by the **Caribbean Tourism Organization**, Sir Frank Walcott Building, Culloden Farm, St Michael, Barbados (Tel: (809) 427-5242, Fax: (809) 429-3065).

carnet *Carnet de passage en douanes*, a **customs** pass issued by **motoring organizations** to their members, authorizing temporary importation of motor vehicles, **trailers** and **caravans** into countries without payment of duties. A carnet is also used for temporary **duty-free** importation of certain other goods, e.g., promotional material of no commercial value, works of art and capital equipment for temporary use in exhibitions.

carousel
(a) Revolving mechanism from which passengers claim **checked baggage** at **airports** and other transport **terminals**.
(b) Food and beverage self-service, in which food and/or drink is displayed on several revolving circular shelves at different heights; from there the **customer** places his/her chosen items on a tray.

carrier Any person or organization that undertakes the conveyance of goods and/or people for hire. The legal term *common carrier* implies an obligation to transport subject to certain conditions (as, e.g., in the case of railways), as distinct from *private carrier* who makes no general offer to the public. The term *designated carrier* refers to an airline identified in a **bilateral** agreement to operate services between two countries.

carrying capacity In tourism, the maximum capacity of a site or area to sustain **tourist** activity without deterioration in the quality of the **visitor** experience or the **environment**. Hence, carrying capacity may be seen to have physical, social (perceptual) and environmental dimensions and is normally expressed in terms of a given number of concurrent users of, e.g., a historic attraction, **beach** or **resort**. The concept was first applied extensively in tourism in the 1960s when it was also incorporated in the planning of such major developments as the Languedoc-Roussillon project in France. It has assumed an enhanced significance more recently with an increasing concern for the **environment**.

carry-on baggage See **checked/unchecked baggage**

cartel A group of **firms** in an **industry** agreeing to act together to minimize competition by such means as regulating prices and output. Cartels and similar agreements are now illegal in the UK, the USA and many other countries as being **monopolies** not in the public interest. A prominent example of an international cartel is the **Organization of the Petroleum Exporting Countries (OPEC)** but many shipping **conferences** are also forms of cartel.

cartography Representation of spatial information in the form of maps; mapmaking.

carvery A **restaurant** where hot roast meals are offered at the **buffet** table for the **customer** to carve his/her own portion or to be served by a **chef** and then to help himself/herself to vegetables and **accompaniments**.

cash and carry A method of selling, originally used by manufacturers or **wholesalers**, whereby retailers would collect goods from warehouses for resale to the general public. Nowadays used, i.a., widely as a popular method of food and drink purchasing at competitive prices by smaller **catering establishments** collecting purchases from a warehouse for which they pay cash.

cash bar A bar provided at a private function where those attending pay for their own drinks. In North America, also called *no host bar*. See also **host bar**.

cash dispensers See **automated teller machines (ATMs)**

cash points See **automated teller machines (ATMs)**

casino Originally, a public room used for social meetings, especially music and dancing, nowadays usually a purpose-built structure for gambling, a major attraction for **tourists** in centres such as Las Vegas and Monte Carlo. Seen by many smaller settlements as a means of attracting tourists, e.g., Sun City in South Africa and a number of Indian reservations in the USA. However, in the UK, under the Gaming Act 1968, casinos can legally only operate as **clubs**.

casual attire Casual dress of a sport shirt, possibly with a jacket, for men and leisure dress, such as slacks, for women. See also **black tie**; **business attire**.

casual employee/worker One engaged for irregular employment by the hour or on a day-to-day basis, and usually paid wages in cash on completion of each particular turn of duty. Sometimes also described as *occasional employee/worker*. What constitutes a casual employee/worker is sometimes defined specifically for statutory purposes or in **collective agreements** between employers and employees or their representatives.

catamaran Originally describing a raft of two boats fastened side by side, nowadays the term is usually used for a twin hull ship or boat, designed to cut through the waves, such as *SeaCat* operated as a **ferry** by *Hoverspeed* between the English coast and the Continent of Europe.

catchment area In the context of travel, tourism and hospitality, an area from which the majority of users of an attraction, facility or service are drawn. Many, such as theatres or swimming pools, are usually local, with most users coming from within a few miles; many **theme parks** and major **leisure** centres have regional catchment areas; some major attractions, such as Alton Towers in England, have national catchment areas.

catering In the USA the term denotes the provision of food and service for specific occasions on particular dates in particular locations. In other countries, including the UK, the term has a wider meaning and refers to all food services.

caveat emptor A legal expression meaning 'let the buyer beware', i.e., a person being assumed to exercise common sense when buying and not being entitled to the protection of the law, if he/she fails to do so. In most **developed countries** the rule is now of limited significance as a result of **consumer** protection legislation, which is particularly relevant in travel, tourism and hospitality, where the buyer is often not in a position to inspect the product before purchase.

caving A general term which has acquired special meaning as active **recreation** exploring caves, particularly in limestone areas, as in the

Peak District National Park in England, where there are interlinked systems of caverns. Problems can occur from the sudden rise in the level of water in the caverns, which may result in cavers being trapped or drowned. Caves may be also **tourist/visitor attractions** in their own right, as with the Carlsbad Caverns in the USA, where the main cave has a maximum height of 285 feet (85 metres).

cay A low sand and coral island, sandbank or reef, common especially in the West Indies and Florida. See also **kay/key**.

Cedi (C) Unit of **currency** of Ghana.

Celsius See **centigrade**

census A method of inquiry, in which data are collected from every member in a specific population, as distinct from **sampling**. It is rarely used in **market research** because of cost reasons. Probably best known are periodic national population censuses nowadays carried out in most countries, which provide a wealth of demographic, economic and social data. They have been carried out every ten years in the UK since 1801 (except 1941) and in the USA since 1790. See also **Census of Population (UK)**.

Census of Population (UK) Comprehensive enumeration of the whole UK population every ten years. Provides information on population size and characteristics, including demographic, economic and social characteristics. It is the most detailed and accurate source of data relating to a particular point in time, i.e., Census day, which also provides **benchmarks** for other surveys, estimates and projections. A **census** with similar objectives is conducted in most countries at more or less regular intervals.

centigrade Measure of temperature using Celsius' thermometer of 100 degrees, with freezing point of water 0° and boiling point 100°, now used almost everywhere except the USA. See also **Fahrenheit**.

central business district (CBD) A concept of American origin to describe the commercial centre of a town or **city** (also called *downtown* in the USA). Its main characteristics are a concentration of retailing, financial, professional and personal services and of transport

facilities, together with high density of land use and high land values. Other common features are high rise buildings, high traffic densities, and high daytime in relation to **resident** population.

central government See **public sector**

central reservation system(s) (CRS) See **computer reservation systems (CRS)**

Central Standard Time A Canadian and US **time zone** based on the standard of the 90th **meridian**. Time equals GMT –6.

certificate of airworthiness Document issued by a national civil aviation authority to certify that an **aircraft** satisfies its safety and other criteria.

certificate of seaworthiness Document issued by a national maritime authority to certify that a ship satisfies its safety and other criteria.

chain unit Individual **establishment** (such as a **hotel**, **restaurant** or shop) that is part of a large group of similar establishments with the same management. Also referred to as **multiple**.

Chamber of Commerce Voluntary nonprofit making organization of businesses in a town or district to protect and promote their interests through representation and providing **services** to members as well as promoting local economic development. In some countries they also perform the functions of a local **tourist board**, especially tourism promotion. Chambers of Commerce are to be distinguished from *chambers of trade*, normally local associations of retailers with more limited purposes, and also from **trade associations**.

Chamber of Trade See **Chamber of Commerce**

Channel Tunnel See **Eurotunnel**

charge card An instrument which enables the card holder to make purchases on credit by presenting the card to the vendor in lieu of cash. Issued by organizations such as American Express and Diner's Club, charge cards (unlike **credit cards**) have no credit limit but accounts have to be settled in full each month. Together with credit cards, charge cards are the fastest growing methods of payment for travel, tourism and hospitality services. See also **credit card**; **debit card**.

charter The hire by contract of the whole or part capacity (*part charter*) of an **aircraft**, ship, train or bus; when several operators share a charter, this is known as *split charter*. Single or several one-off arrangements are known as *ad hoc charters*, regular journeys contracted for as *series charters*; in the case of *time charter* an operator has an exclusive use of the vehicle throughout the period of the charter. In travel and tourism chartering has assumed a particular significance in connection with **inclusive tours** by air, which were responsible for much of the growth of **international travel/tourism** following the Second World War.

château French term for a country home or castle.

check-in

(a) Procedure for registration of guests on arrival in **hotels** and other **accommodation establishments**, commonly by signing a register.
(b) Procedure for passengers completing airline formalities before flight departure, also sometimes applicable in other forms of transport.

check-in time Term most commonly used to denote the latest time by which passengers are required to report at the **airport terminal** before flight departure. The interval between **check-in** and departure times usually differs as between domestic and international flights, but also between **scheduled** and **charter** services to the same destination. The term is also used in relation to other forms of transport and somewhat differently in **hotels** where *latest check-in time* denotes how late a reserved room will be held before it is let to another guest, unless the hotel is notified of **late arrival**.

check-out Procedure for guests vacating their rooms and settling their accounts in **hotels** and other **accommodation establishments**. The term is sometimes also applied to the desk or counter where accounts are settled.

check-out time Latest time by which **hotel** guests are expected to vacate and pay for their rooms on the day of departure, commonly but not necessarily 12 noon. See also **late check-out**.

checked/unchecked baggage Accompanied **baggage** may be either handed over by the passenger to the **carrier** at **check-in time** and claimed at the destination or remain in the passenger's possession during the journey (also called *cabin* or *carry-on baggage*).

chef Person in charge of food preparation in a **hotel** or **restaurant** kitchen, also called *chef de cuisine; sous chef* is the second in command; *chef de partie* is in charge of a section of the kitchen, e.g., soups; *commis chef* is an assistant to a chef de partie. In this 'classical' kitchen organization, *chef entremêtier* = vegetable chef; *chef garde-manger* = larder chef; *chef pâtisser* = pastry chef; *chef poissonnier* = fish chef; *chef potage* = soup chef; *chef rôtisseur* = roast chef; *chef saucier* = sauce chef; *chef tournant* = relief chef de partie.

cheque (check) An order written by the drawer to a bank, in which he/she has an account, to pay on demand a specified sum of money to a bearer or a named payee. An open cheque is payable over the counter; a crossed cheque can only be paid into a bank account. Once a common method of payment for travel, tourism and hospitality services, in most parts of the world the use of cheques has been to a great extent superseded by the use of **charge cards** and **credit cards**. See also **cheque (check) card**; **traveller's cheque (traveler's check)**.

cheque (check) card A card issued by a bank to its **customers** guaranteeing that a **cheque (check)** drawn by a customer up to a specified amount will be honoured by a bank. See also **charge card**; **credit card**; **debit card**.

Chicago Convention An international agreement made in 1944 which, i.a., confirmed the doctrine that air space above sovereign territory was within the jurisdiction of the sovereign country, and defined the so-called **freedoms of the air**. These are strictly speaking not rights but privileges, which may be permitted by **bilateral** agreements between governments. Each country has to conclude a series of bilateral agreements with other countries, which may include all or some of the freedoms of the air codified at Chicago. See also **air services agreement**; **Bermuda Agreement**; **technical rights**; **traffic rights**.

C

Chinese New Year New Year's Day based on lunar calendar observed as a **public holiday** in China and other countries with large Chinese communities. It falls in January or February and is celebrated as the most important annual festival by Chinese communities.

Chinese religions Religious systems primarily concerned with the celebration of major events in the **life cycle** and rituals in recognition of birth and death as rites of passage, with three forms of religious teaching: Confucian ethics (in relation to public life), Taoist teachings (about nature), and Buddhist ideas (about salvation).

Chinese restaurant syndrome Name given to an allergic condition which manifests itself by violent headaches after eating food flavoured with monosodium glutamate, used in Chinese cooking.

Chinook See **föhn**

cholera An intestinal infection causing severe diarrhoea (diarrhea) which may lead to dehydration and even death. Caused by contaminated water and also food in areas of poor sanitation in the **Middle East**, Africa, Asia and South America, but relatively rare among **travellers** even in those areas. It can be avoided by scrupulous attention to food, water and personal hygiene; a vaccine originally offered gave very little protection and none is currently available.

Christianity The monotheistic faith and religion (including Eastern Orthodox, Protestant and Roman Catholic) based on the personal teachings of Jesus Christ, a prophet from first-century Palestine.

Chunnel See **Eurotunnel**

Circle Pacific Fare Special air **fare** offered by several Pacific **carriers**, which allows passengers to fly to **Pacific Rim** destinations including Australia, Asia, North and South America, usually including four **stopovers** with additional stopovers available at an extra charge. One condition is that passengers must travel in either clockwise or anti-clockwise direction. See also **circle trip**.

circle trip A **trip** including more than one destination and return to **origin**, as distinct

from a return or **round trip**, a trip from one point to another and return. Thus, London–New York–Miami–London is a circle trip, London–New York–London is a return or round trip. See also **Circle Pacific Fare**.

circuit tourism Trips involving visits to more than one destination and return to **origin**. See also **circle trip**; **trip index**.

circulation Number of distributed copies of a newspaper or periodical, as distinct from the number of people who read it (**readership**). *Total* circulation consists of *subscribed*, i.e., paid for, and *free*, i.e., distributed free of charge, circulation. Normally quoted is *net* circulation, i.e., the number excluding distributed copies returned unsold or free copies. *Controlled* circulation refers to a free distribution of a publication, which is restricted to specific groups of reader, usually by reference to occupation status. Circulation data are of particular significance to advertisers of goods and **services**, including travel, tourism and hospitality products.

citizen
(a) An inhabitant of a town or **city**.
(b) A member of a state by birth or **naturalization**, as such enjoying certain rights and owing allegiance to it.
See also **national**.

city In **British Isles**, strictly a town which is or has been the seat of a bishop and has a cathedral, but more generally a large town. In the USA, the word is used more loosely as a synonym for town.

city/airport codes Three-letter location identifiers assigned and published by the **International Civil Aviation Organization (ICAO)** for use in timetables, ticketing and other communications. Thus, e.g., LON = London UK; LHR = London Heathrow Airport; NYC = New York, USA; JFK = New York J.F. Kennedy International Airport. See *OAG Flight Atlas* for a full list.

city pair The origin and destination **cities** of an **aircraft** flight.

city terminal Airline office located in town or **city** centre away from the **airport** from which passengers can normally obtain transport to the airport, and sometimes also complete some or all **check-in** procedures for their flight. Also called **air terminal**; see also **airport terminal**.

city tourism See **urban tourism**

class(es)
(a) A division according to quality, e.g., **aircraft** or railway carriage seating.
(b) A division of society according to status, e.g., into working, middle and upper class. Classes are usually represented in **consumer market** analysis by such classifications as **socio-economic groups**, which often reflect the foremost profile characteristics of **tourists**.

classification societies (shipping) Societies providing for the survey and classification of ships to specified standards and according to their construction, place of build, machinery, etc. Steel ships and their machinery are subject to regular surveys in order to maintain their classification. The principal classification societies are Lloyd's Register of Shipping (the first to be established), American Bureau of Shipping, Bureau Veritas, Der Norske Veritas, Germanischer Lloyd, Nippon Kaiji Kyokai, Registro Italiano Navale. Classification is voluntary, but its commercial advantages are so marked that it is generally sought by shipowners.

classified advertisements 'Small ads' grouped together into categories or classifications in one part of the newspaper or periodical, usually small type-set or semi-displayed and not more than one column wide, paid for on a line-by-line basis. This is a common use of **advertising** by smaller **firms** and **establishments** in travel, tourism and hospitality. See also **display advertisements**.

client Strictly speaking, an individual or organization that employs the professional **services** of another but nowadays also used more generally as a synonym for **customer**.

climate The long-term average weather conditions – principally rainfall, sunshine, temperature – over an area. It may encourage or act as a constraint on the development of tourism and is determined by three main factors: **latitude**, distribution of land and sea areas, and relief. Latitude or distance from the **equator** is the dominant influence. Land surfaces heat up and cool more rapidly than large areas of water; the oceans act as a store of warmth; hence, windward coasts and islands enjoy more equable climate, in contrast to extreme variations of continental areas. Relief has a major effect on weather where there are high **mountains**.

climatology Scientific study of the earth's **climates**. See also **meteorology**.

club
(a) Normally an **establishment** providing food and drink, sometimes also entertainment, overnight **accommodation** and other facilities and **services**, for members and not the general public. The exact meaning of the term differs sometimes between the **British Isles**, where the club originated, and other countries. A *night club* denotes a club open during the night hours, usually providing dancing and other entertainment.
(b) For use of the term in relation to air **fares**, see **air fare types**.

cluster Generally, a collection of things of the same kind in close proximity. In **land use planning**, cluster development strategy aims to locate activities, facilities and **services** together in an area. In travel, tourism and hospitality, the term is used when referring, e.g., to a cluster of **tourist attractions**, transport termini or eating **establishments**.

cluster analysis Technique often used in **market segmentation** in travel, tourism and hospitality, which aims to find groups of objects as homogenous as possible with respect to certain criteria within clusters, and as heterogenous as possible between clusters. There are several methods for combining objects into clusters.

coach
(a) A railway carriage.
(b) In the UK, a road passenger motor vehicle operating long distance **services** or tours, to be distinguished from a **bus**, which operates short **scheduled** stage services.
(c) In North America, economy class section of **aircraft**.

Coastal Pacific New Zealand rail service linking Invercargill and Picton in the South Island.

code of conduct A set of guidelines laying down standards to which members of a profession or association are expected to adhere in the exercise of their activities. Thus, e.g., in the UK the **Association of British Travel Agents (ABTA)** provides codes of conduct for retail **travel agents** and for **tour operators**, and individual members of the **Hotel and Catering International Management Association (HCIMA)** are required to observe the Association's code of conduct. The agreement between the **International Hotel and Restaurant Association (IHRA)** and the **Universal Federation of Travel Agents' Associations (UFTAA)** on **hotel** contracts represents a **bilateral** *Code of Practice* at international level. In recent years a number of Codes of Practice have been developed for the regulation and control of the **environment**, e.g., by the **Pacific Asia Travel Association (PATA)**.

code sharing The use of the same airline identification code for two or more **sectors**, which may be operated by different airlines; a practice of relatively recent origin, designed to promote the use of airlines for **connecting flights**. See also **airline codes**.

codes Standard abbreviations used in travel, tourism and hospitality by airlines, **travel agents** and others, in internal as well as external communications, such as reservations, timetables and ticketing. See **aircraft types: codes**; **airline codes**; **city/airport codes**; **country/state codes**; **currency codes**; **ticketing codes**. See also **code of conduct**; **International Hotel (Telegraph) Code**.

coffee shop An informal food and beverage outlet found in **hotels**, serving meals, snacks and refreshments through the day and into the night. The term differentiates a less formal outlet with more limited menu and long opening hours from a more formal hotel **restaurant**. In Asia the term *coffee shop* can also refer to a collection of private food sellers selling cheap meals in one **establishment**.

cognitive mapping Graphical representation of **consumer** perception of the distance to be travelled and the time to be spent in getting from point of **origin** to a **destination**. It is affected by the desirability of the destination and the convenience to reach it.

cohost An operator such as an airline or **hotel company** paying for storage and display of its schedules, availability and prices in the reservation system of another, which may include sharing the cost of development and provision of the system.

collective agreement A written agreement between representatives of employers and the **trade union** specifying the terms and conditions of employment and the procedures for the settlement of disputes. Also known as *union contract*.

collective tourism establishment An **accommodation establishment** providing overnight lodging for the **traveller** in a room or some other unit, but the number of places it provides must be greater than a specified minimum for groups of persons exceeding a single family unit and all the places in the establishment must come under a common commercial-type **management**, even if it is non-profit making. Collective establishments include **hotels and similar establishments**, specialized establishments and other collective establishments [**World Tourism Organization**].

colloquium An academic meeting at which one or more speakers deliver a lecture and answer questions on it.

Colon (₡) Unit of **currency** of Costa Rica.

colonial An inhabitant of a colony, term often used in the derogatory sense. In the USA, often used as an adjective to refer to the seventeenth and eighteenth centuries when the British territories which became the USA were still colonies, e.g., colonial art, colonial architecture, colonial dress.

Columbus Day Public Holiday observed in many countries of the **Americas** (including the Caribbean) towards the middle of October. Also called in some countries *Discovery of America Day*.

Comenius The school education strand of the **European Union Socrates** programme.

comfort index A subjective assessment, based on temperature and relative **humidity**, ranging from extremely cold to very hot, with comfortable conditions occupying a median position. As temperature rises, relative humidity should fall to maintain that sense of comfort. The level of comfort is also affected by wind speed (see **wind chill**). The concept was developed in relation to white Americans, and values for the most comfortable weather vary throughout the world because people have adapted to different conditions; stays by **tourists** are, however, too short for them to become acclimatized. The comfort index also differs at night and in daytime. Air conditioning in rooms and vehicles has lessened the importance of this concept in travel and tourism.

commercial economies See **economies of scale**

commercial freedoms Term used for Third and Fourth **freedoms of the air**, which cover most point-to-point traffic.

commercial hotel A description sometimes used for a transit **hotel** catering for business guests.

commissary A centralized food preparation and production facility, from which food is distributed to satellite kitchens in a number of locations. This is in contrast to self-contained facilities in each location concerned with all stages of food preparation and production.

commission (organization) In relation to organizations, designation normally used by or applied to a body of persons charged with a specified function, but also more loosely as a synonym for association or organization, e.g., Alpine Tourist Commission; Danube Tourist Commission; **European Travel Commission**.

commission (payment) Payment by a supplier to an **intermediary** as a reward for his **services**, usually determined as a percentage of the value of the transaction. Hence, *commission-able*, that for which a commission is payable. In travel, tourism and hospitality this is most commonly the amount received by a retail **travel agent** on ticket sales from airlines and other transport operators, on sales of tours from **tour operators**, and on other products and services from other **principals**. The percentage varies between products and services and to some extent also between countries and operators. Many principals also reward their most productive agents by higher rates or by other

incentive payments. See also **incentive commission**; **overriding commission**.

commissionaire Uniformed door attendant at cinemas, **hotels**, theatres and other public buildings.

commodization A process of human activities acquiring monetary value and effectively becoming goods for sale. In the tourism context the term often has pejorative connotation as, e.g., when cultural or religious events become commercialized.

common carrier See **carrier**

common interest travel/tourism A major segment of travel and tourism to be distinguished from **holiday (vacation)** and **business travel/tourism**, in which the **visitor** and the visited significantly share the common **purpose of the trip/visit**, e.g., **visiting friends and relatives**, education, religion. Relatively price-sensitive and not readily influenced by promotion, common interest travel/tourism often includes a relatively long stay but limited use of commercial facilities and **services** in the place visited.

common rated fares In air transport, identical **fares** available from an **airport** to two or more destinations, e.g., most **normal air fares** at most times of the year from London to Edinburgh and to Glasgow.

common rated points In air transport, two or more destinations to which air **fares** from a common point of origin are the same.

community tourism Term used to describe an approach to tourism in which the needs and views of local **residents** are incorporated in the planning and development process.

commuter A person who travels regularly, usually daily, between his/her places of residence and work. Commuters are not considered **tourists** or **visitors** and, therefore, not included in tourism statistics, but may be included in some travel statistics, e.g., in data relating to passenger transport.

commuter airline An airline (usually a small one) providing regular and reasonably frequent **scheduled** flights between small communities and larger hub airports. See also **hub and spoke system**.

companion fare/rate Charge for additional person(s) sharing a **trip**, journey or **accommodation**, normally requiring concurrent travel and use, often used by airlines and other **carriers**, as well as accommodation providers, as a promotional tool. Also called *spouse fare/rate*.

companion way/companionway A nautical term for the interior staircase between **decks** of a ship.

compactness index Measure of relative compactness and internal accessibility of a **region**, attributed to W.J. Coffey, which depend on the shape of the region. Generally, more compact regions have a greater degree of internal accessibility. See Smith, S.L.J. (1989) *Tourism Analysis: A Handbook*, London: Longman.

company A **corporate** body created in the UK by royal charter or by an Act of Parliament, but more universally registered under and governed by relevant legislation, in which the liability of members may be limited by shares or by guarantee, and which may be private or public (public limited company, abbreviated PLC). In the USA known as *corporation*. See also **partnership**; **sole trader**.

comparative advantage An economic concept which suggests that maximum efficiency is attained if people, **firms** and areas specialize in activities for which they are relatively better suited than for others. Accordingly, in international trade countries should specialize in goods and **services** in which they have a comparative advantage and this may be also applied to **international tourism**, as well as to regional and local tourism development.

compass An instrument used to find direction, in which a needle is fixed to and swings over a dial graduated in degrees.

competition
See **duopoly**
imperfect competition
monopolistic competition
monopoly
non-price competition
oligopoly
perfect competition
price competition

competitive advantage An advantage over competitors gained by offering **consumers** greater value, either by lower prices or by providing greater benefits that could justify higher prices.

competitor analysis The process of comparing the performance and strategies of competitive products or **brands**, in such terms as prices and quality, with a view to determining one's competitive advantages and disadvantages. See also **benchmark**.

complimentary Something offered without charge, e.g., complimentary registration, complimentary room. Also known as *comp*.

comptroller See **controller**

computer bureau A **company** which performs various computing operations for **clients** for a fee as an alternative to their use of **in-house** facilities. When selling time on a computer, two basic approaches are *batch processing* and *real time*. In batch processing, information is sent daily, weekly or at some other interval to a bureau on forms, punch cards or magnetic tape for processing. In real time, **on-line terminals** are used on the client's own premises linked to the bureau computer.

computer reservation system(s) (CRS) Computer-based interactive electronic data systems providing direct access through **terminals** to airline, **hotel** and other operators' computers, to establish product availability, make reservations and print tickets. Also called *automated reservation systems*, especially in North America, and *central reservation systems*. See also **Abacus**; **Amadeus**; **Apollo**; **Axess**; **DATAS II**; **Fantasia**; **Galileo**; **Galileo International**; **Gemini**; **Gets**; **Infini**; **PARS**; **Sabre**; **System One**; **Worldspan**.

concession A contractual arrangement between two parties, in which one party (the owner) grants the other (the concessionaire) the right to use land or premises to carry on a business. The relationships range from the user paying a **rental** as a tenant, to being paid for providing a service, with various fee paying and/or profit sharing arrangements between the two. However, technically rentals denote greater independence than the use of premises on certain conditions, which is the essence of a concession. Examples include newsagents, hairdressers and souvenir shops on **hotel** premises, and **catering** rights in **airports**, public parks and theatres. See also **management contract**.

concierge French term, in common use particularly in Europe, for a member of **uniformed staff** in **hotels**, variously responsible for guests' luggage, the parking of their cars, provision of information and other guest services. Also known as *head (hall) porter* and in America as *bell captain*.

condominium Building in which the interior space of accommodation units is owned individually and the land and building in common by the owners of the individual units. Often located in **resorts** and units are used as a **second home**. Colloquially abbreviated as *condo*. See also **timesharing**.

condotel A portmanteau word combining **condominium** and **hotel** and denoting a hotel wholly or partly consisting of individually owned condominium units, which may be offered with their owners' agreement at particular times for short-term letting.

confederation See **federation**; *confederation* is nowadays mainly used for an alliance of states rather than associations. But the latter use continues, e.g., **Confederation of British Industry (CBI)**; **Confederation of Passenger Transport (CPT)**.

conference
(a) A formal meeting or assembly for information, consultation and discussion purposes, sometimes also called **congress** or **convention**.
(b) In transportation, a formal or informal agreement or alliance between **carriers**, to promote their common interests and, when its scope extends to such matters as route- and rate-making, restrict competition. In shipping, lines acting together to offer standard rates to shippers are referred to as *conference lines*. See also **traffic conference areas**.

configuration As a transport term, most commonly an arrangement of seats in an **aircraft** or another vehicle, with particular size and number of seats in a row and **seat pitch** between seats. Also used to describe, e.g., the arrangement of rail carriages.

Confucianism The doctrines of Confucius (famous Chinese philosopher of the sixth and fifth century BC) and his followers which provide a code of humanistic ethics for the conduct of life.

conglomerate A large **firm** engaged in a wide range of dissimilar activities, normally consisting of a *holding* or *parent company*, which controls a number of **subsidiary companies**. Examples of travel, tourism and hospitality activities of conglomerates include, e.g., P & O Steam Navigation Company (shipping to property).

congress A formal meeting or assembly for information, consultation and discussion purposes, especially a regular periodic meeting of an association or of a body of specialists. See also **conference**; **convention**.

conjunction tickets A set of two or more airline tickets to cover a single **itinerary**, stapled together and issued at the same time, which constitute a single contract of carriage.

connecting flight/train The subsequent flight or train service that will continue the passenger's journey to the next destination. In air transport, a maximum time between connecting flights is sometimes laid down in order to prevent the abuse of rules relating to **stopovers**. A passenger may need to **check-in** again, before joining a connecting flight.

connecting rooms Rooms in a **hotel** or another building adjacent to each other with direct access between them without the need to use a corridor, hall or another area, although they can also be used as separate **accommodation**. See also **adjoining rooms**.

connecting time Although applicable in most forms of transport, of particular importance in air travel, where it is the minimum specified time to be allowed for a passenger between arrival on one flight and departure on a **connecting flight**. The time varies between **airports**, domestic and international flights, **on-line** and **off-line**, and according to other circumstances.

connectivity index Measure of internal **accessibility** of a **region** based on established routes composed of links connecting nodes, which form a transportation network; the higher the level of connectivity, the better for tourism; attributed to S.L.J. Smith (*Tourism Analysis: A Handbook,* London: Longman. 1989).

connoisseur Critical judge in matters of taste, one competent to make judgements in art.

conservation Protection from decay, depletion and destruction, as a positive approach to maintaining, enhancing and managing **natural** and man-made **resources**, for the benefit of future generations. There is a close relationship between tourism and conservation; tourism depends on conservation for the continuing existence and appeal of many attractions, and in turn contributes through the income it generates to their conservation. Conservation is usually distinguished from *preservation*, which implies maintaining something in its present form, and also from *restoration*, which means returning something to its previous appearance or condition.

Conservation Areas Built-up areas in **United Kingdom** considered worthy of protection and designated under the Civil Amenities Act 1967 by **local authorities**, which have a duty to preserve and enhance their character and appearance. Individual areas cover groups of houses and streets, as well as whole towns and villages, and no building may be demolished in them without consent. There were more than 10 000 Conservation Areas in the UK in mid 2000 (over 9000 in England, 600 in Scotland, over 500 in Wales, 50 in Northern Ireland). See **building conservation schemes** for other schemes.

consolidation
(a) The practice of some travel **companies** of combining bookings from several travel companies or individual members of the public with a view to achieving the necessary minimum numbers to benefit from group **fares**. Hence the company is called *consolidator*.
(b) The practice of **tour operators** of combining flight departures to the same destination with a view to achieving higher **load factors**; flights may be consolidated with other flights of the same operator or with flights of another operator.

consortium A voluntary group of independent business or other organizations joined together for a common purpose. This may range from joint ownership of an enterprise to cooperative associations in a particular trade or **industry** involved in a joint approach to **marketing**, purchasing and provision of operational and technical advice and services to members. Main examples in travel, tourism and hospitality are to be found in the **hotel** field (e.g., internationally Best Western, with almost 4000 members in 80 countries in 2001), but there are also national and regional (sub-national) consortia of **visitor attractions** and other tourism-related businesses. See also **joint venture**.

conspicuous consumption Term attributed to American economist Thorstein Veblen to describe purchases that satisfy a psychological (rather than physical) need for esteem of others. Although difficult if not impossible to establish empirically, the choice of travel, tourism and hospitality products as status symbols or to 'keep up with the Joneses' is considered by some as a significant **motivation**. See also **sunlust; wanderlust**.

constant prices See **real terms**; see also **current prices**.

consumer Ultimate user of goods and **services** who may but need not be the **customer**, i.e., buyer. Hence, e.g., *consumer advertising* (advertising directed at individuals and households); *consumer goods and services* (goods and services for use by individuals and households as distinct from business and other organizations); *consumer research* (**market(ing) research** among consumers).

Consumer Price Index In the USA and some other countries term for **cost of living index**.

consumer protection by tour operators (UK) Regulations of the Department of Trade and Industry (see **Package Travel Directive**) provide three ways for **tour operators** to protect their **customers**:
(a) **Bonding**, when tour operators lodge an amount equivalent to a proportion of their turnover with a bond holder who is then responsible for refund or repatriation of the holidaymaker in case of a tour operator collapse.

(b) Insolvency insurance, provided by a specialist company to whom the tour operator pays an annual membership fee and from whom he buys insurance cover notes, which are issued to customers.
(c) Trust fund set up by the tour operator into which all customers' payments are paid and which are held in trust on behalf of the customer until return from holiday.

consumerism An organized social movement to protect the interests of **consumers** in response to the growing **market** power of large business. It has increased its influence in many walks of life, including travel, tourism and hospitality.

consumer expenditure Personal expenditure on goods and **services** consisting of household expenditure on goods and **services** (including income in kind, imputed rent of owner-occupier dwellings and administrative cost of life assurance and superannuation) and final expenditure by non-profit making bodies. Excluded are interest payments, all business expenditure and the purchase of land and buildings [United Kingdom National Accounts]. In 2000 tourist spending in the UK exceeded 6 per cent of total consumer spending.

content analysis Any systematic attempt to examine the subject matter in communications, such as newspapers, books, brochures, films and broadcasts. As a research technique it measures the meaning of communicated material through the classification and evaluation of selected words, themes, concepts and symbols. Applications cover the content of **advertising** and other promotional material, including that used in travel, tourism and hospitality.

continent
(a) One of the main continuous bodies of land on the earth's surface: Europe, Asia, Africa, North America, South America, Australia, Antarctica. The first two are sometimes described as *Eurasia*.
(b) The *Continent* in British parlance denotes mainland Europe, which is also described as 'Continental Europe'.

Continental breakfast Breakfast normally consisting as a minimum of tea or coffee, bread, toast or rolls, butter and preserves, but sometimes also served with juice, cheese and cold meat. See also **American breakfast; Asian breakfast; English breakfast**.

continental divide The main watershed in a **continent**, e.g., in North America where the streams flow on one side of the divide to the Pacific and on the other side to the Atlantic Oceans.

Continental Plan (CP) Hotel tariff which includes room and **Continental breakfast**. See also **Bermuda Plan (BP); European Plan (EP)**.

contour A line on a map joining points on the earth's surface at the same height above sea level.

contraband Illegally exported or imported goods, i.e., goods smuggled out of or into a country.

contract catering Provision of **catering** services by specialist firms under contract to clients whose main activity is in some other field, on clients' own premises for a fee. The major reason for the employment of a contractor is to relieve the parent organization of an unfamiliar service and to draw on the contractor's wider resources. Contract catering is prominent in employee catering but also widespread in education, hospitals and other institutions, as well as increasingly in other fields.

contribution pricing See **marginal cost pricing**

controlled circulation See **circulation**

controller In the USA, the chief accounting executive of an organization, normally concerned with financial reporting, taxation and auditing. Also known as *comptroller*.

conurbation A large continuous urban area formed by the expansion and joining together of previously separate urban areas, also known as *metropolitan area*, especially in the USA. Seven conurbations are officially recognized in **Great Britain**: Central Clydeside, Greater London, Merseyside, South-East Lancashire, Tyneside, West Midlands, West Yorkshire. Conurbations tend to be major **tourism generating areas**.

DICTIONARY OF TERMS

43

convenience foods Foods partially or fully prepared by the manufacturer and used as labour-saving alternatives to raw foods. Three main processing methods – dehydration, canning and freezing – are used for fruit and vegetables, meat, poultry and fish.

convenience products Products bought frequently at a relatively low price, which are widely available, satisfy basic needs, and are likely to be branded, such as breakfast cereals but also, e.g., bank **services**. See also **shopping products**.

convention
(a) A large meeting or assembly commonly so described in the USA, when referring to an association meeting held on an annual basis, whilst **conference** or **congress** is more often used elsewhere.
(b) An agreement or covenant between parties, especially between states and when the outcome of a meeting. See, e.g., **Athens Convention**; **Chicago Convention**; **Warsaw Convention**.

Convention and Visitor(s) Bureau See **Visitor(s) and Convention Bureau**

conventions and treaties
See **Athens Convention**
   Australia New Zealand Closer Economic Relations Trade Agreement (ANZCERTA)
   Berne Convention
   Brussels Convention
   Chicago Convention
   Cotonou Agreement
   General Agreement on Tariffs and Trade (GATT)
   Helsinki Accord
   International Convention on the Travel Contract
   Lomé Convention
   Maastricht Treaty
   North American Free Trade Agreement (NAFTA)
   Schengen Agreement
   Treaty of Amsterdam
   Treaty on European Union
   Treaty of Rome
   Warsaw Convention

conversion rate In **marketing**, the ratio of **customers** who buy a product to the number of enquiries or responses received to an advertisement or another promotion. See also **response rate**.

convertible currency See **currency**

cook–chill A **catering** system in which food is cooked, followed by fast chilling and storage at a low controlled temperature just above freezing point, before it is reheated when required for consumption. Compared with **cook–freeze**, cook–chill has a short shelf life of up to five days.

cook–freeze A **catering** system in which food is cooked, followed by fast freezing and storage at a low controlled temperature of −18 °C or below, before it is reheated when required for consumption. Compared with **cook–chill**, cook–freeze has a long shelf life.

cooperative
(a) A synonym for **consortium**.
(b) An American term for a form of apartment ownership in **cities** when shares are bought in the building in which the apartment is sited, rather than individual apartments, which is the essence of **condominium**.

cooperative marketing An arrangement between two or more parties for joint action and sharing of costs in some aspect of **marketing**, such as destination promotion by a **tourist board** and an airline serving the destination. Thus, e.g., in the 1990s some two-thirds of the **British Tourist Authority (BTA)** expenditure on marketing **campaigns** abroad was contributed by commercial **companies** and **local authorities**. Cooperative marketing is also relevant to firms joining together which operate within the same single **sector**, such as **hotel** companies.

coral reefs Coral reefs are produced by lime-secreting colonial polyps and occur mainly between 30° North and South, in unpolluted waters at temperatures of not less then 21 °C (73 °F) with access to sunlight; they are in part the product of rising sea level in the post-glacial period. They occur as fringing reefs adjoining the shore, as **barrier reefs**, separated from the land by a **lagoon**, and as **atolls**, a ring of coral enclosing a lagoon. Because of the rich variety of fish life, and of forms of coral, accessible reefs are major **tourist/visitor attractions**, particularly the *Great Barrier Reef*, along the coast of Queensland, the islands inside the Reef in the Red Sea, off the coast of East Africa, and around the Caribbean and Pacific islands.

Corbett Scottish term for a **mountain** between 2500 and 3000 ft (762–914 m) high. See also **Munro**.

Cordoba (C$) Unit of **currency** of Nicaragua.

cork charge See **corkage**

corkage A charge per bottle by a **hotel** or **restaurant** for permission to bring in and consume one's own alcoholic liquor on the premises. In the USA also called *cork charge*. See also **Bring Your Own**; **brown bagging**.

corporate Of, or belonging to, a body of people such as a **firm** or organization. Hence, e.g., *corporate advertising* (which promotes the body generally rather than its particular products or activities); *corporate identity* (the outward means by which the body projects itself to the outside world, including, e.g., design, **logos** etc.); *corporate image* (the overall impression people have of the body); *corporate planning* (setting out the longer-term goals and the ways of achieving them); *corporate rate* (discounted price offered as a promotional tool by **hotel**, car hire and other firms to business users); *corporate travel* (synonym for **business travel**).

corporation See **company**

correlation The degree to which two sets of data are related, expressed as a coefficient with values ranging between +1.0 and –1.0. A value of one indicates an exact relationship, the sign + a positive one and the sign – an inverse one; a value of zero indicates no relationship. Thus, e.g., there is likely to be a high positive correlation in the population between the use of telephones and incomes and a high inverse correlation between the use of telephone and telegrams. However, an association between variables does not necessarily mean causation.

corridor
(a) A strip of territory belonging to one country running through the territory of another, e.g., to give the former access to

the sea, such as the Israeli corridor to Elat on the Red Sea.
(b) An international air **route** allowing access by air over the territory of a country to other countries.

corridor train
(a) A train consisting of **coaches** with corridors and individual compartments, as distinct from open plan coaches.
(b) A train service in parts of Continental Europe, which leaves the country of origin and runs through another country without stopping before returning to the country of origin, thus avoiding a long detour between two areas of a country.

cosmonaut See **astronaut**

cosmopolitan A person with a global outlook free from national limitations.

cost benefit analysis (CBA) Systematic evaluation of the costs and benefits of a project, which takes into account not only economic but also social and environmental costs and benefits accruing to the project. May be used for existing situations to determine whether they should be continued or for proposed projects to determine whether they should proceed. This is a technique in increasing use, especially in the assessment of public projects to decide between alternative schemes, as in various forms of transportation. See also **feasibility study**; **investment appraisal**.

cost of living index See **index numbers**; see also **Consumer Price Index**.

costa Spanish term for a coast, especially one on the Mediterranean, developed as a **holiday (vacation) region**, such as Costa Blanca, Costa Brava, Costa del Sol.

cost-plus pricing Any method of setting prices in which a mark-up is added to product cost. When the full cost is used as a mark-up base, the addition represents the expected profit. This approach continues to be used, e.g., in development contracts when it is not possible to estimate eventual costs accurately in advance. When only a part of the total cost is used as a basis, the mark-up has to cover the balance of cost as well as profit as, e.g., in **catering** when a margin is added to food cost;

the margin then serves to cover labour and overhead costs as well as profit.

Cotonou Agreement An accord concluded in Cotonou, Benin, in June 2000 by **European Union** and **ACP** heads of state and governments with 77 ACP countries, for a period of 20 years to continue assistance previously provided under **Lomé Conventions**.

couchette Convertible sleeping **berth** on European Continental trains with four to six places per compartment, each with a sheet, blanket and pillow, but unlike sleeping car accommodation, no toilet or washing facilities. See also **parlor car**; **Pullman**; **roomette**; **Wagon-Lits**.

counter staff Collective term for **front of house** employees who work 'behind the counter' and deal directly face-to-face with **customers**, as in banks, shops and travel agencies.

country house hotel A **hotel** usually operated in a large converted house in the country, often in its own extensive grounds, with an emphasis on personal atmosphere and service. See also **boutique hotel**.

country of residence For purposes of **international tourism** statistics, the country where the **visitor** has lived for most of the past 12 months, or for shorter periods if he or she intends to return within 12 months to live there [**World Tourism Organization**].

country park A public recreational land area in the countryside close to major concentrations of populations, sometimes including water, often with signposted **nature trails** and information provided about the local flora and fauna for **visitors**. May be in public or private ownership and in England, Scotland and Wales designated as a country park by **local authorities**. Strathclyde Country Park in Scotland was by far the most visited country park in the UK in the 1990s.

country/state codes Two-letter standard abbreviations published by the **International Organization for Standardization (ISO)** for use by airlines as well as in other communications. Thus, e.g., GB = United Kingdom, DE = Federal Republic of Germany, US = United States of America. Published state codes cover,

e.g., Australia (total eight, e.g., TS = Tasmania); Canada (total 13, e.g., OT = Ontario); USA (total 51, e.g., NV = Nevada). See, e.g., *OAG Flight Atlas* for a full list.

countryside conservation designation schemes Conservation by designating areas of countryside and providing a framework for development and other controls against undue change.
(a) *International* (**World Heritage Sites**; **Biosphere Reserves, Ramsar Sites**).
(b) *Regional* (e.g., **Special Protection Areas** and **Environmentally Sensitive Areas**, both designated by the **European Community**).
(c) *National*, e.g., within the UK **National Parks, Special Protected Areas** (England), **Areas of Outstanding Natural Beauty** (not Scotland), **Heritage Coasts** (England and Wales), **National Nature Reserves, Sites of Special Specific Interest, National Scenic Areas** (Scotland).
See also **building conservation schemes**.

courier
(a) A person employed by a tour organizer and escorting a group tour, who may also act as a guide. In North America, more commonly described as *tour conductor, director, leader*, or *manager*.
(b) An airline passenger carrying packages for courier **companies** for urgent and safe delivery.

courier fare Return air **fare** available on some **scheduled** flights for passengers taking packages as part of their luggage for **courier** companies.

courtesy bus Free **bus** service provided by a **hotel** between the **airport** and the hotel.

cover In **catering**, utensils laid for each person at a table, hence the number of covers in a **restaurant** denotes its capacity or the number of **customers** served.

cover charge A fixed charge per person made by a **restaurant**, **night club** or similar **establishment** in addition to charges for food and beverages served, especially when entertainment is provided. The additional charge is sometimes made to cover such costs as the bread roll and butter and other items not priced on the menu, but also in lieu of a minimum charge to discourage low-spending **customers** from using the premises.

cream tea **Afternoon tea** served with scones, cream and jam. See also **high tea**.

credit card An instrument which enables the card holder to make purchases on credit up to an amount authorized by the credit card **company**, by presenting the card to the vendor in lieu of cash, or to draw cash from participating banks or **automated teller machines (ATMs)**. The companies normally charge the vendor and the card holder and also interest to the latter on outstanding balances. Together with **charge cards**, credit cards are the fastest growing methods of payment for travel, tourism and hospitality services. See also **cheque (check) card**; **debit card**.

credit rating An assessment of the creditworthiness of an individual or organization, which indicates to what extent it is safe to grant credit.

crewed charter An arrangement in which the hire of a yacht or another vessel includes the crew. This is to be distinguished from **bareboat charter** and **provisioned charter**. See also **flotilla cruising**.

crib A **beach** or lakeside **holiday (vacation)** home in South Island, New Zealand, called a **bach** in North Island.

critical path analysis (CPA) Also called *network analysis*, a technique used in project planning for scheduling of component tasks in such a way as to enable the project to be completed in the shortest possible time. Each task calls for a certain amount of time and some tasks must be completed before others, whilst some may be carried out simultaneously. The critical path shows the sequence of tasks, which minimizes the time between the start and finish of the project. In travel, tourism and hospitality, as elsewhere, common uses of the technique are in such areas as new product development and **marketing** planning, as well as in building and civil engineering projects.

cross border selling/ticketing The practice of writing an international airline ticket with a fictitious point of origin or destination, with a view to undercutting the **fare** which applies between the actual point of origin and destination. Thus, to travel between country Y and country Z, a ticket issued in country X routed via country Y may be cheaper than a ticket issued in country Y, taking advantage of special fares and/or **rates of exchange**. But discarding the first **sector** of the ticket and boarding in country Y breaks **IATA** regulations.

cross-elasticity of demand An economic concept which measures the responsiveness of demand for one product to a change in price of another. If the two products are close substitutes for each other (e.g., beach h**olidays (vacations)** in neighbouring Mediterranean countries), the cross-elasticity is likely to be positive; an increase in the price of holidays in one country may be expected to lead to an increase in the demand for holidays in the other country. If the two products are complementary, the cross-elasticity is likely to be negative; e.g., an increase in fares to a holiday island may be expected to result in a fall in demand for **accommodation** on the island. See also **income elasticity of demand**; **price elasticity of demand**.

cross-subsidy See **subsidy**

cruise A voyage by ship for pleasure – commonly by sea but also on lakes, rivers and **canals** – of varying duration, which may but need not depart from and return to the same **port** or include **scheduled** calls at ports **en route**. The Caribbean and the Mediterranean are the principal *sea cruising areas*, drawing in the main on the North American and European markets; other year-round areas include the Atlantic off the West coast of Africa, southern and western Pacific, and North Pacific off the western coast of North America; the Baltic and Norwegian Seas are popular summer cruising areas.

cruise director See **animator**

cuisine French term for kitchen, cookery or style of cooking. Hence, e.g., *haute cuisine* (high class French cooking); *nouvelle cuisine* (French cooking characterized by light traditional dishes, small portions and attention to presentation with the use of contemporary ingredients and modern equipment).

cultural heritage Monuments and groups of buildings or structures of outstanding universal value from the point of view of history, art or science, and sites of outstanding universal value from the historical, aesthetic, ethnological or anthropological points of view [based on **UNESCO** Convention for the Protection of the World Cultural and Natural Heritage, 1972].

cultural relativism
(a) A sociological term denoting that beliefs are relative to a particular society and are not comparable between societies.
(b) A method of analysing different societies or cultures objectively without using the values of one to judge another. One way is to describe the practices of a society from the point of view of its members.
See also **ethnocentrism/ethnocentricity**.

cultural tourism In a narrow sense, **special interest holidays (vacations)** essentially motivated by cultural interests, such as **trips** and visits to historical sites and monuments, **museums** and galleries, artistic performances and **festivals**, as well as **lifestyles** of communities. In a broad sense, including also activities with a cultural content as parts of trips and visits with a combination of pursuits. See also **wanderlust**.

culture shock The effect sometimes experienced by **travellers** when they leave their own cultural **environment** and enter a new and unfamiliar one.

currency Notes and coins used as a medium of exchange in a country. *Convertible currency* is freely exchangeable for other currencies and for gold. *International currency* is one acceptable for the settlement of international debts and includes gold and certain national currencies, such as the US Dollar. However, countries may impose currency restrictions limiting the amount of currency which may be taken out of a country, and thereby affect **international travel/tourism** flows. See **exchange control**; see also **rate of exchange**.

currency codes Three-letter standard abbreviations of the **International Organization for Standardization (ISO)** for use in, i.a., airline tariffs, ticketing and other applications. Thus, e.g., GBP = Pound Sterling; JPY = Japanese

Yen; USD = US Dollar. At 1 January 1990, the **International Air Transport Association (IATA)** converted its former currency codes to ISO designations. See, e.g., *OAG Flight Guide Supplement* for full list.

currency control See **exchange control**

currency surcharge See **surcharge**

current prices Money values (such as **tourism expenditure**) not adjusted for **inflation**. See also **constant prices**.

customer The actual buyer of goods and **services** who may but need not be the **consumer**. Thus, e.g., a **tourist** buying an **inclusive tour** for him/herself is both customer and consumer. On the other hand, the **business travel department** of a **company** is the customer of **carriers** and **hotels** making travel arrangements for employees who are the actual consumers.

customer mix See **business mix**

customer satisfaction questionnaire (CSQ) Self-completion questionnaire used as an instrument of quality control for service products. Completed, e.g., by **customers** at the end of an airline flight, **hotel** stay or **package holiday (vacation)**, often as part of periodic sample surveys carried out to provide primarily regular monitoring of customer perceptions of satisfaction/value for money received. It may be also used to measure the effectiveness of **marketing** activities.

customs
(a) Established patterns of behaviour and belief of a society relating both to routines of daily life and to features which distinguish one culture from another. They are of significance as **motivations** in tourism and in interactions between **tourists** and **residents**.
(b) The government agency responsible for collecting duties on imports, including goods acquired abroad and brought into a country by **visitors** and returning **residents**. Hence, *customs duty*, the duty levied on imports, and *customs declaration*, the process of declaring such goods to customs and also the official document used for the purpose.

customs channels

(a) Green channel for passengers with nothing to declare.
(b) Red channel for passengers with goods liable for duty.
(c) Blue channel for passengers arriving in a member country from within the **European Union**.

cutting in line North American term for the practice of *queue jumping*.

cyclic(al) menus A series of menus repeated by a **catering establishment** at set periods of time, sometimes weekly but more commonly three- or four-weekly.

cyclone A circular storm circulating anticlockwise in the northern **hemisphere** and clockwise in the southern hemisphere round a centre of low barometric pressure.

D train (*Durchgehender Zug*) German term for an express train.

dacha A Russian country cottage, commonly owned or part-owned through a **cooperative**, or rented by **city** dwellers for **holidays (vacations)**.

dahabeeyah Originally sailing boat on the Nile, now motorized.

Dalasi (D) Unit of **currency** of The Gambia.

dale A broad open valley mainly in northern England, a term often used in place names.

dam A structure built across a river to hold back water for such purposes as flood control, irrigation or storage. Sometimes a distinction is drawn between a dam and a **barrage**, the former but not the latter being used for power generation. A well-known example is *Hoover Dam* on the border of Arizona and Nevada, USA, which is a major **tourist/visitor attraction**, and *Lake Mead*, created by the dam, a large water **recreation** area. In some countries, e.g., in Australia, a dam denotes a man-made body of water or **reservoir**, not just the structure itself.

damper Australian expression denoting a **bush** loaf made from flour and water. It symbolizes **outback** tourism where **travellers** gather around a camp fire with tea boiled in a tin container called a *billy*.

database Collection of data nowadays commonly stored on a computer and retrievable from a shared file for different purposes. Hence, *database marketing*, the collection, storage, analysis and use of a database, which enables **customer** behaviour to be predicted through analysis of customer characteristics and past behaviour. See also **direct response marketing**.

DATAS II US **computer reservation system (CRS)** owned by Delta Airlines, which merged with **PARS**; both were replaced by **Worldspan** system in 1990.

datum level/line The zero **altitude** base for the measurement of elevation. For British official maps heights above the sea level are derived from the mean sea level at Newlyn, Cornwall, England.

day rate
(a) The rate available in some **hotels** for daytime use of bedrooms, particularly common in **airport** hotels.
(b) The rate charged to **conference** delegates for a day's attendance, which normally includes morning coffee, lunch and tea, in addition to participation in conference sessions.

day visitor A **visitor** who does not stay overnight in the country or place visited. Also known as an *excursionist*. See also **same-day visitor**.

Day Visits Survey (DVS/UK) Household **sample** survey conducted every second year since 1992 (pilot) and 1994 (full year) and sponsored by a **consortium** led by the **Countryside Agency** and the **Department of Culture, Media and Sport**.

daylight saving time Local time observed by certain countries for part of the year, normally one hour in advance of the local **standard time**, in order to extend the period of daylight at the end of the working day; in the UK known as **British Summer Time (BST)**.

days of service For most purposes the calendar week in travel and tourism begins on Monday. In timetables and other published material, days of service are often designated by numerals 1-7, beginning with Monday = 1.

deadhead

(a) **Aircraft** or another vehicle travelling without passengers or cargo. Hence, e.g., *deadhead flight.*

(b) Airline or another **carrier's** employee travelling free.

See also **ferry mileage**.

deadweight tonnage See **tonnage (shipping)**

debit card An instrument issued mainly by banks, which enables the card holder to pay for goods and **services** and to obtain cash advances by **electronic funds transfer (EFT)** from his/her current bank account. *Delta* and *Switch* are the most widely used debit cards. See also **charge card**; **credit card**; **cheque (check)**.

debus To alight from a **bus** or **coach**.

deck A nautical term for floor of a ship.

decreasing returns An economic term to describe a situation when less than a proportionate increase in output can be observed, after a certain point has been reached, from a given increase in inputs. Also known as *diseconomies of scale*, these are internal and external. *Internal diseconomies* often arise from problems of **management** and coordination, as the size of the **firm** or **establishment** continues to increase. *External diseconomies* arise from such problems as shortage of labour or traffic congestion. See also **economies of scale**; **law of diminishing returns**.

dedicated line A communication or transportation link used exclusively for a particular purpose as, e.g., a telephone line connecting a **travel agent** and a **tour operator** in a **viewdata** system, or a high-speed railway line connecting a **city** centre and an **airport**.

deferred demand See **demand for tourism**

deflation A sustained reduction in general price level in a country, often accompanied by a decline in the output of goods and **services** and in employment. See also **inflation**.

deforestation See **acid rain**; **Amazonia**; **land resources depletion**

de-industrialization The decline in goods-producing **secondary industries** and an increase in **services (tertiary industries)**, marked by the movement of employment from the former to the latter, a phenomenon common to a greater or lesser extent to most **developed countries** in the twentieth century. Travel, tourism and hospitality services are prominent examples of the change. See also **industrialization**.

Delhi belly Commonly used term for a diarrhoea (diarrhea) suffered when travelling abroad as a result of eating unwashed fruit or drinking contaminated water. Also called **Montezuma's revenge**. See also **traveller's diarrhoea (traveler's diarrhea)**.

Delphi technique A method of forecasting future developments by a group of experts, in which a sequence of questionnaires and feedback of information representing a group view is used to reach a consensus. The method uses the advantages of group decision-making without such disadvantages as the influence of dominating members and the reluctance of members to change their views. Well-known applications of the method include, i.a., studies of future trends in tourism in Austria, Switzerland and Canada. Although the technique originated and has been most extensively used in forecasting, it has been also used to identify and assess other complex problems.

delta A broadly triangular area at the mouth of a river formed by deposits of solid material on the river bed which build up faster than they are moved by tide or other currents.

demand for tourism Normally defined in terms of the number of **tourists**. In this a distinction may be drawn between *actual* (those currently participating in tourism) and *potential* (those who do not participate currently but may so do in the future); for **marketing** purposes both have to be backed by the necessary purchasing power for the demand to be *effective*. Unsatisfied demand, which may exist due to such reasons as absence of a suitable product to meet a particular need or shortage of supply, is referred to as *latent* or *deferred* demand.

demarketing Term to describe activities aimed at reducing demand for a product, which may be undertaken to discourage **customers** in general or certain groups of customers in particular, by such methods as **differential pricing**, **trading up** and reduced promotion. Demarketing has an important role in travel, tourism and hospitality in case of excess demand for particular destinations or products or to discriminate against particular **market** segments.

demi-pension Half-board **hotel tariff**, which includes room, breakfast and one main meal per day, usually dinner. See also **Modified American Plan (MAP)**.

democratization A process whereby opportunities are extended to wider strata of society, as has been the case with travel and tourism.

demography The statistical study of populations. Such characteristics as geographical distribution and age, sex and household composition are known as *demographics* and are of particular importance in tourism planning, development and **marketing**, as they provide the basis for **market segmentation**. Such data are available in most countries from population **censuses**.

demonstration effect Tendency for an individual or a group to imitate the behaviour of another and to assimilate it as one's own. This process is often observed in tourism, especially in **developing countries**, when local **residents** are influenced by the behaviour of **tourists** and assume their characteristics. Thus, they may change their mode of dress and consumption patterns, e.g., demand goods imported for the use of tourists.

Denar Unit of **currency** of Macedonia.

dengue An infection, also known as *breakbone fever* owing to its painful symptoms in the bones and joints, and which may give rise to a spotty rash; it is not fatal in adults. It is transmitted by the bite of an infected mosquito and occurs in the **tropics**, especially the **Far East**. There is no vaccine available; the only prevention is to avoid mosquito bites.

denied boarding compensation Payment by an airline to a passenger with a confirmed reservation for a specific flight not honoured by the airline, commonly for such reasons as

overbooking. Most airlines also reimburse passengers for reasonable expenses incurred by them as a result of not being able to travel as **scheduled**. As a result of a **European Community** Regulation, since April 1991 passengers with a valid ticket for a scheduled flight from an **airport** within the **European Union (EU)** denied boarding because the flight was already full, have been entitled to an immediate cash compensation, the amount depending on the distance to be flown and the amount of delay caused. See also **bumping**.

departure tax Tax levied on passengers leaving a country. Varies in its scope and application; e.g., it may be levied at **airports** only but sometimes also at other exit points; it may be levied on all passengers or only foreign **visitors** or only **residents** travelling abroad. Also known in some countries as *exit tax*, **Air Passenger Duty** in UK, *Passenger Movement Charge* in Australia. See also **airport service charge**.

dependant pass/permit/visa Terms used for a permit to stay in a country issued to the spouse of a non-national working in that country.

deplane To leave an **aircraft**. See also **enplane**.

depressed area An area with high unemployment, low income per head, **migration** (especially of young people) out of the area, declining traditional **industries**, and an unattractive **environment**. A major need in such areas is to attract new economic activities and in many of them tourism is seen to have a major potential. See also **ghost town**.

deregulation Removal or relaxation of regulation of economic activities by governments and public authorities, usually in order to introduce or increase competition. Like **privatization**, deregulation has been pursued by many countries in recent years, including such travel- and tourism-related fields as various forms of transport. The Airline Deregulation Act 1978 in the USA marked a major break in the growth of regulation since the Second World War and the beginning of the trend to deregulation generally.

derived demand The demand for a particular product that is dependent on the demand for another product. For example, the demand for air travel depends on the **demand for tourism**; the demand for **restaurants** on the demand for eating out; the demand for **conference** interpreters on the numbers of international **conferences** held.

designated carrier See **carrier**

desk research Collecting and drawing on **secondary data**, including published and other readily accessible sources, such as internal **company** records, as distinct from **field research**.

destination See **tourism destinations**

destination management company See **ground arrangements**; **incoming tour operator**

destination marketing organization (DMO) A national, regional or local organization whose major function is the promotion of its destination.

determinants of tourism Factors determining the scale and patterns of participation in tourism. Demand determinants of private travel include such economic and social influences as the **standard of living**; supply determinants include the availability, quality and price of **tourist attractions**, facilities and **services**, and their promotion. The volume of **holidays (vacations)** abroad is additionally strongly influenced by the size of the country of residence, its geographical location and the relative costs of domestic and foreign holidays. See also **motivations**.

detrain To alight from a train.

devaluation See **rate of exchange**

developed countries Also called *advanced countries* and *industrialized countries*, these are countries with a relatively high level of economic and social development reflected in their **standard of living**, usually taken as the member countries of the **Organisation for Economic Co-operation and Development (OECD)**. Most of these have high **holiday (vacation) propensities** and high levels of **domestic travel/tourism**, are leading generators of **international travel/tourism**, and also significant international **tourism destinations**. See also **developing countries**.

developing countries Also referred to as *underdeveloped, less developed* and *Third World*, these are countries with a relatively low level of economic and social development reflected in their **standard of living**. According to **United Nations** lists they number some 180 (including OPEC member countries) in various stages of development and with widely varying incomes. Most of them have low **holiday (vacation) propensities** but many are significant international **tourism destinations**. In recent years they have increased their share of **international tourist** arrivals and account for around 30 per cent of all **international tourism receipts**. See also **developed countries**.

development plans
(a) More or less comprehensive plans for a particular development, e.g., tourism development.
(b) Overall plans for the land use and development in a particular area. See **land use planning**; **land use planning systems (UK)**

DG XXIII Department of the European Commission with a responsibility for tourism.

diet A generic term denoting the amount and range of food a person eats. Hence, e.g., *balanced diet* (one that includes the right amount and variety of basic nutrients); *dietetics* (study of food and its nutritional value).

differential pricing See **price discrimination**

dime US ten-cent coin.

Dinar Unit of **currency** of Algeria (DA), Bahrain (BD), Iraq (ID), Jordan (JD), Kuwait (KD), Libya (LD), Sudan (SD), Tunisia (TD) and Yugoslavia (New Dinar).

dine-around The provision of a range of restaurant opportunities, which allows **hotel** or **restaurant** guests a choice of dining at different **establishments** when staying on *full-pension* or *demi-pension* terms (see **en pension**).

diner
(a) Small **restaurant**.
(b) A person eating in a restaurant.
(c) Also American term for a restaurant car on a train.

dinkies Term derived from *double income no kids* and denoting an affluent childless married couple who may be expected to be large spenders on goods and **services**, including travel, tourism and hospitality products.

diphtheria Until the 1930s, one of the most important causes of childhood death worldwide, but the mass immunization of children since the 1940s has effectively eradicated the disease in **developed countries**. However, it remains a serious disease, especially in tropical countries where there is overcrowding and poor hygiene. It is caught by close contact with an infected person. For unimmunized adults a special low-dose vaccine is available.

direct flight A flight between two points with or without stops on the same **aircraft**.

direct mail Mailing of promotional material to selected prospects. These may be previous **customers** but increasing use is made by many **firms** and other organizations of available lists of specifically targeted prospects. Lists, which may be purchased, are used to do own mailing; in the case of lists owned by third parties, such as **credit card** and other membership organizations, the names and addresses are not released, but material is normally distributed with routine mailings to members.

direct response advertising The use of **advertising** inviting a direct contact by the **customer** with the advertiser by telephone, letter or commonly by means of a return coupon, to order the advertised product or request information or a call by a representative, without the use of intermediate **distribution channels**. This is a common approach in travel, tourism and hospitality, which avoids the use of **travel agents**, although it may be also used to direct the customer to contact the travel agent.

direct response marketing Also called *database marketing*, an approach to **marketing** in which producers and **customers** are linked in a two-way communication through a computer database, which records details of actual and prospective customers and their buying behaviour. The primary objective is to achieve more cost-effective marketing on the basis of knowledge of customers and direct communication with them made possible by **information**

technology. See also **direct selling**; **target marketing**; **telemarketing/telephone marketing**.

direct selling Selling goods and **services**, which involves direct communication between the producer and **customers**, without the use of retail outlets, distributors, wholesalers or any other type of **middleman**. Often includes **direct mail** and **telephone selling**. An airline selling a seat to a **customer** calling at its office, a **hotel** selling rooms by telephone to a **business travel department**, or a **tour operator** selling a **holiday(vacation)** through a brochure and a booking form sent out by direct mail, are common examples in travel, tourism and hospitality. Called *bypass* in North America.

directional bias index Measure of the travel patterns of an **origin** in relation to its destinations, attributed to R.I. Wolfe [Smith, S.L.J. (1989) *Tourism Analysis: A Handbook*, London: Longman].

Directive A legislative decision of the **European Union** Council of Ministers, which is binding on member states but allows them to decide how to enact their own required legislation.

Dirham Unit of **currency** of Morocco (DH) and United Arab Emirates (Dh).

Disabled Railcard See **British railcards**

discount ticket agency See **bucket shop**

Discovery of America Day See **Columbus Day**

discretionary income Personal **disposable income** of individuals or households remaining after spending on necessities, such as food, clothing and housing, i.e. freely disposable or **threshold** income, from which spending can take place on non-essential goods and **services**. This is the most important income concept for **holiday (vacation)** and other forms of travel and tourism, which involve discretionary use of money and time, as spending on them is more closely correlated with discretionary income than with disposable income.

diseconomies of scale See **decreasing returns**

disembark To leave a ship, **aircraft** or another vehicle.

dish of the day A special dish served on the day not appearing on the printed menu. Often referred to by the French term *plat du jour*.

displacement effect Term used to describe the effect of one activity being displaced by another as, e.g., agriculture and fishing being displaced by tourism, which draws away labour from them, as has occurred in many destinations.

display advertisements Press advertisements using layout, typography and sometimes also illustration to enhance the impact of the message. *Semi-display advertisements* are more limited in size, variety of typeface and graphics. See also **classified advertisements**.

disposable income Personal income of individuals or households after income **tax** and other compulsory deductions, i.e., income from which spending and saving are generated. Estimates of disposable income are published by many countries and there is usually a relatively close **correlation** between levels of and changes in disposable income and **holiday (vacation) propensities**. See also **discretionary income**.

distance decay A geographical term measuring the (generally exponential) decline in the level of interaction between phenomena with distance. An important tool in tourism and recreational planning, by relating the population of generating areas and the attractiveness of destinations, in order to permit predictions of likely volumes of tourist flows and recreational travel (which usually decrease as the distance increases). See also **gravity model**.

distance learning A form of learning usually undertaken at home, away from the teaching centre, such as correspondence courses, sometimes combined with attendance of a study centre or short courses. In a number of countries, including the UK, distance learning methods are available for education and training in travel, tourism and hospitality.

distribution channels Marketing term describing channels through which goods and services are transferred from producers to **consumers** and which provide **points of sale** or access for consumers. In travel and tourism, providers of **tourist attractions**, facilities and services may sell direct to consumers (at their place of operation or through their own retail outlets) or use one or more **intermediaries** (such as **tour operators** and **travel agents**). Most large producers use a combination of distribution channels for their products and this combination is described as the **distribution mix**.

distribution mix See **distribution channels**; **marketing mix**

diversification Introduction of new products into existing **markets** or of existing products into new markets, also but less frequently of new products into new markets. Commonly undertaken to increase sales and more particularly to reduce reliance on a too narrow range of products and/or limited market. Thus, e.g., an airline may enter **hotel** operations and other more or less related activities, and a hotel company may diversify geographically and operate in countries where it was not represented previously.

Diwali Hindu festival celebrated in October or November each year and observed in India and other countries with Hindu populations.

Dobra (Db) Unit of **currency** of São Tome and Principe.

Dollar Unit of **currency** of Australia (see **Australian Dollar**), Bahamas (B$), Barbados (Bds$), Belize (BZ$), Bermuda (B$), Brunei (B$), Canada (C$), Cayman Islands (CI$), Fiji (F$), Guyana (G$), Hong Kong (HK$), Jamaica (J$), Liberia (L$), Namibia (N$), New Zealand (see **New Zealand Dollar**), Singapore (S$), Solomon Islands (SI$), Taiwan (now New Taiwan Dollar, NT$), Trinidad and Tobago (TT$), United States of America (see **United States Dollar**), Zimbabwe (Z$). See also **Eastern Caribbean Dollar**.

dome car A railway carriage with a glass roof designed for **sightseeing**. Also called *bubble car* or *observation car*.

domestic airline An airline operating **services** entirely within one country.

domestic beer/wine Beer or wine produced in the country where it is consumed.

domestic escorted tour (DET) American term for an **inclusive tour** with a **courier** within one's own country.

domestic independent tour (DIT) American term for an unescorted **trip itinerary** within one's own country prepared by a **travel agent** for an independent traveller.

domestic same-day visitor For statistical purposes, a **domestic visitor** who does not spend the night in a collective or private accommodation in the place visited [**World Tourism Organization**]. Also known as a *domestic day visitor* or *excursionist*.

domestic tourism expenditure Defined for statistical purposes as expenditure received as a direct result of **resident visitors** travelling within their country of residence [**World Tourism Organization**]. Thus, e.g., the spending of Australian residents travelling within Australia, of British residents within **Great Britain** or Canadian residents within Canada, all represent domestic tourism expenditure in those countries.

Domestic Tourism Monitor (DTM/Australia) Annual survey of overnight and day trip travel behaviour of Australians aged 14 years and over conducted since 1978 by AGB McNair for the **Bureau of Tourism Research (BTR)**, to provide estimates of volume of **domestic travel**, periodic comparisons of tourism activity, and information about characteristics and behaviour of **domestic travellers**.

domestic tourist For statistical purposes, a **domestic visitor** whose visit is for at least one night and whose main **purpose of visit** may be classified under one of the following three groups: (a) leisure and holidays; (b) business and professional; (c) other tourism purposes [**World Tourism Organization**].

Domestic Travel Study (New Zealand) Annual study by personal interviews of residents over 15 years of age as part of the McNair Omnibus Survey. Results are published in the form of separate regional reports, a demographic report, accommodation and transport reports, origin/destination report, and a general report.

domestic travel/tourism Travel/tourism by **residents** of a country to other areas within the same country, as distinct from **international travel/tourism**. Resident **aliens** are treated as residents in travel and tourism statistics.

domestic traveller Any person on a **trip** within his/her own country of residence (irrespective of the purpose of travel and means of transport used, even though he/she may be travelling on foot) [**World Tourism Organization**].

domestic visitor For statistical purposes, any person residing in a country, who travels to a place within the country, outside his/her usual environment for a period not exceeding 12 months and whose main **purpose of visit** is other than the exercise of an activity remunerated from within the place visited. This definition covers two classes of visitors: '**domestic tourist**' and '**domestic same-day visitor**' [**World Tourism Organization**].

domicile The country or place of a person's permanent home, which may differ from that person's **nationality** or country or place of residence.

Dong Unit of **currency** of Vietnam.

dormette See **sleeper seat/sleeperette**

dormitory town/village A town or village from which many **residents** travel regularly to work in a nearby town or **city**. Some of them are former thriving **resorts**, e.g., Southend-on-Sea and Tunbridge Wells in England. See also **commuter**.

double Adjective used, i.a., with such nouns as *bed* (standard approx. 54 × 75 in.); *room* (a room with such bed); *occupancy* (by two persons); *occupancy rate* (charge for two persons occupying a room). See also **double double**; **single**; **twin**.

double booking See **duplicate reservation**

double double American term for a room with two **double** beds.

double occupancy rate
(a) Per person **hotel tariff** for a shared room, commonly used for organized tours. See also **single supplement**.

(b) Ratio of rooms to guests calculated by dividing the total number of guests by total number of occupied rooms, which may be expressed as a percentage or as guests per room. For example, 50 rooms occupied by 75 guests gives a double occupancy of 50 per cent or 1.5 guests per occupied room. This is also described as *double occupancy factor* to differentiate it from (a).

down time An aviation term used in two different ways:
(a) as the time period an **aircraft** is on the ground;
(b) to indicate the time of landing.

down-market Colloquial term denoting **market** with lower prices, expectations of quality and/or level of service. See also **downgrade**; **trading down**.

downgrade To change to an inferior standard, as in moving an airline passenger or **hotel** guest or their reservations to an inferior seat or accommodation, whether initiated by the airline or **hotel** or by the passenger or guest. See also **upgrade**.

downsizing Contraction of the activities of a **firm** with a view to creating a smaller, more flexible organization better able to respond to changes in its **markets**.

downtown See **central business district (CBD)**

Dram Unit of **currency** of Armenia.

draught (draft) As a nautical concept, the depth of water which a vessel draws, i.e., the depth of the bottom of a ship below the water surface.

dress code Suggested acceptable dress. See also **black tie**; **business attire**; **casual attire**.

drive-in (restaurant) Type of **establishment** in which food is ordered by and served to motorists in their parked vehicles, to be found mainly in North America, and to be distinguished from **drive-through (restaurant)**.

drive-through (restaurant) Type of establishment in which food may be normally

ordered and served indoors but also through a window to motorists without leaving their vehicles for consumption elsewhere, to be found mainly in North America and to be distinguished from **drive-in (restaurant)**.

dry/wet lease Hire of a yacht, or another vessel without crew, fuel or supplies is described as *dry lease*; when these are included in the hire, this is described as *wet lease*. See also **aircraft leasing**; **bareboat charter**; **provisioned charter**.

dry rent See **wet rent**

dual career families Families in which both husband and wife have careers, also sometimes called *two-income families*, of significance as a **segmentation** criterion in the **marketing** of travel, tourism and hospitality.

dude ranch A cattle-breeding **establishment** in North America providing **tourist** accommodation, riding expeditions and the opportunity to sample the cowboy **lifestyle**.

dumb waiter
(a) Waiter's sideboard in a **restaurant**.
(b) Small food lift between kitchen and dining room located on separate floors.

dumping Term used in international trade to describe selling for export at a significantly lower price than in the domestic **market** and often below the cost of production. The practice tends to be adopted for two main reasons. One is the desire of the exporting country to penetrate a foreign market, another is to dispose of surpluses in order to avoid price reductions in the domestic market. Dumping is prohibited under the **Treaty of Rome** and by the **World Trade Organization**. See also **price discrimination**.

dune A ridge or hill of sand, deposited by the wind and characteristic of coasts and deserts. Where it is not stabilized by vegetation it can migrate downwind. Of significance for tourism and **recreation** because of their vulnerability to human pressure which can cause severe **erosion**, particularly in coastal locations backing popular **beaches** or where used by off-road **recreation(al) vehicles**, such as dune buggies.

duopoly In economics, a **market** situation

which exists when the whole supply of a single product is in the hands of two suppliers, who between them dominate the market, determine the quantity supplied and control the price. See also **monopoly**; **oligopoly**.

duplex Accommodation unit on two **floors** connected by a private stairway. When consisting of two rooms, one is normally used as a bedroom and the other as a living room, or both may be used as bed-sitting rooms.

duplicate reservation Two or more reservations of a **hotel** room or passenger seat for the same person for the same night or journey when only one will be used. Also called *double booking*.

duty-free Term applied to (a) goods on which **tax** or **customs** duty is not levied, and (b) shops at international **airports**, **ports** and ships in which passengers travelling abroad can buy such goods. *Duty-free allowance* denotes the quantity of dutiable goods allowed to be taken into a country without paying tax or duty. Duty-free allowances between **European Union** countries were abolished in 1999.

dwell time In transport, the period of time a vehicle is at rest at a **terminal**.

e-commerce Business transactions conducted by electronic means via the **Internet**. In essence, a form of **direct selling**, which enables even small **firms** to compete with large ones and offer the **customer** the convenience of shopping from home.

e-ticket Electronic ticket issued from a passenger operated machine.

early arrival One who arrives at a **hotel** or another **establishment** before the date of reservation or before the arranged time.

early-bird rate A special rate for early booking.

Earth Summit United Nations *Conference on Environment and Development* held in Rio de Janeiro, Brazil, in June 1992, concerned with the impact of world population and economic activities on the biosphere. Agreements reached at the Summit included Agenda for Action in the 21st Century, known as AGENDA 21, a framework of principles to guide international action on the **environment**. Although travel, tourism and hospitality were not specifically identified as key **industry sectors**, the Summit and AGENDA 21 are equally relevant for them. See also **environmental issues**; **Kyoto Agreement**.

easement A right, such as a right of way, that one owner of land has over the land of another.

East Anglia The area of England originally comprising the counties of Suffolk, Norfolk and the old county of Cambridgeshire but in recent times the term has come to include also Essex and what used to be Huntingdonshire (now part of Cambridgeshire). This was also the area covered by the East Anglia Tourist Board, one of the English **Regional Tourist Boards**, before its scope was enlarged to cover also Bedfordshire and Hertfordshire following the demise of the Thames and Chilterns Tourist Board, to be subsequently renamed East of England Tourist Board. **The Broads**, **heritage** and the coast are major attractions of the **region**.

Eastern Caribbean Dollar (EC$) Unit of **currency** of Anguilla, Antigua and Barbuda, Dominica, Grenada, Montserrat, St Kitts and Nevis, St Lucia, St Vincent and Grenadines.

Eastern Orient Express Luxury rail service linking Bangkok, Kuala Lumpur and Singapore, a major **tourist** attraction.

Eastern Standard Time A Canadian and US **time zone** based on the standard of the 75th **meridian**. Time equals GMT –5.

ecology See **ecosystem**

econometrics Application of mathematical techniques to the solution of economic problems, using **models** describing economic relationships, testing the hypotheses and estimating the parameters. Forecasting **international tourist** flows with the use of **regression analysis models** is a prominent example of the econometric approach in travel and tourism.

Economic and Monetary Union (EMU) Unification of the economies of member countries of the **European Union** through such steps as the introduction of a single currency.

economic climate The external conditions in which **firms** and other organizations operate, over which they have no control, but to which they need to respond, e.g., changes in interest rates or **rates of exchange**. Also called *economic environment.*

economies of scale Advantages accruing from an increase in the size of an **establishment**, **firm** or **industry**. *Internal economies* are open to a single establishment or firm as a result of an increase in the scale of output independently of the action of others and are of five main types: technical, managerial, commercial (marketing and purchasing), financial and risk-spreading. They are present, i.a., in **hotel and catering services** and various forms of transport. *External economies* are shared by firms when an industry as a whole expands, particularly when it is concentrated geographically, as is evident, e.g., in the case of **hotels** in a large **resort**.

ecosystem Ecological system, a system in which living organisms interact with each other and with the **environment** in which they live. *Ecology*, the study of the interrelationships, is of importance in the context of tourism, which, like most human activities, may disturb the ecological balance of an area. An **environmental impact assessment (EIA)** is increasingly required in many countries for certain types of development.

ecotourism Open to differences in interpretation but commonly denoting ecologically sustainable **trips** and visits to enjoy and appreciate nature, which promote **conservation**, have low **visitor** impact, and include involvement of local populations. It generally focuses on small-scale activities in well-defined areas, often under some designated form of protection, and on retention of the local traditional economy as a major employer.

educational trips/visits
(a) **Trips**/visits undertaken primarily for education purposes, e.g., by school parties.
(b) **Familiarization trips** or 'fam trips'.

effective demand See **demand for tourism**

efficiency American term for a **hotel** or **motel** room or apartment with cooking facilities.

egocentrism The perspective of one preoccupied with oneself and relatively insensitive to others, i.e., self-absorption and self-centredness.

Eighth freedom In civil aviation a right (not specified in the **Chicago Convention**) to carry traffic between two points within the territory of a foreign country, more commonly known as **cabotage** rights. E.g., Air France had such rights for many years on internal domestic **routes** in Morocco. The incidence is increasing in Europe under **European Union** liberalization measures; one of the first such rights has been taken by British Airways to fly between (London)–Hanover–Leipzig.

elapsed flying time The actual time spent in flight between two points, i.e., after allowing both for time on the ground and for any time changes. See also **elapsed travel time**.

elapsed travel time Of particular relevance in air travel, the actual time taken to travel between two points, after allowing for any time changes. To calculate the elapsed time, i.e., how long the journey actually takes, it is necessary to convert the local departure and arrival times into equivalent **Greenwich Mean Time (GMT)**. See also **elapsed flying time**.

elasticities of demand Measures of the responsiveness of demand to changes in the determining factors. See **cross-elasticity of demand**; **income elasticity of demand**; **price elasticity of demand**

elderhostel (US) Study programmes for men and women over 60 years of age which enable them to learn with travel experiences.

electronic funds transfer (EFT) Transfer of money between accounts through an electronic communication system, which provides direct links between **terminals** in retail outlets and computers in **banks**. Such systems are in growing use in **hotels**, **restaurants** and **travel agents**. See also *Delta* and *Switch* **debit cards**.

electronic mail (e-mail) The transfer of communications between computers, which are connected by cables or telephone lines, using a modem.

electronic ticketing First introduced by low-cost US **domestic airlines** in the early 1990s, electronic ticketing was extended to international flights by the mid 1990s. Commonly operated with cards issued by airlines, which enable passengers to book a flight by telephone or through **travel agents** and obtain a **boarding pass** from a machine at the **airport**, having paid with a **credit card**.

embargo Restriction or prohibition by a government or another authority, originally of shipping and of goods entering or leaving a country. Now used in a wider sense, e.g., when referring to a ban on airline flights and on release of information.

embark To go on board a ship, **aircraft** or other vehicle.

embarkation card See **boarding pass**

emigrant See **migration**

employee buyout See **management buyout**; **leveraged buyout**

employment
See **all found**
    casual employee/worker
    collective agreement
    employment pass/permit/visa
    family employee/worker
    flexitime
    fringe benefits
    full-time
    full-time equivalent
    ghosting
    greeter
    guest worker
    holiday leave loading
    holidays with pay
    industrial awards (Australia)
    job sharing
    long service leave
    moonlighting
    occasional employee/worker
    part-time
    seasonal employee/worker
    self-employed
    Social Chapter
    Social Charter
    split shift
    spreadover of hours
    teleworking
    union contract
See also **occupations**.

employment pass/permit/visa Terms used for a permit to stay and work in a country issued to non-nationals, also known as *labour permit* or *work permit* and under other names in different countries.

empty leg An empty flight between two consecutive **scheduled** stops. This occurs, e.g., when an **aircraft** chartered to take passengers in one direction returns empty rather than waiting for a **return load**. Similarly **tour operators** chartering **aircraft** for the **season** are faced with empty legs on the first return flight and the last outward flight. See also **back-to-back**.

empty nesters An American term for couples whose children have left home, when more time and money tends to be available to be spent on non-essentials, including tourism and eating out.

en pension Inclusive terms for **hotel** stays. En pension or *full-board* terms normally include room and three meals per day (breakfast, lunch, dinner); see also **American Plan (AP)**. **Demi-pension** or *half-board* terms normally include room, breakfast and one main meal, usually dinner; see also **Modified American Plan (MAP)**.

en route On the way (to, for).

en suite Term used in such descriptions as 'bedroom with bathroom en suite' or 'bedroom with en suite bathroom', i.e., with private bathroom attached.

enclave A small territory within a state belonging to another state; e.g., until 1990 West Berlin was from the point of view of the German Democratic Republic an enclave of the Federal Republic of Germany. The term is also used for other small areas surrounded by larger ones (see **tourist enclave**) or for distinct **ethnic** groups surrounded by others (e.g., Chinese quarters in many **cities**). See also **exclave**.

endemic Adjective denoting that which is regularly found in certain places, such as an *endemic disease*.

energy crisis The situation created in the mid 1970s and early 1980s by the intervention of the principal oil-producing countries in the **market** for oil, which led to sharp and successive increases in the price of petrol, aviation fuel and other products based on oil. The effects extended far beyond increases in transport costs, to reduced industrial activity and high unemployment worldwide. Travel and tourism stood up to the effects of the first **recession** in

61

1974–75 relatively well but the 1980–81 recession produced a greater impact and travel and tourism declined or stagnated until well into 1983.

energy management Systems and processes used by **companies** and other organizations to reduce their use of electricity, fuel and other energy resources for cost or environmental reasons. Such approaches are core components of cost control and environmental programmes in travel, tourism and hospitality operations.

Engel's law One of the generalizations put forward by German political philosopher Friedrich Engels, stating that as income increases, the proportion of it spent on food declines (and the proportion spent on **consumer** goods and **services** increases). See also **income elasticity of demand**.

English breakfast Breakfast commonly served in the **British Isles**, normally consisting of juice and/or cereal, main dish, toast, butter and preserves, tea or coffee. The main dish usually consists of meat, fish or eggs or combinations of these. In Scotland, called *Scottish breakfast*. See also **American breakfast**; **Asian breakfast**; **Continental breakfast**.

English service Style of **restaurant** table service, mainly used for private functions, in which food is not portioned in the kitchen, but first presented to guests, as, e.g., whole joints of meat, before carving by the host or by staff. See also **American service**; **family-style service**; **French service**; **Russian service**.

enplane To board an **aircraft**.

enterprise agreements See **industrial awards (Australia)**

entertainments director/officer See **animator**

entrain To **board** a train.

entrée In menu terminology, originally a dish served before the joint of meat; nowadays the main dish, which may be meat, fish, poultry or any other.

entrepreneur A person who undertakes an enterprise, makes decisions on and controls its conduct, and bears the risk.

entry requirements Travel documentation required to enter a country, specified by its government, which may include a **passport** or another proof of citizenship, **visa** and other documents such as **vaccination** certificates. Compared with international trade in goods, much **international tourism** is a relatively free **market** with a high degree of freedom of movement of people between countries. This freedom is increasing, as border controls are reduced and simplified, but entry requirements of varying intensity continue to be applied by most countries to control immigration and for political or other reasons.

entry tax Tax levied on passengers entering a country, usually foreign **visitors**, at **airports** but sometimes also at other entry points.

entry visa See **visa**

environment The surrounding conditions or influences. May refer to physical, e.g., natural or built environment or some other set of conditions or influences as, e.g., economic, social, cultural or political environment. *Environmental impact* usually refers to the effects of some development, such as tourism, on the natural environment. Concern for the protection of the natural environment finds an expression in *environmentalism*, a concept or philosophy which forms the basis of the so-called *Green movement*.

environmental audit A formal evaluation to assess the impact of a **company's** activities on the **environment**. A *site* audit focuses on a location such as a **leisure** complex; an *operations* audit examines the environmental impact and performance of a company's business processes; *associate* audits examine the environmental performance of the company's partners such as suppliers; an *issue* audit assesses potential impact of emerging issues on the business.

environmental impact assessment (EIA) A set of procedures to assess in advance the likely environmental effects of a development project. Such an assessment is required by law in many countries for certain types of development, including the USA and the countries of the **European Union**; it is also sometimes made voluntarily in the absence of a legal requirement.

environmental issues
See **acid rain**
  air quality
  Amazonia
  global warming
  Green Globe
  land resources depletion
  ozone layer depletion
  pollution
  water resources depletion and pollution
See also **building conservation schemes**; **countryside conservation designation schemes**; **Earth Summit**; **ecosystem**; **ecotourism**; **energy management**; **environment**; **environmental audit**; **environmental impact assessment**; **environmental management systems**; **Environmentally Sensitive Areas**; **green holidays (vacations)**; **International Hotels Environmental Initiative**; **Kyoto Agreement**; **Queen's Awards**; **recycling**; **waste management**; **water management**.

environmental management systems (EMS) Range of techniques used to monitor or manage the impacts of business and **industry** operations on the **environment**, such as **environmental audit** and **environmental impact assessment**, as well as **carrying capacity** assessment and **cost benefit analysis**.

Environmentally Sensitive Areas (ESA) **Conservation** areas designated by the **European Community** as part of the scheme to halt overproduction on farms, in which farmers are encouraged to farm voluntarily in a traditional way for the benefit of the landscape and wildlife. By the end of 1999, more than 19 000 farmers in the UK signed ESA management agreements to promote environmentally beneficial farming. See **countryside conservation designation schemes** for other schemes.

epicure
(a) One devoted to a life of ease and luxury and to sensuous enjoyment.
(b) One who cultivates a taste for good food and drink. See also **gourmand**; **gourmet**.

equator The longest **parallel of latitude**, equidistant between the north and south poles, where the sun is overhead at the spring and autumn **equinoxes**. Traditionally, passengers by sea crossing the **equator** for the first time undergo a ritual immersion by Neptune, God of the Sea. See also **hemisphere**.

equinox Time when sun is directly overhead at noon along the **equator** and day and night are equal length: *vernal* equinox about 21 March and *autumnal* equinox about 22 September. See also **solstice**.

equity In business terminology the net worth of a business as a difference between its total assets and total liabilities. It represents the owners' capital, and according to the form of ownership, is represented by the shareholders' capital in a **company** and by capital accounts in a **partnership** or **sole proprietorship**.

Erasmus The **Higher Education** strand of the **European Union Socrates** programme, designed to encourage student and staff mobility, inter-university and other **higher education** cooperative activities.

ergonomics Systematic study of the relationship between man and his working **environment** with the application of anatomy, physiology and psychology. Aspects studied include, for example, human body measurements, the use of energy, and effects of light, heat and noise on work performance, with a wide scope in **hotel and catering services**, transportation, and other **tourism-related industries**.

erosion The wearing away of the land surface by the action of running water, ice and waves to produce a sequence of landforms. This is a slow and inexorable natural process, the rate of which depends on slope, **climate** and rock composition and structure; thus soft coasts of sand and clay are particularly vulnerable, with measurable retreat of the coast in historic time. Often used as a synonym for accelerated erosion through removal of soil, resulting from human actions in removing or disturbing vegetation cover; areas in the **tropics**, underlain by deep weathered rock and subject to torrential rain, and semi-arid areas subject to overgrazing, are particularly vulnerable. See also **canyon**; **dune**.

errors and omissions insurance See **professional indemnity insurance**

escarpment Also shortened to *scarp*, a steep slope usually in areas of gently dipping sedimentary rocks where more resistant rocks overlie more easily eroded rock. Can give rise to striking scenery as, e.g., with Table Mountain in South Africa and the Brecon Beacons in Wales. The term is also applied to any steep slope.

escrow An arrangement whereby payment for goods or **services** is held in a separate bank account or by a third party and released only when the goods or services have been supplied. Thus, e.g., some contracts in travel and tourism require that **tour operators** and **travel agents** keep **customers'** deposits and prepayments in escrow accounts.

Escudo Unit of **currency** of Cape Verde.

esky A portable insulated box-like container used in Australia to transport and keep food and drink cold for picnics, barbecues and other outdoor functions.

esplanade A levelled raised ground along the sea front in a coastal **resort**, carrying a road and a promenade between the road and the seashore.

establishment A separate place of business at a separate address, in which one or more economic activities are carried on, e.g., a factory, a **hotel**, a retail shop. An establishment does not necessarily coincide with the ultimate unit of ownership and control; see **firm**.

ethical investment An investment opportunity offered to investors, which does not compromise their ethics, usually in the form of unit trusts that avoid, e.g., investing in alcohol, tobacco and weapons or in countries with oppressive regimes. Such investments are also available in **companies** that adopt positive policies to the **environment** and to **Third World** development.

ethnic Relating to a particular racial, national or other group with a common background.

ethnic food Food of a particular country, region or racial group, such as Caribbean, Chinese or Indian; hence ethnic **restaurant**, serving such food.

ethnic tourism
(a) Visits to places inhabited by indigenous and other exotic people, to observe their **lifestyles** and cultures, e.g., the Assam hill tribes in India, the Lapps in Northern **Scandinavia**, the San Blas Indians in Panama.
(b) Travel whose primary **motivation** is **ethnic** reunion, e.g., travel to the country of one's ancestry. Thus UK, Greece, Ireland and Poland are among the principal countries with significant ethnic **tourist** arrivals from abroad, as a result of emigration of earlier generations. Ethnic arrivals are also important in countries such as Australia, New Zealand, Canada and Israel, all destinations of major **migrations**.

ethnocentricism/ethnocentricity The belief that the attitudes and behaviour of one's own **ethnic** group are superior to those of others, and the tendency to apply the standards of one's group to other groups. As tourism brings together people of different backgrounds and cultures, it is sometimes claimed to create a better appreciation of other people and their ways of life and to be a lever for change of attitudes and behaviour on the part of **residents** as well as **visitors**. However, the effect of visitors on **host communities** is a contentious issue, especially for many **developing countries**. See also **cultural relativism**.

Eurailpass First class rail ticket for **residents** other than those of Europe and North Africa for unlimited travel within 17 countries for 15 days to 3 months of consecutive travel. Different prices apply to those under 12, 12–25 and over 25 years of age. See also **rail passes**.

Eurail Selectpass First class rail ticket for **residents** other than those of Europe and North Africa for unlimited travel in three adjoining European countries for a maximum of 10 days. Different prices apply to those under 12, 12–25 and over 25 years of age. See also **rail passes**.

Eurasia See **continent**

euro A **currency** introduced in the **European Union** on 1 January 1999 and since adopted by 12 member countries (excluding Denmark, Sweden and the UK). The twelve countries agreed to link their own currencies to the euro for three years to 31 December 2001, during which time the national currencies continued to be traded alongside the euro. Euro notes and coins were introduced in January 2002; after a short transitional period the euro became the only currency in which payments can be made. See also **eurozone**.

Eurobudget Special return air **fare** available on **scheduled** flights in Europe as a promotional **business class** fare. Must be booked and paid for at the same time. A cancellation charge applies; the booking may be changed on payment of the difference between Eurobudget and normal business class fares. See also **air fare types** for other promotional fares.

EuroCity European rail network of fast comfortable trains, which replaced *TEE (Trans Europe Express)* trains.

Eurodollars Dollars deposited with commercial banks outside the USA, which constitute the Eurodollar **market**. The main use of short-term Eurodollar loans is the financing of international trade and longer-term loans are used to finance investment. Eurodollars are subject to less regulation than **currencies** in domestic markets; they are often easier and also less expensive to borrow. The same applies to other Euro-currencies, such as Euro-Sterling or Euro-Swiss Francs, which are balances held outside the UK or Switzerland respectively.

EuroDomino Pass Unlimited travel rail ticket for those **resident** in Europe for at least six months available in first or standard class for three to eight days in a one-month period within one of 28 countries in Europe and North Africa. Different prices apply to those under 12, 12–25 and over 25 years of age. See also **rail passes**.

Eurolines The name of a network of **scheduled** international motor **coach** lines introduced by the **International Road Transport Union** in cooperation with 40 European coach operators.

Europabus International network of motor **coach services** of European railways providing **inclusive tours** by luxury coaches with multilingual guides and using quality **hotels**.

Europass First class ticket for **residents** other than those of Europe and North Africa for unlimited travel in France, Germany, Italy, Spain and Switzerland for between 5 and 15

days within a two-month period. Different prices apply to those under 12, 12–25 and over 25 years of age. See also **rail passes**.

European Cities of Culture A programme for the designation of **cities** by the **European Union**. The annual title was first awarded by the Council of Ministers of the **European Community** to Athens in 1985, then to Florence in 1986, Amsterdam 1987, Berlin (West) 1988, Paris 1989, Glasgow 1990, Dublin 1991, Madrid 1992, Antwerp 1993, Lisbon 1994, Luxembourg 1995, Copenhagen 1996, Thessaloniki 1997, Stockholm 1998, Weimar 1999. Nine cities shared the designation in 2000: Avignon, Bergen, Bologna, Brussels, Cracow, Helsinki, Prague, Reykjavik, Santiago de Compostella; Rotterdam and Oporto followed in 2001, Bruges and Salamanca 2002, Graz 2003, Genoa and Lille 2004. A new programme of *European Capitals of Culture* was announced to begin in 2005. See also **European Cultural Months**.

European Cultural Months A programme for the designation of **cities** by the **European Union**. The first city to host the programme was Cracow in 1992, followed by Graz 1993, Budapest 1994, Nicosia 1995, St Petersburg 1996, Ljubljana 1997, Linz and Valetta 1998, Plovdiv 1999, Riga and Basle 2001. (There were no designations in 2000 and 2002.)

European Currency Unit (ECU) Unit of account of the **European Community (EC)** introduced as part of the **European Monetary System (EMS)** in 1979; it was replaced in January 1999 with the introduction of the **euro** as part of the **Economic and Monetary Union**.

European Economic Area (EEA) A free trade area with the free movement of goods, **services** and capital, implemented on 1 January 1994 by the **European Union (EU)** with five members of the **European Free Trade Association (EFTA)** – Austria, Finland, Iceland, Norway and Sweden. Austria, Finland and Sweden have since joined the Union and Liechtenstein the EEA. By the end of 2000 the EEA covered 18 countries with more than 370 million **consumers**.

European Monetary System (EMS) Monetary system introduced by the **European Community (EC)** in 1979 with the broad aim of promoting monetary stability in Europe, to which all member states belonged. Its key elements included the **European Currency Unit (ECU)** and the **Exchange Rate Mechanism (ERM)**. The system was replaced in January 1999 by the exchange rate arrangements of the **Economic and Monetary Union**.

European Plan (EP) Hotel tariff which includes room only and no meals. See also **American Plan (AP)**; **bed and breakfast**; **Bermuda Plan (BP)**.

European Prize for Tourism and the Environment An award established by the European Commission in 1995, which aims to identify the perfect balance between tourism and the **environment**. The award is made to the destination that most innovatively and effectively develops a tourism policy that respects the environment.

European Year of Tourism 1990 The year marked as such under the auspices of the European Commission, aimed at heightening the awareness of the political, economic and social importance of tourism. A total of 18 European countries were involved and more than 2000 related events were held in the UK alone. See also **International Tourist Year 1967**.

Eurostar Passenger rail service operating through **Eurotunnel** between London and Brussels, Lille and Paris, jointly by Eurostar (UK) Ltd, French Railways and Belgian Railways under the commercial direction of Eurostar Group.

Eurostat *Statistical Office of the European Communities*, which collects, analyses and publishes data on the **European Union** and its member states, including travel and tourism.

Eurotunnel The name of the tunnel between **Great Britain** and France, which opened to traffic in 1994, popularly known as the Channel Tunnel, and of the British-French group operating the tunnel, which has a 65-year operating **concession** from British and French governments. The railway system connecting **terminals** at Coquelles near Calais and Folkestone in Kent carries three types of traffic:

(a) *Le Shuttle*, operated by Eurotunnel for cars and **coaches**;

(b) separate Eurotunnel freight **shuttles** for heavy goods vehicles;

(c) passenger trains and freight operated jointly by Eurostar (UK) Ltd and national railways of France (SNCF), and Belgium (SNCB).

In 2000 Eurotunnel claimed 60 per cent of the total cross-Channel traffic.

eurozone The 12 countries of the **European Union** which have adopted the **euro currency**: Austria, Belgium, Finland, France (including French Guiana, Guadeloupe, Martinique, Mayotte, Monaco, Réunion, St Pierre Miquelon), Germany, Greece, Irish Republic, Italy (including San Marino), Luxembourg, Netherlands, Portugal, Spain together with Andorra and Spanish North Africa (January 2002).

event attractions See **tourist/visitor attractions**

everglades Wetlands with small islands, such as those found in the Everglades **National Park** in Florida, USA.

ex gratia As an act of grace. Hence, e.g., *ex gratia payment*: payment made as a sign of goodwill, without legal obligation.

Excellence Through People (ETP) British **accreditation** scheme launched by the **British Hospitality Association (BHA)** in January 1998 with initial Government funding to encourage employers in the **hospitality industry** to introduce basic best employment practices. See also **Best Practice Forum (BPF)**; **Hospitality Assured (HA)**; **Investor in People (IIP)**.

excess baggage Amount of **baggage** (luggage) exceeding **baggage allowance** set by the **carrier**, which may be carried on payment of an additional charge. Under the *weight system* used by many airlines, the normal charge for every kilo of excess weight is one per cent of the applicable one-way first-class **fare**; under the piece system, the excess charge depends on the distance flown, with additional charge for the actual weight and size.

excess mileage Percentage supplement payable by an airline passenger if the **maximum permitted mileage (MPM)** between two points is exceeded. The additional amount is assessed at 5, 10, 15 or 25 per cent, corresponding broadly to the additional mileage. See also **more distant point principle**.

excess value Amount which may be declared by airline passengers at the time of **check-in** and by which, on payment of a fee to the airline, the possible compensation in the event of **baggage** loss or damage is increased. Excess value is applicable to both **checked** and **unchecked** baggage but is not an insurance: the airline will not necessarily compensate to the full amount and negligence has to be proved on its part. See also **Warsaw Convention**.

excess weight See **excess baggage**

exchange controls Restrictions on the purchase and sale of **foreign exchange** operated in various different forms by many countries. The UK abolished all exchange controls in 1979.

exchange rate See **rate of exchange**

Exchange Rate Mechanism (ERM) An arrangement introduced by the **European Community (EC)** as part of the **European Monetary System (EMS)** in 1979, under which the participating countries kept their **currencies** within agreed limits against each other with a view to maintaining **exchange rate** stability. A new exchange rate mechanism (EMS) was introduced in 1999 to regulate the relationship between the single currency and the currencies of member states not participating in monetary union.

exclave An outlying part of a state separated from it and surrounded by the territory of another state. E.g., until 1990 West Berlin was from the point of view of the Federal Republic of Germany its exclave in the German Democratic Republic. See also **enclave**.

excursion Generally a short pleasure trip, also a **sightseeing trip** (usually optional) as part of an **inclusive tour**.

Excursion fares Special return air **fares** by airlines on **scheduled** flights, which are subject to various restrictions, such as specifying minimum and/or maximum length of stay,

and thus preventing dilution of full-fare revenue. They are less restrictive than APEX or PEX fares and, e.g., allow **stopovers** if specified at the time of booking. Whilst more expensive than APEX and PEX, they are fully refundable. See also **Advance Purchase Excursion (APEX)**; **Public Excursion (PEX)**; **Seat Sale**.

excursionist A synonym for *day visitor*. See also **same-day visitor**.

exile A person compelled by political or other circumstances to live away from his/her native country. See also **refugee**.

exit tax See **departure tax**

exit visa See **visa**

expatriate A person living voluntarily away from his/her country of citizenship, not necessarily permanently but relatively long-term. In statistics of **domestic** and **international travel/tourism**, expatriates are treated as **residents** of the country in which they live. See also **alien**; **migration**; **nomad**; **refugee**.

export tourism See **inbound travel/tourism**.

expressway An American multi-lane divided highway designed for fast **through** traffic, with limited access and no surface crossroads, which may be a **freeway** or **tollway**. See also **motorway**.

external diseconomies See **decreasing returns**

external economies See **economies of scale**

externalities The impact of the actions of one individual or body on another, over which the affected individual or body has no direct control. The effects may be *positive* (i.e. beneficial) or *negative* (i.e. adverse). E.g., a new **tourist/visitor attraction** may create positive externalities for **residents** of the area by bringing additional spending power and employment but also negative externalities, such as increased traffic and congestion.

extrapolation Calculation from known terms, such as predicting a future situation on the basis of past data or events. E.g., one approach to forecasting future **visitor** numbers to a destination is to project past trends into the future.

face to face selling See **personal selling**

facilitation Generally, action or process of moving forward, promoting or rendering something easier. In travel and tourism, facilitation usually refers to measures taken by authorities to remove restrictions on movement, such as reduction and simplification of border controls, or *marketing facilitation*, as provided by **tourist boards** to support **firms** engaged in tourism through, e.g., organization of trade shows and workshops, **familiarization trips**, and provision of travel trade manuals.

facsimile transmission (fax) High speed electronic transmission of an exact copy of a document from one location to another using the national or international telephone networks, which was the fastest growing means of business communication in the 1980s.

factory tourism Trips and visits by members of the public to working factories to observe processes, which may also enable them to purchase products from a factory shop. See also **industrial tourism**.

Fahrenheit (F) Measure of temperature using Fahrenheit's thermometer, with freezing point of water 32 °F and boiling point 212 °F; now largely superseded by **centigrade** except in the USA.

fair An event usually held periodically for a limited duration to provide a location for promoting and selling one or more type of goods or **services**. Prominent are, e.g., *agricultural fairs*, which are normally of local or regional significance, and *trade fairs*, which may have a national or international appeal, and thus a tourism significance.

fale See **Polynesian bure**

fall Term used with the name of a large waterfall, such as *Niagara Falls* in America or *Victoria Falls* in Africa.

familiarization trip Trip commonly arranged by **tourist boards** and similar organizations for journalists, **tour operators** and **travel agents** in generating areas to visit destinations and to become acquainted with their attractions, facilities and **services**. These trips, popularly known as *fam trips*, may be viewed as part of **sales promotion** and as one of the **facilitation** techniques used by tourism organizations to assist the **tourism industry**. They also have a **public relations** role in providing opportunities for influencing communication and **distribution channels** for travel and **tourist products** and through them ultimately potential **customers**. They are also referred to as *educational trips* or *educationals*, and as **agency tours**.

family employee/worker One in the employ of relatives who usually lives in the same household.

Family Expenditure Survey (FES) Continuous household sample inquiry into the expenditure patterns of private households in the UK, based on a sample of about 12 000 households. The results of the survey are used for such major purposes as the calculation of the weights given to various items of the **cost of living index** and as a source of data on **consumers' expenditure**. Results are published in annual *Family Expenditure Survey Reports*.

Family Railcard See **British railcards**

family room Hotel room large enough to accommodate a family, usually with four or more beds.

family table service See **family-style service**

family-style service Style of **restaurant** table service in which bowls and platters of food are placed on the table from which guests help themselves. See also **American service**; **English service**; **French service**; **Russian service**.

Fantasia One of two main **computer reservation systems (CRS)** serving the Asian and Pacific region, owned by QANTAS, Japan Airlines and American Airlines, using **Sabre** software and giving its subscribers access to the Sabre system in the USA. See also **Abacus**.

Far East (FE) Term used to describe collectively but not precisely countries of east and south-east Asia, including China, Korea, Japan and countries to the south of these. This is the fastest growing destination region of the world in **international tourism** with rates of growth well above the global average; it is also an increasingly important **tourism generating area**. See also **Pacific Rim**.

fare Generic term for the price charged by a **carrier** and the cost of a ticket for travel by public transport. Hence, e.g., *air fare* or *bus fare*; *concessionary fare* (reduced fare for certain passengers such as **senior citizens**); *full fare* (adult full price); *single fare* (US one-way fare); *return fare* (US round trip fare).

Fare Construction Unit (FCU) The basis of air **fare** calculations established by the **International Air Transport Association (IATA)**, and in use between 1974 and 1989, replaced by **Neutral Unit of Construction (NUC)** on 1 July 1989.

farm tourism/farm stay tourism Holiday **(vacation)** tourism centred on a working farm, which takes various forms but invariably includes **accommodation** and often other **services** for users. The two main forms are with serviced accommodation in or adjacent to the farm premises and with **self-catering accommodation** based on the farm land, e.g., cottages, **caravans** and **camping sites**. Farm tourism may be seen as a form of **rural tourism** and is also called *agritourism, agricultural tourism, agrotourism, farm stay tourism* and *vacation farm tourism,* especially in North America.

fast food Food prepared, served and consumed quickly on the premises or taken away. Hamburgers, fish and chips, and pizzas are typical examples. See also **fast food outlet**.

fast food outlet A limited menu retail outlet offering quick, often counter, service and take-away service. Usually based on systems with standard recipes, procedures and products, many **fast food** outlets are chain-operated with **brand** names.

fast lane
(a) The outer traffic lane on a **motorway**.
(b) Slang term for high living.

fathom A nautical measure of depth of water, based on the span of the outstretched human arms, equivalent to 6 feet or 1.829 metres.

feasibility study A systematic assessment of the prospects for a new venture, which normally consists of market feasibility and financial feasibility studies. Thus, e.g., a **market** feasibility study for a new **hotel** may identify the best market opportunity, a gap in the market, a location or choice between alternative locations, for a particular hotel concept; or, given a particular location, the study can determine the most appropriate hotel concept. The financial feasibility of the project is then determined by using one or more **investment appraisal** methods. See also **cost benefit analysis**.

featherbedding A practice of creating additional jobs or spreading work by placing limits on production, requiring more people than necessary to do a job, or requiring the performance of superfluous work.

federation Designation normally used by or applied to organizations with institutional rather than individual membership, in which each constituent member retains control over its own affairs. Thus, e.g., an international organization may consist of national associations, such as the **Federation of Nordic Travel Agents' Associations**.

fee-based pricing An approach to **travel agent's** remuneration in which a mark-up is added to the cost of **services** provided according to an agreed schedule, i.e., **cost-plus pricing**, as an alternative to **commission** payment.

feeder airline A local airline operating **scheduled services** between outlying **airports** and a major airport. See **hub and spoke system**

feeder route A local **route** of **scheduled** airline **services** between outlying **airports** and a major airport. See **hub and spoke system**

feeder vessel A small ship used to carry loads discharged at a **port** from larger vessels, to various destinations.

fens Area of low-lying **wetlands** in eastern England.

ferry A boat (ferryboat) or an **aircraft** (air ferry) used to transport passengers, goods and/or vehicles on a regular **route** between two points, usually across a river, lake or other body of water. Because the coast of Europe is highly indented, the ferry in general and the car ferry in particular are especially prominent features of European travel and tourism along the coast between the Baltic in the north and the Aegean Seas in the south.

ferry mileage The distance a ship, **aircraft** or another vehicle has to travel without passengers
(a) to return to its base;
(b) to deliver it from one location to another;
(c) to move it to and from a maintenance base.
See also **deadhead**.

festival A celebratory event normally held at regular intervals with a particular religious or secular theme, such as art, food or music, which may range from local to national or international and, therefore, tourism significance.

fête Small local **festival** of a day's or half-day's duration, such as a school or village fête.

fictitious fare construction points See **hypothetical fare construction points**

field research Obtaining information by methods requiring direct contact with respondents, such as existing or potential **customers** or members of the public, including face-to-face, telephone or postal contact, as distinct from **desk research**. Also referred to as *fieldwork*, although some limit the meaning of fieldwork to face-to-face interviews.

field sports A general term, especially in the **United Kingdom**, to cover angling, hunting and shooting, conducted largely on or over private land, frequently in some form of **multiple land use**. Angling and shooting, as well as being undertaken by landowners and their friends, are let commercially to **visitors**, particularly angling for game fish and shooting of grouse, pheasant and red deer; angling and shooting may also be available to those staying at **hotels**. Apart from stag hunting on Exmoor, England, hunting takes place in winter over farmland and is both a participant and spectator sport. Large tracts of the uplands, especially in Scotland, are devoted to field sports, notably deer stalking and grouse shooting.

fieldwork See **field research**

fiesta Term of Spanish origin, denoting a festivity or **holiday**.

Fifth freedom See **freedoms of the air**

financial economies See **economies of scale**

fiords/fjords Heavily glaciated coastal valleys that have been invaded by the sea, characteristically deep, but with a shallow threshold at the seaward end. They share many of the characteristics of glaciated lakes and often provide spectacular scenery, as in the western coasts of Norway and Scotland, British Columbia and South Island, New Zealand. They are important tourism resources, both for cruising and for those touring by land.

firm A more or less independent business unit, in which final decisions are made and ultimate control is exercised; it raises capital, employs and organizes productive resources, and is the ultimate unit of accountability and profitability. A firm may operate more than one **establishment** and in more than one **industry**. See also **conglomerate**; **holding company**; **parent company**; **subsidiary company**.

First freedom See **freedoms of the air**

First World Collective term for the countries of Western Europe, North America, **Australasia** and Japan with a predominantly **market economy**, as distinct until recently from countries of Eastern Europe and the USSR with a **planned economy**. See also **Second World**.

firth Scottish term for an area of coastal water, e.g., arm of the sea, an estuary.

fixed wing aircraft See **aircraft types: wings**

flag carrier A **carrier** designated by a government to operate international **services**. Hence, e.g., *flag airline* of a country.

flag of convenience The practice of shipowners of registering their ships in countries other than those of their own home **ports**, for such reasons as avoiding **taxes**, government regulations, high wage rates and manning requirements.

flagship Originally ship having an admiral on board, nowadays the largest or best ship of the fleet, whether that of the navy or of a shipping **company**. The term is also used to denote the leading member of a group or chain of properties, when referring, e.g., to **hotels** or stores.

flexitime Flexible working arrangement, under which each employee can choose within limits his/her working hours, as long as they cover 'core' times and the total weekly hours of work. Thus in offices with a working week of 35 hours, common 'core' times are sometimes set between 10 a.m. and 4 p.m. and employees may begin as early as 8 a.m. and finish as late as 6 p.m.

flight attendant Member of **cabin crew** of an **aircraft**, also known as *air steward(ess)* or *air hostess*.

flight coupon The portion of a passenger ticket which covers a flight between particular points, surrendered at **check-in time**. In addition to one or more flight coupons, the ticket contains issuing office and airline audit copies.

flight deck crew The pilots, flight engineers and navigators responsible for flying an **aircraft**, as distinct from **cabin crew**.

flight numbers Flight designations normally consisting of two letters **(airline codes)** and three figures. Some domestic and also intra-European flight numbers have four figures. See also **code sharing**.

flight recorder Device carried in the **aircraft** which records technical information about the flight and which should be recoverable in case of an accident. Also known as *in-flight recorder* and referred to as the *black box*.

floor As a designation for the same level of a building, the floor numbering differs in the UK and the USA: in the UK the floor at street level is called the ground floor and in the USA the first floor.

floor service See **room service**

Florin See **Guilder/Florin**

flotilla cruising An arrangement in which a group of yachts sails in a fleet under the guidance of a lead boat with a small crew usually consisting of a skipper in overall charge, an engineer, and sometimes also a **hostess**. See also **bareboat charter**; **crewed charter**; **provisioned charter**.

fly cruise A **holiday (vacation)** arrangement consisting of **scheduled** or **charter** flight to and/or from a **port** and a sea **cruise**.

fly drive An arrangement of **scheduled** or **charter** flight and car hire **(rental)**, normally booked at the same time or as a **package** at an inclusive price.

fly rail An arrangement consisting of air and rail travel, normally booked at the same time, or as a **package**; it may include a **rail pass**, which entitles the holder to unlimited rail travel at the destination for a specified period of time.

flying boat An **aircraft** that can land on and take off from water, in which a boat serves as both **fuselage** and float. See also **seaplane**.

föhn A warm dry wind characteristic of mountainous **regions**, sometimes given its own name. E.g., *Chinook* blows down the eastern slopes of the Rocky Mountains over the adjacent US and Canadian plains, and causes snow in winter to disappear rapidly, hence its nickname, the 'snow eater'. *Santa Ana* blows from east to north east, west of Sierra Nevada Mountains, especially in the pass and river valley near Santa Ana, California.

food
See à la carte	Asian breakfast
accompaniment	bill of fare
afternoon tea	brunch
American breakfast	buffet
American service	café complet

food cont.

catering	grub
Continental breakfast	gueridon
convenience foods	halal
cook–chill	haute cuisine
cook–freeze	health food
cream tea	high tea
cuisine	hors-d'oeuvre
cyclical menus	junk food
diet	kosher
English breakfast	nouvelle cuisine
English service	organic produce
entreé	plat du jour
epicure	plate service
ethnic food	portion
family-style service	recipe
fast food	Russian service
food cycle	smörgåsbord
French service	supper
gastronomy	table d'hôte
gourmand	tapas
gourmet	vegetarianism

food court A **catering** concept in which a number of different food outlets share a common eating area. Usually comprising **self-service fast food outlets**, food courts are often located in shopping malls, transport **terminals** and other places with a high density of pedestrian traffic, and also major **holiday (vacation)** centres. See also **hawker centre**.

food cycle The sequence of stages in the food operation of a **hotel** or **restaurant**, usually seen for control purposes as purchasing, receiving, storing and issuing, preparing, selling.

food service contracting See **contract catering**

footpaths Narrow, unpaved **routes** for pedestrians across countryside in England and Wales. Most are public **rights of way** across farmland and through woodlands; **local authorities** have had to prepare definitive maps of such paths. Mainly used for informal walking in the countryside by **day visitors**. Since 1949, long-distance footpaths have been created around parts of the coast and on hills and uplands, linking existing paths and creating new ones where necessary, to give opportunities for long-distance travel; the oldest and longest is the *Pennine Way* (opened 1965, 256 miles or 412 kilometres long). Other footpaths have been created along **canals** and abandoned railway lines. In countries of more recent settlement, such paths are largely confined to public lands. See also **long-distance footpath**.

force majeure An event or effect that cannot be reasonably anticipated or controlled, such as an earthquake, war or strike. See also **act of God**.

Forces Railcard See **British railcards**

foreign escorted tour (FET) American term for an **inclusive tour** abroad with a **courier**.

foreign exchange Foreign **currency**, i.e., currency of another country that is purchased for one's own currency. See also **exchange controls**; **exchange rate**.

foreign independent tour (FIT) American term for an unescorted **trip itinerary** abroad prepared by a **travel agent** for the independent traveller.

Forint Unit of **currency** of Hungary.

Form E111 Form used in the **European Economic Area (EEA)**, which entitles **residents** of a member country to free or reduced-cost medical treatment in another country.

forward Originally a nautical term, now denoting front part of a ship or **aircraft**. See also **aft**; **abaft**; **(a) midship(s)**; **astern**; **bow**.

forward buying *Inter alia*, buying **foreign exchange** for a future date, to cover a payment that has to be made in foreign **currency** at a later date, e.g., by **tour operators** to **hotels** and other suppliers abroad.

forwarding address Address to which mail may be sent after a person or business has left their current address. May be arranged by a guest with a **hotel** or in most countries with the Post Office.

four Ps See **marketing mix**

Fourth freedom See **freedoms of the air**

Fourth World Term sometimes used for the least developed countries of the world, i.e., countries with the lowest **gross domestic**

product **(GDP)**, share of manufactures in the economy, and literacy rate. In recent years the **United Nations** listed between twenty and thirty such countries, most of them in Africa and Asia.

Franc Unit of **currency** of Burundi, Comoros, Congo Dem. Rep., Guinea (FG), Liechtenstein (SF), Madagascar, Rwanda, Switzerland (SF). See also **Franc CFA**; **Franc CFP**.

Franc CFA *Franc de la Communauté financière africaine* (African Franc), unit of **currency** in Benin, Burkina Faso, Cameroon, Central African Republic, Chad, Congo Rep., Côte d'Ivoire, Equatorial Guinea, Gabon, Guinea-Bissau, Mali, Niger, Senegal, Togo.

Franc CFP *Franc des Comptoirs Français du Pacifique* (Pacific Franc), unit of **currency** in French Polynesia, New Caledonia, Wallis and Futuna.

France Railpass Unlimited travel rail ticket available in first or standard **class** for three to nine days within a one-month period in the French National Railways network. Different prices apply to those under 12, 12–25, 26–60 and 60+ years of age, as well as with a French Saverplan when two to eight people travel together. See also **rail passes**.

franchising A contractual relationship between two parties for the distribution of goods and **services**, in which one party (the franchisee) sells a product designed, supplied and controlled by and with the support of the other party (the franchisor). Although interdependent, both parties are legally and financially independent business units. Franchising is particularly prominent in filling stations, **fast-food outlets**, retailing, repairs and other personal **services**, also increasingly in civil aviation. It is also common in **hotels**, particularly in the USA, where franchising is most developed generally. See also **management contract**.

free circulation See **circulation**

free house Term most commonly used in relation to a **public house** in **Great Britain** owned by a proprietor other than the brewery who is under no obligation to obtain supplies from any particular source. See also **tied house**.

free port A **port** in which cargo may be unloaded and stored without the imposition of import duties and **taxes**, which is of particular value when imported goods are to be re-exported. Several hundred such ports have been established in various parts of the world, with a view to assisting international trading and the **balance of payments** of the countries in which the ports operate, Hong Kong, Rotterdam and Singapore being the largest.

freedom of the seas A principle of international law that no state has any imposing right in the open seas and navigation on the open seas must be free of any interference.

freedoms of the air Privileges agreed by the **Chicago Convention** which may be included in **bilateral air services agreements** between countries.

First: Overflying a country without landing (e.g., a British non-stop flight London–Rome overflying France).
Second: Landing for technical reason (e.g., to refuel).
Third: Setting down passengers, cargo or mail.
Fourth: Picking up traffic, as for the Third.
Fifth: Setting down and picking up passengers in the territory of a third country (e.g., a US airline flying between New York and Athens and carrying passengers boarding in London and disembarking in Rome).

See also **Bermuda Agreement**; **Sixth freedom**; **Seventh freedom**; **Eighth freedom**; **technical rights**; **traffic rights**.

free-market economy See **mixed economy**

freesale An arrangement that enables a **tour operator** to sell an agreed number of **hotel** rooms without first checking availability with the hotel, whereby reservations can be confirmed immediately to the client.

freeway See **turnpike road**

French Canada Term used for the Province of Quebec, one of Canada's 12 provinces.

French service Style of **restaurant** table service, in which the food is portioned and arranged on silver salvers in the kitchen; the salvers are placed in the restaurant on a **gueridon** with a small heater, and the food is served from the salvers on to the guest's plate. See also **American service**; **English service**; **family-style service**; **Russian service**.

frequent flyer programmes (FFPs) See **frequent user programmes**. **Brand** names of some major airlines' programmes are: AAdvantage (American Airlines), Flying Dutchman (KLM), Mileage Plus (United Airlines), Miles and More (Lufthansa), Worldperks (North West Airlines), Freeway (Virgin Atlantic).

frequent user programmes Promotional programmes, also known as *loyalty schemes*, typically targeted at business travellers and operated by **carriers**, **hotel** and car hire as well as other **companies**, in which the frequent (loyal) user of the company's services earns free or discounted travel, hotel stays or other benefits. Some programmes are operated by a single company, others jointly by two or more companies, e.g., an airline and a hotel. See also **airline clubs**.

fringe benefits Benefits received by employees in addition to normal remuneration, such as free meals, medical insurance, pension arrangements. See also **all found**.

front of house The operational areas and staff, e.g., all parts of a **hotel**, **motel** or **restaurant** in direct contact with the **customer**, such as foyers, bars and dining rooms. Staff in these areas are critical to the **customer's** quality perception of the **tourist product**, which is largely experiential and involves much customer–supplier interaction. See also **back of house**.

FTO Bonding Scheme **Bonding** scheme of the **Federation of Tour Operators (FTO)**, which covers any **inclusive tour (IT) holiday (vacation)** not covered by **ATOL Bonding Scheme**. See **bonding schemes (UK)** for other schemes.

fuel surcharge See **surcharge**

full-board See **en pension**

full-time (FT)
(a) Generally normal hours of work excluding overtime and main meal breaks considered to constitute a full working week in a

particular **industry** or **occupation**. However, what is full-time employment is usually defined for particular purposes; thus, e.g., full-time workers are defined for statistical purposes by the UK Department for Education and Skills as people normally working for more than 30 hours a week.
(b) The term is variously defined in the context of education.
See also **part-time**.

full-time equivalent (FTE) Standardized unit arrived at by converting **part-time** employment into **full-time** for accounting and statistical purposes. When data are available, this is usually done on the basis of hours worked. However, a common approximation is to convert numbers employed into full-time equivalent persons employed on the assumption that **part-time** employees work on average half the hours of full-time employees, and that the **self-employed** work full-time.

funicular (railway) A cable railway constructed for the ascent of a **mountain**, in which the weight of an ascending car is partly or wholly counterbalanced by the weight of the descending car.

Further Education (FE) In the UK, generally defined as all non-advanced education outside schools, i.e., following the period of compulsory education after the age of 16 up to and including the Advanced level of General Certificate of Education (GCE) and its equivalent, excluding those studying in **higher education (HE)** at universities and certain colleges. In Australia this public sector education provision is known as *Technical and Further Education (TAFE)*. See also **Adult and Continuing Education**.

fuselage The main body of an **aircraft** containing the passenger and cargo compartments and the flight deck, i.e., excluding the wings, tailplane and undercarriage.

futures
(a) Contracts to sell or buy commodities or **currencies** at a future date, to provide a hedge against price changes or for speculative reasons.
(b) The study of the future, which seeks to identify, analyse and evaluate possible

future developments. Futures research, using various forecasting techniques, is of growing importance in many fields, including travel, tourism and hospitality, in providing a basis for decision-making. See also **futurism**.

futurism Term originally used to refer to a movement in art and literature representing a radical departure from traditional methods. Nowadays used also to describe an outlook emphasizing contemplation of and planning for the future. See also **futures**.

Galileo One of two main European **computer reservation systems (CRS)** established in 1987 by a **consortium** led by Alitalia, British Airways, KLM and Swissair and including also Aer Lingus, Austrian Airlines, Olympic Airways, SABENA and TAP, with US Covia Corporation supplying initial software and United Airlines being a partner in the system. In 1992 Galileo and **Apollo** merged to form **Galileo International** as a **global distribution system**.

Galileo International A global **computer reservation system (CRS)** formed in 1992 by the merger of the **Apollo** network in the USA and the **Galileo** network in Europe, owned in equal shares by three North American carriers (United Airlines, USAir and Air Canada) and European partners of the former **Galileo** system, including SAS, former founder of **Amadeus**. In Canada **Gemini** acts as the local distribution **company** for Galileo; in the USA, Mexico and Japan Galileo uses the Apollo **brand** name.

galley Originally ship's kitchen, nowadays also **aircraft** area used for food preparation, as distinct from **in-flight** kitchen, a ground food preparation facility.

gallon (gal.) An English cubic measure of capacity for liquids and a dry measure for such substances as corn. The imperial gallon contains 277¼ cubic inches and equals 4.55 litres; the wine-gallon of 231 inches is the standard in the USA and equals 3.79 litres. A gallon is divided into 4 quarts or 8 pints; 1 bulk barrel is 36 gallons.

game reserve An area designed and managed to conserve wildlife, which may be also used for research and to provide controlled access for **visitors**. There are no game reserves in the UK, but see **National Nature Reserves**.

gaming Playing games of chance for money or money's worth. In **Great Britain** gaming is, subject to certain exceptions, generally prohibited in premises to which members of the public have access (such as **public houses**, **restaurants** or **hotels**), unless the premises are licensed for gaming under the law.

gangway
(a) Passage between rows of seats in an auditorium.
(b) **Ramp** for **embarking** and **disembarking** ship passengers.
(c) Staircase on wheels used to load and unload **aircraft**.

gasoline/gas US term for petrol, hence *gasoline/gas station*.

Gasthaus/Gasthof A small **hotel** or **inn** in Austria, Germany and Switzerland.

gastronomy Art and science of good eating. Hence *gastronome*, expert on or judge of food and drink.

gateway A **city** or another main point of access to a country or **region**, usually because of its location and/or transport links. Thus, e.g., London is the main gateway to the UK and Copenhagen the main gateway to **Scandinavia**; Nairobi performs an analogous role for East Africa and Nadi in Fiji for most islands of the South Pacific.

gazebo A structure on the roof of a house, a projecting window, balcony or similar, with extensive views, also one erected on the ground.

gearing See **capital gearing**

Gemini Computer reservation system (CRS) owned by Air Canada, Canadian Airlines International and **Galileo International**, which acts as the local distribution **company** for Galileo in Canada.

genealogy A study of one's descent from ancestors, a pedigree.

General Agreement on Tariffs and Trade (GATT) International agreement on reducing restrictions on trade between countries superseded by *World Trade Organization (WTO)* on 1 January 1995 as the legal and institutional foundation of the **multilateral** trading system. The WTO also administers and implements multilateral agreements with a total coverage of all internationally traded **services**.

General Delivery See **poste restante**

General Household Survey (GHS) Multipurpose continuous survey of all adults in a household designed to provide information on a large number of topics about private households in **Great Britain**, based on a sample of about 12 000 households. The flexible form of the questionnaire enables the Survey to meet specific needs and interviews carried out as a **trailer** to the survey have been, e.g., used in recent years for **day visits surveys (DVS)**. Findings of the GHS are published in reports by the *Office for National Statistics (ONC)*.

General National Vocational Qualifications (GNVQs) A framework of vocational qualifications for England, Wales and Northern Ireland developed primarily for young people between the ages of 16 and 19 as work-related education in schools and colleges and as a vocational alternative to academic qualifications. Based on broad occupational areas, they provide both preparation for employment and a **route** to higher qualifications, including **higher education**; areas covered include hospitality and catering and leisure and tourism. GNVQs are offered at three levels – Foundation, Intermediate and Advanced (the last equated to two GCE A-levels) – and the Scottish equivalent is General Scottish Vocational Qualifications.

General Sales Agent (GSA) Agent appointed by an airline or another **principal** to handle variously promotion, reservations, ticketing and enquiries for that airline or other principal in a particular territory, and then may be also known as *sole agent*. See also **overriding commission**.

generating country For purposes of **international tourism** statistics, the country whose **residents** travel to other countries. See also **receiving country**.

geo-demographic segmentation See **ACORN**

geographical mile See **mile**

geographical names
See **ABC Islands**

Amazonia	Levant
Americas	Low Countries
Antarctic	Melanesia
Arctic	Metropolitan France
Australasia	Micronesia
Balkans	Middle East
Baltic States	Near East
Benelux	New England
Britain	Nordic countries
British Isles	Oceania
Broadlands/The Broads	Orient
East Anglia	Pacific Rim
Eurasia	Polynesia
Far East	Riviera
French Canada	Scandinavia
Great Britain	Seven Seas
Great Lakes	Silk Road
Gulf States	Spice Island
Heart of England	Sub-Saharan Africa
Iberia	United Kingdom
Indian Subcontinent	West Country
Lapland	West Indies
Latin America	Yugoslavia

Gets A **computer reservation system (CRS)** designed principally to meet the needs of smaller airlines and operated by *Société Internationale des Télécommunications Aéronautiques*.

geyser A hot spring that emits columns of water intermittently, to be found in volcanic areas, especially Iceland, New Zealand and the United States, where geysers are major **tourist/visitor attractions**.

ghetto Historically, the part of a town or **city** in which Jews lived in Europe. Nowadays commonly used to refer to an area where members of a minority live or where **tourists** are concentrated **(tourist ghetto)**.

ghost town A term applied to a formerly thriving town, which has been abandoned by all or most of its inhabitants. Such towns, to be found particularly in Australia and North America, many of them former mining settlements, are now sometimes historical **tourist/visitor attractions**. See also **depressed area**.

ghosting Term used, i.a., for the incidence of not declaring one's sole paid employment to the authorities for taxation purposes, to be distinguished from **moonlighting**. See also **black economy**.

gîte French name for self-catering **holiday (vacation) accommodation** in a countryside location, which may be an apartment, cottage or the whole or part of a house. Many are converted from farm outbuildings, flats in former presbyteries or school houses, and wings of a **château**. There are around 10 000 gîtes throughout France. *Gîte de France* and *Gîte Ruraux de France* designations indicate that the accommodation meets the standards set by those organizations.

giveaway A promotional gift item given free to **customers** and/or **industry** contacts, such as branded travel bags, T-shirts, stationery and souvenirs. Also called *promotional items*.

glacier A large mass of ice, resulting from the compaction and crystallization of snow and moving slowly downslope under the influence of gravity. There is a distinction between *piedmont* and *valley* glaciers, the former spreading out over a broad front and the latter being narrowly confined and often moving more rapidly. Glaciers are now found mainly in mountainous country in high and middle **latitudes**, particularly **Scandinavia**, the Alps, the northern Rockies and South Island, New Zealand, where they left their mark in the rugged scenery, overdeepened valleys and **fjords** of **mountain** country; such areas are hence attractive to **visitors**.

glen Gaelic term for a deep narrow valley, usually forming the course of a stream, as distinct from **strath**.

global distribution system (GDS) Worldwide **computer reservation system (CRS)**, such as **Galileo International**, also called **global reservation system (GRS)**, which has the capacity to distribute airline and other travel services throughout the world.

global reservation system (GRS) See **global distribution system**

global tourism regions Grouping of countries in conformity with the six Regional Commissions of the **World Tourism Organization**, used for statistical purposes: Africa; Americas; East Asia and the Pacific; Europe; South Asia; **Middle East**.

global warming Increase in global temperatures caused by the release and accumulation in the atmosphere of certain gases, which allow solar radiation to penetrate but prevent heat from escaping. Described as the *greenhouse effect*, it may cause increases in sea levels, which could destroy low-lying coastal **resorts**, but also affect ski resorts, and damage **coral reefs** and other **tourist/visitor attractions**.

globalization Growth of global **markets** and **multinational companies** to service them, with a convergence in world tastes, product preferences and **lifestyles** leading to increasing standardization and market homogenization. Travel and tourism provides a stimulus, especially to globalization of culture, and also displays many of its features.

Golden Age Passport Card available to those of 62 years of age and over, which allows unlimited access to parks and sites operated by US *National Park Service*.

golden era of bus and coach travel Description given in **Great Britain** to the inter-War period 1918–1938 when more passengers were carried on **buses** and **coaches** then ever before or after.

Golden Week Term used for a week in May in Japan, in which several **public holidays** occur, resulting in heavy Japanese demand for tourism facilities and services both in and out of Japan, when tour, transport and **accommodation** prices rise sharply in response to the excessive peaking of demand.

gondola Light flat-bottomed boat with a high point at each end worked by one oar at **stern**, used as a means of transport on Venetian **canals**.

gorge Deep steep-sided narrow river valley.

go-show American term for airline **standby** passenger.

Gothic Architectural style of the twelfth to sixteenth centuries in Europe, of which the main characteristics are the pointed arches and ribbed vaulting. The term is also applied to the painting and sculpture of the period.

Gourde Unit of **currency** of Haiti.

gourmand One fond of eating, one who eats greedily, glutton. See also **epicure**; **gourmet**.

gourmet A connoisseur of food and drink. See also **epicure**; **gourmand**.

gram(me) (g) A metric measure of weight equal to one-thousandth of a **kilogram(me)**.

Grand Tour Term to describe travel by the younger members of the English society in countries of Continental Europe, increasingly in evidence between late sixteenth and early nineteenth centuries. Undertaken for what may nowadays be labelled as **wanderlust motivations** to become 'educated and civilized' by exposure to European art, manners and society; much of it took place with tutors and servants, often over two or three years. Together with early travel to **spas** and coastal **resorts**, the Grand Tour represents the beginnings of tourism as we know it today.

gratuity A sum paid voluntarily by a **customer** in addition to normal price, to one rendering a personal service as in **catering**, hairdressing and taxi transport. See also **service charge**; **tip**; **tronc**.

gravity model Based on Newton's law of gravitation, one of several attempts to explain the factors which affect **tourist** flows and determine the volume of flows between **regions**. The two main factors are 'the mass' of the regions (e.g., the population) and the distance between them (in linear, time or cost terms): the larger 'the mass' and the smaller the distance, the greater the flows. Mathematically, in its simple form, flows between two regions are predicted by multiplying their mass and dividing it by the square of a measure of distance. See also **distance decay**.

greasy spoon Term describing a small, inexpensive and often unsavoury-looking **café**.

Great Britain (GB) England, Wales and Scotland, also referred to ambiguously as **Britain**, which is sometimes used erroneously for **British Isles** and **United Kingdom (UK)**.

Great Lakes Name given to five linked lakes on the border of the USA and Canada: Lakes Superior, Huron, Michigan, Erie and Ontario.

green audit See **environmental audit**

Green Belt An area of countryside, which may comprise farmland, woodland as well as other land, surrounding a large built-up area, in which building development is strictly controlled in order to prevent unplanned spread of urban areas, and neighbouring towns merging, as well as to preserve the special character of historic towns and to assist in urban regeneration. In **Great Britain** Green Belts have been established around major cities, including London, Edinburgh, Glasgow, Liverpool and Greater Manchester, as well as several smaller **cities** and towns.

green field site An undeveloped plot of land, usually in a rural area, for which development is intended or in progress.

Green Globe Global environmental **management** and awareness programme for travel and tourism **companies** committed to environmental practice improvement, developed by **World Travel and Tourism Council (WTTC)**.

green holidays (vacations) Holidays **(vacations)** spent in the countryside on work to improve the **environment**, usually sponsored by public and voluntary agencies.

green tourism See **alternative tourism**

greenhouse effect See **global warming**

Greenwich Mean/Standard Time (GMT)/(GST) The local time at the zero **meridian** of Greenwich, England, and the **standard time** for the **British Isles**, from which the standard time round the world is calculated.

greeter American term for a male employee who receives guests in a **restaurant** and shows them to their tables. Such a female employee is called a **hostess**.

DICTIONARY OF TRAVEL, TOURISM AND HOSPITALITY

grid route system A network of airline **routes** based on a number of **airports** from which flights are scheduled to operate on a number of combined routes. See also **hub and spoke system; line route system**.

gringo Term, usually derogatory, for a foreigner in Spain or Spanish America, especially an American or an Englishman.

grockles Disparaging term applied to tourists in **Great Britain**. It originated in Torbay, Devon, and is reputed to mean that tourists look like little Grocks. (Grock was an internationally famous circus clown whose typical prop was a suitcase.)

gross domestic product (GDP) A measure of the value of the goods and **services** produced by an economy over a period of time, normally a year or a quarter, in **value added** terms, i.e., excluding the value of intermediate products. The ratio of tourism receipts to GDP is sometimes used as an indication of the relative importance of tourism to an economy. Thus, e.g., in the 1990s UK income from tourism was in the region of 4 per cent. However, it has to be borne in mind that tourism receipts usually include expenditure on imported goods and services and **taxes** on expenditure and, therefore, unless these are allowed for, the ratio tends to overstate the contribution of tourism to GDP.

gross national product (GNP) A measure of the value of output of an economy equal to **gross domestic product (GDP)** *plus* the income of the country's **residents** from economic activity abroad and from property held abroad *minus* the income earned in the domestic economy accruing to non-residents.

gross registered tonnage See **tonnage (shipping)**

grotto Small picturesque cave or room decorated with shells in imitation of a cave.

ground arrangements Local services provided for **tourists** at destinations, such as **hotel transfers**, car hire **(rental)** and **sightseeing**, by a person or organization variously known as *ground operator, ground handling agent*, **incoming tour operator** and *destination management company*. In USA, also called **land arrangements**.

ground breaking A ceremonial turning of the first piece of earth at a construction site.

ground handling agent See **ground arrangements, incoming tour operator**

ground operator See **ground arrangements; incoming tour operator; land arrangements**

grounding See **aircraft grounding**

group inclusive tour (GIT) An **inclusive tour** for members of an organized group qualifying for a group-based air **fare** offered by **scheduled** airlines; the members must travel together on the same outward and return flights.

grub Colloquial term for food. Hence, e.g., **pub** grub, food typically served in pubs, such as sandwiches, pies, salads and **fast food**.

Grundtvig The adult and other education strand of the **European Union Socrates** programme.

Guarani (G) Unit of **currency** of Paraguay.

guaranteed payment reservation Advance **hotel** booking with payment guaranteed even if the guest does not take up the **accommodation**.

gueridon Trolley from which final preparation and service of a dish is performed in a **restaurant**. Hence, gueridon service. See also **French service**.

guest house
(a) Small owner-managed **establishment** normally providing **accommodation**, food and drink to residents only, also known in Continental Europe as a **pension**. See also **boarding house**.
(b) In the **Far East** a small state-owned **hotel** for official guests.

guest questionnaire See **customer satisfaction questionnaire (CSQ)**

guest worker A person who moves temporarily to another country for employment. Such temporary **migration** normally takes place from a country with high unemployment to one with labour shortages, as was the case, e.g., until recently between Mediterranean countries and countries of Central and Northern Europe. As **travellers** whose main **purpose of visit** is the exercise of an activity remunerated from within the place visited, guest workers are not included in tourism statistics.

Guilder/Florin Unit of **currency** of Aruba (AFl), Netherlands Antilles (NA Fl), Suriname (Sf).

Gulf States
(a) American states bordering the Gulf of Mexico: Alabama, Florida, Louisiana, Texas.
(b) States bordering the Persian Gulf: Bahrain, Iran, Iraq, Kuwait, Qatar, Saudi Arabia, United Arab Emirates.

habitat An ecological term describing the physical conditions required and used by species of plants and animals. A major aim of **nature reserves** is to preserve examples of all the main habitats and species in the national territory. Human activity has had major impacts on natural habitats, through grazing, forest clearance for cultivation, draining and burning, and what is thought of as natural is often semi-natural, e.g., much of the remaining grasslands of the world.

hacienda Spanish-American term for an estate, plantation or ranch building.

HAG Colloquial **acronym** for 'Have-a-go' passenger who has checked in late but is allowed to proceed to departure gate.

Hague Declaration on Tourism Declaration adopted by the Inter-parliamentary Conference on Tourism held at The Hague, Netherlands, in April 1989, organized jointly by the Inter-Parliamentary Union (IPU) and the **World Tourism Organization (WTO)**. The Declaration comprises ten principles for tourism development and emphasizes the necessity of a global approach and international cooperation involving both governments and the **private sector**.

Hajj Pilgrimage to **Mecca**, which all Muslims must make at least once during their lifetime, which takes place during the last month of the Moslem calendar (which varies from year to year) and represents a major example of **religious travel/tourism**.

halal (Of food, shop or **restaurant**) fulfilling requirements of Muslim law.

Hales Trophy See **Blue Riband of the Atlantic**

half-board See **demi-pension**

handbill A printed sheet handed to potential **customers** or posted through their letter boxes and used to advertise a variety of products and **services** including, e.g., **restaurants**.

hansom (cab) A two-wheeled one-horse carriage for two passengers, with a driver mounted behind the reins going over the roof, nowadays used mainly for **sightseeing** rather then transport between two points.

happy hour A promotional device to encourage **customers**, denoting the time when drinks are offered at reduced prices in **hotels**, **restaurants** and other **establishments**, usually early evening.

hard class See **soft class**

hard currency A **currency** in high demand in relation to its supply, with a stable or rising **rate of exchange**, typified, e.g., by the US Dollar in the 1960s and 1970s and by the German Mark and the Japanese Yen in the 1980s and 1990s. See also **soft currency**.

hard tourism Term used in contrast to **soft** or **alternative tourism**, to describe large-scale tourism and indiscriminate tourism development motivated by economic considerations and neglecting its social, cultural and environmental impacts. See also **sustainable tourism**.

haute cuisine See **cuisine**

hawker centre A collection of privately operated food stalls with shared tables and seating, synonymous with inexpensive simple local food, often in an **alfresco** or makeshift semi-outdoor setting. Food is ordered from different hawkers who deliver dishes to **customers** who may share tables. Common in South-East Asia and seen as a local experience for **tourists**. See also **food court**.

(head) hall porter See **concierge**

head wind Wind blowing towards a ship or **aircraft** and making it travel at a slower speed. See also **tail wind**.

headland A relatively high steep projection of land into the sea or a lake.

health club A **club** or area in a **hotel** or apartment block with fitness equipment and often including a swimming pool, frequented by people who wish to improve their health by taking exercise.

health declaration form A form required by some countries to be completed by arriving **visitors** declaring good health, freedom from disease and no recent contact with specified **regions** where certain diseases are **endemic**. Increasing concern about **AIDS** spread by **tourists** has prompted some authorities to ask for health forms to include an HIV clause. Exact requirements are available in *OAG Guide to International Travel* and other travel reference manuals.

health farm Residential clinic in the countryside where people stay with a view to improving their health and appearance by dieting, exercise and relaxation.

health food Term used to describe natural foods or food with no additives, such as cereals, fruit and vegetables, yoghurt, considered beneficial to one's health.

health resort A **resort** with health-giving qualities, such as air, sun and mineral waters, and special facilities, visited for treatment, convalescence and relaxation. See also **health tourism**.

health tourism Also known as *health-care tourism*, **trips** and visits to **health resorts** and other destinations whose main purpose is health treatment, ranging from therapeutic treatments for various diseases to fitness and relaxation programmes. Some of these services are also offered by many **hotels** and **cruise** lines and by such **establishments** as **health farms**.

Heart of England The name given to the **region** within the scope of the Heart of England Tourist Board, one of ten English **Regional Tourist Boards**, which covers the counties of Derbyshire, Gloucestershire, Herefordshire, Leicestershire, Lincolnshire, Northamptonshire, Rutland, Shropshire, Staffordshire, Warwickshire, Worcestershire and certain districts. The Cotswolds, Shakespeare's Country and the Marches are the major **tourism destinations** in the region.

hectare (ha) A metric unit of area, equivalent to 10 000 square **metres** or 2.471 **acres**; 100 hectares equals 1 square **kilometre**.

hedonism Philosophy stating that pleasure is the chief good or the proper end to one's actions. Hence, *hedonist, hedonistic*.

helicopter See **aircraft types: wings**

helipad Small area of **tarmac** for the landing and take-off of helicopters. See also **heliport**.

heliport Landing and take-off area used solely for **helicopters**. See also **aircraft types: take-off and landing; aircraft types: wings**.

Helsinki Accord A declaration of principles adopted by the European Conference on Security and Cooperation held in Helsinki, Finland, 1975. As well as acknowledging the significance of **international tourism**, the 35 participating countries declared themselves, i.a., in favour of simplification and harmonization of administrative formalities in the field of international transport, and expressed their intention to encourage increased tourism in several specific ways.

hemisphere One of the halves into which the globe is divided by a plane passing through its centre. The earth's surface is commonly divided by the **equator** into the northern and southern hemispheres, and by the **meridians** 20° West and 160° East into the eastern and western hemispheres.

hepatitis A (infectious hepatitis) An infection of the liver, which causes fever and abdominal pain and may cause jaundice. It is usually caused by consuming contaminated food and water and may also be spread in faeces. The risk exists worldwide, especially in warm **climates** where sanitation is primitive. The main precautions are care with food and water and personal hygiene; immunoglobulin or another vaccine gives short-term immunity.

hepatitis B (serum hepatitis) An infection of the liver with symptoms similar to **hepatitis A** but rarer and more dangerous, which may lead to chronic liver disease. It is commonly spread through contaminated blood or body fluids, e.g., infected equipment or sexual contact. This occurs worldwide but more likely in **developing countries** in areas with poor hygiene. The best way to prevent infection is to avoid exposure; a vaccine is also available.

hepatitis C An infection of the liver spread in the same way as **AIDS** and **hepatitis B**. There is no vaccine. The best way to avoid infection is to take the precautions recommended against AIDS and hepatitis B.

heritage Those aspects of the **environment** consisting of **natural** and man-made **resources** of outstanding value and interest considered worthy of **conservation** for the benefit of future generations. See also **cultural heritage; natural heritage**.

heritage attraction Tourist/visitor attraction based on **cultural** or **natural heritage**.

Heritage Coasts Stretches of undeveloped coast of particular scenic beauty in England and Wales defined jointly by government countryside bodies with **local authorities**. By mid 2000 45 coasts of 1540 km (960 miles) had been so defined. See **countryside conservation designation schemes** for other schemes. Coastline of great natural beauty and recreational value is also protected in England, Wales and Northern Ireland by the **National Trust** through its Enterprise Neptune, and in Scotland by the National Trust for Scotland.

heritage tourism Holiday (vacation) special interest tourism with a particular focus on visits to **heritage attractions**. See also **cultural tourism**.

hidden economy See **black economy**

high seas The open seas beyond the three-mile limit of the shore outside the jurisdiction of any state. See also **territorial waters**.

high tea A large meal eaten in the late after-noon in the North of England, Scotland and Wales, commonly consisting of a cold or hot main dish, cakes and tea. See also **afternoon tea; cream tea; supper**.

Higher Education (HE) In the UK generally defined as education leading to qualifications above the General Certificate of Education Advanced Level, Scottish Certificate of Education Higher Grade and their equivalent, which is provided mainly in universities and colleges of higher education. See also **Adult and Continuing Education, Further Education**.

hiking Recreational walking, particularly in open and wild country, and covering both **day trips** and extended **vacations**. The word also appears in a number of guises depending on the kind of terrain and vegetation, as with *bush walking, hill walking* and *trekking*, which are both a physical challenge and a way of seeing much attractive scenery. See also **backpacking**. *Hitch-hiking* denotes travel by obtaining lifts from car and lorry drivers.

hill station A settlement at a high **altitude** usually founded by Europeans in former colonial territories as a retreat to escape the summer heat and **humidity** of lowlands, e.g., by the British in India and the Dutch in Indonesia.

Hinduism The Asian polytheistic religion and social system of the Hindus with beliefs in the transmigration of the soul and veneration of the cow, formulated between 500 BC and 500 AD as sacred texts in Sanskrit by the Brahmans, from which Hinduism developed.

hippie Term describing those who reject middle-**class** values and conventions, many of whom adopt communal and/or nomadic **lifestyles**.

hitch-hiking See **hiking**

hold A nautical term originally, now denoting **baggage** or cargo/freight storage space below **aircraft** or ship **deck**.

hold baggage Accompanied checked baggage stored in the **hold** of a ship or **aircraft**, which is not available to passengers during the journey.

holding bay Area of the **airport** where **aircraft** wait until they receive permission to take off.

holding company See **parent company**

holiday
(a) A day on which work is suspended by law or by custom.
(b) Outside the USA, a **vacation** or time away from home.

In most countries the number of days of **public holiday** appears to have stabilized at around ten a year, but for many people in the longer term both annual and weekly **leisure** time continues to increase through increased holiday entitlements and reductions in working hours. However, after a point, holidays away from home increase much more slowly than available leisure time.

holiday camp An **establishment** first developed around the coasts of **Great Britain** in the 1930s by commercial **entrepreneurs** offering inexpensive self-contained **holidays (vacations)** in chalet **accommodation**, with meals, recreational facilities and a wide variety of entertainment. Facilities have been upgraded considerably since 1945 to meet competition from **package holidays (vacations)** in Mediterranean coastal **resorts** and rising expectations and the term ceased to be used. A major post-war development has been self-contained holiday centres and villages throughout the world, notably by organizations such as *Club Méditerranée*.

holiday home See **second home**

holiday insurance See **travel insurance**

holiday leave loading Payment in Australia of a 17.5 per cent **supplement** over an employee's normal wage during the main annual **holiday (vacation)** of four weeks. Originally introduced to supplement otherwise reduced income for workers reliant on overtime and providing them with the resources to go away on holiday, the loading has become an entitlement for most Australians.

holiday (vacation) frequency The ratio of the total number of **holiday (vacation) trips** to the number in the population who make at least one trip in a given period (usually 12 months), i.e., the average number of trips taken by those who make any trips. See also **additional holiday (vacation)**; **holiday (vacation) propensity, net**; **holiday (vacation) propensity, gross**.

holiday (vacation) ownership See **timesharing**

holiday (vacation) propensity, gross The total number of **holiday (vacation) trips** made in a given period (usually 12 months) in relation to total population. As distinct from net propensity, this measure shows the number of trips per 100 population, and reflects the tendency for individuals to make more than one trip in a given period. See also **additional holiday (vacation)**; **holiday (vacation) propensity, net**; **holiday (vacation) frequency**.

holiday (vacation) propensity, net The proportion of the total population or a particular group in the population (e.g., income group or age group) who make at least one **holiday (vacation) trip** in a given period (usually 12 months). This is a basic measure of participation in tourism and is derived from **national holiday (vacation)/travel/tourism surveys**. Highest propensities in Europe have been recorded in Germany, Sweden and Switzerland (70 per cent or more), Denmark, Netherlands and the UK (60 per cent or more). See also **holiday (vacation) frequency**; **holiday (vacation) propensity, gross**.

holidays (vacations) forms/terms/types
See **activity holidays (vacations)**
   additional holiday (vacation)
   adventure holidays (vacations)
   campus holidays (vacations)
   fly cruise
   fly drive
   fly rail
   green holidays (vacations)
   long holidays (vacations)
   main holiday (vacation)
   short breaks
   short holiday (vacation)
   special interest holidays (vacations)
   water sports holidays (vacations)
   winter sun
See also **travel/tourism forms/terms/types**.

holidays with pay (UK) Annual leave entitlements generally determined by negotiation, but see **Working Time Regulations**.

holistic Term used to denote the whole produced from the ordered grouping of separate units or as a system of interacting parts. Thus holistic definitions of tourism embrace its essential elements as, e.g., formulated by the Australian author Neil Leiper: 'The elements of the system are **tourists**, generating regions, transit routes, destination regions and a tourist **industry**. These elements are arranged in spatial and functional connections. Having the characteristics of an open system the organization of the five elements operates within broader **environments**: physical, cultural, social, economic, political, technological, with which it interacts' [*Annals of Tourism Research*, 6(4), 1979].

Hollywood American term used to describe (a) **twin** beds joined by a common headboard (*Hollywood bed*) or (b) extra long bed, approx. 80–85 in. instead of 75 in. (*Hollywood length bed*).

honeypots Places of strong appeal, which attract large numbers of **visitors** and tend to become congested at peak times. Honeypots may develop naturally or as a matter of planned policy, with a view to providing facilities for visitors and/or drawing visitors away from sensitive areas. See also **intervening opportunity**.

horizontal integration See **integration**

hors-d'oeuvre French term for a cold dish served at the beginning of a meal, consisting of such items as pâté, hard-boiled eggs with mayonnaise, salad or several items brought together as mixed hors-d'oeuvres.

hospitality See *Preface* p. vii.

Hospitality Assured (HA) British **accreditation** scheme established by **Hotel and Catering International Management Association (HCIMA)** in June 1998 to encourage higher standards of **customer** service together with higher standards of professional organization in the **hospitality industry**. See also **Best Practice Forum (BPF)**; **Excellence Through People (ETP)**; **Investors in People (IIP)**.

hospitality industry Imprecise term, most commonly used as a synonym for **hotel and catering industry/services**.

host bar American term for a bar provided at private functions where those attending are entitled to free drinks; also called *open bar*. See also **cash bar**.

host community The local inhabitants of **tourism destinations**. Their culture, **environment** and values may be influenced by **tourists**, both adversely and favourably; hence there is an increasing awareness on the part of planners and developers of the need to involve host communities in the planning and development process **(community tourism)**.

hostel An establishment providing inexpensive **accommodation** and often also food, usually for specific groups, rather than the general public, such as employees of a **firm**, students, young **travellers** (*youth hostel*).

hostelry Term of mediaeval origin for an **inn**, nowadays especially used to describe a traditional inn.

hostess A woman who looks after passengers (e.g., *air hostess* or *ground hostess*) or guests (e.g., in the USA, an employee who receives guests in a **restaurant** and shows them to their tables). See also **greeter**.

hot springs Continuous flow of water, at temperatures between 20 and 100 °C (65–212 °F) in areas of present or recent volcanic activity and contrasting with the periodic and forceful ejection of water from **geysers**. Common in, e.g., Iceland and North Island, New Zealand. Sometimes called *thermal springs*. Also occur in some non-volcanic areas as, e.g., in Bath, England.

hotel Establishment providing **accommodation**, food and drink for reward mainly to **travellers** and temporary **residents**, usually also meals and refreshments to other users, and often other facilities and **services**. More specific meaning is sometimes attached to the term in particular countries for legislative or other purposes, thus, e.g., 'an establishment held out by the proprietor as offering food, drink and, if so required, sleeping accommodation, without special contract, to any traveller presenting himself who appears able and willing to pay a reasonable sum for the services and facilities provided and who is in a fit state to be received' [**Great Britain**: Hotel Proprietors' Act 1956]. In 2000 there were estimated more than 60 000 hotels and **guest houses** in the UK.

hotel and catering industry/services Collective term for **firms** and **establishments** providing **accommodation**, food and drink away from home for payment, variously defined for particular purposes in various countries. See, for example, **Standard Industrial Classification (SIC)**. See also **hospitality industry**.

hotel classification The categorization of **hotel accommodation** by type and range of available facilities and **services**, which may be extended also to other **tourist** accommodation. Normally administered by **tourist boards**, **motoring organizations** and similar bodies, classification schemes often include minimum standards for each type or **class** of accommodation and may be combined with **hotel grading**.

hotel garni Type of **hotel**, particularly common on the Continent of Europe, with restricted facilities and **services**, normally confined to the provision of **accommodation** with breakfast, but sometimes also with limited service of drinks, snacks and light refreshments to **residents**.

hotel grading Quality assessment of **hotel** facilities and **services**, which may be operated also for other **tourist** accommodation. The assessment may extend to physical features, food and drink, and/or other services, and may be expressed individually for each or collectively for the **establishment** as a whole by letters, numbers or symbols.

hotel industry Collective term most commonly applied to **hotels** and **motels** but sometimes also variously extended to include such **establishments** as **guest houses** and **boarding houses**. See also **lodging industry**.

hotel licence
(a) A **licence** for the sale of alcoholic liquor in residential premises in Scotland granted by licensing boards under the Licensing

(Scotland) Act 1976. See also **on-licence**; **public house licence**.
(b) The same term is used for licences for hotel operation in various other countries.

hotel registration
(a) Registration of guests on arrival in **hotels**.
(b) Listing of **hotels** resulting in an inventory which may be extended also to other **tourist accommodation**. In order to be comprehensive, registration normally has to have legal authority and be administered by a government or statutory body, which may require compliance with certain minimum standards. Registration schemes are operated in most countries under fire prevention, or other health and safety **consumer** protection legislation, for planning purposes, and/or as a basis for **hotel classification** and **grading**.

hotel representative A person or organization retained by **hotels** to provide reservation services for **travel agents** and individuals. Such arrangements are of particular value to independent hotels but also to hotel groups in lieu of maintaining own reservation offices abroad.

hotel tariff List or schedule of prices of **hotel services**. Prices of **accommodation** and related charges may be quoted on a 'per room' or 'per person' basis, as separate charges or more or less inclusive terms, with or without service and **taxes**. Different prices may apply to individuals and to groups, during the week and at weekends, and at different times of the year. See **hotel tariff terms**

hotel tariff terms
See **American Plan**
 bed and board
 bed and breakfast
 Bermuda Plan
 Continental Plan
 demi-pension
 en pension
 European Plan
 full-board
 Modified American Plan

hotel tax Tax levied by **central** or **local government** or another agency on staying **visitors**, collected at the place of stay, as a means of raising revenue; sometimes the proceeds are applied to tourism purposes. May be also called *bed tax*, *room tax* or *visitor tax*. See also **resort tax**; **tourist tax**.

hotel transfer See **transfer**

hotel types

See **albergo**	motel
all-suite hotel	motor hotel
apartment hotel	motor inn
beehive-style hotel	motor lodge
boatel/botel	parador
boutique hotel	pousada
commercial hotel	residential hotel
condotel	ryokan
country house hotel	townhouse hotel
Gasthaus/Gasthof	transit hotel
hotel garni	

hotel voucher Coupon usually issued by a **tour operator** or **travel agent** to cover such prepaid elements of a **trip** as **accommodation** and meals, surrendered by the guest on arrival at the **hotel**, which then claims payments from whoever issued it.

hotels and similar establishments Term used by tourism organizations normally to include **hotels**, **motels**, **inns**, **guest houses** and **boarding houses**. According to the **World Tourism Organization (WTO)**, hotels and similar establishments are typified as being arranged in rooms, in number exceeding a specified minimum; as coming under a common **management**; as providing certain services, including **room service**, daily bed-making and cleaning of sanitary facilities. However, the exact meaning of the term tends to differ between countries, and essentially reflects the designation given to **accommodation establishments** in each country. See also **supplementary tourist accommodation**.

houseman American term for an employee performing general duties in an **hotel**.

hovercraft Vessel moving above the water surface on a cushion of air maintained by a 'skirt', thus achieving substantially higher speeds than a conventional ship, as well as greater manoeuvrability and faster turn-round in **ports**. However, it has limited capacity and range of operation, and also less stability in rough seas and winds. Thus the hovercraft is particularly suitable for relatively short sea crossings, including shallow water. See also **hydrofoil**.

Hryvna Unit of **currency** of the Ukraine.

hub and spoke system A network of airline **routes** through a major **airport** (hub) used as a staging point for feeder services to and from outlying airports (the spokes). This approach is conducive to higher **load factors** than the provision of direct **services** between a large number of airports, and applies also to other transport modes. Its greatly increased incidence in air transport is one of the main outcomes to emerge from airline **deregulation** in the USA and from the liberalization of **competition** on international routes.

Hubbart formula Method of pricing **hotel** accommodation, as a particular form of **rate-of-return pricing**, developed for the American Hotel and Motel Association.

humidity Amount of moisture in the air. As air can hold more moisture at higher and less at lower temperature, the maximum possible moisture content is expressed as a percentage at a given temperature, i.e., relative humidity. Low humidity results in rapid evaporation; perspiration evaporates easily and wet clothes dry quickly. Those conditions prevail in hot and dry **climates**, as in North Africa, inland Western USA and mid Western Australia, in contrast to hot humid climates, as in Central Africa, Central America and the Caribbean, South-East Asia and the Pacific Islands. Humidity varies seasonally and throughout the day, even in hot humid climates.

hunting Term differently interpreted on the two sides of the Atlantic. In the USA, hunting is one of the most popular sports, and involves shooting a variety of birds and animals, albeit with controls over the numbers that can be shot. In the **United Kingdom**, hunting involves the pursuit of foxes, hares and stags by much smaller numbers of people on horseback or on foot, aided by a pack of dogs; fox hunting in particular is also important as a spectator sport. There are moves to ban or restrict it by licensing. See also **field sports**.

hurricane A powerful tropical storm with torrential rain and high winds capable of causing widespread damage on land as well as representing a serious hazard to shipping. Hurricanes form mainly in the **West Indies** and Gulf of Mexico and in the Indian and Pacific Oceans.

hydrofoil Vessel moving above the water surface on retractable submerged fins or foils similar to **aircraft** wings. Its derivative *jetfoil* is propelled by a turbine engine pushing water through a jet at the back of the craft, thus providing a further enhancement of speed advantage over a conventional ship and also over **hovercraft**.

hygrometer An instrument for measuring **humidity**.

hypothetical fare construction points Airline term to describe points (i.e., **airports**) included in an **itinerary** in order to construct a lower air fare, also known as *fictitious construction points*. The passenger does not actually fly to these points; they are shown in the fare construction part of the airline ticket, which does not include a **flight coupon** for them. Example: It is less expensive to fly London–Milan–Madrid–London by using Ibiza as a hypothetical fare construction point between Milan and Madrid, although the ticket is written out for a straight London–Milan–Madrid–London routing.

IATA Bonding Scheme Bonding scheme operated by **International Air Transport Association (IATA)**, to protect the IATA airlines and ensure that they receive payment in case of a **travel agent** failure. The scheme covers **scheduled** flights with IATA airlines booked through IATA appointed **agents**. For other schemes, see **bonding schemes (UK)**.

Iberia Name of the peninsula in south-west Europe shared by Spain and Portugal, a favourite **holiday (vacation)** destination for northern Europeans since the 1960s. Spain was one of the first countries to enter the **mass inclusive tour (IT) market** and tourism has made a major contribution to the country's economic development; more recently Spain has attempted to move away from its **mass tourism image**. Portugal was a later entrant into tourism, has made a determined effort to avoid some of the worst excesses of Spanish tourism development, to control the impact of tourism, and to attract the more affluent **tourist** from the outset.

image A composite mental picture of an organization or its products, how they portray themselves to people or how they are perceived as portraying themselves.

immigrant See **migration**

immunization Protection by **vaccination** against a particular disease.

immunization for travellers
(a) For all areas:
if not previously immunized: **diphtheria, poliomyelitis, tetanus**
(b) For all areas except North and Western Europe, North America, Australia and New Zealand:
poliomyelitis (booster dose if immunized more than 10 years ago)
(c) For areas where standards of hygiene and sanitation may be less than ideal:

hepatitis A, typhoid
(d) For infected areas:*
Antimalarial tablets and precautions against insect bites
Yellow fever (compulsory for some countries)
(e) In certain circumstances:*
diphtheria booster, **hepatitis B, Japanese encephalitis, measles/MMR, meningitis, rabies, tickborne encephalitis, tuberculosis**
* Consult doctor or health clinic
Source: Department of Health, *Health Advice for Travellers*, February 2001

imperfect competition In economics, a **market** situation which departs from **perfect competition**. This may be because there are few sellers and the actions of each affect the others or because there is product differentiation, so that the products are no longer perfect substitutes for each other in the eyes of the buyers. Imperfect competition exists in most markets for travel, tourism and hospitality products. See also **duopoly**; **monopoly**; **monopolistic competition**; **oligopoly**.

imperfect oligopoly See **oligopoly**

implant Travel trade term for a travel agency business travel team located in a large **firm** or organization to make travel arrangements for its employees, as distinct from *outplant*, dedicated staff dealing with the account on the travel agency premises. See also **business travel department**.

import content of tourism expenditure Imports of goods and **services** from abroad to provide for tourists' needs, which enter into purchases made by **tourists**. At sub-national (regional and local) level the import content includes also goods and services bought from other parts of the country. See also **leakages**.

import substitution The replacement of

imported goods by home produced goods. The term is usually applied in a **balance of payments** context to goods rather than **services**. However, it is equally applicable to services and there is the same favourable balance of payments effect when, e.g., domestic **holidays (vacations)** are substituted for holidays (vacations) abroad.

import tourism See **outbound travel/tourism**.

impulse buying Product purchase without previous intention to buy and usually without evaluation of competing **brands**.

inaugural In travel and tourism, term used in relation to formal ceremonial introduction of a new ship, **aircraft** type or **route**, as in *inaugural voyage* or *inaugural flight*. See also **maiden**.

inbound travel/tourism Travel/tourism to a given country by residents of other countries. See also **international travel/tourism**; **outbound travel/tourism**.

incentive commission Additional **commission** paid by a **principal** (such as an airline or **tour operator**) to a **travel agent** as a bonus or incentive to generate high sales. See also **overriding commission**.

incentive travel/tourism Travel by employees, dealers or **agents**, often with spouses, paid by a **firm** as a reward for achieving sales or other targets, for outstanding performance, or as a stimulus to future attainment. Specialist businesses known as *incentive companies* exist to organize *incentive travel programmes* for clients, and many airlines offer discounted **fares** known as *incentive fares* for *incentive groups*.

inclusive tour (IT) A **package** of transport, **accommodation** and possibly other travel **services** such as **sightseeing**, sold as a **holiday (vacation)** for an inclusive price, which is usually significantly lower than could be obtained by the **customer** booking the individual elements separately. Inclusive holidays by air are the most conspicuous form, but in practice inclusive tours may be constructed using any form of transport and also any form of **accommodation** with various other services. See also **tour operator**.

inclusive tour fare (ITX) A tour-basing fare made available by some airlines to operators producing minimum quantities of promotional literature for **inclusive tours**.

income elasticity of demand An economic concept which measures the responsiveness of demand to changes in income. When a given change in income leads to a more than proportionate change in demand, the demand for a product is said to be income-elastic; when a given change in income leads to a less than proportionate change in demand, the demand is said to be income-inelastic. Much demand for travel, tourism and hospitality **services** is income-elastic and income elasticity is of practical importance in assessing their future growth. See also **cross-elasticity of demand**; **price elasticity of demand**.

incoming tour operator A person or organization providing local **services** for **tourists** at destinations, such as **hotel transfers**, car hire (**rental**) and **sightseeing**, also known as **inbound tour operator**, *ground operator, ground handling agent* and *destination management company* according to the scope of its functions and services, which may include, e.g., arrangements for **conferences** and exhibitions.

index numbers Summary numbers which measure relative changes over time in relation to a base, usually equated to 100. Thus an index number at a particular time indicates the relative value at that time compared with the value at the time taken as a base. Probably the best known example is the **cost of living/Consumer Price Index** (*Retail Price Index*), which represents the trend of a series of prices paid by households for a representative sample of goods and **services**. See also **real terms**.

Indian Pacific Australian rail service linking Sydney and Perth.

Indian Subcontinent The area of South Asia comprising Afghanistan, Bangladesh, Bhutan, India, Nepal, Pakistan and usually also Sri Lanka. An area of limited **international tourism**, attracting less than one per cent of world arrivals and receipts, more than half of the total accounted for by India.

Indian Summer A period of calm, dry, mild weather with clear skies but hazy atmosphere occurring in the late autumn in the UK and the USA.

indigenous tourism Term used to describe tourism activities, in which indigenous people are involved, i.e., people in their original **habitats**, and in which indigenous culture represents a major attraction.

indirect route principle Airline term used to describe the general rule allowing passengers paying full **fares** on **IATA** airlines to deviate from the direct **route** between any two points without extra payment, as long as the **maximum permitted mileage (MPM)** for the route listed in the tariff manuals is not exceeded. Example: The direct mileage between Montreal and London is 3484, the MPM is 3902. Hence the passenger may travel (and **stopover**) via Dublin, Glasgow and Manchester at the same price as the normal Montreal–London one-way full fare.

industrial awards (Australia) The centralized system of wages and associated benefits prevalent in Australia. The minimum rate for a particular activity or function is described as the 'award wage'. Decentralization of the existing system is occurring as so-called *enterprise agreements* are arrived at to cover terms and conditions at the enterprise level, including some in the travel, tourism and hospitality **sectors**. Enterprise agreements sometimes involve the payment of rates above the award wage for enhanced **productivity** and may also include the waiver of 'penalty rates' in travel, tourism and hospitality businesses for work undertaken outside 'traditional' hours.

industrial heritage attractions Tourist/ **visitor attractions** based on former industrial **establishments**, such as coal mines or shipbuilding yards, with exhibits of products and sometimes working processes.

Industrial Revolution Process of change from an agricultural and handicraft economy to an industrial and manufacturing economy, which spread from England in the eighteenth century to other parts of the world from the early nineteenth century onwards. Major facets of the change of relevance to travel and tourism included population growth and **urbanization**, structural changes in the society, increases in the **standard of living** and devel-

opments in transport and communications. See also **developed countries**; **developing countries**.

industrial tourism **Trips** and visits to places of work, such as breweries and distilleries, food manufacturing and textile factories, but also to mines and power stations, to observe processes. See also **factory tourism**.

industrialization The process of change from an agricultural and handicraft economy to a manufacturing economy, marked by the movement of employment from the former to the latter and internal **migration** from rural to urban areas, which are of major importance for the generation of tourism. See also **de-industrialization**; **Industrial Revolution**; **urbanization**.

industrialized countries See **developed countries**

industry In practice, there are usually certain economic activities carried on by a number of **firms** and **establishments** which have a bond of interest among themselves, and which come to be regarded as an industry. The bond may be one of the type of product, use of materials or process, or a still looser one – such as their general function and place in the total economic activity. The industry in which an individual is engaged is determined (whatever may be his/her **occupation**) by reference to the business or other **establishment** for the purpose of which his/her occupation is followed. See also **Standard Industrial Classification (SIC)**; **tourism industry**; **hotel and catering industry**; **hospitality industry**.

Infini A **computer reservation system (CRS)** owned by All Nippon Airways with cooperation agreements with **Abacus** and **Worldspan**.

inflation A sustained increase in general price level and decline in the value of money in a country when the volume of purchasing power runs ahead of volume of available goods and **services**. See also **deflation**.

in-flight On board an **aircraft** during the flight as, e.g., *in-flight catering, in-flight entertainment, in-flight magazines*. These passenger **services** may be provided free or in some cases for payment. See also **galley** for meaning of *in-flight kitchen*.

informal economy See **black economy**

information technology Use of computers and other electronic means to process and distribute information.

infrastructure All forms of construction required by an inhabited area in communication with the outside world, which support and make economic development possible. It includes roads and railways, harbours and **airports**, as well as **public utility services** of water supply, drainage and sewage disposal, power supply and telecommunications. The infrastructure has to precede other development and has to be adequate to serve the needs of both **residents** and **visitors**; it is commonly provided by the **public sector**. See also **superstructure**.

in-house Within a **firm** or organization, as e.g., *in-house laundry* (laundry provided internally in a **hotel** as distinct from an outside laundry); *in-house research* (research conducted by own staff as distinct from research commissioned or bought from an external source); *in-house travel agency* (see **business travel department**).

inland waterways Navigable rivers and **canals** in countries (mainly in Europe) with extensive canal networks built primarily for commercial traffic but now increasingly used for water-based **recreation** and cruising **holidays (vacations)**. In **Great Britain** more than one-half of the network of 3200 km (2000 miles), for which **the British Waterways Board** is responsible, is known as *cruising waterways*, and is being developed for boating, fishing and other **leisure** activities.

inn Unlike in earlier times when the term was used, sometimes with legal sanction, to differentiate **establishments** providing overnight **accommodation** from **taverns** and ale-houses, no specific meaning attaches to it at present. It is used more or less indiscriminately for **hotels** and also eating outlets without overnight accommodation. Although probably more commonly applicable to smaller establishments, it is not confined to them, as shown by such **companies** as Holiday Inns.

inner city An area within a large urban area often characterized by economic and social problems. In recent years tourism has been seen in many countries as a means to inner city renewal by attracting **tourism-related industries** and activities and by bringing spending power to the area.

innkeeper's lien Legal right of **hotels** to detain in certain circumstances guests' property against unpaid bills. Based on English common law, the right has been given statutory authority in most English-speaking countries, which usually also gives the right to sell the goods held on lien.

inoculation See **vaccination**

in-plant agency See **business travel department**

input–output analysis Means of tracing systematically flows between **sectors** of the economy by determining the sources of purchases of each sector (inputs) and the destination of its outputs. The resulting tables show each sector's input from each of the others in a column and the distribution of its output to each of the others in a row. The tables present a bird's-eye view of the working of the economy and enable the effects of changes in one part to be traced through to other parts. Input–output analysis is a widely used technique for measuring **tourism expenditure impacts** on the economy.

INSPASS An **acronym** for *Immigration and Naturalization Service Passenger Accelerated Service System*, an experimental **automated immigration lane** project introduced at J.F. Kennedy **airport** in New York in 1993, available to US and Canadian **nationals** and nationals of the countries in the US **visa** waiver scheme. See **biometrics** for the basis of the system.

instruments
See **altimeter**   **hygrometer**
anemometer   **pedometer**
barometer   **seismograph/seismometer**
compass   **tachograph**
flight recorder

integrated resort Generally, a **resort** development where all components, including **infrastructure**, **superstructure** and supporting services, are planned, developed and operated

DICTIONARY OF TERMS

in an integrated and complimentary way, e.g., a number of **hotels** may share elements of infrastructure, recreational and other facilities. The term is used in contrast to ad hoc resort development where individual aspects are built and operated independently. In some countries resort-specific legislation is relevant: e.g., in the state of Queensland, Australia, the Integrated Resort Development Act (Qld) 1987 established a special category of resort called 'integrated' and specified the roles of **public** and **private sectors** in managing the land covered by such resorts.

integration In business usage, the merging of two or more **firms**. If in the same line of business, e.g., two **hotel companies**, it is known as *horizontal* or *lateral* integration. If the merger is of firms in successive stages of production and distribution, it is known as *vertical integration*. When a firm integrates to secure the sources of supply, as when a **restaurant** company acquires a food manufacturing company, it is *vertical backward integration*. When a firm integrates towards the **market**, as when a **tour operator** acquires retail **travel agents**, it is *vertical forward integration*.

intercontinental Between two **continents**, e.g., *intercontinental flight*. See also **transcontinental**.

inter-governmental organization (IGO) International organization established by treaty between states, in which the states are members represented in it by delegates of member governments. The treaty which provides for the creation also defines the organs, functions and competence. The organization normally possesses legal personality and enjoys certain privileges in international law. **World Tourism Organization (WTO)** is an example. See also **non-governmental organization (NGO).**

interline Anything involving two or more passenger or cargo **carriers**, particularly in air transport. Hence, e.g., *interlining*, an arrangement in which a **trip** involves more than one airline. Such arrangements are normally governed by agreements between the carriers, which enable one carrier to include the **services** of another carrier in its tickets and to share the revenue. See also **on-line/off-line**.

intermediary A person or organization acting between parties, e.g., a **travel agent** selling a **tour operator's holidays (vacations)** to **tourists**.

intermediate technology See **appropriate technology**

intermodal Anything involving two or more modes, e.g., in transport **fly cruise, fly drive, fly rail** represent intermodal journeys. *Intermodal substitution* refers to one mode replacing another as, e.g., the motor car replacing the train. *Intermodal transfer* refers to a change from one mode to another as occurs, e.g., at points of interchange between rail and **bus**.

internal diseconomies See **decreasing returns**

internal economies See **economies of scale**

internal travel/tourism From the point of view of a country, comprises for statistical purposes **domestic travel/tourism** plus **inbound travel/tourism**, e.g., French **residents'** and foreign **visitors'** travel/tourism in France.

international airport Any **airport** designated by the contracting state in whose territory it is situated as an airport of entry and departure for international air traffic, where the formalities incident to **customs**, immigration, public health, animal and plant **quarantine** and similar procedures are carried out [**International Civil Aviation Organization**].

international company See **multinational company/corporation**

International Convention on the Travel Contract International agreement adopted in Brussels in 1970 to harmonize different legal provisions with a view to the **tourist** obtaining maximum information and protection in his/her relations with **travel agents** and **tour operators**. Few countries ratified the Convention; as a result the approach to this continues to differ from one country to another. To be distinguished from the **Brussels Convention**.

international currency See **currency**

International Date Line An imaginary line broadly corresponding to the **meridian** of 180°

from Greenwich, England, with some deviations to accommodate certain land areas, at which the calendar day is assumed to begin and end, so that at places east and west of it the date differs by one day. The calendar on the western (Asian) side of the Date Line is always one day ahead of the eastern (American) side. Hence travellers crossing the Date Line in the eastern direction 'gain' a day and those crossing in the western direction 'lose' a day. See also **standard time**; **time zones**.

International Direct Dialling (IDD) Direct dial telephone facility not requiring the assistance of an operator, which can be slow and costly. Although a few of the more remote places in the world still cannot be dialled directly, virtually all international calls from a country such as the UK can use IDD.

international fare expenditure Defined for statistical purposes as any payment made to **carriers** registered abroad by any person resident in the compiling country. This category corresponds to 'Transportation, passenger services, debits' in the standard reporting form of the **International Monetary Fund** [**World Tourism Organization**]. Thus, e.g., international fare expenditure of the UK includes amounts paid by UK **residents** to foreign transport companies.

international fare receipts Defined for statistical purposes as any payment made to **carriers** registered in the compiling country of sums owed by non-resident **visitors**, whether or not travelling to that country. This category corresponds to 'Transportation, passenger services, credits' in the standard reporting form of the **International Monetary Fund** [**World Tourism Organization**]. Thus, e.g., UK international fare receipts include amounts received by UK airlines and shipping lines from overseas visitors to the UK and also from other non-residents of the UK using their services.

International Hotel (Telegraph) Code A letter **code** initially introduced for telegraph communications and designed to reduce to a minimum the number of words required to make a **hotel** reservation, as well as to help overcome language barriers. There is little evidence of its use nowadays.

International Hotels Environment Initiative (IHEI) An international network of **hotel** executives committed to making the **environment** a priority in their business operations, launched in London in 1993 as part of the Prince of Wales Business Leaders Forum (PWBLF), an international network to promote **corporate** responsibility. IHEI helps members by facilitating access to the experience of others.

International Load Line A mark on the hull of a ship showing the maximum permitted level to which the ship may be submerged by the weight of the cargo. Also called *Plimsoll Line*.

international nautical mile See **mile**

International Passenger Survey (IPS) The principal source of statistics of incoming and outgoing travel and tourism to and from the **United Kingdom** since 1964, carried out as a continuous sample survey by personal interviews at air, sea and tunnel ports with passengers entering and leaving the country by the *Office for National Statistics*. The results are published in *Travel Trends* (annually), *MQ6 – Overseas Travel and Tourism* (quarterly) and in the *First Release* series *Overseas Travel and Tourism* (monthly), as well as in the *Digest of Tourist Statistics* by the **British Tourist Authority (BTA)**, and online from the Office for National Statistics.

international same-day visitor For statistical purposes, an **international visitor** who does not spend the night in collective or private **accommodation** in the country visited. This definition includes:
(a) **Cruise** passengers who arrive in a country on a cruise ship and return to the ship each night to sleep on board even though the ship remains in **port** for several days. Also included in this group are, by extension, owners or passengers of yachts and passengers on a group tour accommodated in a train.
(b) Crew members who do not spend the night in the country of destination; this group also includes crews of warships on a courtesy visit to a port in the country of destination, and who spend the night on board ship and not at the destination.
[**World Tourism Organization**]

International Tourism Exchange An annual international travel and tourism trade **fair** held in Berlin in March each year since 1966, usually abbreviated ITB from the German name.

international tourism expenditure Defined for statistical purposes as expenditure of outbound **visitors** in other countries including their payments to foreign **carriers** for international transport. It should in practice also include expenditure of **residents** travelling abroad as **same-day visitors**, except in cases when these are so important as to justify a separate classification. It is also recommended that, for the sake of consistency with the **balance of payments** recommendations of the **International Monetary Fund**, **international fare expenditure** be classified separately [**World Tourism Organization**].

international tourism receipts Defined for statistical purposes as expenditure of international inbound **visitors**, including their payments to national **carriers** for international transport. They should also include any other prepayments made for goods/**services** received in the destination country. They should in practice also include receipts from **same-day visitors**, except in cases when these are so important as to justify a separate classification. It is also recommended that, for the sake of consistency with the **balance of payments** recommendations of the **International Monetary Fund**, **international fare receipts** be classified separately [**World Tourism Organization**].

international tourist For statistical purposes, 'an **international visitor** who travels to a country for at least one night and whose main **purpose of visit** may be classified under one of the following three groups: (a) leisure and holidays; (b) business and professional; (c) other tourism purposes' [**World Tourism Organization**].

International Tourist Year 1967 The year designated as such by the XXI United Nations General Assembly when it formally acknowledged the importance of tourism with an unanimous resolution recognizing that 'tourism is a basic and most desirable human activity deserving the praise and encouragement of all peoples and all governments'. See also **European Year of Tourism 1990**.

international travel/tourism Travel/tourism between countries, i.e., foreign travel/tourism by **residents** of one country to, from and within other countries, as distinct from **domestic travel/tourism**; for statistical purposes residents include resident **aliens**. From the point of view of a country, international travel/tourism consists of **inbound** and **outbound travel/tourism**, e.g., in the case of France, foreign **visitors** to France and French residents abroad.

international traveller Any person on a **trip** outside his/her own country of residence (irrespective of the purpose of travel and means of transport used, and even though he/she may be travelling on foot) [**World Tourism Organization**]. See also **traveller**.

international visitor For statistical purposes, 'any person who travels to a country other than that in which he/she has his/her usual residence but outside his/her usual **environment** for a period not exceeding 12 months and whose main **purpose of visit** is other than the exercise of an activity remunerated from within the country visited. This definition covers two classes of visitors: **international tourist** and **international same-day visitor**' [**World Tourism Organization**].

International Visitor Survey (IVS) Australian study conducted annually since 1969 by A.G.B. McNair for the Australian **Bureau of Tourism Research** to provide a profile of the characteristics, behaviour and expenditure of **international visitors** to Australia.

Internet An international computer network linking computers of educational institutions, government agencies, industrial and other organizations and individuals. The network can be accessed with a personal computer, a modem and a telephone line by subscribing to a service provider who supplies the software and the host computer. In addition to accessing different sources of information, subscribers can interact with other users, take part in discussions and send electronic mail (**e-mail**) messages. By 2001 there were estimated to be some 30 million Internet users around the world. See also **TRINET**.

interpretation centre **Visitor** facility located at or near a **heritage attraction**, such as a historic monument or a **nature reserve**, providing display, information and interpretation of the meaning, significance and other aspects of the attraction. Frequently used as a means to educate and to enhance the visitor experience, interpretation centres also serve as an instrument for managing visitor flows and minimizing damage.

Inter-Rail Pass Unlimited travel rail ticket available to those resident in Europe for at least six months, valid for 12/22 days in eight geographical areas in up to 28 countries of Europe and North Africa. Different prices apply to those under and over 26 years of age. See also **rail passes**.

interstate/intrastate Between/within states, terms used particularly in relation to one or more states of the United States of America. Thus, e.g., an airline or a **bus company** providing **services** between two or more states is an *interstate carrier*, and one operating within a state, an *intrastate carrier*.

interval ownership American term for **timesharing**.

intervening opportunity A geographical concept denoting, i.a., locations between the home or tourist base of prospective **visitors** and a major recreational resource, particularly one that is vulnerable to, or has been adversely affected by, recreational pressure. They are important as a tool for managing **tourist** flows: by creating or promoting existing intermediate attractions, pressure may be relieved at a more distant destination. Examples in England include the construction of **country parks** between major **cities** such as Manchester and the Lake District National Park. See also **honeypots**.

Intranet Private computer network within a single organization similar to **Internet** but only accessible to authorized individuals.

intrastate See **interstate/intrastate**

investment appraisal Evaluation of the anticipated costs and revenues of a prospective investment in a capital project to determine whether it should proceed. This is a common approach to assessing the viability of **private sector** projects, including **tourist attractions** and facilities, normally using one or more of three basic appraisal methods – pay back period, average rate of return on capital invested, discounted cash flow. See also **cost benefit analysis (CBA)**; **feasibility study**.

investment incentives Measures of government assistance to encourage **firms** to invest, either generally or in particular **industries** or in particular locations. Forms of assistance common in travel, tourism and hospitality range from *financial* (e.g., grants, loans, loan **subsidies**) and *quasi-financial* incentives (e.g., loan guarantees, **exchange rate** guarantees) to *fiscal* incentives (e.g., tax exemption or reduction). The main effect of financial incentives is to reduce the investment outlay for the recipient; the main effect of fiscal incentives is to reduce operating costs; quasi-financial incentives act to secure the investment.

investment intensity The relationship between fixed assets, such as land, buildings and equipment, and current assets, such as cash, debtors (accounts receivable), stocks (inventories). Most transport and **hotel companies** have high investment intensities (i.e., a high proportion of total investment in fixed assets), which contributes to high fixed costs of their operation through depreciation and other expenses of property ownership. Tour operations and travel agencies on the other hand display low investment intensities.

Investors in People (IIP) British **accreditation** scheme for organizations that pursue business success through the continuous development of their **management** and staff. It is based on a national standard, providing indicators to which an organization can work and a **benchmark** against which progress can be measured. See also **Best Practice Forum (BPF)**; **Excellence Through People (ETP)**; **Hospitality Assured (HA)**.

invisibles Receipts and payments included in the current (as distinct from capital) **balance of payments** account, from **services** (as distinct from goods), investments abroad, private transfers and government transactions with other countries. Receipts and payments arising from **international travel/tourism** and comprising spending in the countries visited represent invisible exports and imports and appear as separate items; international fare payments are included in the current account with transport.

Iron Curtain A term coined by Winston Churchill in a speech in 1946 describing the divide (which continued until 1989) between the USSR and associated communist states in Eastern Europe on the one hand and the countries of Western Europe on the other hand. Although there was a large volume of travel and tourism within the countries of Eastern and Western Europe respectively, for the greater part of the period after the Second World War, the Iron Curtain was a barrier between East and West in travel and tourism as in other walks of life. Following the overthrow of communism in Eastern Europe in the late 1980s, Europe entered an era of major growth in East–West tourism.

Islam The monotheistic Muslim faith as revealed by Mohammed in the Koran, the sacred book of Mohammedans.

iso- A prefix for lines drawn on a map connecting points of equal value or quantity, e.g., *isobar* (atmospheric pressure), *isohel* (sunshine), *isohyet* (rainfall), *isotherm* (temperature).

ISO 9000 See BS 5750

isthmus A narrow strip of land, with water on each side, connecting two larger land areas.

itinerary Description of a journey, showing dates and times, mode of transport, places visited and activities.

Jainism The Asian religious system of the East Indian sect holding doctrines closely resembling those of **Buddhism** and also dating from the sixth and fifth century BC.

Japanese encephalitis A viral inflammation of the brain, which can be fatal. It is transmitted by mosquitoes, which have bitten infected farm animals, and occurs in South-East Asia, mainly in rural areas and during the **monsoon season**. A vaccine is recommended for **travellers** who stay in risk areas for a month or more and all **visitors** should avoid mosquito bites.

Japanese religions Religious traditions of Japan are based on **Buddhism**, **Confucianism** and **Christianity**, and local tradition of *Shinto* as the religion of emperor-worship, which became the official state religion in the nineteenth century with an emphasis on the loyalty to the state as a religious duty. But the post World War II constitution promotes religious freedom and separation of state and religious institutions.

jet boating A form of **recreation** and a significant **tourist/visitor attraction** on rivers using jet boats (fast moving boats with a shallow draft invented by a New Zealander), which offer to participants an exhilarating experience often in scenic settings.

jet lag A condition experienced by people flying long distances across a number of **time zones** and caused by the disruption of the natural rhythms of the human body. It commonly manifests itself in sleeplessness and other disorders and is usually found to be more prominent on eastbound than westbound flights, but the effect varies between individuals.

jetfoil See **hydrofoil**

jetty A structure projecting into the sea, lake or river, usually constructed to protect the shore or harbour or to serve as a landing stage.

jitney A motor vehicle akin to a **bus** providing passenger transport for a small **fare** over a flexible **route** picking up and setting down passengers anywhere **en route**. It is a common form of public transport, e.g., in the Caribbean Islands.

job rotation An approach to multi-skilled employment by rotating staff through a range of jobs, in order to reduce boredom, increase motivation and improve staffing flexibility. Thus, e.g., in a **hotel** the same people may alternate as maids, barmaids and waitresses.

job sharing Arrangement whereby a **full-time** job is performed by more than one person, each working **part-time**.

joint venture A contractual arrangement involving two or more separate parties in the joint ownership of business units and joint participation in their financial outcome, as well as usually an involvement of the parties in the **management** and operation of the venture, as defined in the agreement. This is a common arrangement in **hotel** and property fields and is increasingly used in joint projects between **public** and **private sectors** as, e.g., in **resort** development. See also **concession**; **consortium**; **management contract**.

Judaism The monotheistic belief system documented in the Bible and the Jewish Law taught by the ancient Hebrew priests as a revelation of the divine will; the profession and practice of Jewish religion.

jumbo jet See **aircraft types: bodies**

jump seat A stowable seat in an **aircraft**,

often in the cockpit, which a passenger may be allowed to use if a flight is full.

junior suite See **suite**

junk food Term used for food relatively high in calories but low in nutritional value. Also a derogatory term for **fast food**.

junket In travel and tourism, colloquially a business **trip** that is in fact a pleasure trip, often at public expense. In **casino** terminology, an arrangement to attract high spending **customers** with the offer of a **complimentary** trip, which includes free transport and **hotel** stay.

K

kay/key Variation of **cay** as, e.g., in Florida Keys.

keelage A fee paid by ship owners for permission to dock in certain **ports** and harbours.

kibbutz Israeli communal living **establishment**, often providing opportunity for working **holidays (vacations)** and sometimes also **guest house** accommodation for paying **tourists**.

kilogram(me) (kg) A metric measure of weight, equal to 2.20462 pounds. A kilogram(me) is divided into 1000 **grammes (g)**; 1000 kilogrammes = 1 **tonne** (t).

kilometre (km) A metric unit of length, equal to 0.62 of a **mile** or 3280.84 feet. A kilometre is divided into 1000 **metres**. In measures of area one square kilometre equals 100 **hectares** each of 10 000 square metres.

Kina (K) Unit of **currency** of Papua New Guinea.

king room A **hotel** room with a **king (size)** bed.

king (size) Term used to describe an extra wide, extra long **double** bed, min. 72 × 80 in. (180 × 200 cm). See also **queen (size)**.

Kip (K) Unit of **currency** of Lao PDR (now New Kip).

Kiwi A flightless bird widely recognized as an emblem of New Zealand; a colloquial term for a New Zealander.

knocking copy Advertising copy that attacks a rival product.

knot A measure of speed equivalent to one **international nautical mile** (1.852 **kilometres** or 6076 feet) per hour.

Konvertibilna Marka (KM) Unit of **currency** of Bosnia and Hercegovina.

Koori tourism Tourist activity which incorporates an element of culture of the indigenous population of south-east Australia called Kooris. Unlike the **aborigines** of northern Australia, many of whom have a traditional **lifestyle**, Kooris are more concentrated in urban areas, and Koori tourism often involves purpose-built 'cultural centres' which portray historic and contemporary Koori life.

Koruna Unit of **currency** of Czech Republic (Kč) and Slovakia (Sk).

kosher (Of food, shop or **restaurant**) fulfilling requirements of Jewish Law.

Krona (Kr) Unit of **currency** of Iceland and Sweden.

Krone (Kr) Unit of **currency** of Denmark (also Faroe Islands and Greenland) and Norway.

Kroon Unit of **currency** of Estonia.

Kuna Unit of **currency** of Croatia.

Kwacha (K) Unit of **currency** of Malawi and Zambia.

Kwanza (KZ) Unit of **currency** of Angola.

Kyat (K) Unit of **currency** of Myanmar (Burma).

kyle Gaelic term for a narrow channel between two islands or between an island and the mainland as, e.g., in *Kyles of Bute*, a significant **tourist/visitor attraction** in Scotland. See also **sound**.

Kyoto Agreement Following the **Earth Summit**, agreement by **developed countries** reached at the Conference held in Kyoto, Japan, in 1997, for legally binding targets to reduce emissions of the basket of six main greenhouse gases

labelling of alcoholic beverages European Commission **Directive** of April 1987 concerns the indication of alcoholic strength by volume in the labelling of alcoholic beverages for sale to the ultimate **consumer** in member countries.

Labor Day American national **holiday** celebrated as a **public holiday** on the first Monday in September.

Labour Force Survey (LFS) British household sample survey conducted every three years to 1983 and then annually until 1991, for which interviews were normally carried out in the late spring, using a sample size of approx. 60 000 addresses. From spring 1992 the Survey has been quarterly. Provides estimates of employees, **self-employed** and unemployed at national and regional level. Summary results are published in *Labour Market Trends (incorporating Employment Gazette).*

labour permit See **employment pass/permit/ visa**

labour productivity See **productivity**

labor union American term for **trade union**.

labour-intensive An economic activity is labour-intensive when it calls for a high labour contribution in comparison with other productive resources, such as capital. Tourism is generally considered to be labour-intensive, but such **tourism-related industries** as transport are highly **capital-intensive**. However, on the whole a given level of **tourist** spending supports more employment than a comparable sum of **consumer** spending in many other economic activities. See also **productivity**.

lagoon
(a) A shallow area of coastal water separated from the open sea by a low sandbank or a **coral reef**.
(b) An area of water enclosed in an **atoll**.

laissez-faire French term for government abstention from interference, especially in business.

lanai A Hawaiian term for veranda, hence room with a patio or a balcony, usually with a scenic view or overlooking a landscaped area.

land arrangements American term for **ground arrangements**.

land operator American term for **ground handling agent**.

land resources depletion There is an increasing depletion of minerals, fossil fuels, fertile soil, forests, **wetlands** and wildlife as a result of human activities. Serious long-term implications for travel, tourism and hospitality include potential loss of new destinations, deterioration of existing ones, and higher fuel prices leading to operational price increases in **tourism-related industries**.

land use planning The process of designating land for specific uses on the basis of environmental, social and economic considerations to meet present and future needs, e.g., industrial, housing or recreational. In such planning, tourism may be subsumed with **recreation** or represent a separate element when meeting **visitors'** needs is important, as in **resort** areas. See also **development plans**; **land use planning systems (UK)**; **physical planning**; **zone**.

land use planning systems (UK) In *England and Wales, structure plans* prepared by county planning authorities, some unitary and National Park authorities set out broad policies; *local development plans* prepared by some unitary and National Park authorities and district councils provide detailed guidelines for development expected to start within about ten years, in general conformity with structure plans; *unitary* *development plans* combine broad policies and detailed guidelines for metropolitan districts and boroughs. In *Scotland*, structure plans are prepared by regional and islands authorities, local plans by districts, general planning or islands authorities. In *Northern Ireland*, development plans are prepared by the Department of the Environment for Northern Ireland.

landau Term of German origin for a four-wheeled horse-drawn carriage with a two-part top, which may be fully closed or half- or fully opened, sometimes used for town and **city sightseeing**.

landbridge Term used in Ireland to refer to travel by sea to/from continental Europe via **Great Britain**.

landing card Card given to passengers to fill in and to be handed to immigration and **passport** control.

landing fee Payment made by an airline to **airport** authorities for landing an **aircraft**.

landlocked country A country without a coast and hence direct access to the sea, e.g., Switzerland in Europe, Zambia in Africa, Nepal in Asia, Paraguay in South America. See also **corridor**.

landscape From a Dutch term for the representation of scenery in a painting, term used to describe the totality of the scenery or the land defined by a particular type of scenery. In England the landscape garden movement in the eighteenth century, particularly associated with the names Humphrey Repton and Capability Brown, attempted to devise a harmonious whole in the park surrounding a large country house; an important feature of gardens and associated parks open to the public, as at Blenheim Palace, now important **tourist/visitor attractions**.

landside **Airport terminal** area before **passport** and security checks with free access. See also **airside**.

Langlauf German term for cross-country **skiing**, a winter sport particularly popular in **Scandinavia**.

Lapland The area of northern Finland, Norway, Sweden and Kola Peninsula in Russia, lying mainly in the **Arctic** Circle, inhabited by the Lapp race with its own language.

Lari Unit of **currency** of Georgia.

Lats (LVL) Unit of **currency** of Latvia.

late arrival Term used by **hotels** to apply to a guest who arrives or is **scheduled** to arrive after the latest **check-in time** specified by the hotel, usually after undertaking of guaranteed payment and/or prior notification of late arrival is received by the hotel.

late cancellation Cancellation of **accommodation**, transport or another reservation after the designated time limit. This may incur a charge if the cancelled room or seat cannot be resold.

late check-out Check-out by a guest in a **hotel** later than the stipulated time, commonly but not necessarily noon. Hotels may make an additional charge, but it is common practice to extend a guest's **check-out time** on request, if the room is not required for another guest.

latent demand See **demand for tourism**

lateral integration See **integration**

Latin America Collective term for countries of the **New World** where Spanish or Portuguese is spoken, comprising South America (except Guyana, French Guyana, Suriname), Central America (except Belize), Cuba, Dominica and Spanish-speaking islands of the **West Indies**. Mexico and the Caribbean are the most important **international tourist destinations** in the **region**, which owe their tourism growth to their proximity to the large wealthy North American **market**.

latitude The angular distance of any point on the earth's surface north or south of the **equator**, as measured from the earth's centre in degrees, minutes and seconds. There are 90 degrees from the equator to each of the poles, each degree is subdivided into 60 minutes and each minute into 60 seconds. See also **parallel of latitude**; **longitude**.

Laundromat US term for *launderette*, an **establishment** with coin-operated washing machines for public use.

law of diminishing returns This economic law states that sooner or later additional units of an input, whilst other inputs are held constant, can be expected to result in less than a proportionate increase in output. Thus, e.g., in a given situation, for a time the more workers are employed, the greater the increase in output, until after a time output begins to increase less than proportionately to the number employed.

layover Scheduled interruption of a journey, usually overnight, which may be at the passenger's request or necessary, e.g., in the absence of connecting **services**. Also called **stopover**. Same terms apply to crews, especially airline crews on **long haul** flights.

league A measure of distance, varying in different countries, but usually three **miles**, the land league in the UK and the USA being three **statute** miles, the nautical league being three **nautical miles**.

leakages Withdrawal of demand from an economy when money is spent on buying goods and **services** from another economy or when money is put into savings. If many goods and services used by the **tourism industry** have to be imported, tourism is said to have import leakages. The same concept applies to **regions** and other geographical areas. In general, the smaller the economy, the greater the likelihood that tourism needs have to be supplied from outside the area. See also **linkages; tourism expenditure impacts; tourism multipliers**.

lease A contract between the owner of an asset (the lessor) and another party (the lessee) allowing the latter to hire the asset. The lessor retains the ownership and the lessee acquires the right to use the asset for a specific period of time for payment.

leaseback An arrangement in which the owner of an asset, such as land or buildings, sells it to another party and enters into a **lease** agreement with the buyer to acquire the right to use the asset. This is a common method for a **hotel company** to raise funds.

leeward A nautical term denoting the side opposite to that against which the wind is blowing, i.e., the sheltered side of a ship. See also **windward**.

leg See **sector**

Legionnaires Disease An uncommon form of pneumonia which occasionally occurs in holiday-makers. It is spread through aerosols of water containing the Legionella germ, usually through poorly maintained cooling towers or air conditioning systems. There is no vaccine but it is treatable with antibiotics.

leishmaniasis A disease which manifests itself with a persistent skin sore; it can also damage the spleen, liver and bone marrow. It is spread by sandfly bites and is common in many tropical countries, the **Middle East** and the Mediterranean basin; walkers and campers are particularly at risk. The only prevention is to avoid sandfly bites.

leisure Generally considered to be the time remaining after work, travel to and from work, sleep and necessary personal and household tasks, i.e., 'discretionary time', which may be put to various uses, including travel and tourism. Leisure scholars call this the *time* definition of leisure, one of several in their repertoire, but probably the most meaningful in the context of travel and tourism. Others define leisure as a *type of activity* or as a *type of experience*. See also **recreation**.

leisure industry Organizations, **firms** and **establishments** with a common function of providing goods and **services** for use in **leisure** time. In economic terms the **industry** serves leisure **markets** and attracts the expenditure of **disposable income**. Leisure spending represents a large and growing proportion of **consumer expenditure** in most **developed countries**.

Lek (Lk) Unit of **currency** of Albania.

Lempira Unit of **currency** of Honduras.

Leonardo da Vinci The **European Union** vocational training programme designed to improve the skills and competences of people, especially young people, in initial vocational training; to improve the quality of, and access to, continuing vocational training and the lifelong acquisition of skills and competences; to reinforce the contribution of vocational training to the process of innovation in business. The programme is open to 31 countries (I5 **EU**, 3 **EFTA/EEA**, 13 **EU** candidate countries including Malta and Turkey).

Leone (Le) Unit of **currency** of Sierra Leone.

less developed countries (LDCs) See developing countries

letter of credit A document issued by a bank or another financial institution authorizing the person named in it to draw money up to an agreed amount. As elsewhere, of declining importance in travel, tourism and hospitality. See also **banker's draft**; **bill of exchange**.

Leu Unit of **currency** of Moldova and Romania.

Lev Unit of **currency** of Bulgaria.

Levant See **Middle East**

leverage US term for **capital gearing**.

leveraged buyout The acquisition of a business by another with the use of borrowed funds, in which the acquiring business uses its own assets as security for a loan to be repaid from the cash flow of the acquired business.

licence Generally an authority to do what is specified by the licence, which would be illegal without it, granted by a government agency or another regulatory body. In most countries various forms of transport operations, as well as other travel and tourism activities, require a licence.

licences for sale of liquor in England and Wales There are five main types of **licence** applicable to retailers:
(a) **on-licence**, authorizing sale on or off the premises;
(b) residential licence, permitting sale only to residents;
(c) **restaurant** licence, for sale only to persons taking a substantial meal on the premises;
(d) residential and restaurant licence, a combination of (b) and (c) above;
(e) **off-licence**, for sale for consumption off the premises only.
See also **licences for sale of liquor in Scotland**.

licences for sale of liquor in Scotland There are seven main types of **licence** applicable to retailers:

(a) **hotel licence**, for residential premises;
(b) restricted hotel licence, similar to residential and restaurant licence in England and Wales;
(c) **restaurant** licence, similar to restaurant licence in England and Wales;
(d) **public house** licence;
(e) **off-sale licence**, the Scottish equivalent of the English **off-licence**;
(f) refreshment licence, for **café**-style premises;
(g) entertainment licence, for places like cinemas and dance halls.
See also **licences for sale of liquor in England and Wales**.

life cycle The sequence of phases in life from childhood to old age. Often applied more meaningfully to families than individuals, as a process in the family history, which includes, e.g., the influence of children on family behaviour. The concept provides a useful basis for **consumer market segmentation** in travel, tourism and hospitality. From this should be distinguished the life cycle concept as applied to products and in the case of travel and tourism to destinations, which are seen to pass through an exploration, development, consolidation, stagnation and either a decline or a rejuvenation stage.

lifestyle Concept used to describe the way of life of individuals and groups reflected, for example, in consumption and other behaviour, of importance in **market segmentation**.

light refreshment voucher (LRV) Voucher handed out at the **airport** by the airline to departing passengers in the event of a long delay.

Lilangeni (E) Unit of **currency** of Swaziland.

limo American abbreviation for *limousine*, a motor car hired with a chauffeur.

line route system A network of airline **routes** in which **aircraft** set out from base **airport** and make a number of intermediate stops to refuel or to pick up passengers **en route** to their ultimate destination. See also **grid route system**; **hub and spoke system**.

liner Large sea-going ship engaged in providing a regular **scheduled** service for passengers and/or cargo on given **routes**.

Lingua The language teaching and learning strand in the **European Union Socrates** programme, designed to promote language training and skills.

lingua franca
(a) A mixture of French, German, Italian and Spanish used in the **Levant**.
(b) Any common language used in communication between different people, such as **pidgin-English** in the Pacific Islands.

linkages The extent to which **industries** use goods and **services** available from other **sectors** of the same economy rather than importing them. If most goods and services used by the **tourism industry** are produced domestically, tourism is said to have strong linkages with other sectors of the economy. The same concept applies to **regions** and other geographical areas. In general, the smaller the economy, the fewer the linkages between **firms** and the greater the likelihood of **leakages**. See also **tourism expenditure impacts**; **tourism multipliers**.

liquidity Accounting term to describe the availability in a business of cash and its ability to convert other assets into cash to meet its financial obligations. Commonly measured by dividing current liabilities – such as creditors (accounts payable) and bank overdraft – into current assets – such as cash, debtors (accounts receivable) and stocks (inventories); this is known as *current ratio*. Where stocks are high and/or not readily saleable, it is preferable to exclude them and to calculate the ratio on the basis of other current assets; this is known as *acid test* or *quick ratio*.

Lira Unit of **currency** of Malta (LM) and Turkey (TL).

Listed Buildings Buildings considered worthy of protection and listed in England by the **Department for Culture, Media and Sport (DCMS)** advised by **English Heritage**, and in Scotland and Wales by the Scottish and Welsh Offices advised by their own Councils. Listed buildings may not be demolished or altered without prior consent of the **local authority**. There were more than half-a-million listed buildings in the UK in 2000 (450 000 in England, 45 000 in Scotland, 23 500 in Wales, in addition to 8400 in Northern Ireland). See

building conservation schemes for other schemes.

Litas Unit of **currency** of Lithuania.

litre A metric unit of capacity, equal to 0.220 of an imperial **gallon** or 1¾ **pints**; 100 litres = 1 hectolitre (hl). US liter equals 0.264 of a US gallon or 2 pints.

livery As used in relation to airlines, the term applies to the distinctive visual **corporate** identity projected by an airline through such means as design and house style on its **aircraft**, uniforms, merchandise, printed matter and wherever it is seen by the **customer**. The need for maintaining and enhancing an airline's **corporate** identity stems from the need to distinguish it from other airlines and livery is used as an instrument of **non-price competition**.

load factor The percentage relationship of transport capacity sold to capacity operated. *Passenger load factor* (also known as *passenger seat occupancy*) relates passenger **kilometres** to **seat kilometres** and *revenue load factor* relates **load tonne-kilometres** to **capacity tonne-kilometres**. Load factor is the measure of utilization analogous to **occupancy** in **hotels** and other **accommodation establishments**.

load-tonne kilometres A measure of transport sales calculated as the product of revenue load in **tonnes** and the distance in **kilometres** over which it is carried. See also **capacity tonne-kilometres**.

load-tonne miles A measure of transport sales calculated as the product of revenue load in **tonnes** and the distance in **miles** over which it is carried.

local authorities/government See **public sector**

local development plans See **land use planning systems (UK)**

location factor A measure of concentration of an **industry** in an area, attributed to P. Sargant Florence, which relates the proportion of the economically active population of a given area engaged in an industry to the proportion engaged in the country as a whole. Location factors thus provide a measure of comparison between different areas.

location quotient A statistical measure of the share of an area of some activity in comparison with its share of another aggregate such as population. For example, if an area receives 10 per cent of a country's tourist arrivals and accounts for 20 per cent of the country's population, the location quotient is 0.50.

locator map Map used in guide books and other travel reference books, usually covering a town, **city** or another limited area with attractions and **accommodation** highlighted. Grids are used to aid location rather than degrees of **latitude and longitude** common to conventional maps.

loch A Scottish, Gaelic and Irish term for a lake, e.g., Loch Lomond in Scotland or Loch Erne in Ireland; also a narrow arm of the sea with steep sides.

lock Section of **canal** or river enclosed by gates, into which boats enter to be raised by water being let in or lowered by water being let out. In this way boats can pass from one reach of canal or river to another at different levels.

lodging industry American term used as a synonym for **hotel industry**, but also in a wider sense to include to a varying extent all or most other **establishments** of commercial hospitality, such as **guest houses** and also **condominia**.

logo Unique design, symbol or another representation of the name of a **firm** or another organization used to identify it and distinguish it from competitors.

Lomé Convention A **convention** first signed at Lomé, the capital of Togo, in 1975 by the **European Economic Community (EEC)** and **developing countries** of Africa, the Caribbean and the Pacific (**ACP States**), which provided for duty-free access for most ACP countries' exports to the EEC and financial and technical aid. The latest Convention – Lomé IV – covered the ten years 1991–2000. Meeting in Cotonou, Benin, in June 2000, **EU** and ACP heads of state and governments concluded a new 20-year partnership accord with 77 ACP countries, called the **Cotonou Agreement**.

long haul/short haul travel/tourism Distinction of particular relevance in civil aviation, where it stems from difference in **aircraft types**, operational and traffic handling techniques and in **marketing**. Sometimes used synonymously with travel/tourism between/ within **continents** or between/within global **regions**. However, the distinction is most appropriately based on the measurable length of haul. Thus, e.g., the **Consumers' Association's** *Holiday Which?* defines long haul travel as flights lasting more than about five hours.

long holidays (vacations) A term variously defined for particular purposes, e.g., in most **national holiday (vacation)/travel/tourism surveys** in Europe, as **holidays (vacations)** of four nights/five days or more away from home. See also **short holidays**.

long service leave Entitlement to 13 weeks' leave on full pay for Australian employees in continuous employment with a single **public sector** employer over a ten-year period. This benefit has enabled Australians to take long **holidays (vacations)** away from home, to explore Australia and/or travel overseas to such **long haul** destinations as the UK and the rest of Europe.

long ton (lgt) See ton (tonne)

long-distance footpath A long linear pedestrian **route**, typically across **open** or forested hill **country**. **Accommodation** may be sought in nearby settlements, in huts or tents along the **route**. Introduced in England and Wales by the National Parks and Access to the Countryside Act 1949 and in Scotland by the Countryside (Scotland) Act 1967. Known in North America as a **trail**, e.g., Appalachian Trail, extending over 2000 km (1200 miles). However, it is not known what proportion of users walk the whole length of any **footpath** or trail.

longitude The angular distance of any point on the earth's surface east or west of the zero **meridian**, which runs through Greenwich, England, as measured in degrees, minutes and seconds. There are 180 degrees in each direction, each degree is sub-divided into 60 minutes and each minute into 60 seconds. See also **latitude**.

loss leader A good or service sold at a very low price to attract **customers** to purchase other items, a practice particularly common in grocery retailing, but also used, e.g., in **restaurants** and other eating **establishments**.

Loti Unit of **currency** of Lesotho.

Low Countries Belgium, Holland and Luxembourg. See also **Benelux**.

loyalty programmes/schemes See **frequent user programmes**

luggage See **baggage**

luncheon vouchers Tickets issued by employers to employees to use in payment for food in **restaurants** which accept the vouchers. Vouchers are commonly provided to employers by specialist firms, such as *Luncheon Vouchers Ltd* in the UK, which redeem them from restaurants for cash.

M

Maastricht Treaty Popular name for the **Treaty on European Union** signed by representatives of the 12 countries of the **European Community (EC)** in Maastricht, Netherlands, on 7 February 1992, establishing a **European Union (EU)**, which introduced European Union citizenship for **nationals** of member countries. The Treaty aims to increase intergovernmental cooperation in economic and monetary matters; to establish a common foreign and security policy; to introduce cooperation in justice and home affairs.

macadam Term used in road-making, after Scottish road engineer John Loudon McAdam, one of the three great road-makers (the others being John Metcalf and Thomas Telford), who revolutionized road building in **Great Britain** in the late eighteenth century. The term is applied to the compressed broken stone forming a hard surface and the roads so built are described as macadam roads or macadamized roads. *Tarmacadam*, a later development, refers to the material consisting of stones or iron slag coated with tar or tar and creosote, used also, e.g., for **airport runways**, hence *tarmac*.

MAGLEV *Magnetic levitation*, a technique by which a train moves suspended above the track. It is a high speed means of surface transport in use in **Great Britain**, e.g., between Birmingham International railway station and Birmingham Airport, and at London Gatwick Airport.

maiden In travel and tourism (and elsewhere), term denoting, i.a., first of its kind or first use, especially in transport. Thus, e.g., *maiden voyage* denotes first voyage of a new ship, *maiden flight* first flight of a new **aircraft** type or first use of a new route, although the latter is more commonly referred to as *inaugural flight*.

main activity index Measure of the relative importance of various activities participated in by **tourists** developed by T.C. Huan [Huan, T.C. and O'Leary, J.T. (1999) *Measuring Tourism Performance*, Champaign, IL: Sagamore Publishing].

main holiday (vacation) Term used in some **holiday (vacation)** surveys, e.g., **British National Travel Survey (BNTS)**: 'Where only one is taken, this is the main holiday; when two or more are taken, the main holiday is the longest or, if two or more are of equal length, the one in or nearest to the peak summer period.' See also **additional holiday (vacation)**.

maitre d'hôtel French term for head waiter or **restaurant** manager, a term in wide use worldwide. Often abbreviated in speech to 'maitre d' (pronounced *matr' dee*).

major operated departments Primary revenue-earning **hotel** activities grouped for accounting and control purposes and comprising rooms, food and beverages, as distinct from **minor operated departments** and also **rentals** and **concessions** [**Uniform System of Accounts for Hotels**].

malaria One of the most common travel-related diseases, causing high fever, jaundice and coma; cerebral malaria can be fatal. It is spread by infected mosquitoes, which usually bite after dark. Main areas of infection extend from the Mediterranean to South-East Asia, **Sub-Saharan Africa** and South America. Prevention takes the form of antimalarial tablets taken before, during and after travel, and avoiding mosquito bites.

man-made attractions See **tourist/visitor attractions**. Most popular man-made attractions in **Great Britain** charging **admission** in 2000 were: Millennium Dome (6.5 million visitors), British Airways London Eye (3.3 million visitors) and Alton Towers, Staffordshire (2.45 million visitors).

management Among many definitions in existence, the following represents the British Standard: 'Management, as a subject, may be seen as the process of utilizing material and human resources to accomplish designated objectives, involving the activities of planning, organizing, directing, co-ordinating and controlling. Management, as a group of people, are those who perform the functions described above. Levels of management authority are usually expressed as top, middle and lower management' [BS 3138: 1979].

management buyout The purchase of the whole or part of a **company** by its senior executives, usually with the backing of the banks and institutional investors. Normally undertaken when a company is in difficulty or to prevent a takeover by another company or when a company wishes to dispose of part of its business. To be distinguished from an *employee buyout*, when the company is acquired by employees who become shareholders as, for example, when employees took majority shareholding in United Airlines in 1994. Recent management buyouts in **Great Britain** have included Wallace Arnold travel chain and other activities from Barr and Wallace Arnold Trust.

management contract A contractual arrangement between two separate parties for the provision of organizational and operational expertise, in which one party (the owner or **principal**) engages the services of another (the contractor or **agent**) to manage a business for an agreed remuneration. The contract defines the respective duties, rights and obligations of the parties and provides for the payment of expenses, management fees and/or the sharing of profits. Management contracts are used for various tourism facilities, in particular **hotel** and **catering establishments**. See also **franchising**.

managerial economies See **economies of scale**

Manat Unit of **currency** of Azerbaijan and Turkmenistan.

manifest An official list of passengers or cargo carried in a ship or **aircraft**.

Manila Declaration Declaration adopted by the World Tourism Conference held in Manila, Philippines, in 1980. It clarifies the nature of tourism and the role of tourism in a dynamic and changing world, and considers the responsibility of states for the development and enhancement of tourism. The Declaration forms the basis of other agreements and pronouncements on issues related to tourism development.

Mardi gras The last Tuesday before Lent, celebrated in France and French-speaking countries with **festivals**; in the UK, called *Shrove Tuesday* and celebrated by eating pancakes, hence also called *Pancake Day*.

marginal cost pricing Method of setting prices to cover the direct (variable) costs of a product and make a contribution to fixed costs. Claimed to be particularly suitable for **hotels and similar establishments** with high fixed costs (which have to be covered anyway) and elastic demand. Thus, when deciding whether to accept a particular piece of business, what matters is (a) whether it covers its direct cost, and (b) what contribution it makes to fixed costs.

marina A small sea, lake or river harbour with docking facilities for motor and sailing boats, usually with maintenance and supply **services**. Most marinas provide **berths** for long- and short-term use and some also offer boat **charter**.

marine park A park created on the sea bottom where **visitors** can observe marine life from observation chambers under the sea. See also **oceanarium**.

mark down Reduction in selling price to stimulate demand for a product, to take advantage of reduced costs or force competitors out of a **market**.

market In *economics*, a network of dealings between the sellers and buyers of a product; a particular market is defined by reference to the product, the sellers who supply it, and the buyers who exercise the demand for it. Hence, **tourist** markets are defined by reference to **tourist products**, their suppliers and tourists who buy them. In *business usage* buyers are seen to constitute the market: *actual (existing)* *market*, which comprises those who currently buy the product in question, or *potential market*, which includes those who may buy it in the future. Correspondingly, tourist markets focus on existing and potential tourists.

market economy See **mixed economy**

market intelligence The process of gathering and analysing information relevant to the business, normally undertaken as a continuing activity.

market(ing) research The terms *market research* and *marketing research* are often used indiscriminately to denote all systematic investigations to provide information both about **markets** and about **marketing** activities. However, *market research* is most appropriately confined to the measurement and analysis of markets, whilst *marketing research* embraces anything to do with the marketing of goods and **services**, including, e.g., product and price studies, **promotional** and **distribution channels**.

market segmentation See **segmentation**

market share The ratio of sales of a **firm's** product to total sales of that type of product in a particular **market** or of the firm's sales to total **industry** sales. Both may be measured in physical or value terms. Thus, e.g., in the 1990s Thomson Holidays enjoyed a share of around 30 per cent of the air **inclusive tour (IT) market**.

marketing Most modern definitions view marketing as a concept (or philosophy of business) and as a process: 'The marketing concept holds that the key to achieving organizational goals consists in determining the needs and wants of target **markets** and delivering the desired satisfactions more efficiently than competitiors' [P. Kotler, leading US author]; 'The **management** process responsible for identifying, anticipating and satisfying **customer** requirements profitably' [**Chartered Institute of Marketing**, leading UK **professional body**].

marketing facilitation See **facilitation**

marketing mix The combination of the elements or variables which make up the total **marketing** operation of an enterprise with a view to best achieving its objectives. One of the most widely known explanations is in terms of four elements described as the **four Ps**: product, price, promotion, place. ('Place' in this context means the place of purchase and includes distribution.) These may be further sub-divided; thus, e.g., the combination of product lines of a **firm** is referred to as the *product mix*, the combination of marketing communications, or *promotional channels*, used as the *promotional mix*, and the combination of **distribution channels** as the *distribution mix*.

marketing orientation Term used to describe the approach to the conduct of business, in which **marketing** is the dominant consideration. Sometimes used in contrast to *product orientation*, with the main emphasis on output in a **seller's market** when demand exceeds supply. Also used in contrast to *sales orientation* when supply exceeds demand and the main focus of the business is on increasing sales. With a marketing orientation, **customer** needs are always a central concern in the planning, design and provision of goods and **services** because selling alone may not be enough in itself to secure profitability in a **buyer's market**.

marketing strategy See **strategy**

mark up Increase in selling price, also amount added to product cost to arrive at the selling price (mark-up). See also **cost-plus pricing**.

marquee In most countries, a tent used for social occasions or exhibitions; in the USA, mainly a long narrow tent without sides used for sheltering walkways.

Marshall Plan A popular name for the *European Recovery Programme (ERP)*, after General G.C. Marshall, then US Secretary of State, under which aid was provided by the USA to countries of Europe between 1948 and 1952. The programme was administered by the Organisation for European Economic Co-operation (OEEC), which subsequently became the **Organisation for Economic Co-operation and Development (OECD)**. Several countries, notably Austria and Italy, recognizing the importance of tourism to their economies, applied a substantial proportion of the ERP funds to investment in their **hotel industries**.

Maslow's needs theory A theory of individual development and **motivation** postulated by behavioural scientist Abraham Maslow in 1954, whose pyramid of the human hierarchy of needs can be related in terms of motivators to the demand for travel, tourism and hospitality. See also **self-actualization**.

mass A very large amount, quantity or number, often used as an adjective as, e.g., in mass **advertising** (using the mass media to reach markets); mass **market** (very large market for **consumer** products); mass **media** (channels of communication reaching very large markets). See also **mass tourism**.

mass media See media

mass tourism Term to describe participation in tourism in large numbers, a general characteristic of **developed countries** in the second half of the twentieth century, in contrast to earlier times and to the situation in **developing countries**, as well as limited participation of people in such activities as mountain trekking or sailing.

master of ceremonies (MC) A person who introduces speakers or parts of a formal event, such as a banquet.

Maximum Permitted Mileage (MPM) Airline term for maximum mileage between any two points (i.e., **airports**) listed in the tariff manuals, which exceeds the actual direct mileage by approx. 20 per cent, and which provides for passengers paying full **fares** a choice of routings and **carriers**. Example: The direct mileage between London and Milan is 584, MPM is 700. Therefore, the permitted **round-trip** mileage is 1400 (although unused mileage on the outward **sector** cannot be used on the return sector). Thus the passenger may fly (and **stopover**) via Brussels and Geneva or via Paris and Zurich, at the same return fare as London–Milan. See also **indirect route principle**.

measures

Area	see **acre**; **hectare**
Atmospheric pressure	see **millibar**
Capacity	see **barrel**; **gallon**; **litre**; **pint**; **quart**
Earthquake	see **Richter scale**
Length	see **kilometre**; **league**; **metre**; **mile**; **yard**
Nautical	see **fathom**; **knot**; **tonnage** (shipping)
Speed	see **knot**
Temperature	see **centigrade**; **Fahrenheit**
Transport	see **available seat kilometres**; **available seat miles**; **available tonne-kilometres**; **capacity tonne-kilometres**; **capacity tonne-miles**; **gross registered tonnage**; **load tonne kilometres**; **load tonne-miles**; **load passenger kilometre**; **passenger kilometre**; **revenue passenger kilometre**; **revenue passenger mile**; **revenue tonne kilometre**; **seat kilometre**; **seat mile**; **tonnage** (shipping)
Weight	see **avoirdupois**; **gram(me)**; **kilogram(me)**; **ton** (tonne)
Wind force	see **Beaufort scale**

measures of tourism distribution and impact
See **comfort index**
  compactness index
  connecting index
  directional bias index
  main activity index
  tourism activity index
  tourism attractiveness index
  tourism barometer
  tourism concentration index
  tourism peaking index
  tourism ratio index
  tourist function index
  tourist intensity
  trip index

Mecca
(a) Birthplace of Mohammed and place of **pilgrimage** for Muslims in Saudi Arabia.
(b) Any place which it is the aspiration of one's life to visit.
(c) Colloquial synonym for **honeypot**.

media Plural form of *medium*, a channel or vehicle of communication, a term of particular significance in the context of **advertising**. May be specifically designed for advertising purposes (e.g., a poster) or may be used, i.a., for advertising (e.g., the press, radio, television). *Mass media* may refer to channels which reach very large **markets**, such as national newspapers, radio and television.

media advertising See **above-the-line advertising**

meeting (and conventions) planner
Organizer of meetings and travel arrangements for **companies** and associations, as an employee or as an outside consultant, in conjunction with **hotels**, **resorts** and **conference** centres.

mega- Prefix used with some nouns to denote very large scale. Thus, e.g., a very large airline may be called a *mega-carrier*, a very large event such as the **Olympic Games** as a *mega-event*, a very large **resort** as a *mega-resort*.

Melanesia See **Australasia**

Memorandum of Understanding (MOU)
A document signed by two or more parties expressing their wish to work together towards a common goal. Usually broad in intention and not legally binding (hence the term 'understanding'), the MOU may be followed by a more formal document subsequently.

meningitis An inflammation of the membranes covering the brain and spinal cord, which affects particularly children and can result in death. The main symptoms are a rash and a severe headache. It is contracted by droplet infection, i.e., bacteria from cough and sneezing of an infected carrier. The main areas are hot dry parts of Africa and Asia but it is not confined to them and there are occurrences also in Europe and elsewhere. Saudi Arabia requires the **immunization** of all those going on **Hajj**, the annual Muslim **pilgrimage** to **Mecca**.

mental map Image of an area carried in the head, differing from an actual map in that distances and shapes are likely to be distorted and there may be errors and omissions. It is important in a recreational and tourism context in that it controls images of where places are and what they are like, and so influences choices of destinations. Also plays a part in finding one's way in the absence of a guide book or map.

merchandising Activities directed to influencing prospective **customers** once products reach the **point of sale**, also known as *point-of-sale promotion*, such as display, packaging, sampling, special offers. The fact that in much travel, tourism and hospitality the act of consumption takes place on the sellers' premises, provides particular opportunities for merchandising as, e.g., in **hotels**.

meridian A line drawn on a map linking the North Pole and the South Pole and intersecting the **equator** at right-angles. Meridians are numbered east and west from the zero meridian, which runs through Greenwich, England, to 180° in each direction, and 180° East coincides with 180° West. See also **longitude**.

Meridian Day See **Antipodean Day**

meteorology Scientific study of weather. See also **climatology**.

method study See **work study**

Metical (MT) Unit of **currency** of Mozambique.

metre (m) A basic metric unit of length, equal to approx. 39.37 inches. A metre is divided into 10 decimetres (dcm) or 100 centimetres (cm) or 1000 millimetres (mm). In measures of area, 1 square metre (10.8 square feet) equals 10 000 square centimetres or 1 million square millimetres. In measures of volume, 1 cubic metre (35.315 cubic feet) equals 1 million cubic centimetres.

metric ton See **ton (tonne)**

metro Term used in some **cities** for the underground railway system, e.g., in Brussels in Belgium, Paris in France, Liverpool and Newcastle-upon-Tyne in **Great Britain**.

Metroliner High-speed train operated by **Amtrak** between Washington, DC and New York City.

metropolitan area See **conurbation**

Metropolitan France The home country (which includes Corsica), as distinct from overseas territories of France, such as Martinique and Guadeloupe in the Caribbean or French Polynesia and New Caledonia in the Pacific.

MICE **Acronym** for Meetings, Incentive Travel, Conventions and Exhibitions, commonly used by the travel **industry** when referring collectively to group **business travel**.

Micronesia See **Australasia**

microstates Very small sovereign states, some with populations of less than 10 000, such as island states in the Caribbean (e.g., Antigua and Barbuda, Dominica, St Kitts and Nevis) and the Pacific (e.g., Kiribati, Nauru, Tuvalu). Population of less than 1 million is sometimes used to define a microstate; there are almost 100 island and non-island territories within this definition.

midcentric See **allocentric/psychocentric**

Middle East (ME) Strictly speaking, the Middle East includes countries around the Persian Gulf, to be distinguished from those facing the Mediterranean, known as the *Levant* or *Near East*. However, nowadays the term is commonly used to describe collectively countries of southwest Asia and northeast Africa, from Iran through Iraq and Arabia to those along the eastern shores of the Mediterranean, including Egypt. Most of the countries command significant tourism resources, but their tourism development has been retarded by conflicts and terrorist activity, whilst oil-based wealth has generated an increasing volume of **international travel** from the **region**.

middleman A person or organization acting as an **intermediary** between parties, e.g., a **travel agent** acting between the **tour operator** and the **customer**.

midnight sun Sun or light to be seen above the horizon at midnight in **Arctic** (higher than 63° 30′ north) **latitudes** between mid-May and end July and **Antarctic** (higher than 63° 30′ south) latitudes between mid-November and end January.

migration Movement of people from one place (country, **region**) to another, both between countries (international) and within countries (internal), to take up permanent or long-term residence, which distinguishes it from tourism, as a temporary short-term movement of people outside their normal place of residence and work. Hence *migrant, emigrant, immigrant*. See also **alien; expatriate; nomad; refugee**.

mile A unit of linear measurement, which has several different meanings:

(a) *Statute mile* (the legal mile in the UK, USA and most **Commonwealth** countries) is 1760 yards or 5280 feet or approx. 1.609 km.
(b) *Geographical mile* (one minute of arc measured along the **equator**) is 6087 feet, rounded to 6080 feet or approx. 1.852 km.
(c) *Nautical mile* (one minute of arc standardized in the UK at 48° N) is 6080 feet or about 1.15 statute miles or about 1.852 km.
(d) *International nautical mile* (also known as *air mile*, used by the USA and other countries) is 6076 feet or about 1.15 statute miles or about 1.852 km.

In measures of area, 1 square mile (2.59 square **kilometres**) equals 640 **acres** each of 4840 square **yards**.

mileage system See **Maximum Permitted Mileage (MPM), Ticket Point Mileage (TPM)** and **excess mileage** for the three main elements of the system of air **fare** calculation. See also **basing point; common rated fares; common rated points; fictitious/hypothetical fare construction points; indirect route principle; more distant point principle**.

mileage-based fare system Method of calculating **fares** in various forms of transport based on distance without reference to demand and **competition**.

millibar Unit of measurement of atmospheric pressure.

Minerva The **European Union Socrates** action programme for open and distance learning, information and communication technologies in education.

minimum connecting time See **connecting time**

minimum land package See **minimum-rated package tour**

minimum-rated package tour Inclusive **tour** by air providing only minimum **accommodation** to satisfy regulations and qualify for **tour-basing fare**. In USA, called *minimum land package*. See also **throwaway**.

minor operated departments (MOD) Miscellaneous revenue-earning **hotel** services grouped for accounting and control purposes and including, i.a., telephones, guest laundry and valeting, **casino** and **leisure club** operations under direct management, as distinct from **major operated departments** concerned with rooms, food and beverages, and also from **rentals** and **concessions** [**Uniform System of Accounts for Hotels**].

Miscellaneous Charges Order (MCO) An all-purpose voucher issued by an airline and drawn on any organization willing to accept it in prepayment for **services** or charges, such as **accommodation**, meals, **sightseeing** and **transfers**, in connection with transportation covered by the airline ticket. See also **travel voucher**.

mise en place French term used in **catering** to denote 'everything in place', e.g., all items needed to prepare a dish before food preparation begins, or all items needed before the **restaurant** opens, to be at hand.

mixed economy National economy in which economic activities are undertaken by both private and public enterprise, and the **market** is to some extent controlled and regulated by government, as is the case in most **developed countries**. By contrast, in a *market economy* on the one hand, market forces determine what is produced at what prices, and in a *planned economy* on the other hand, these matters are determined by the state. See also **First World**; **Second World**.

mobile home American term, originally used to describe a **trailer caravan**, now a similar structure, which can be moved, although not truly mobile, but is fully equipped with heating, lighting, water, drainage and sewage services.

models Systems of hypotheses relating one or more dependent variables (such as numbers of v**isitors** or their expenditure) to one or more independent variables (such as **standard of living** or distance from generating sources), to explain past variations and predict future variations in **consumer** behaviour.

Modified American Plan (MAP) Demi-pension or *half-board* **hotel tariff** which includes room, breakfast and one main meal per day, usually dinner.

monopolistic competition In economics, a form of **imperfect competition**, which exists in

markets with large numbers of sellers who seek to differentiate their products by such means as **branding** and **advertising**; the products are then close but no longer perfect substitutes for each other. In broad terms, this applies, e.g., in large **cities** and **resorts** where many **restaurants** compete offering similar services at similar prices. See also **duopoly**; **monopoly**; **oligopoly**; **perfect competition**.

monopoly In economics, a **market** situation which exists when the whole supply of a single product, for which there is no substitute, is in the hands of one seller. In hospitality services the local character of hotel and catering markets makes monopoly more common than is the case with products that can be transported. E.g., a **hotel**, **restaurant** or **public house**, which is the only hotel, restaurant or public house within a wide geographical area, may be said to enjoy a monopoly market. See also **imperfect competition**; **perfect competition**.

monorail A railway of one rail, on which carriages move or from which they are suspended. See also **MAGLEV**.

monsoon A regular periodic wind blowing at definite **seasons** of the year as a result of seasonal reversal of pressure over land and neighbouring oceans. Most commonly applied to the area of the **Indian Subcontinent** and South-East Asia, where southwest moist winds bring rains in the summer (wet monsoon) whilst northeast dry winds blow in the winter (dry monsoon).

moonlighting Working in one or more separate jobs in addition to one's normal employment, often on one's own account and without declaring the income for taxation purposes. Moonlighting is a growing feature of many economies with the gradual reduction in working hours in many **industries** and **occupations**. There are many opportunities for it in travel, tourism and hospitality activities, which provide much scope for **part-time** employment. See also **black economy**; **ghosting**.

Montezuma's revenge Commonly used term for a diarrhoea (diarrhea) suffered when travelling abroad as a result of eating unwashed fruit or drinking contaminated water. Also called **Delhi belly**. See also **traveller's diarrhoea (traveler's diarrhea)**.

more distant point principle Airline term for the general rule which in certain circumstances enables an air fare to be reduced by including a point in an **itinerary** further away than the passenger wants to fly. Example: As the actual mileage London–Athens–Lagos is 4006 and the **Maximum Permitted Mileage (MPM)** is 3562, a 25 per cent supplement would have to be added to the one-way direct fare. However, with the inclusion of Enugu (beyond Lagos) the MPM increases to 3859, which means only a 15 per cent **surcharge**. The passenger does not have to go to Enugu, although he/she can choose to do so.

motel An **establishment** providing **accommodation** and often also other facilities and **services** primarily for motorists. Originating in North America as a response to growth in motor travel, early motels were distinguished by low-rise buildings with rooms normally accessible from the outside, adjacent car parking and location in relation to highways. These features are still characteristic of many motels today but other establishments so called do not differ significantly from **hotels** with extensive parking facilities, and are sometimes also known as *motor hotels, motor inns* and *motor lodges.*

motion sickness Sickness caused by the movement of a vehicle, especially in car travel (car sickness), which manifests itself by abdominal pain, nausea and vomiting. Also called *travel sickness.*

motivations Generally, psychological stimuli which move or activate individuals to act in a particular way. Thus, whilst *determinants* explain the factors which stimulate the growth of tourism, why people wish to become **tourists** is the subject of *motivations*. Motivational research, the study of psychological reasons underlying human behaviour, particularly in relation to buying situations, provides useful insights for travel, tourism and hospitality planning and development as well as **marketing**. See also **sunlust; wanderlust.**

motor home See **caravan; recreation(al) vehicle (RV)**

motor hotel See **motel**

motor inn See **motel**

motor lodge See **motel**

motoring organization Individual membership organization providing **services** to motorists, such as the **Automobile Association (AA)**, the Royal Automobile Club (RAC) and the Royal Scottish Automobile Club (RSAC) in **Great Britain**, or the **American Automobile Association (AAA)** in the USA. In Australia the motoring organizations are organized at State and Territory level, e.g., the Royal Automobile Club of Victoria (RACV). See also **automobile club**.

motorway A wide multi-lane road with up and down lanes separated by a central strip, with limited access without surface crossroads and restricted to certain types of vehicle. By 2000 the network in **Great Britain** covered 3316 km (2060 miles) and other **trunk roads** 12 150 km (7750 miles). See also **autobahn; autopista; autostrada; expressway.**

mountain A descriptive term with no precise meaning. An elevated area, usually at least 2000 feet (600 m), rising sharply above the surrounding terrain and occurring both as isolated features, such as Mt Egmont on North Island, New Zealand, or as ranges of mountains, as with the Himalayas. Mountains are the main element of some of the world's most striking scenery, often conserved against development and a major recreational resource for climbing and **skiing**. Marked by zonation of vegetation as **climate** changes with elevation and subject to rapid changes of weather for which **visitors** are often unprepared; such zonation and changeability are particularly marked on isolated peaks in areas of oceanic **climate**.

mountain sickness See **altitude sickness**

Mountain Standard Time A Canadian and US **time zone** based on the standard of the 105th meridian. Time equals GMT –7.

mountaineering The sport of **mountain** climbing, a significant activity in **Alpine** countries, where it originated, but nowadays also in the Himalayas, Andes and Rocky Mountains.

mull Scottish term for a promontory or **headland**.

multicultural Concerning more than two races or cultures when referring, for example, to communities or societies composed of several races or cultures, as found in Hawaii and Singapore with their mixed populations.

multilateral Concerning more than two sides or parties as, for example, in *multilateral agreements* between more than two countries, without discrimination between those involved. Some aspects of **international travel** and **tourism** subject to regulation are covered by multilateral agreements, which include much transport and communications between countries. See also **bilateral**.

multinational company/corporation A large business enterprise operating in a number of countries, also called *international company* and *transnational corporation*. Most examples in travel, tourism and hospitality are to be found in the **hotel** field (e.g., Hilton International, InterContinental Hotels Corporation, Sheraton) but also in such fields as car hire (**rental**) (e.g., Avis, Eurodollar, Hertz) and elsewhere.

multi-ownership See **timesharing**

multiple Term most commonly describing a shop or store, which is one of the same kind under the same **management** in different locations. Its plural form, *multiples*, came into common usage in the UK in the 1980s also applied to **travel agent companies** with branch outlets, following their rapid growth.

multiple land use In **land use planning**, use of land for more than one purpose, of which recreation (private and public) is often one. Characteristic of areas of low intensity use, especially in upland grazed by domestic livestock and also used for **field sports**, water collection and informal recreation. Uses may be incompatible but can coexist if they do not coincide seasonally. Also applies to areas of intensive cultivation in which shooting and **hunting** occur.

multipliers See **tourism multipliers**

municipal Of or under **local authorities/ government**. In **Great Britain** many travel and tourism undertakings, such as **museums**, galleries and other **tourist/visitor attractions**, as well as much public passenger transport, are municipally owned.

Munro Scottish term for a mountain over 3000 feet (914 m) high. The sport of trying to climb as many Munros as possible is known as *Munro-bagging*. See also **Corbett**.

Murphy American term used to describe a bed that folds or swings into a cabinet or wall when not in use.

museum An institution for the collection, **preservation**, display and interpretation of exhibits, originally of art, history, religion and natural history. Nowadays, most branches of human endeavour are represented in museums, many of which are important **tourist/visitor attractions**. Thus there are museums with a focus on many sports, hobbies and other activities.

Naira (₦) Unit of **currency** of Nigeria.

Nakfa Unit of **currency** of Eritrea.

named trains
See **Al Andalus Express** (Spain)
  Bay Express (New Zealand)
  Blue Train (South Africa)
  Coastal Pacific (New Zealand)
  Eastern Orient Express
    (Thailand/Malaysia/Singapore)
  Eurostar (Belgium/France/UK)
  Indian Pacific (Australia)
  Metroliner (USA)
  Orient Express (UK/France/Italy)
  Overland (Australia)
  Overlander (New Zealand)
  Queenslander (Australia)
  Southerner Express (New Zealand)
  Trans-Siberian Express (Asia)
  Xplorer (Australia)
  XPT Express (Australia)
See also **nostalgic trains**.

Nansen Passport Internationally recognized identification document for **refugees**, named after Fridtjob Nansen, Norwegian statesman and humanitarian.

narrow boat Long narrow covered boat used on **canals** as permanent or temporary **holiday (vacation)** accommodation.

narrow body aircraft See **aircraft types: bodies**

national A person who is a **citizen** of a country, by birth or **naturalization**.

National Estate Defined by the *Australian Heritage Act 1975* as 'those places being components of the natural **environment** of Australia or the cultural environment of Australia, that have aesthetic, historic, scientific or social significance or other special value for future generations as well as for the present community'. Such places are listed on the Register of the National Estate and are often major **tourist/visitor attractions**. See also **cultural heritage**; **natural heritage**.

national holiday (vacation)/travel/tourism) surveys Sample inquiries of households or individuals measuring the volume, value and characteristics, in some cases of **holiday (vacation) trips**/visits, in others of all or most trips, of the **residents** of a country. Most countries of Western Europe have regular annual surveys and several more than one; such surveys are also conducted in Australia, USA and several other countries. Guidelines for national holiday surveys have been published by the **OECD** Tourism Committee with a view to facilitating survey comparability but these are followed to a varying extent in individual countries.

National Nature Reserves More than 300 areas in the UK managed so as to conserve natural **habitats** and their plant and animal species or distinctive geological or physiographic features, and to provide opportunities for research with controlled access, by **English Nature**, Scottish Natural Heritage, Countryside Council for Wales and Department of the Environment for Northern Ireland. See **countryside conservation designation schemes** for other schemes.

National Parks Large countryside areas commonly in public ownership designated as such by government in order to protect and conserve their natural beauty and other features. The concept has its origin in the Yellowstone National Park established in 1872; the US National Park Service now manages more than 300 parks, historic sites and **recreation** areas. However, the 15 National Parks in existence or scheduled for designation by 2002 in **Great Britain** (10 in England, 3 in Wales, 2 in Scotland) are largely in private ownership and recreational use in them exists side by side with agriculture and other activities on land on which there are public rights of access, within a framework of building development and other controls. See **countryside conservation designation schemes** for other schemes.

National Readership Survey British continuous sample survey conducted by the *Joint Industry Committee for National Readership Surveys (JICNARS)* with a sample of more than 50 000 individuals. It provides an analysis of the average issue **readership** of major publications, as well as analysis of ITV viewing, listening to commercial radio, cinema-going and of special interest groups such as car-owning households. Findings are published in reports by JICNARS and selected summary findings also in *Social Trends*.

National Scenic Areas (Scotland) Forty areas of predominantly privately owned land in Scotland designated in order to conserve their scenic beauty through strict planning control over development, but with no explicit recreational role. Analogous to **Areas of Outstanding Natural Beauty (AONBs)** in other parts of the UK, they cover more than one-eighth of the area of Scotland. See **countryside conservation designation schemes** for other schemes.

National Tourism Administration (NTA) Defined by the **World Tourism Organization** as:
(a) The Central Government body with administrative responsibility for tourism at the highest level, or
(b) Central Government body with powers of direct intervention in the **tourism sector**.
(c) All administrative bodies within national government with powers to intervene in the tourism sector.
Other governmental or official bodies of lower rank – either incorporated within a higher body or autonomous – may be regarded as *NTA executive bodies*. These may also include central organizations legally or financially linked to the NTA. See also **National Tourism Organization (NTO)**.

National Tourism Organization (NTO) Also referred to as *National Tourism (or Tourist) Office*, an official body variously concerned with the development, promotion and coordination of tourism in a country, recognized and also to a varying extent financed by its government. Three main types are: governmental (government department), semi-governmental (statutory body set up by government), non-governmental (voluntary association). Designation may differ accordingly, e.g., Ministry of Tourism, Tourist Board, Tourist Association.

National Tourist Boards (UK) Statutory bodies set up under the Development of Tourism Act 1969 responsible for tourism development in their respective countries and for their promotion within the UK: **English Tourist Board (ETB)**, now **English Tourism Council (ETC)**, **Scottish Tourist Board (STB)**, now **VisitScotland**, **Wales Tourist Board (WTB)**. These were preceded by the **Northern Ireland Tourist Board (NITB)** established under the Development of Tourist Traffic Act (Northern Ireland) 1948.

national travel/tourism From the point of a country, comprises for statistical purposes **domestic travel/tourism** plus **outbound travel/tourism**, e.g., French **residents'** travel/tourism in France and abroad.

National Travel Survey British continuous sample survey carried out for the **Department for Transport, Local Government and the Regions** by *Office for National Statistics*, which collects data on personal travel patterns in **Great Britain** and relates different kinds of personal travel with the characteristics of **travellers** and their families. Findings are published by the Department in *Transport Statistics Great Britain*. To be distinguished from **British National Travel Survey (BNTS)**.

National Vocational Qualifications (NVQs) A comprehensive framework of vocational qualifications for all **occupations** and professions in England, Wales and Northern Ireland, intended primarily for young people between the ages of 16 and 19 who have left **full-time** education, providing job-specific skills and knowledge. There are five levels ranging from foundation to professional and **management** and the sectors include, i.a., arts and entertainment, **catering** and hospitality, environmental **conservation**, sport and **recreation**, travel services, warding and **visitor** services. The Scottish equivalent to NVQs are Scottish Vocational Qualifications (SVQs).

nationality The nationality of a **traveller** is that of the Government issuing his/her **passport** (or other identification document), even if he or she normally resides in another country [**World Tourism Organization**].

natural attractions See **tourist/visitor attractions**

natural heritage Natural features consisting of physical and biological formations of outstanding universal value from the aesthetic or scientific point of view; geological or physiographical formations and **habitats** of threatened species of animals and plants of outstanding universal value from the point of view of science or **conservation**; natural sites or areas of outstanding universal value from the point of view of science, conservation or of natural beauty [based on **UNESCO** Convention for the Protection of the Cultural and Natural Heritage 1972].

natural resources Resources provided by nature and available for human use, including, e.g., animals, plants, natural scenery. A distinction is drawn between *renewable* and *non-renewable* resources. The former are inexhaustible and capable of replenishment but may be adversely affected, e.g., air and water by **pollution**; the latter are finite and irreplaceable, e.g., minerals and soils.

naturalization Admission of an **alien** to the rights and privileges of citizenship of a country. See also **citizen; national**.

nature reserve An area of land or water set aside to be so managed as to protect and conserve its animal and plant life and other features, and often used for research. In the UK there are both local and **National Nature Reserves**, some owned and managed publicly, some privately, and others by voluntary bodies, such as the Royal Society for the Protection of Birds.

nature tourism See **ecotourism**

nature trail Designated **route** in the countryside with signposting to draw attention to animals, birds, plants and other interesting features.

naturism Synonym for *nudism*, belief in and practice of going about naked. Hence *naturist* (person believing in and practising going about naked); *naturist beach* (beach where the practice is allowed); *naturist colony* (**club** or centre for naturists).

nautical mile See **mile**

nautical terms

See **abaft**	**flagship**
(a)midship(s)	**forward**
abeam	**gangway**
aft	**hold**
anchorage	**knot**
astern	**leeward**
beam	**mile**
berth	**port**
bow	**ramp**
catamaran	**starboard**
companion way/	**stern**
companionway	**tonnage**
deck	**wharf**
draught (draft)	**windward**
fathom	

Near East See **Middle East**

Neoclassical Style of architecture and design of late eighteenth and early nineteenth centuries representing a return to classical Greek and Roman forms as a reaction against **Baroque** and **Rococo**.

neo-colonialism The term used to describe the influence a powerful country exercises over the affairs of another, commonly over economic and political affairs of a **less developed country**. This may include technical and development assistance and the activities of **multinational companies** in travel, tourism and hospitality.

net circulation See **circulation**

net tonnage See **tonnage (shipping)**

network analysis See **critical path analysis**

Network Card See **British railcards**

networking An informal system of communications between members of a group, usually with a view to providing mutual self-help as, e.g., between the alumni of a university or between members of an association.

Neutral Unit of Construction (NUC) The basis of air **fare** calculations established by the **International Air Transport Association (IATA)**, which replaced the **Fare Construction Unit (FCU)** on 1 July 1989. In the new system individual amounts in local **currencies** are converted to NUC by the use of NUC conversion factors and the total NUC amount is converted back to the local currency of sale. The conversion factors are normally adjusted four times a year.

New Australian A recent immigrant to Australia, often a euphemism for an Australian of non-British descent. See also **Pom/Pommie/Pommy**.

New England Collective term for the six US states of Connecticut, Maine, Massachusetts, New Hampshire, Rhode Island and Vermont.

New World Normally understood to denote the western **hemisphere**, i.e., the North and South American **continents** and the Caribbean islands. See also **Old World**.

New Zealand Dollar ($NZ) Unit of **currency** of Cook Islands, New Zealand, Niue, Tokelau.

Newly Independent States (NIS) See **Commonwealth of Independent States (CIS)**

Ngultrum (Nu) Unit of **currency** of Bhutan.

niche marketing See **target marketing**

nickel US five-cent coin.

night club See **club**

no host bar See **cash bar**

no show Term used in the business for a **hotel** guest or passenger with a reservation who fails to take it up without notifying the **hotel** or **carrier**. See also **overbooking**.

nomad Member of a race or tribe which moves from place to place to find pasture, hence one who lives a wandering life. Nomads

are normally excluded from travel and tourism statistics. See also **alien**; **expatriate**; **migration**; **refugee**.

non-discretionary income Personal income of individuals or households over the spending of which the recipient has no discretion. Examples include income tax and other compulsory deductions, other enforced long-term spending such as mortgage payments, spending on necessities such as food and housing. See also **discretionary income**; **disposable income**.

non-endorsable Not valid for travel on another **carrier**.

non-governmental organization (NGO) International organization established by individuals, associations or **firms** (i.e., not by inter-governmental agreement), in which members are individuals or **corporate** bodies. The organization creates its own statutes, cannot claim any privileged position, and is normally subject to the law of the state where its headquarters or secretariat are located. **European Travel Commission (ETC)**, **International Hotel and Restaurant Association (IHRA)** and **Pacific Asia Travel Association (PATA)** are well-known examples. See also **inter-governmental organization (IGO)**.

non-price competition A generic term describing factors other than price, which differentiate the products of one seller from those of another and influence the buyers' choice. There is much evidence to suggest that suppliers of many goods and **services** prefer to compete on factors other than price and this is also increasingly the case in travel, tourism and hospitality. For such facilities as **hotels**, location is a common competitive factor. Reservation services constitute a competitive convenience for buyers of many **tourist products**, as do credit arrangements, which enable accounts to be settled without the payment of cash. See also **price competition**.

non-refundable Cannot be returned for cash or credit. Some changes may be allowed but a fee is normally charged.

non-transferable Can only be used by the passenger named at the time of booking.

Nordic countries Collective term for the five countries of Denmark, Finland, Iceland, Norway and Sweden. With a combined population of 24 million and a high **standard of living**, the **region** represents one of the richest **holiday (vacation) markets** in the world. See also **Scandinavia**.

normal air fares See **air fair types**

Norman (architecture) See **Romanesque**

North American Free Trade Agreement (NAFTA) A treaty between Canada, Mexico and the USA, which came into effect on 1 January 1994, beginning a gradual process of eliminating tariffs and other barriers to trade between the three countries. While it does not deal specifically with travel, tourism and hospitality, they are covered more generally under such headings as trade in **services**, investment and temporary entry, as well as under environmental and labour issues. Importantly, tourism is expected to grow as a result of the strengthened economies of the countries and NAFTA stimulates increased cooperation between their **National Tourism Administrations (NTAs)**.

Northern Lights (aurora borealis) A shifting coloured glow seen near the horizon in the night sky in high **altitudes** in northern parts of **Scandinavia** and elsewhere in the northern hemisphere. The corresponding phenomenon in the southern hemisphere is *aurora australis*.

Northern Summer Term used in Australia and New Zealand for the summer **season** in the northern **hemisphere** (usually referring to the months of June, July and August), which coincides with winter in Australia and New Zealand.

nostalgic trains US term for trains restored to former state and operated as special tours and tourist attractions rather than means of transport, such as *Orient Express*. See also **named trains**.

notice of proposed rule making A public announcement by a government agency, such as a civil aviation authority, that it is considering amending its existing regulations, providing an opportunity for interested parties to make their views known.

notifiable disease Serious infectious disease, such as **cholera**, **meningitis** or **typhus**, which has to be reported by a doctor to the appropriate authority (the Department of Health in the case of **Great Britain**), from whom the full current list of notifiable diseases is available.

nouvelle cuisine See **cuisine**

nudism See **naturism**

observation car See **dome car**

occasional employee/worker See **casual employee/worker**

occupancy The percentage relationship of **accommodation** capacity used to available capacity in **hotels and similar establishments**, a measure of utilization analogous to **load factor** in transport. *Bed/guest/sleeper occupancy* relates occupied beds to available beds, and *room occupancy* relates occupied rooms to available rooms; hence **single/double** occupancy denotes room occupancy by one/two persons.

occupation The occupation of any person is the kind of work he or she performs, due regard being paid to the conditions under which it is performed; this alone determines the particular group in an occupational classification to which the person is assigned. The nature of the factory, business or organization in which the person is employed has no bearing upon the classification of his/her occupation, except that it may enable the nature of his/her duties to be more clearly defined. See **Standard Occupational Classification (SOC)**

occupations

See **aboyeur**	commissionaire
activities host(ess)	comptroller
air hostess	concierge
air steward(ess)	controller
air travel organizer	counter staff
animator	courier
back of house	cruise director
bell boy	entertainments
bell captain	director/officer
bell hop	flight attendant
bellman	front of house
blue-collar	greeter
busboy/busgirl/busser	ground handling
car hop	agent
chef	ground operator
head (hall) porter	toastmaster
hostess	tour conductor
hotel representative	tour director
houseman	tour guide
incoming tour operator	tour leader
land operator	tour manager
maitre d'hôtel	tour operator
meeting and conventions	tour wholesaler
planner	tourism police
plongeur	travel agent
purser	uniformed staff
resort representative	valet
retail travel agent	white-collar
sommelier	

Oceania Term used to denote (a) the Pacific Islands and the adjacent seas or (b) the region including Australia, New Zealand and the Pacific Islands. See also **Australasia**.

oceanarium A large saltwater aquarium where marine animals can be observed. See also **marine park**.

off-licence A shop selling alcohol for consumption off the premises, also the name for one of two main **licences** for sale of alcoholic liquor in England and Wales, authorizing sale of all classes of liquor but only for consumption off the premises for which the licence is granted. The licence is granted by licensing justices operating in each licensing district. The Scottish equivalent is *off-sale licence*; the US equivalent, *package store*. See also **on-licence**.

off-line See **on-line/off-line**

Old World Normally understood to denote the eastern **hemisphere**, especially Europe, Africa and Asia eastwards as far as the Malay **archipelago**. See also **New World**.

oligopoly In economics, a form of **imperfect competition**, which exists when there are only a few sellers in the **market**. If their products are homogenous – each a perfect substitute for the others – the oligopoly is described as *perfect*; if the products are differentiated, it is *imperfect* oligopoly. The former is rarely found in practice, but many **accommodation** and **catering** markets tend to fit the description of imperfect oligopoly. E.g., in many towns a few **hotels** represent most of the accommodation capacity of the location, and offer similar facilities at similar prices. See also **duopoly**; **monopolistic competition**; **monopoly**; **perfect competition**.

Olympic Games A quadrennial international sport meeting held in various places (the first in modern times in Athens in 1896) and a major **tourist/visitor attraction**. The first games after World War II were held in London in 1948, then Helsinki 1952, Melbourne 1956, Rome 1960, Tokyo 1964, Mexico City 1968, Munich 1972, Montreal 1976, Moscow 1980, Los Angeles 1984, Seoul 1988, Barcelona 1992, Atlanta 1996, Sydney 2000; the 2004 Games are scheduled to be held in Athens. See also **Winter Olympic Games**.

omnibus survey Regular repeat survey using a standardized methodology and covering a number of topics for different clients at the same time. Individual clients commission a limited number of questions each from a **market research company** operating such surveys at monthly or other regular intervals. This is significantly less expensive for them than purpose-designed separate surveys and a particularly cost-effective approach for much market research in travel, tourism and hospitality, but it provides limited scope for detailed findings.

one-way ticket American term for single ticket.

Oneworld Global **airline alliance** of (June 2001) Aer Lingus, American Airlines, British Airways, Cathay Pacific, Finnair, Iberia, Lan Chile and Quantas, formed February 1999 with American, British Airways, Quantas and Cathay Pacific as founding partners.

on-licence One of two main **licences** for the sale of alcoholic liquor in England and Wales, which permits the sale of all or some classes of liquor for consumption on the premises and also sanctions sale for consumption off the premises for which the licence is granted. The licence is granted by licensing justices operating in each licensing district. See also **off-licence**. The Scottish **hotel licence** and the **public house licence** are in effect equivalent to the on-licence in England and Wales.

on-line/off-line
(a) In transport generally, countries or places through which a **carrier** operates with rights to pick up passengers are described as *on-line*; those through which a carrier does not operate or does not have rights to pick up passengers as *off-line*.
(b) In air transport, using the same airline, e.g., changing planes with the same airline, is described as *on-line connection*, as distinct from changing planes as well as airlines, described as *off-line connection*. See also **interline**.
(c) In computing, connected to and communicating with a computer as, e.g., travel agency equipped with a **terminal** linked to a **carrier's** computer is on-line.

onward connection See **connecting flight/ train**

open bar See **host bar**

open country A descriptive term for uncultivated land covered with non-tree vegetation, including grasses and shrubs, particularly in upland and **mountain** areas. In England and Wales given legal definition in the National Parks and Access to the Countryside Act 1949 as 'mountain, moor, heath, down, cliff or foreshore', but subsequently extended to include woodland.

open rate Air transport term describing a situation which exists when **conferences**, governments or **carriers** fail to agree uniform rates for particular **routes**, leaving the parties concerned to agree their own **fares**.

open return A return (**round trip**) ticket issued by a **carrier** without a reservation to use a particular service on the return journey.

open skies The concept of a free **market** for international aviation, which allows airlines to fly anywhere without restrictions, e.g., American and British airlines between the two countries. However, existing open skies agreements concluded separately between member states of the **European Union** with the USA aimed at liberalizing air traffic between the USA and a single European country have been challenged by the European Commission as discriminating against other member states and acting against free trade within the Union.

open(-date) ticket A passenger ticket issued by a **carrier**, usually an airline, without a reservation to use a particular service, such reservation to be made at a later date.

open-jaw trip A return (**round trip**) journey with different originating and terminating points (e.g., London/New York/Paris) *or* with a departure point for the return different from the arrival point (e.g., Chicago/London and Paris/Chicago).

operational lease See **aircraft leasing**

operational/operations research (OR) A multidisciplinary approach to the solution of quantifiable business or administrative problems, using mathematical processes, usually with the aid of computers.

opportunity cost The cost of an opportunity foregone as, e.g., the loss of revenue that would be earned from an alternative use of the sum of money. This is an important concept of practical value to be applied in investment decisions when a choice has to be made about the commitment of scarce capital resources to different projects.

option
(a) Activity, item or services not included in the basic price, which may be chosen by the **customer** for an additional charge, e.g., **sightseeing**, or a **single** room on a tour, for which prices are based on two persons sharing a room. See also **add-on**.
(b) A reservation made and held by an operator, such as a **carrier**, **hotel** or **tour operator** for a limited period of time, by the end of which the reservation must be confirmed or it is cancelled.

organic food Food grown on farms which do not use conventional agrichemicals but natural fertilizers and natural forms of pest control. Farmers wishing to qualify for recognized organic labels must conform to a strict set of rules. Using organic produce is a **unique selling proposition** of some **restaurants**.

organization and methods (O&M) See **work study**

Orient The countries east of the Mediterranean or of Southern Europe, including variously those of South-West Asia, the **Far East** or Asia generally, most of them with much potential for tourism development.

Orient Express Named train service inaugurated 1883, closed down 1977 and resurrected 1982 as the Venice Simplon–Orient Express, between London and Venice via Paris and the Alps, travelling by Pullman between London and Folkestone, SeaCat to Boulogne, and thence in refurnished original carriages to Venice.

orienteering A competitive sport of Scandinavian origin of cross-country running by map and compass.

origin In air transport, the starting point of a passenger journey. When a journey comprises more than one **leg**, **segment** or **sector** using more than one airline, the airline carrying a passenger on the first portion of the journey is called *the originating airline*.

origin country For purposes of **international tourism** statistics, the country where the **visitor** has lived for most of the previous 12 months or has lived for a shorter period and intends to return within 12 months [**World Tourism Organization**].

Ouguiya (UM) Unit of **currency** of Mauritania.

outback Term used for relatively remote and sparsely populated areas of Australia, called *beyond the black stump* and also *Back O'Bourke* in Australian English. See also **bush**.

outbound travel/tourism Travel/tourism by **residents** of a given country to other countries. See also **inbound travel/tourism**; **international travel/tourism**.

outdoor advertising Advertising medium consisting of posters, illuminated signs and outdoor displays. Advertising sites in railway and underground stations and advertising spaces in **buses**, trains and other vehicles are described separately as *transport advertising*.

outplant See **implant**

outside cabin A ship **cabin** with porthole or window.

outsourcing The buying in of products and **services** from outside suppliers instead of making them available internally. Common reasons include lack of expertise, investment capital or physical space, as well as the ability to buy in more cheaply or more quickly than supplying **in-house**. See also **convenience foods; contract catering**.

overbooking Reservation of more seats by a transport **carrier** or rooms by a **hotel** than are available, sometimes deliberate to compensate for anticipated **no shows**. In North America, also called *oversale*. See also **bumping; denied boarding compensation**.

overflights of Antarctica Non-stop flights of 10–12 hours aboard QANTAS Boeing 747 **aircraft** departing from Australian **airports** and overflying the Australian, New Zealand and French **Antarctic** territories. The 'flightseeing' **charter trips** spend 3–4 hours over Antarctica but do not involve any landings on the **continent**.

overland Travel or transport across land by road or rail, e.g., across North America from Atlantic to Pacific Coast.

Overland Australian rail service linking Melbourne and Adelaide.

Overlander New Zealand rail service linking Auckland and Wellington in the country's North Island.

overriding commission Additional **commission** paid by a **principal** (such as an airline or **tour operator**) to a **travel agent** in certain circumstances, e.g., as a bonus or incentive. The term is also used to describe the commission allowed by a principal to a **General Sales Agent (GSA)** in respect of bookings originated by an ordinary travel agent, the GSA acting as a **middleman** between the principal and the travel agent.

oversale American term for **overbooking**.

overtrading A situation arising when a **firm** increases its output and sales without having adequate additional funds available to finance the additional working capital required.

ownership of business For the three most common forms, see **company; partnership; sole trader**.

ozone layer depletion Depletion of a thin layer of oxygen-related gases that circles the earth and filters harmful cancer-causing ultraviolet rays from the sun. Caused primarily by manufactured gases, the likely effects of the depletion are such health hazards as increased incidence of skin cancer and eye damage, which might lead to a decline in traditional **beach holidays** and many water sports, as well as **mountain**-based tourism.

P

Pa'anga ($T) Unit of **currency** of Tonga (also called Tongan Dollar).

Pacific Rim General name given to countries bordering the Pacific Ocean, particularly in the northern **hemisphere**, where the volume of trade and **tourist** movement, notably between east Asia and North America and within the **region**, is growing rapidly. See also **Far East**.

Pacific Standard Time A Canadian and US **time zone** based on the standard of the 120th **meridian**. Time equals GMT –8.

package Generally, a combination of two or more elements sold as a single product for an inclusive price, in which the costs of the individual product components are not separately identifiable. In travel and tourism, the term is used as a popular synonym for **inclusive tour**, as in *package holidays (vacations)* or *package tour*.

package store American term for a liquor store selling alcohol for consumption off the premises, equivalent to an **off-licence** in **England and Wales**.

Package Travel Directive European Community Council **Directive** to approximate the laws and regulations of member states relating to the sale, or offer for sale, of package holidays, which was agreed by EC Consumer Affairs Ministers in June 1990 and came into operation on 1 February 1993. The Directive defines the terms **package**, travel organizer and travel retailer, and lays down requirements for the protection of the **consumer**. The Department of Trade and Industry (DTI), responsible for implementing the Directive in the UK, produced the *Package Travel, Package Holidays and Package Tours Regulations 1992*, agreed by Parliament in December 1992. See also **consumer protection by tour operators (UK)**. Relevant legislation in the Republic of Ireland is the *Package Holidays and Travel Trade Act, 1995*.

Pan-American Comprising North, Central and South America.

parador A **hotel** in Spain, one of a chain owned and controlled by the state, providing a high standard of **tourism accommodation** in traditional Spanish style, often converted from a castle, monastery or another historic building.

parallel economy See **black economy**

parallel of latitude A line drawn on a map linking all points on the earth's surface with the same angular distance from the **equator** and, therefore, encircling the earth parallel to the equator. There are 90 divisions or degrees between the equator and each of the poles, each degree is subdivided into 60 minutes and each minute into 60 seconds. See also **latitude**.

parent company A **company** which controls one or more **subsidiary companies**. Also known as *holding company*. See also **conglomerate**.

park-and-ride A scheme which enables drivers to park their cars and continue their journey by public transport, increasingly used to reduce traffic congestion in urban areas and in fragile rural areas.

parlor car See **Pullman**

PARS US **computer reservation system (CRS)** owned by Trans World Airlines (TWA) and Northwest Airlines, merged with **DATAS II** and both were replaced by **Worldspan** system in 1990.

part charter See **charter**

participation rate The proportion of a population who take part in a particular activity, such as outdoor **recreation** or tourism, as distinct from **activity rate**, which refers to employment. See also **holiday (vacation) propensity, net**.

partie French term for a section of a **hotel** or **restaurant** kitchen. See also **chef**.

partnership
(a) Form of ownership of business carried on by two or more people in common, sharing risks, profits and losses. Normally each partner is responsible for the debts and for the actions of others to the full extent of his or her own possessions. This is a common form of ownership in the professions and in activities with relatively small capital requirements, as in some **catering** and retailing. In many countries partnerships are governed by legislation, as, e.g., in the UK by the Partnership Act 1890. See also **company; self-employed; sole trader**.
(b) Association of complementary parties, e.g., airline and car hire (**rental**) or **public** and **private sector**.

part-time (PT)
(a) Generally, shorter hours than constitute a full working week in a particular **industry** or **occupation**. However, what is part-time employment is usually defined for particular purposes; thus, e.g., part-time workers are defined for statistical purposes by the UK Department for Education and Skills as people normally working for not more than 30 hours a week. Travel, tourism and hospitality activities are large employers of part-time labour.
(b) The term is variously defined in education. See also **full-time**.

passenger designations
(a) *Through passenger* – one scheduled to travel on the same vehicle to its final destination.
(b) *Transfer passenger* – one who changes vehicle to continue a journey by connecting service.
(c) *Transit passenger* – one who breaks a journey at an intermediate point, to change vehicle or for another reason; if travelling between countries, not leaving the transit area of the **airport** or **port** and, therefore, not officially entering a country; such a passenger is not subject to entry formalities, such as **customs** control. See also **standby; transit traveller**.

passenger kilometre A measure of transport output denoting a passenger carried over a distance of one **kilometre**.

passenger load factor See **load factor**

Passenger Movement Charge See **departure tax**

Passenger Name Record (PNR) See **record locator**

passenger seat occupancy See **load factor**

passenger space ratio (PSR) Also known as *ship density*, the ratio of gross registered **tonnage** (GRT) and passenger capacity, of particular significance in **cruise** ships: low density ships normally provide more space in **cabins**, public rooms and on **decks**, and *vice versa*.

passport An official document issued by a government to a **citizen** of a country, verifying his/her identity and citizenship, for travel abroad. See also **travel document; visa**.

Pataca Unit of **currency** of Macau.

paying guest A person staying with a family in their home and paying a rent.

payload The revenue-producing load of an **aircraft**, including both passengers and cargo. It equals the total take-off weight less the empty weight including equipment and operating load (fuel, supplies and flight crew). The responsible government authorities fix the maximum take-off payload capacity of each aircraft.

pedalo Small boat with seats for two people who propel it by pedalling two twin paddle wheels.

pedometer An instrument for measuring walking distance.

peninsula A piece of land projecting into a body of water, almost surrounded by water, and only attached at one end to other land.

pension Establishment common in Continental Europe, usually described in English-speaking countries as a **guest house**,

DICTIONARY OF TRAVEL, TOURISM AND HOSPITALITY

normally owner-managed and providing **accommodation**, food and drink to **residents** only. See also **boarding house; en pension**.

penthouse Accommodation, often a **suite**, on the top **floor** of a high building.

per capita Well established, although erroneous, term used instead of the correct *per caput*, meaning 'a head' or 'each', as, e.g., per capita income (average income per head), and per capita expenditure (average expenditure per head), both common statistics derived from **consumer market** surveys, including **visitor** surveys.

per diem Payment made as a fixed amount per day by **firms** and other organizations to employees and others, such as consultants, who spend time away from their base, to cover their living expenses.

perfect competition In economics, a **market** situation with a large number of sellers of a homogeneous product. Each seller supplies only a small fraction of the total output, so that no seller can alone affect the market price. Each seller supplies a product identical with the products of all the other sellers, for which it is a perfect substitute, so that buyers can have no preference between products of different sellers. Few markets in travel, tourism and hospitality or elsewhere even approach perfect competition but the model is helpful for understanding markets generally and various forms of **imperfect competition** in particular. See also **monopoly**.

perfect oligopoly See **oligopoly**

personal income Income received by persons from employment, investments and transfer payments in the form of wages, salaries, other labour earnings, dividends, interest and rent.

personal selling Also referred to colloquially as *face-to-face selling*, the term describes personal contact with oral presentations to potential buyers. Although such forms as sales calls by representatives to **consumers** are not common in travel, tourism and hospitality, they are used in negotiating group sales, as with **conference** and exhibition organizers, and by producers *vis-à-vis* **intermediaries** as, e.g., by **tour operators** *vis-à-vis* retail **travel agents**.

personnel association An association of employees in a particular **occupation** to promote their common interests which, depending on its scope and functions, may but need not be a **professional body** or a **trade union**. Examples include *Association of Conference Executives (ACE), Association of National Tourist Office Representatives (ANTOR)*.

person-trip A standard measure of tourism activity, recording each person making a **trip**; for example, three persons making a trip, equals three person-trips.

Peso Unit of **currency** of Argentina, Chile, Colombia, Cuba, Dominican Republic (RD$), Mexico, the Philippines, Uruguay.

PHARE Acronym originally formed from the French term for *Poland and Hungary; Assistance for Economic Restructuring*, a scheme launched by the **European Community (EC)** in 1989 to help the reform process, initially in Hungary and Poland. Subsequently other Central and Eastern European Countries (CEEC), including the **Baltic States**, have also benefited. Programmes of technical assistance have extended to tourism development.

physical planning The process of preparing proposals for, and regulating the use of land in a given area. *Urban* (town) planning refers to physical planning in a built-up area, *rural* (country) planning to physical planning outside a built-up area. The term is sometimes used in conjunction with *development* when building and other operations or changing the use of land or buildings is involved. *Planning and development*, together with **marketing**, are the principal functions in tourism, and this is reflected in the scope and structure of national, regional and local tourism organizations. See **development plans**.

Piazza In Italy a square or **market** place.

pickup point
(a) Place where individuals or groups are collected by a **coach** or another vehicle by prior arrangement.
(b) Slang term for a place where prostitutes congregate to meet **customers**.

pidgin-English Spoken language consisting largely of English words, often corrupted in pronunciation, originally mainly used for communication between the Chinese and Europeans, now throughout the Pacific Islands where it is the most common **lingua franca** between various local groups speaking many local languages.

pied-à-terre French term for somewhere to stay, a temporary lodging.

pier Structure extending into the water used as a landing place or as a place of entertainment. See also **quay**; **wharf**.

pike A **mountain** peak in the English Lake District, e.g., Scafell Pike.

pilgrimage Movement of believers to distant holy places. The most widespread of these is probably the journey to **Mecca**, which all Muslims must make at least once during their lifetime. Formerly made on foot, by camel or by ship, but now increasingly by air, on **scheduled** services and by **charter**, from West Africa, Indonesia and elsewhere. Hindus similarly travel to Varanasi (Benares) in India, Japanese to ancestral shrines throughout the country, and Christians and Jews to Jerusalem. Visits to religious sites from the developed world are now more likely to be made because of the historical or architectural interest of the holy places rather than primarily or exclusively for religious purposes. However, Lourdes in France and Knock in Ireland are examples of modern shrines that have arisen from visions and attract large numbers of religious **visitors**. See also **religious travel/tourism**.

Pink Dollar Term used to refer to spending by gay and lesbian **consumers** who have emerged as a significant and identifiable **tourist market** segment, in some countries served exclusively by specialist tourism and hospitality operators.

pint Cubic measure of capacity for liquids equal to one-eighth of a **gallon**. British pint is equal to 0.568 of a **litre**, US pint to 0.473 of a litre.

pitch
(a) The distance between rows of **aircraft** seats.
(b) The rise and fall of the **bow** of a ship that contributes to seasickness. See also **roll**.

pizzeria **Restaurant** which sells wholly or mainly pizzas.

planetarium A working model of the planetary system, usually enclosed in a domed building, a significant **tourist/visitor attraction** in many **cities**.

planned economy See **mixed economy**

plastic money A colloquial term for **debit**, **credit** and **charge cards**.

plat du jour French term meaning *dish of the day*, a dish not appearing on a printed menu and normally varying from day to day.

plate service See **American service**

Plaza In Spain, a square or a **market** place, but the term is also used elsewhere to refer to a wide open space that forms a pedestrian forecourt to one or more buildings.

Plimsoll line See **International Load Line**

plongeur French term for an employee who washes dishes in a **restaurant**.

point of sale (POS) Any location where selling takes place. For most travel, tourism and hospitality products *external* points of sale include retail travel agencies and operators' booking offices; *internal* or **in-house** points of sale include, e.g., **hotel** reception offices, bars and **restaurants**. Display and other promotion material used there is also referred to as point-of-sale.

polar Of, near or referring to the pole. Hence, e.g., *polar regions* lie between the poles and the tree lines; *polar wind* is a very cold wind blowing from the north or south polar regions.

polder An area of low-lying land at or below sea level reclaimed from the sea, lake or river by dykes and draining; common, e.g., in the Netherlands.

polio(myelitis) A viral disease of the nervous system, causing muscle pains, fever and paralysis; can cause permanent disability and is sometimes fatal. It is spread by faecal–oral means and by droplet infection (coughs and sneezes) in areas of poor hygiene (outside North and Western Europe, North America, Australia and New Zealand). May be prevented by **immunization**, which has to be followed by a booster dose every 10 years.

pollution Direct or indirect alteration of the properties of any part of the natural **environment** in such a way as to present a hazard or potential hazard; alternatively, presence of material in the wrong place at the wrong time and in the wrong form. Pollution can thus affect the **atmosphere** through harmful gases or particulate matter, the land through the dumping of waste or noxious matter, and the sea, rivers and lakes through discharges or deposition. **Tourists** have been both adversely affected by pollution, e.g., by traffic in **cities**, by adulteration of water supply and the discharge of sewage on bathing **beaches**, and been a source of pollution, especially where numbers are large and tourism planning is inadequate. See also **environmental issues**.

Polynesia See **Australasia**

Polynesian bure Thatched, cottage-style **accommodation** found throughout the South Pacific and in island **resorts** of Australia in village-style resort settings. Although the term has become an almost generic expression, terminology in particular countries varies: e.g., the same accommodation is known in Samoa as *fale*.

Pom/Pommie/Pommy In Australia and New Zealand, a person of English descent, an immigrant from the UK. See also **New Australian**.

pooling In air transport, sharing the revenue to be obtained on a particular **route** between two or more airlines, on a predetermined basis by agreement between them, which may also cover matters such as cooperative flight scheduling and joint **marketing**.

population change The main components of change in the size of the population of an area are *natural change* (i.e., the difference between births and deaths) and *net migration* (i.e., the difference between immigration and emigration). Trends in these are of travel and tourism significance because the size of population is a basic determinant of the volume of travel and tourism generated by an area.

port
(a) Harbour or town possessing a harbour.
(b) Left side of a ship or **aircraft** when facing forward, with red navigation lights on the bridge or wings. See also **starboard**.

portion The size or weight of a food item served to the **customer** in an eating **establishment**.

poste restante French term in international use for the post office department where mail so addressed is kept until called for by the addressee, hence applied to the service, which is of particular benefit to **travellers**. *General Delivery* is the US equivalent.

post-industrial society The term used to describe a stage reached by society in the late twentieth century in North America, Western Europe and several other parts of the developed world, as a result of technological progress and economic and social change. Main characteristics include the relative decline of goods-producing **industries**, the growth of **services** and increases in professional and technical **occupations**. The growth of travel and tourism is a prominent feature of the post-industrial society.

potential demand See **demand for tourism**

Pound (£) Unit of **currency** of Cyprus (C£), Egypt (£E), Lebanon (£L), Syria (£S), United Kingdom, including Channel Islands and Isle of Man (£), Falkland Islands (FI£), Gibraltar (G£), St Helena. See also **Sterling**.

pousada A **hotel** in Portugal, one of a network of strategically located **establishments** to meet the needs of touring motorists, providing **tourism accommodation,** often in converted historic buildings.

power boating Craft powered principally by petrol engines, both as an end in itself, whether for speed boating or cruising, or as a source of traction for **water-skiing** and paragliding. Both forms are often a source of conflict with other forms of **recreation** on or in, or on the banks of, water, as well as sources of **erosion** of soft banks from wash, and of **pollution** from the discharge of oil, sewage and other waste.

precipitation All forms of moisture falling on the ground, whether in the form of rain, snow, sleet, hail or fog drip. All forms are measured as the melted equivalent of rain, one foot (approx. 30 cm) of snow being broadly equivalent to one inch (approx. 2.5 cm) of rain.

preclearance Provision of **customs** and immigration procedures in a foreign country of departure to ease the demand for such facilities in the country of arrival. Such arrangements exist, e.g., between some Caribbean countries and the USA.

predatory pricing The practice of a **firm** temporarily selling at very low prices with the objective of driving out competitors or keeping out new entrants from a **market**; once the objective has been achieved, prices can be raised and higher profits made. This is what Laker Airways claimed several airlines were doing in the late 1970s and early 1980s when they cut their **fares** on North Atlantic **routes** on which Laker operated its *Skytrain* service, and what Virgin Atlantic complained of more recently. The practice is difficult to prove but has been also alleged to exist, e.g., in Europe in the competition between **scheduled** and **charter** airlines.

Prepaid Ticket Advice (PTA) Notification by an **agent** or **carrier** that a person has paid for another person's transportation, usually from a place other than the one in which the **fare** was paid, thereby authorizing the issue of an airline ticket by the recipient.

pre-registration Term to describe procedures for completion of registration prior to the guests' arrival, used for **conferences**, exhibitions, tours and other large groups by **hotels**, as well as event and travel organizers, to save time and avoid congestion on arrival.

preservation See **conservation**

press relations See **public relations**

price/rate hike American synonym for price/rate increase/rise.

price competition Market situation in which **firms** compete on price rather than quality of product or other factors to influence the buyer's choice. Price competition features strongly in travel, tourism and hospitality markets, especially in air transport, **hotel and**

catering services and tour operations. Price competition is sometimes chosen as a deliberate strategy but often it is the result of unforeseen market conditions, in which planned capacity or sales exceed **actual demand**. See also **non-price competition**.

price cutting Reducing prices below the commonly accepted level for the product concerned, with a view to undercutting competitors and achieving increases in **market share**.

price discrimination Practice of charging different prices to different **customers** for the same product for reasons not associated with differences in the cost of supply. Common examples include situations where different customers have different **elasticities of demand**. Thus, e.g., **normal air fares** may be charged to business **travellers** and **promotional air fares** to holiday (vacation) travellers on the same flights; in order to prevent the dilution of revenue by business travellers making use of promotional fares, the latter have various conditions or restrictions attached. See also **dumping**.

price elasticity of demand An economic concept which measures the responsiveness of demand to changes in price. When a given change in price leads to a more than proportionate change in **consumer** demand, the demand is said to be elastic; when a given change in price leads to a less than proportionate change in demand, the demand is said to be inelastic. Much demand for travel, tourism and hospitality **services** is price-elastic and elasticity is of practical importance in **pricing**. See also **cross-elasticity of demand**; **income elasticity of demand**.

price pegging Keeping selling price at a stable level. Thus a **firm** may prevent the price of its product from rising by absorbing increased costs in order to remain competitive; a firm may sell surplus output abroad by **dumping** in order to avoid reducing the price of its product in the domestic **market**; a country's central bank may buy/sell **currency** to prevent its **rate of exchange** from falling/rising.

price skimming Setting high initial prices in **markets** with price-inelastic demand, commonly with a view to achieving a quick return.

pricing

See **backward pricing**
    contribution pricing
    cost-plus pricing
    differential pricing
    dumping
    fee-based pricing
    Hubbart formula
    marginal cost pricing
    predatory pricing
    price cutting
    price discrimination
    price pegging
    price skimming
    rate-of-return pricing
    recommended retail price (RRP)
    Resale Price Maintenance (RPM)

primary data Information collected specifically for a particular purpose, often by means of a survey, as distinct from **secondary data** collected and recorded already.

primary impacts See **tourism expenditure impacts**

primary industries See **services**

principal Person who gives authority to an **agent** who may then act for or represent the principal. In travel, tourism and hospitality, **hotels**, transport operators and **tour operators** are principals when they sell their products through **retail travel agents**.

private carrier See **carrier**

private cost See **social cost**

private sector That part of the economy in which economic activity is carried on by private enterprise, including households and individuals, businesses and non-profit-making bodies other than those included in the **public sector**. See also **mixed economy**.

privatization Transfer of **industries**, enterprises and activities owned by government into private ownership, which has been pursued by many countries by such means as sales of shares and subcontracting of work by **public** and **private sector**. In the 1980s the main travel- and tourism-related activities privatized in the UK included the British Airports Authority, British Airways and Sealink, and in the 1990s, the railways. See also **deregulation**.

product See **tourist product**

product life cycle See **life cycle**

product mix See **marketing mix**

product orientation See **marketing orientation**

productivity The relationship between outputs of goods and **services** and inputs required to produce those outputs, such as labour or capital. The most common but partial measurement is *labour productivity*, the relationship between output and the labour resources employed. *Total productivity* measurement is concerned with the contribution to output of all productive resources. Labour productivity levels in the main **tourism-related industries** differ: those in the **hotel and catering industry** are substantially below, whilst those in transport are similar or even higher than those in most other **industries**. See also c**apital-intensive**; **labour-intensive**.

professional body An organization of individuals engaged in a particular **occupation**, normally a vocation or calling requiring a long period of training or learning, which seeks to provide standing for its members, and which controls admission, usually by examination. Therefore, professional bodies adopt certain defined standards, and members qualify for admission by formally meeting those standards and by agreeing to observe them once they are admitted into membership. The standards are normally based on standards of competence shown in knowledge and experience, and may also include standards of conduct in the exercise of the occupation. See also **Professional bodies in travel, tourism and hospitality (UK)**.

professional indemnity insurance Insurance which covers organizations and their employees against mistakes and negligence. Also called in North America *errors and omissions insurance*.

Programme Evaluation and Review Technique (PERT) Technique used in planning and monitoring complex activities such as large construction projects and large events.

promotional air fares See **air fare types**

promotional channels See **marketing mix**

promotional mix See **marketing mix**

proof of citizenship A document such as a birth certificate or **passport** which certifies that a person is a **citizen** of a state.

propensity
See **holiday (vacation) frequency**
holiday (vacation) propensity, gross
holiday (vacation) propensity, net

Property Irregularity Report (PIR) Term used in air transport for the form completed by airline passengers at the **airport** in respect of missing **baggage**, which provides the airline with a description of the baggage, a brief list of contents and an address to which it can be forwarded. It is important that passengers do not leave the airport without first reporting the loss and completing the PIR and, when claiming compensation, produce a copy of the PIR, their ticket and the **baggage check**.

protected areas Areas designated by appropriate national, regional or international authorities because of their archaeological, cultural or environmental significance. See **building conservation schemes**; **countryside conservation designation schemes**

protected commission A **commission** guaranteed by a supplier to an **intermediary** regardless of cancellations, e.g., by a **tour operator** to a **travel agent** whether a tour takes place or not.

provisioned charter An arrangement in which the hire of a yacht or another vessel for a specified period includes fuel and provisions. This is to be distinguished from **bareboat charter** and **crewed charter**. See also **flotilla cruising**.

PSA Bonding Scheme Bonding scheme operated by **Passenger Shipping Association** (PSA) in the UK, which requires all firms wishing to join the Association to put up a bond as a condition of membership. The scheme covers any **inclusive tour (IT) holidays (vacations)** from the UK with the bonded **ferry** and **cruise companies**. For other schemes, see **bonding schemes (UK)**.

psychocentric See **allocentric/psychocentric**

psychographics Measurement of an individual's psychological attributes as distinct from demographics (see **demography**), which studies such physical population characteristics as age, sex and household composition. Both provide a basis for **market segmentation** and are of major importance in product formulation and promotion, but whereas, e.g., the **life cycle** is the subject of demographics, **lifestyle** is the province of psychographics.

pub Colloquial abbreviation of **public house**.

public corporations See **public sector**

Public Excursion (PEX) Special instant purchase air **fare** offered by airlines on **scheduled** flights between certain **cities** subject to certain restrictions. Thus, e.g., reservation, payment and ticketing must be completed at the same time, although not necessarily a minimum period in advance, and a cancellation charge applies. See also **Advance Purchase Excursion (APEX)**; **Seat Sale**.

public holiday A day observed as a **holiday** in a country. A few apply in many countries, e.g., New Year's Day, May Day or Labour Day, Christmas Day. Most vary between countries or groups of countries, such as religious holidays according to major religions. Many countries also observe a National or Independence Day under that or a similar name. There are commonly 8–12 public holidays in most countries. See **Bank Holidays** for those observed in the **United Kingdom**; also entries for **public holidays** in Australia, Canada, India, New Zealand, Republic of Ireland, South Africa and USA.

public holidays (Australia) New Year's Day, Australia Day (26 January), Good Friday, Easter Monday, Anzac Day (anniversary of 1915 landing at Gallipoli, 25 April), Queen's Official Birthday (June), Christmas Day,

Boxing Day. These eight are national holidays, which some states observe on different days; there are also some individual state holidays.

public holidays (Canada) New Year, Good Friday, Easter Monday, Victoria Day (May), Canada Day (July), Labour Day (September), Thanksgiving (October), Remembrance Day (November), Christmas Day, Boxing Day (total 10). Other days may be also proclaimed holidays by individual provinces.

public holidays (India) Public holidays observed in India vary locally. As religious holidays depend on astronomical observations, holidays are usually declared at the beginning of each year.

public holidays (New Zealand) New Year, Waitangi Day (anniversary of 1840 treaty, 6 February), Good Friday, Easter Monday, Anzac Day (anniversary of 1915 landing at Gallipoli, 25 April), Queen's Official Birthday (June), Labour Day (October), Christmas Day, Boxing Day (total 9). In addition each region celebrates its anniversary day.

public holidays (Republic of Ireland) New Year's Day, St Patrick's Day (17 March), Good Friday, Easter Monday, May Day (first Monday in May), June Bank Holiday (first Monday in June), August Bank Holiday (first Monday in August), October Bank Holiday (last Monday in October), 25–28 December (Christmas) (total 12).

public holidays (South Africa) New Year's Day, Human Rights Day (21 March), Good Friday, Family Day (9 April), Freedom Day (27 April), Workers' Day (1 May), Youth Day (June), National Women's Day (9 August), Heritage Day (24 September), Day of Reconciliation (December), Christmas Day, Day of Goodwill (26 December) (total 12).

public holidays (United States of America) New Year's Day, Martin Luther King Day (January), President's Day (February), Memorial Day (May), Independence Day (4 July), Labor Day (September), Veterans' Day (November), Thanksgiving Day (November), Christmas Day (total 9). Federal legal public holidays are designated by presidential proclamation or congressional enactment, but need not be observed in individual states, which have legal jurisdiction over their public holidays.

public house **Establishment** prominent in the **British Isles** wholly or mainly supplying alcoholic liquor and other drinks for consumption on the premises to the general public, to which the supply of food is ancillary, and the provision of overnight **accommodation**, if any, subordinate. Colloquially abbreviated as *pub*. Also often described as an **inn** but, e.g., in Australia public houses commonly trade as **hotels**. See also **free house**; **tied house**. In 2000 there were more than 50 000 public houses in the UK and their number was gradually declining.

public house licence A **licence** for the sale of alcoholic liquor in **public houses** in Scotland granted by licensing boards. See also **hotel licence**; **on-licence**.

public relations (PR) The British *Institute of Public Relations* defines public relations practice as 'the planned and sustained effort to establish and maintain goodwill and mutual understanding between an organization and its publics'. This definition highlights the systematic and continuous nature of the activity and its concern with all groups of people of relevance to the well-being of the organization; such groups include not only **customers** but also, e.g., employees, shareholders and local communities. Public relations activity aimed at establishing and maintaining a relationship with and through the press is *press relations.*

public sector That part of the economy consisting of central government, **local authorities** and public corporations. The exact demarcation may differ from one country to another. In the UK, *central government* includes activities for which a Minister of the Crown or other responsible person is accountable to Parliament. *Local authorities* are public authorities of limited geographical scope; in the UK they include county, borough, district and parish councils, and joint boards and committees formed by two or more councils. As a result of **local government** reorganization in 1996, some new **unitary** authorities combine the functions of the county, borough and district councils. *Public corporations* comprise public trading bodies, including the nationalized industries. See also **private sector**.

public utilities Industries supplying essential basic public **services**, such as electricity, gas, water and telephones, i.e., providing **infrastructure** for economic development, which often have a character of natural **monopoly**.

public works Social **infrastructure** such as roads and housing, financed by Government. Such spending is often advocated during a depression, in order to alleviate unemployment and stimulate economic activity.

publicity Means of securing public attention, other than **advertising**, through news value, artistic, entertainment or other merit, e.g., in feature articles in the press, books and broadcasting programmes. Unlike in advertising, which represents the purchase of advertising space or time and where the advertiser has control over the message, no charge is made by the **media**, which decide whether or not and how information is used by them.

Pula (P) Unit of **currency** of Botswana.

Pullman Named after the designer **G.M. Pullman**, term applied to a railway carriage providing seating and sleeping accommodation of high standard on American as well as European trains, described in North America as *parlor car*. Also sometimes used as name of the **company** providing such accommodation, e.g., the Pullman Car Co. Ltd, owned by the *British Transport Commission*, operated some 200 Pullman cars over British Railways lines as

a separate organization until the early 1960s. See also **couchette; roomette; Wagon-Lits**.

purpose of trip/visit The reason for which a **trip**/visit is undertaken. In surveys data are usually collected on the main purpose, i.e., the reason in the absence of which the trip/visit would not take place, although it may be supplemented or expanded by another purpose, e.g., business as main purpose followed by holiday (vacation). Three main groups of reasons are evident in literature: **holiday (vacation), business, common interest**. Six major groups are recommended by the **World Tourism Organization** for statistical purposes: **leisure, recreation** and **holidays; visiting friends and relatives;** business and professional; health treatment; religion/**pilgrimage;** other.

purser A passenger ship's officer responsible for accounts, supplies and various passenger services.

push–pull theory Theory first used in connection with **migration**, which suggests that people are pushed by adverse conditions (such as unemployment or political repression) to leave an area, and are at the same time attracted by an area with favourable conditions (such as employment prospects or freedom). The theory has been more recently extended to explain by analogy tourism, where it seems equally self-evident (whether on climatic or other grounds). See **determinants of tourism; sunlust; wanderlust**.

quadrennial Every four years.

Qualiflyer Group Airline alliance of (June 2001) Air Europe, Air Liberté, Air Littoral, AOM, Crossair, LOT Polish Airlines, PGA Portugalia, Swissair/Sabena, TAP Air Portugal, Turkish Airlines, Volare, formed March 1998.

quango An **acronym** formed from abbreviation of quasi-autonomous non-governmental organization, a semi-public body in the UK appointed and financed by government, but not a government department. Examples include the **British Tourist Authority** and other statutory **tourist boards**.

quarantine Isolation imposed by health authorities on persons or animals that might spread infectious disease. When a ship is under quarantine, no one is allowed to go on board or **disembark**. Particularly strict restrictions are applied by UK authorities to animals brought into the country.

quart Measure of cubic capacity equal to a quarter of a **gallon** or two **pints**. A British quart equals 1.136 **litres**, a US quart 0.946 of a litre.

quay A solid structure, usually of stone or iron alongside or projecting into water, used as a landing stage and for loading and unloading ships. See also **pier; wharf**.

queen room A **hotel** room with a **queen (size)** bed.

queen (size) Term used to describe an extra wide, extra long **double** bed, approx. 60 × 80 in. (150 × 200 cm). See also **king (size)**.

Queen's Awards Annual awards to British **firms** and other organizations to recognize outstanding performance in their respective fields, initially for export and technological achievement; the Queen's Award for Environmental Achievement was launched in 1993. Following a review in 1999, the scheme was renamed the Queen's Awards for Enterprise. In 2002, 131 organizations received awards: 85 for International Trade, 37 for Innovation, 9 for Sustainable Development. In most recent years awards were made to firms in **travel, tourism** and **hospitality industries**.

Queenslander Australian rail service linking Brisbane and Cairns.

Quetzal (Q) Unit of **currency** of Guatemala.

queue jumping Practice of going ahead of one's turn in a queue or waiting list, known in USA as *cutting in line*.

quicksand A mass of loose fine sand, sometimes mixed with mud, supersaturated with water to be found on some coasts and near river mouths, which tends to suck down any heavy object, including a person.

quinquennial Every five years.

rabies An acute viral infection of the nervous system. Symptoms include delirium, paralysis and painful muscle spasms in the throat; it is usually fatal. It is most commonly contracted by being bitten by a dog or another infected animal and occurs in Europe and North America as well as **less developed countries (LDCs)**. The main precaution is avoiding contact with animals and a vaccine is also available.

rack rate Standard full or published price per **hotel** room, to be distinguished from various special (discounted) rates at which rooms may be actually sold, and also from **average room rate (ARR)**. See also **hotel tariff; hotel tariff terms**.

rail(way) gauge The width between the top of the rails, which varies in different parts of the world as follows:
(a) The standard gauge used in Europe (except Spain, Portugal, former USSR and certain countries linked to USSR), North America and parts of Australia is 1.435 metres (4 ft 8½ in.)
(b) Broad gauges of 1.6 metres (5 ft 3 in.) and 1.65 metres (5 ft 6 in.) are used in Spain, Portugal, former USSR, parts of the **Indian Subcontinent**, Australia and South America.
(c) Narrow gauges, especially 1.066 metres (3 ft 6 in.) or less, are used in South Africa and parts of Australia.
(d) The metre gauge (3 ft 3⅜ in.) is used in many parts of the world.

rail passes

See **abonnement**	**EuroDomino Pass**
Amtrak Rail Passes	**Europass**
Britrail Pass	**France Railpass**
Eurail Pass	**Inter-Rail Pass**
Eurail Selectpass	**ScanRailpass**

railway mania Description given in **Britain** to the decade of the 1840s (when more **miles** of track were opened than during any other decade).

Ramadan Ninth month of the Mohammedan year when fasting is observed and able-bodied Muslims over 14 years of age are required to refrain from eating, drinking and smoking from dawn to sunset. According to the Islamic calendar the period comes about 11 days earlier each year. It is observed in much of the **Middle East**, several other countries in Africa, and in Turkey and Pakistan.

ramp
(a) A sloping plane joining two levels of ground.
(b) A plane connecting a **roll-on/roll-off ship** to the shore or **quay**, which may be *bow ramp* (at front), *stern ramp* (at end) or *side ramp* (at side of ship).
(c) Staircase on wheels used to load and unload an **aircraft**. See also **gangway**.

Ramsar Sites Conservation areas of marsh and other **wetlands** of international importance for their wildlife, named after an Iranian town, in which the international **convention** for their protection was held. Designated by official nature conservation authorities, a total of close on 150 sites existed in the UK by early 2000. See **countryside conservation designation schemes** for other schemes.

Rand (R) Unit of **currency** of South Africa; also Namibia.

random sample See **sampling**

rate of exchange The price at which one **currency** is exchanged for another. At any particular time in the absence of controls, the actual rates are determined by supply and demand for currencies in **foreign exchange markets**. A currency is said to appreciate/depreciate when its *floating* rate of exchange increases/falls in terms of other currencies; changes in *fixed* rates of exchange are called revaluations/devaluations. Movements in exchange rates exercise an important influence on **international travel and tourism** flows.

rate-of-return pricing Method of setting prices with a view to achieving a predetermined rate of return on invested capital.

readership Number of people who read a newspaper or periodical as distinct from the number who buy or receive it (**circulation**). A readership figure can normally be expected to be higher than a circulation figure. Both figures are of particular significance to advertisers of goods and **services**, including travel, tourism and hospitality products.

real terms A money value at **constant prices**, i.e., adjusted for changes in prices. To eliminate the effects of price changes, data at **current prices** are converted to constant prices by using **index numbers**. **Tourism expenditure** data are commonly converted by using the *Retail Price Index* (**cost of living index**). However, as this measures changes in **consumer** prices paid by households, in a number of countries an increasing use is made of specially constructed indices of tourist prices, which reflect more accurately tourist spending patterns.

receiving country For purposes of **international tourism** statistics, the country that receives **visitors** who are **residents** of another country. See also **generating country**.

recession General decline in economic activity reflected in the national income, employment and other aggregates. A widely accepted technical definition is at least two consecutive quarters of falling output in **real terms**. This has occurred three times in recent years worldwide: 1974–5, 1980–1, 1990–2, the last being the longest recession since World War II. See also **business cycle**.

recipe A formula for producing a particular dish including the ingredients and the method of preparation; when used in **catering**, it may also include such information as the costing of the dish and its nutritional value.

recommended retail price (RRP) Price at which a manufacturer suggests the product should be sold by the retailer.

reconfirmation It is a requirement of some airlines if an international journey (other than within Europe) is broken for more than a given length of time, that the passenger should reconfirm the intention to use the seat reserved for the next **leg** of the journey. Failure to reconfirm may result in the cancellation of the next and any subsequent reservation and the seat being sold.

record locator Also called *PNR (Passenger Name Record)* number, an identification number or **code** provided by an airline or **computer reservation system (CRS)** for each booking.

recovery rate A performance indicator of public and voluntary **sector** organizations such as **tourist/visitor attractions** obtained by dividing total income by total operating expenditure (×100).

recreation Particular use of **leisure** or activity undertaken during leisure, which may include travel and tourism. Some major distinctions are indoor/outdoor, home-based/away from home, active/passive recreation. Hence *recreation centre, recreation development, recreation facilities.*

recreation(al) vehicle (RV) Term used for several types of vehicle, such as a motorized **caravan** for **holiday (vacation)** use, also called *camper* and *motor home*, and for a truck or van or another vehicle equipped or modified for off-the-road pleasure use, such as **dune** buggy, off-road motor bicycle and snowmobile. The latter three are often a source of conflict with conservationists because of the damage and disturbance they cause, with **residents**, and with those who seek quiet enjoyment in remote areas.

recycling Re-use of materials after further processing, which would otherwise be thrown away, including both industrial and domestic waste, such as bottles, can metal and paper.

red light district American term for a town or **city** area known as the location of brothels and prostitutes.

referral In general, the act of one person or organization recommending another, with or without a payment, known as *referral fee* or *referral commission*. Thus, e.g., each **hotel** in a group may promote other hotels in the group and generate business for them by onward reservations. Hence a hotel **consortium** is sometimes referred to as a *referral system*, especially in the USA.

refugee The United Nations, in the 1951 Convention relating to the Status of Refugees, extended in its application by the 1967 Protocol relating to the Status of Refugees, defined a refugee as a person who 'owing to the well-founded fear of being persecuted for reason of race, religion, nationality, membership of a particular social group or political opinion, is outside the country of his [or her] nationality and unable or, owing to such fear, is unwilling to avail himself [or herself] of the protection of the country'. See also **alien; expatriate; migration; nomad**.

regatta A boat or yacht race, or commonly an organized series of such races, forming a sporting and social event, derived from the name of certain boat races on the Grand Canal in Venice. Notable regattas, such as the Henley Regatta in England, are major **tourist/visitor attractions**.

region
(a) A major area within a country, which has certain attributes in common, such as **climate** or **topography**, and then is usually described as a *natural region*, and/or which forms a unit for political or administrative purposes. Catalonia in Spain, the Highlands in Scotland, Languedoc-Roussillon in France, are well-known examples in Europe.
(b) An area of the world with defined characteristics or a group of countries in geographical proximity, e.g., the **Balkans**, the Caribbean, **Middle East**. See also **global tourism regions**.

regional carrier A **carrier** serving a **region**, which may be an area within a country or a global region.

regional development Growth in economic and social terms of a defined major area, usually an administrative entity, particularly one suffering problems, in which often government plays a role, directly or indirectly, by stimulating, planning, co-ordinating and/or financially supporting such development. In areas with climatic, scenic or other attractions and deficient in resources for other forms of economic activity, tourism often represents an important element in regional development, as is the case in many coastal and mountainous **regions**. See also **regional planning**.

regional planning A systematic and comprehensive approach to planning the economic and social development of a defined major area, usually undertaken by governments, for areas which represent administrative units and broader in scope than statutory **land use planning** areas. Some of the best known examples of regional planning of tourism significance in Europe have been on the Adriatic coast of former **Yugoslavia**, Languedoc-Roussillon in France, and parts of the Iberian coast. See also **regional development**.

Regional Tourism Authorities (RTAs) Seven regional organizations in the Republic of Ireland with a membership of local authorities and individuals, associations and firms, providing **visitor** servicing, regional **marketing**, and development coordination and planning.

regional tourism organization Intermediate level of tourism organization between national and local levels, variously concerned with the development, promotion and coordination of tourism in its area. See, e.g., **Regional Tourist Boards (RTBs)** for England, **Area Tourism Companies (ATCs)** for Wales, **Regional Tourist Associations (RTAs)** for Northern Ireland, **Regional Tourist Authorities (RTAs)** for the Republic of Ireland.

Regional Tourist Associations (RTAs) Voluntary bodies operating within Northern Ireland with membership drawn from the **public** and **private sectors** and operating with the support of the **Northern Ireland Tourist Board (NITB)** to develop, promote and coordinate tourism in their respective areas of the Province.

Regional Tourist Boards (RTBs) Network of ten voluntary bodies with a tripartite structure of **local authorities**, the **tourism industry** and the **English Tourism Council (ETC)** covering the whole of England. Formed following the setting up of the national board for England under the Development of Tourism Act 1969, to develop, promote and coordinate tourism in their respective areas of England.

regression analysis A statistical technique for establishing a relationship between a dependent variable and one or more independent variables, which would explain past variations in the former and predict future variations in terms of changes in the latter. A simple regression **model** is used for a two-variable relationship, such as **holiday (vacation)** participation and income. Multivariate regression models are required for more than two variables. E.g., to forecast tourist flows to several destinations, population size and income **per capita** of each of the generating countries, relative distance and travel times may be used.

regular body aircraft See **aircraft types: bodies**

relais See **brasserie**

religions of the world
See **Buddhism**   **Jainism**
Chinese religions   **Japanese religions**
Christianity   **Judaism**
Confucianism   **Shinto(ism)**
Hinduism   **Sikhism**
Islam   **Taoism**

religious travel/tourism In a narrow sense, **trips** and visits whose main purpose is the religious experience, e.g., **pilgrimages** to Jerusalem, Lourdes and **Mecca**. In a broad sense, also **trips** and visits whose major **motivation** is religious **heritage**, such as churches and cathedrals.

remittances *Inter alia*, money sent by immigrants from the country in which they work to relatives in their country of origin; these amounts appear as 'private transfers' among **invisibles** in the **balance of payments** current account.

Ren Min Bi Yuan See **Yuan**

rent it here, leave it there American term used to describe a car **rental** arrangement for

picking up a car at one location and leaving it at another.

rental
(a) Amount paid by tenant or received by owner as rent for occupation and use of space. See also **concession**.
(b) US synonym for **hire**, as, e.g., in *automobile rental*.

representative See **hotel representative**; **resort representative**

repeat customer **Customer** who buys products or **services** from the same supplier, e.g., guest staying at the same **hotel** or **traveller** using the same airline. Hence *repeat tourist* or *visitor* is one who returns to the same destination.

re-route To change an **itinerary**.

Resale Price Maintenance (RPM) The practice of suppliers setting specific or minimum prices for their products and requiring the distributors to sell them at those prices. The practice is subject to legislation in many countries. E.g., in the UK all resale price arrangements are assumed to be against the public interest unless proved otherwise, and **tour operators** cannot legally enforce **inclusive tour** prices against retail **travel agents**, but suppliers may publish a **recommended retail price (RRP)** and agree with distributors to what extent such prices may be discounted.

reservoir An artificial body of water, created in upland valleys by the construction of a **dam** or **barrage**, and in the lowlands by the building of a wall or bund to enclose the water. Reservoirs are created for a number of different purposes and these and their location and characteristics affect their suitability for recreational use: direct supply of drinking water, control of flow in a river for extraction lower down, generation of hydroelectric power, irrigation and the maintenance of water levels in **canals**. Apart from the first, there is no reason why the water should not be used for **recreation**, and modern purification plant makes some forms of recreation acceptable on the direct supply reservoirs, notably sailing and angling.

resident For purposes of **international tourism** statistics, a person is considered to be a resident in a country if the person

(a) has lived for most of the past year (12 months) in that country, or

(b) has lived in that country for a shorter period and intends to return within 12 months to live in that country.

For purposes of statistics of **domestic tourism**, a person is considered to be a resident in a place if the person

(a) has lived for most of the past year (12 months) in that place, or

(b) has lived in that place for a shorter period and intends to return within 12 months to live in that place.

[World Tourism Organization]

residential hotel A description sometimes used for a **hotel** accommodating long-term guests who may make it their home.

resort

(a) Place to which people go for **holidays (vacations)** and **recreation**, hence *holiday (vacation)* and *health* resorts, also *inland* and *coastal/seaside* resorts. Historically the evolution of tourism has been closely identified with the beginnings and subsequent development of resorts. Nowadays the term often has its literal meaning to denote any **visitor** centre to which people resort in large numbers and **capital cities** tend to be the largest and most prosperous resorts in their countries, especially for **international tourists**.

(b) In the USA and the Caribbean, also a **holiday (vacation) hotel** providing extensive entertainment and **recreation** facilities.

resort representative A **tour operator's** employee based in a **resort** and providing a formal point of contact between the **firm** and **clients** and resort facilities and services, as well as entertainment and other arrangements.

resort tax Tax levied by **local authority** or another agency on staying **visitors**, usually in the form of *bed, hotel* or *room tax*, as a means of raising revenue; sometimes the proceeds are applied to tourism purposes. See also **tourist tax**.

resource-based resources Resources devoted to **recreation** and tourism, which depend for their attraction on their quality irrespective of their location. Their character

attracts from considerable distance and their appeal is national or international rather than local or regional. See also **user-oriented resources**.

response rate In surveys, the ratio of the number of people responding to the total number of people approached. In **marketing**, more specifically, the number of replies or enquiries received in response to an advertisement (or another promotion), used as a measure of **advertising** effectiveness. See also **conversion rate**.

responsible tourism See **alternative tourism**

rest room US term for a public toilet.

restaurant Establishment providing food for consumption on the premises to the general public, to which the supply of alcoholic liquor, if any, is ancillary, as a separate unit or as part of a **hotel** or another **establishment**. Beyond this generalization, some restaurants operate under designations such as **cafés**, **snack bars** and the like; in some countries the designation of restaurants and other eating establishments is regulated by law. In 2000 there were around 45 000 restaurants, cafés and take-away food shops operating in the UK. See also **restaurant types**

restaurant types

See **auberge**	**drive-in restaurant**
bistro	**drive-through restaurant**
bodega	**fast food outlet**
brasserie	**food court**
Bring Your Own	**pizzeria**
café	**relais**
cafeteria	**snack bar**
carvery	**speciality restaurant**
coffee shop	**trattoria**
diner	**truckshop**

restoration See **conservation**

Retail Export Scheme Scheme administered by Customs and Excise in the UK, which enables overseas **visitors** to receive a refund of **value added tax (VAT)** paid on some goods bought while in the UK. From 1 January 1993 European Community (EC) **travellers** have no longer been eligible to use the scheme but it continues to be available to others and also in certain circumstances to UK **residents** departing abroad and to crew members of ships and **aircraft**.

Retail Price Index (RPI) See **cost of living index**

retail travel agent See **travel agent**

return load Paying load carried by a vehicle on a return journey to the place from where its previous load came. Also called *back load*. See also **back-to-back**.

revalidation sticker An amendment attached to the **flight coupon** of an airline ticket, showing a change such as change of flight made to the original reservation.

revenue load factor See **load factor**

revenue passenger kilometre (RPK) A measure of transport output denoting one paying passenger carried one **kilometre**.

revenue passenger mile (RPM) A measure of transport output denoting one paying passenger carried one **mile**.

revenue tonne kilometre (RTK) A measure of transport output calculated as the product of revenue earning load in **tonnes** and the **kilometres** over which it is carried.

Rial Unit of **currency** of Iran (IR) and Oman (RO).

ribbon development Building along main roads extending outwards from built-up areas, a common direction of much urban growth, including many coastal and inland **resorts**. Also used to describe more generally a linear building development along a coastline, valley or **route**.

Richter scale A numerical scale used to measure the magnitude of earthquakes, ranging from 0 (slight) to over 8 (very severe), with earthquakes from 5 upwards causing increasingly severe damage. The measuring instrument used is a *seismograph/seismometer*.

rickshaw Light two-wheeled carriage drawn by a man on foot between two shafts, used in Hong Kong and some other Asian **cities** as a form of tourist transport. See also **trishaw**.

Riel Unit of **currency** of Cambodia.

right of way A legal right of passage across the property of another, usually by a defined **footpath**. Of particular importance in **Great Britain** where there is a dense network of footpaths throughout areas used for farming, representing a major recreational resource. See also **trespass**.

ring-and-ride A term used in community transport for a scheme which enables users such as disabled and elderly people to telephone and arrange for door-to-door transport, usually by taxi or minibus.

Ringgit (RM) Unit of **currency** of Malaysia.

risk-spreading economies See **economies of scale**

Riviera The Mediterranean coastal **region** facing the Ligurian Sea and extending between the departments of Alpes-Maritimes in southern France and Liguria in northern Italy. The French Riviera is known as the Côte d'Azur and includes such well-known **resorts** as Nice, Cannes and Monte Carlo in the Principality of Monaco. The term Riviera is sometimes also applied to other important tourism areas with an attractive **climate** and scenery, usually for **marketing** purposes, e.g., Cornish Riviera in England.

Riyal Unit of **currency** of Qatar (QR), Saudi Arabia (SR) and Yemen.

roads

See **autobahn**	**freeway**
autopista	**motorway**
autoroute	**scenic route**
autostrada	**tollway**
beltway	**trunk roads**
bypass	**turnpike road**
expressway	

Rococo Elaborate, florid and light style of architecture and interior design forming the last phase of **Baroque** in Europe.

roll The side to side motion of a ship that contributes to seasickness. See also **pitch**.

rollaway bed A portable collapsible bed, which can be rolled under another, when not in use.

rolling stock Term used for passenger carriages and goods wagons of railways.

roll-on/roll-off ship A vessel operating primarily as a vehicular **ferry** on which vehicles are loaded and unloaded by means of **ramps**.

Romanesque Architectural style of the late tenth to mid thirteenth centuries in Western Europe, of which the main characteristics are round-headed arches and geometrical precision. In England, more often referred to as *Norman*. The term is also applied to the painting of the period.

room safe A small guest-operated safe provided in a **hotel** bedroom, in which guests may keep their valuables, as an alternative to a centralized **safe custody** facility provided through hotel reception.

room service Food and beverage service provided by **hotels** in guests' rooms, also called *floor service.*

room tax Tax levied by **central** or **local government** or another agency on staying **visitors**, collected at the place of stay, as a means of raising revenue; sometimes the proceeds are applied to tourism purposes. May be also called *bed tax*, *hotel tax* or *visitor tax*. See also **resort tax; tourist tax.**

room types/descriptions

See **adjoining rooms**
cabana
cabin
connecting rooms
double
double double
duplex
efficiency
en suite

family room
king room
lanai
queen room
single
studio room
suite
triple room
twin

roomette In North America a small sleeping compartment on a train with a toilet and a washbasin. See also **couchette; parlor car; Pullman; Wagon-Lits.**

rooming house US term for a house with rooms to let.

rooming list List of names of members of a group provided by the travel organizer in advance of arrival and used by the **hotel** to assign rooms.

roots tourism See **ethnic tourism**

Rouble/Rubl/Ruble (R) Unit of **currency** of Belarus and of the Russian Federation.

round-the-world ticket **Long haul** airline ticket based on the combined networks of two or more airlines. Usually available for economy, business and first class travel and valid for a year, allowing travel in one direction with **stopovers**.

round trip A synonym for a return journey. For civil aviation purposes, the **International Air Transport Association (IATA)** defines round trip as travel from point of origin to another turnaround point and return via the same air **route** used outbound, regardless of whether the outbound and inbound **fares** are identical, *or* by an air **route** different from that used outbound, for which the same normal all-year one-way fare exists. See also **open-jaw trip**.

rounding Procedure for discarding digits representing small numbers or decimals considered insignificant as, e.g., 'rounding to the nearest whole number'. When a digit to be discarded is below 5, it is customary to round down, and when it is 5 or above, to round up. However, showing numbers to fewer digits may give rise to a discrepancy when they are, e.g., added up, and this is known as *rounding error*. Hence tables may be accompanied by a note such as 'Totals may not agree with the sums of items because of rounding'.

route
(a) A way, road, course; a certain direction taken in travelling from one place to another.
(b) To travel, send or forward by a certain route as, e.g., (in aviation parlance) **AT** (via the Atlantic) or **AF** (via Africa).

Rufiyaa Unit of **currency** of Maldives (Maldivian Rupee).

runway The **airport** area used for **aircraft** take-offs and landings.

Rupee Unit of **currency** of India (Rs), Mauritius, Nepal (NR), Pakistan (Rs), Seychelles (SR), Sri Lanka.

Rupiah (Rp) Unit of **currency** of Indonesia.

rural planning See **physical planning**

rural tourism Mainly **holiday (vacation)** tourism with a focus on countryside destinations. Although not a new phenomenon, rural tourism development has been receiving much attention in recent years as a means of income and employment generation and of **diversification** of local economies. It is often identified with **farm tourism** but rural tourism is a wider concept and includes also such specific features as the development of **nature trails**, picnic sites, **interpretation centres** and agricultural and folk **museums**.

Russian service Style of **restaurant** table service, in which the food is portioned and placed on silver salvers in the kitchen, and served in the restaurant from the salvers on to the guest's plate. See also **American service; English service; family-style service; French service**.

ryokan A traditional Japanese **inn,** commonly with a garden, private **suites** or guest rooms with shared bathrooms, and meals normally served in rooms. Also spelt *Royakan*.

Sabre Global **computer reservation system (CRS)** owned by American Airlines.

safari Term originally describing a hunting expedition in Africa, nowadays also applied to **trips** to observe wildlife, highly developed in East and South Africa, sometimes referred to as *camera safari*.

safe custody Facility offered by banks to their **customers** and by **hotels** to their staying guests to deposit valuables and documents for safe keeping. See also **room safe**.

sailing card/list A list of sailings issued by a shipping **company** showing for each of its ships receiving, sailing and arrival dates at **ports** at which the ships call.

sale and lease-back An arrangement whereby a **company** sells its land and buildings to an investor and leases the same property back for an agreed term. A common means of financing **hotel** investment, the effect is to release capital tied up in the property for other purposes, as the hotel company is then normally only required to finance investment in interior assets and to pay a rent.

sales mix Term used to describe the composition of total sales, usually expressed in percentage terms. Thus, e.g., the sales mix of a **hotel** may be made up of room, food, beverage and other sales. See also **business mix**.

sales orientation See **marketing orientation**

sales promotion Generally activities designed to stimulate sales other than **advertising** and **publicity**. Common incentive sales promotions in travel, tourism and hospitality include price cutting, discount vouchers, extras, free gifts and **frequent user programmes**, as well as **point-of-sale** promotion.

sales tax A **tax** levied by governments at the **point of sale** as a proportion of the retail price of goods and **services**. It may be levied by **central governments** (as, e.g., by the Federal Government of Canada) or state or regional governments (as, e.g., in the USA and some provinces in Canada). It may apply to all sales or to particular goods and **services**. To be distinguished from **value added tax (VAT)**.

salvage In **hotels** and **restaurants**, revenue derived from the sale of such items as used cooking oil, waste paper and other waste or obsolete material, to dealers.

same-day visitor For statistical purposes, a **visitor** (either **domestic** or **international**), or *excursionist*, who does not spend the night in collective or private **accommodation** in the place visited [**World Tourism Organization**].

sampling A method of inquiry in which data are collected from a proportion of the population to provide information on the whole population, as distinct from a **census**, in which data are collected from the whole population. When each person or item has an equal chance of being chosen, the sample is known as *simple random sample*; when the population consists of various groups, a *stratified random sample* may be used, i.e., specified proportions of the sample are drawn at random from different groups or strata. Sample surveys are the main form of survey in travel and tourism.

sanatorium **Establishment** for the treatment of invalids, especially consumptives and convalescents, commonly located in high **altitudes** and other locations with health-giving properties, e.g., the Alps and along the sea coasts.

Santa Ana See **föhn**

satellite account Term developed by the **United Nations** to measure the size and structure of economic **sectors** not included in their own right in national accounts. Hence a *tourism satellite account* measures the **tourism sector**. The account runs alongside as a subset of national accounts and enables the provision of reliable estimates of the contribution of tourism to the country's economy, which can be accurately compared with other sectors.

Scandinavia The term is used variously and often erroneously to include (a) the **peninsula** shared by Norway and Sweden, (b) the three countries of Denmark, Norway and Sweden, (c) often these and also Finland, (d) sometimes also Iceland. Strictly speaking, Scandinavia consists of Denmark, Norway and Sweden, and the five countries including Finland and Iceland are correctly described as **Nordic countries**. With a combined population of more than 18 million (Scandinavia) and 24 million (Nordic countries), and a high **standard of living**, the **region** represents one of the richest **holiday (vacation) markets** in the world.

ScanRailpass Unlimited travel rail ticket available for various periods in first or standard class to non-residents of **Scandinavia** on the national railways of Denmark, Finland, Norway and Sweden and certain other services. Different prices apply to those under 12, 12–25, 26–60 and 60+ years of age. See also **rail passes**.

scenic route Generally a minor road passing through attractive countryside relatively little used by commercial traffic and hence well suited to pleasure motoring. Often identified by **local authorities** and publicized not only as a **tourist/visitor attraction** but also to attract **tourists** off major roads.

scheduled An adjective used, e.g., in transport when referring to a regular service between two points operated according to the publicized timetable (schedule), available for use by members of the public. Hence, e.g., in air transport *scheduled flight*, also *scheduled airline*, an airline operating such flights.

Scheduled Ancient Monuments Castles, fortifications, other structures and archaeological sites scheduled and protected in the **United Kingdom** in similar ways as **Listed Buildings**. In mid 2000 the inventory included over 43 000 ancient monuments (31 500 in England, 7200 in Scotland, 3300 in Wales and 1400 in Northern Ireland). See **building conservation schemes** for other schemes.

Schengen Agreement Treaty signed in Luxembourg village of that name in June 1985 by France, Germany and the three **Benelux** countries on the gradual abolition of controls at the common frontiers. It took more than 10 years for it to come into force. The Schengen **zone** covers 13 EU states including Denmark, Sweden and Finland and two non-EU countries (Norway and Iceland), which joined in March 2001, as a free travel area of 310 million people allowing crossing borders without showing **passports**. The UK and the Republic of Ireland have opted out of most of the agreement. The system also includes a **database** to combat crime and illegal immigration.

schistosomiasis See **bilharziasis**

Scottish Vocational Qualifications See **National Vocational Qualifications (NVQs)**; **General National Vocational Qualifications (GNVQs)**

scuba diving Water sport of swimming under water, using self-contained underwater breathing apparatus, called *scuba*.

sea breeze A coastal breeze blowing from sea to land, caused by the temperature difference when the land surface is warmer than the sea surface, and exercising a cooling effect.

sea cruising areas See **cruise**

sea fog A type of fog formed when air that has been lying over a warm surface is transported over a colder surface. See also **steam fog**.

sea-legs Ability to walk on **deck** while the ship is pitching and rolling without becoming seasick.

seaboard Coastline, seashore.

seaborne Conveyed by a ship on sea.

seamen's fares Reduced air **fares** to which seamen are commonly entitled when travelling to join or leave a ship.

seaplane Aircraft equipped with floats in place of undercarriage for landing on and taking off from water. See also **flying boat**.

Seaside Awards A UK scheme for **beaches** meeting the standards of the **EC Bathing Water Directive**, comprising two tiers: *Seaside Awards* given to beaches that meet the minimum or 'mandatory' standards of the **Directive** and *Premier Seaside Awards* given to beaches that meet stricter 'guideline' standards. A list of UK **Blue Flag** and Seaside Awards is available from Encams, 5 Chalk Hill House, Rosary Road, Norwich NR1 1SZ, Telephone 01603 766076.

season A division of the year normally associated with **climate** and related factors. There are four seasons of similar duration in the middle **latitudes**, but effectively two in the **tropics** (wet and dry) and in the polar **regions** (winter and summer), and three in the **monsoon** regions (cold, hot and wet); there is little differentiation of season in equatorial regions. See also **seasonal adjustment**; **seasonality**.

seasonal adjustment Process of adjusting statistical time series to remove fluctuations which show a regular seasonal pattern over the year, and which may be estimated from previous years. The adjusted series gives a clearer view of the underlying trend, although any remaining changes may also comprise cyclical movements, as well as irregular and exceptional variations. As many travel, tourism and hospitality services are subject to **seasonality**, seasonal adjustment is widely used in related monthly and quarterly statistics. See also **season**.

seasonal employee/worker One engaged for temporary employment at times of peak activity in the high **season**. May be **full-time** or **part-time**, depending on the hours worked. Payment of wages depends on agreement between employer and employee and commonly takes place weekly; if at less than weekly intervals and, particularly if daily, such an employee may be described as a **casual** seasonal **employee**.

seasonality Variation according to the time or **seasons** of the year, which tends to exhibit a similar pattern from year to year, and affect activities such as agriculture, construction, tourism and related employment. When associated with climatic and related factors, this is sometimes described as *natural seasonality*, to differentiate it from *institutional seasonality*, such as that reflected in the calendar of the churches and such events as **pilgrimages**. An important aspect of institutional seasonality is patterns of **holiday (vacation)** taking, in part dictated by school holidays and considerably reducing the period when climatic conditions are favourable. See also **seasonal adjustment**.

seat kilometre A measure of transport capacity denoting a passenger seat carried over a distance of one **kilometre**.

seat mile A measure of transport capacity denoting a passenger seat carried over a distance of one **mile**.

seat pitch The distance between the front edge of an **aircraft** seat and the front edge of the seat behind when both seats are in the upright position.

seat rotation An arrangement whereby **coach tour** passengers change seats in order to have an equal opportunity of viewing from the best seats.

Seat Sale Special return air **fare** offered by airlines on European **scheduled** flights for travel during periods of low demand, subject to various restrictions, for a maximum stay of one month. Cannot be changed or cancelled.

seat turnover A measure of utilization of a **catering establishment** capacity, showing the number of times each seat is used by **customers** over a period of time. Thus, e.g., when in a **restaurant** seating 100 customers, 250 are served in a day, the daily seat turnover is 2.5.

seaworthiness See **certificate of seaworthiness**

Second freedom See **freedoms of the air**

second home A house, apartment or another building used for **holidays (vacations)** and other temporary stays by owners whose main residence is normally elsewhere. Also known as *holiday/summer/vacation home*. Second homes are also frequently used by owners' friends and relatives and let by owners to others. Second home ownership is highly developed in North America, several parts of Eastern and Western Europe, including France and **Scandinavia** and, if static **caravans** are included, also in **Great Britain**. See also **condominium**; **timesharing**.

Second World Collective term formerly used for the countries of Eastern Europe and the USSR with centrally **planned economies**, as distinct from countries of Western Europe, North America, **Australasia**, and Japan with **market economies**. See also **First World**.

secondary data Existing information which may be drawn upon for a particular purpose, e.g., published official statistics, as distinct from **primary data**.

secondary impacts See **tourism expenditure impacts**

secondary industries See **services**

sector
(a) Part of the economy as, e.g., **private sector**, **public sector**, **tourism sector**, generally comprising a number of **industries**.
(b) A portion of a journey by air, which may consist of one or more legs or segments. A *leg* is a portion of a journey between two consecutive **scheduled** stops on a particular flight. A *segment* is the portion of a journey on a particular flight from the passenger's boarding point to the disembarkation point; a segment may consist of one or more legs.

security check A **baggage** or body check carried out commonly at **airports** by professional security staff using security checking equipment.

security surcharge See **surcharge**

security tax Tax levied by many governments and **airport** authorities at airports to help defray additional security costs in recent years. The term is also sometimes used for a **security surcharge** levied by airlines to compensate for increased security measures as, e.g., by some US airlines on transatlantic flights.

segment See **sector**; **segmentation**

segmentation In **marketing**, the process of dividing the total **market** into more or less homogeneous groups (*segments*), each of which shares certain characteristics and product preferences and may be expected to behave similarly. The purpose of segmentation is to facilitate cost-effective marketing by focusing on the needs of identified target groups. Typical breakdowns are based on age, sex, income, status and other demographic and socio-economic criteria; all of these are used in segmenting travel, tourism and hospitality markets, together with **psychographic** criteria.

seismograph/seismometer An instrument for measuring the force of earthquakes. See also **Richter scale**.

self-actualization Term used in explaining needs and **motivations**, to describe the highest level in a hierarchy of needs postulated by psychologist Abraham Maslow (after physiological, safety, belonging and love, and esteem needs have been satisfied). Travel and tourism motivations are sometimes explained in terms of this hierarchy: self-actualization represents personal self-fulfilment and particular types of **holidays (vacations)** are seen as contributing to it by offering an opportunity for personal exploration, evaluation and self-discovery. See also **Maslow's needs theory**.

self-catering accommodation Overnight **accommodation** provided without meals in many holiday centres, rented rooms, houses, apartments, and similar **establishments**, where cooking and other facilities are provided for guests' use. Large self-catering complexes often provide retail outlets for provisions, as well as **restaurants** as optional facilities. See also **serviced accommodation**; **supplementary tourist accommodation**.

self-employed One employed in his/her main job on his/her own account, with or without any employees. A large part of employment in travel, tourism and hospitality is in small businesses and includes many self-employed; although there has been a growth in the concentration of ownership and in the scale of operation, small businesses and the self-employed continue to be prominent. See also **sole trader**; **partnership**.

self-service Form of selling, in which the

customer serves herself/himself, common in retailing and **catering**. In catering a **restaurant** sometimes operates on a *semi-self-catering* basis when, e.g., starters and hot beverages are served by waiting staff, and the main course and dessert are selected by **customers** from the servery.

sellers' market A **market** for goods and **services** in which prices are rising, usually as a consequence of a shortfall in supply compared with demand. See also **buyers' market**.

semi-display advertisements See **display advertisements**

semiotics Also known as *semiology*, the study of signs or the way objects, words or pictures convey concepts or **images**. Of particular significance in **advertising**, semiotics has a contribution to make in the promotion of **tourist products** and **tourism destinations**.

senior citizen Term used to describe the population group of the retired who represent a growing **market** of increasing importance in travel, tourism and hospitality in **developed countries**, as people tend to live longer and retire earlier. Originally interpreted as comprising those above the normal retiring age, it has become more meaningful for both product development and **marketing** purposes to include those over 60, or even 55, and to differentiate between sub-groups (e.g., 55–64, 65–74, 75 and over), which tend to share common attitudes to travel and display similar **holiday (vacation)** patterns. See also **Third Age**.

Senior Railcard See **British railcards**

series charter See **charter**

series tour An **inclusive tour (IT)** that is one of a series of departures for the same tour.

service charge A percentage (usually between 10 and 15 per cent) added to **hotel** and **restaurant** bills as a **gratuity** in lieu of direct tipping. *Service compris*, a French term, indicates that the gratuity is included with the price of the room or meal. See also **tip**; **tronc**.

serviced accommodation Overnight **accommodation** usually provided by **hotels and**

similar establishments with meals and service, and often also by holiday centres and others. See also **self-catering accommodation**.

services The output of economic activities resulting in intangible products (as distinct from physical goods), such as **accommodation**, transport and communications, financial services, as well as education, health and various personal services. Hence, *service industries*, also described as *tertiary industries*, as distinct from *primary* (agriculture and extractive) and *secondary* (manufacturing and construction). By their nature travel, tourism and hospitality products are largely made up of services and supplied by the service industries. As an example of their significance, UK service industries contribute about 65 per cent of **gross domestic product (GDP)** and over 70 per cent of employment. See also **invisibles**.

Seven Seas The **Arctic**, **Antarctic**, North and South Atlantic, North and South Pacific and Indian Oceans.

Seven Wonders of the World

1 The Pyramids of Egypt (at Giza near Cairo).
2 The Hanging Gardens of Babylon (south of Baghdad).
3 The Tomb of Mausolus (at Halicarnassus in Asia Minor).
4 The Temple of Artemis (at Ephesus in Asia Minor).
5 The Colossus of Rhodes (according to legend, bestriding the harbour).
6 The Statue of Zeus (at Olympia, Greece).
7 The Pharos of Alexandria (a lighthouse on the island of Pharos).

Seventh freedom In civil aviation a right (not specified in the **Chicago Convention**) to operate stand-alone services entirely outside the territory of the airline's home country, to carry traffic between two foreign countries. A US airline had such rights for many years to operate a shuttle service between Tokyo and Seoul. The incidence is increasing in Europe under **European Union** liberalization measures; one of the first Seventh freedom rights has been taken up by the Belgian airline Sabena to fly between Barcelona and Venice.

sex tourism Trips and visits primarily motivated by the prospect of sexual encounters, a significant activity in a number of **developing countries**, especially in South-East Asia.

shared commission Commission received from **principals** and shared by non-appointed **travel agents** who obtain tickets from appointed agents. Also called *split commission.*

Shekel/Shequel Unit of **currency** of Israel (now New Shekel/Shequel).

Shilling Unit of **currency** of Kenya (Ks), Somalia (So.sh), Tanzania and Uganda.

Shinto(ism) Japanese religion based on reverence for natural spirits and the spirits of ancestors.

ship density See **passenger space ratio (PSR)**

shopping products Products bought relatively infrequently and at a high price; most **consumer** capital goods are in this category but also, e.g., **holidays (vacations)**. See also **convenience products**.

shore excursion A tour provided for cruise passengers at a **scheduled** stop on a **cruise**, usually by **bus** or **coach**, normally optional and therefore paid for separately.

short breaks See **short holiday (vacation)**

short haul See **long haul/short haul travel/ tourism**

short holiday (vacation) A term variously defined for particular purposes, e.g., in most **national holiday (vacation)/travel/tourism surveys** in Europe as **holiday (vacation)** of one to three nights/two to four days away from home. Also sometimes described as *short breaks*. In recent years short holidays represented over a half of all holidays of UK residents in the UK [**United Kingdom Tourism Survey**].

short take-off and landing (STOL) See **aircraft types: take-off and landing**

short ton See **ton (tonne)**

shoulder periods Times of year between peak and low **seasons**, often identified as such by providers of **tourist/visitor attractions**, facilities and services and reflected in prices, which are lower than in the peak and higher than in the low season.

shuttle Frequent transport service between two points on high density **routes** for which no reservations are required. Airlines operating shuttle services normally offer late **check-in times** close to flight departure, and some also a back-up service if a particular flight is full as, e.g., British Airways between London and several UK **cities**. See also **Eurotunnel**.

siesta Rest taken in the middle of the day and/or early afternoon in the Mediterranean and some other hot countries when shops and offices may be closed.

sightseeing One of the most popular forms of passive **recreation** in **developed countries** and an important **holiday (vacation)** activity on foot, by car, in **coach** tours, **cruises**, excursions from holiday bases, and travel in small groups or alone using a variety of transport. The attractions may be attractive countryside, spectacular scenery, archaeological sites and historical monuments, wildlife and way of life of other people. **Tourists** are increasingly adventurous in how far they travel to see unusual features, such as **Antarctica**, Galapagos Islands or the **Silk Road**.

Sikhism A religious movement originally established as a sect in the Punjab, India, in the early part of the sixteenth century, based on doctrines produced by a line of gurus, opposed to the traditional caste structure of **Hinduism**, placing emphasis on communal equality, and rejecting mysticism and asceticism as necessary for salvation.

Silk Road Name given to a number of historic trade **routes** from East China to central Asia but now a tourist **route** by train and **bus** from Xian, through Langzhou and Urumchi, to Almaty (Alma Ata) or Tashkent.

single Adjective used, i.a., with such nouns as *bed* (standard approx. 36 × 75 in. or 90 × 188 cm), *room* (to accommodate one person), *occupancy* (by one person), *rate* (charged for one person occupying a room). See also **double**; **twin**.

Single European Market Defined by the Single European Act 1987 as 'an area without internal frontiers in which free movement of goods, persons, **services** and capital is ensured in accordance with the provisions of the **Treaty [of Rome]'**. The Act included some 300 measures for removing barriers. Those of particular significance for travel, tourism and hospitality were concerned, i.a., with frontier controls, harmonization of **VAT** rates and **deregulation** of air and **coach** travel.

single supplement Additional payment by a guest for **single occupancy** of a **hotel** room, usually on an organized tour for which charges are specified on the basis of sharing a room. See also **double occupancy**.

sirocco/scirrocco Hot south or southeasterly wind which blows from the Sahara over North Africa and the Mediterranean to Malta, Sicily and Italy.

sister ship Ship of the same design belonging to the same **company** as another ship.

site attractions See **tourist/visitor attractions**

Site(s) of Special Scientific Interest (SSSI) More than 6700 areas in the UK (2000) designated as having some outstanding natural feature worthy of protection, such as rare animals, birds, plants or geology, by **English Nature**, Scottish Natural Heritage, Countryside Council for Wales and Department of the Environment for Northern Ireland, and managed by owners under various arrangements with the **conservation** agencies. See **countryside conservation designation schemes** for other schemes.

situational analysis Examination of the internal strengths and weaknesses and of external opportunities and threats affecting an organization. Also known as **SWOT** analysis.

Sixth freedom In civil aviation, term sometimes used although not specified in the **Chicago Convention**, to describe the combination of Third and Fourth **freedoms of the air** services, so as to provide a service between two foreign countries via the country in which the airline is registered. Thus, e.g., a German airline may carry traffic between London and Athens by operating a service from London to Frankfurt and thence from Frankfurt to Athens, either by the connection of two separate services or by a **through** service.

skiing Movement over snow on skis (for **water skiing** see below). *Cross-country* (*Langlauf*) skiing is more a recreational pursuit on level ground, whether on tracks in forests and across cultivated land or on plateau surfaces in the uplands, particularly common in **Scandinavia** and Canada. *Downhill* skiing, using longer skis, requires steep slopes, good and reliable snow cover (although snow making machines can be used), and uplift facilities, in the form of ski tows, chairlifts and gondolas, hence a major public and private capital investment; the Alps are the main area in Europe and the Rockies in North America. Skiing has the advantage of being a winter activity and so complements summer **recreations**, when most people take their **holidays (vacations)** using common **accommodation** and other facilities as well as easy access to high areas.

Skyteam Global **airline alliance** of (June 2001) AeroMexico, Air France, CSA Czech Airlines, Delta Airlines, Korean Airlines, formed June 2000.

sleeper seat/sleeperette A reclining transport seat usually provided in the first class **cabin** on **long haul** flights, designed to be adjustable to a sleeping position. Also called *dormette*.

slip American term for ship or boat **berth**.

slot Set time assigned to a flight for take-off and landing at an **airport**. At busy airports availability of slots is a major constraint on **airport capacity**.

smörgåsbord Scandinavian buffet of **hors-d'oeuvres**.

smuggling Illegal import or export of goods through both official and other cross-border points, much through the former accounted for by **tourists**.

snack bar Establishment providing simple food and non-alcoholic refreshments to the general public for consumption on the premises where **customers** commonly sit or stand at a counter.

snorkelling Water sport of swimming with a snorkel, a tube which enables the swimmer to breathe in air while observing underwater fauna and flora.

snowbird Term used for people who live in cold winter **climates** and go to warmer climates to escape the cold weather, e.g., **residents** of northern **latitudes** in North America going to Florida or in Europe to the Mediterranean.

snowline The lowest level of permanent snow cover in **mountain** areas, varying with location, orientation, **climate** and **topography**. However, in the northern **hemisphere** much of the lower ground is also snow-covered in winter, providing opportunities for a variety of snow-based **recreations**.

snowmobiling Movement over snow, mainly in the lowlands, on a motorized sledge, capable of travelling at speed. Also used as a more general form of transport in winter and in permanently snow-covered areas. Characteristic of both tourism areas and the more settled areas, and often a source of conflict with other forms of **recreation** and with **residents** because of noise **pollution** and adverse effects on other forms of traffic. In addition to the use of paths and tracks, travel by snowmobile occurs over snow-covered farm land, where accidents have occurred because of unseen fences.

Social Chapter See **Social Charter**

Social Charter Short name for *Charter on the Fundamental Social Rights of Workers* proposed by the **European Commission**, covering freedom of movement, fair remuneration, improvement of working conditions, the right to social security, freedom of association and collective wage agreements, the development of participation by workers in management, and sexual equality. The Charter was approved by heads of government of all Community members except the UK in December 1989. On the insistence of the UK, the chapter on social affairs was omitted from the **Treaty on European Union** negotiated in December 1991 and formed a separate protocol until 1999 when it was integrated into the Treaty following its adoption by the UK.

social cost The cost of an economic activity to society. Whereas *private costs* are borne directly

or indirectly by the owner, operator or user, e.g., the cost of petrol and the wear and tear on the car by the car owner, the social cost of car use, e.g., the wear and tear on the roads, is not paid by the car owner, unless it is incorporated by taxation into private costs.

social director/officer See **animator**

social tourism Tourism participation of people of limited means and those disadvantaged through age, disability or family circumstances, encouraged and made possible by special measures. These include in practice **subsidies**, particular facilities and other measures, sometimes of a cooperative nature, sometimes by the state or another third party. Social tourism is highly developed in Belgium, France and Eastern European countries in particular.

socio-economic groups Groups or **classes** comprising people with important characteristics in common, to which they are principally allocated according to their **occupation** and employment status. The approach provides one of the main bases for **consumer segmentation** in many **markets**, including travel, tourism and hospitality. The most common systems in the UK are those used by the Registrar General in the analysis of **Census of Population** data and in the **National Readership Survey**.

Socrates European Union programme established to contribute to the development of quality education and encouragement of lifelong learning. Specific objectives are strengthening the European dimension of education at all levels; improving knowledge of European languages; promoting cooperation and mobility in all areas of education; encouraging innovation in education. The programme is open to 31 countries (15 **EU**, 3 **EFTA/EEA**, 13 EU candidate countries). Separate action strands within Socrates include **Comenius**, **Erasmus**, **Grundtvig**, **Lingua**, **Minerva**.

sofa bed Couch with back and arms, serving as a sofa by day and as a bed by night. See also **studio bed**.

soft class Term used in some parts of Asia for comfortable more expensive seating on trains, in contrast to *hard class* to refer to the cheapest and most basic category.

soft currency A **currency** with a falling **rate of exchange**, usually because of long-term **balance of payments** problems, and hence not attractive to be held by countries in their **foreign exchange** reserves. See also **hard currency**.

soft loan A concessional loan bearing no interest or an interest rate below the **market** rate. Such loans are made, e.g., to **developing countries** by the **World Bank Group** through the **International Development Association (IDA)** and by regional development banks.

soft tourism See **alternative tourism**

Sol Unit of **currency** of Peru (now Nuevo Sol).

solar power Energy from sunshine converted to make electricity and to provide water and space heating, a growing source for domestic and institutional (e.g., **hotel**) use in appropriate **climates**.

sole agent See **General Sales Agent (GSA)**

sole proprietorship See **sole trader**

sole trader Individual ownership of business by a person who trades on his or her own account, with or without employees. In this common form of ownership of many small businesses there is no separation in law between the business and its owner who is personally responsible for all debts of the business to the full extent of his or her personal possessions. See also **company; partnership**.

solstice Time when sun is furthest from the **equator**, in northern **hemisphere** about 21 June (summer solstice, longest day) and about 22 December (winter solstice, shortest day). See also **equinox**.

Som Unit of **currency** of Kyrgyzstan.

sommelier French term for wine waiter in charge of wine service in a **restaurant**.

Somoni Unit of **currency** of Tajikistan.

Son et Lumière Performance combining sound and lighting effects to enhance and interpret mainly **heritage** sites. Outstanding examples are multi-lingual presentations in such locations as the Acropolis in Athens, the Forum in Rome and the Giza Pyramids in Egypt.

sound A narrow channel between two islands or an island and the mainland. See also **kyle**.

sourcing Selection by a **firm** of its sources of supply. See also **outsourcing**.

Southerner Express New Zealand rail service between Christchurch and Invercargill via Dunedin in the South Island.

spa A **resort** with mineral or thermal water used for drinking and bathing; in American parlance, any resort providing health-care facilities and services. The term derives from the name of a town in Belgium and has been applied to resorts worldwide, as well as being incorporated in many of their names, especially in Europe. The revival and growth in popularity of spas from the end of the sixteenth century onwards, and their transformation into fashionable pleasure resorts subsequently, represents together with the **Grand Tour** and the emergence and growth of coastal resorts, the beginnings of tourism as we know it today.

space travel/tourism Trips and visits to outer space, the first having been undertaken by a paying American in a Russian capsule to a space station in 2001.

Special Group Inclusive Tour fare (SGIT) European **inclusive tour (IT) fare**, in the UK available to **tour operators** holding the **Air Travel Organiser's Licence (ATOL)**, which may be used for groups of not less than ten passengers.

special interest holidays (vacations) A generic term for **holidays (vacations)** for people with particular interests, such as arts, education, various hobbies, sports and outdoor activities. These are some of the fastest-growing **segments** of tourism, with many specialist providers. See also **activity holidays (vacations)**.

Special Protected Areas Countryside areas in England designated by government for special protection against development where the **management** authorities have powers and responsibilities similar to those of the **National Park** authorities. To be distinguished from **Special Protection Areas**. See **countryside conservation designation schemes** for other schemes.

Special Protection Areas Conservation areas designated for the protection of rare bird species listed by the **European Community Directive** on wild bird conservation. There were more than 200 such sites in the UK by 2000. To be distinguished from **Special Protected Areas**. See **countryside conservation designation schemes** for other schemes.

speciality restaurant Restaurant which specializes in particular food, e.g., pasta, seafood or steaks, or in national foods, such as Chinese, Indian or Mexican.

Spice Island Term used for Zanzibar, off the east coast of Tanzania.

split charter See **charter**

split commission See **shared commission**

split payment Payment made by different forms, e.g., part in cash and part by **cheque (check)** or by different **credit cards**.

split shift A term used in **hotels** and **restaurants**, but also in other employment, for a work pattern of two working periods separated by a long interval between them (i.e., longer than a normal rest or meal time), e.g., 11 a.m. to 3 p.m. and 6–10 p.m. See also **spreadover of hours**.

sponsored event A sporting, cultural or other event, the costs of which are covered in full or in part by a **firm** as part of its **public relations** to promote the name and image of the organization or its products. Sponsorship of major events of national or international significance is understandably undertaken by large organizations but the same approach is often used by small firms to local events.

sports tourism Trips and visits motivated by participation in sport or by spectator attendance at sporting events.

spouse fare/rate See **companion fare/rate**

spouse programme An **accompanying** persons'** programme of **sightseeing** or other events during a **conference**.

spreadover of hours A term used in **hotels** and **restaurants**, but also in other employment, for the total number of hours over which work extends in a day. E.g., in a **split shift** 11 a.m. to 3 p.m. and 6–10 p.m. there are 8 working hours and the spreadover is 11 hours.

Stabilizer An exclusive dealing arrangement introduced in 1965 by the **Association of British Travel Agents (ABTA)** whereby **tour operators** would sell their tours only through ABTA **travel agents** and ABTA travel agents would not sell tours of non-ABTA tour operators. Following a challenge by the Office of Fair Trading, Stabilizer was upheld by the Restrictive Practices Court in 1982 as operating in the public interest. However, by 1993 the need for its continuation became increasingly doubtful as a result of the **EC Package Travel Directive**, the implementation of which made the protection afforded by Stabilizer superfluous, and its demise followed.

stabilizers Retractable fins extending from the sides of a ship below the waterline to reduce rolling.

stages of economic growth A theory of economic development formulated by American economic historian Walt Whitman Rostow, who proposed that societies passed through five stages: (a) the traditional society; (b) pre-conditions for take-off; (c) take-off; (d) the drive to maturity; (e) maturity/the stage of high mass consumption. The **model** was based on what has occurred in **developed countries**. It is less likely to predict what might happen in currently **developing countries**, many less dependent on technology for economic growth, particularly those with successful **tourism industries**.

stakeholders Those with an interest in an organization, such as employees, shareholders, suppliers or **customers**.

stalactites/stalagmites Complementary features of caves in limestone areas, caused by the evaporation of water containing calcium bicarbonate which is deposited as calcium carbonate. *Stalactites* begin at the roof of the cave and grow downwards as a slender pointed feature; *stalagmites* grow upwards from the floor and are much broader and dumpier. Eventually they may join to form a column. Caves containing these features have been developed as **tourist/visitor attractions** in many such areas because of the shapes they take, which may be accentuated by artificial lighting. See also **caving**.

Standard Industrial Classification (SIC) An official categorization of economic activities, in which activities of a similar nature are grouped into **industries**, providing a framework for the collection, presentation and analysis of data, with a view to promoting uniformity and comparability of statistics. Such classifications are produced by UK, US and other governments; there is also *General Industrial Classification of Economic Activities within the European Communities (NACE)* and the United Nations' *International Standard Industrial Classification of All Economic Activities (ISIC)*. These are to be distinguished from national and international classifications of **occupations**, which relate to jobs rather than to the industries in which they are performed.

Standard International Classification of Tourism Activities (SICTA) A supply-based structure of tourism activities developed by the **World Tourism Organization (WTO)** and adopted as a provisional classification by the **United Nations** Statistical Commission in March 1993. SICTA was published jointly by the UN Statistical Commission and the WTO in the full report on *Recommendations on Tourism Statistics* in 1994.

Standard Occupational Classification (SOC) An official categorization of **occupations**, which relates to the work performed by individuals rather than to the **industries** in which it is performed, as is the case with the **Standard Industrial Classification (SIC)**. Thus workers classified to a particular industry fall into a number of different categories of an occupational classification and the workers in some occupations may be found in a number of different industries. *Standard Occupational Classification* (London, The Stationery Office, 2000) is an example of a national classification; the **International Labour Organisation (ILO)** published *The International Standard Classification of Occupations* (Geneva, ILO, 1993).

standard of living Standard of material well-being commonly measured by national income per head of population (**gross domestic product** or **gross national product per capita**). Other indicators include household ownership of consumer durables (e.g., motor cars, refrigerators, TV sets) and social indicators (e.g., food consumption, life expectancy, literacy). The standard of living is generally considered to be the most important single determinant of **holiday (vacation) propensity**. See also **developed countries**; **developing countries**.

standard time Local time in any of the 24 **time zones** in the world, the time in each being generally one hour different from the next. The standard time at zero **meridian** is **Greenwich Mean/Standard Time (GMT/GST)**. The standard times of places in the western **hemisphere** are designated with a minus number, as so many hours behind GMT/GST (e.g., New York is GMT –5), and in the eastern hemisphere with a plus number, as so many hours ahead of GMT/GST (e.g., Singapore is GMT +8). See also **daylight saving time**; **International Date Line**.

standby In travel and tourism, most commonly used in relation to a would-be passenger without a reservation taking a chance and waiting for a seat to become available; hence *standby passenger*, also *standby fare*, a reduced fare available for standby passengers on some **routes**. See also **go-show**; **waiting list/waitlist**.

Star Alliance Global **airline alliance** of (June 2001) Air Canada, Air New Zealand (including Ansett Australia), All Nippon Airways, Austrian Airlines (including Tyrolean and Lauda Air), bmi british midland, Lufthansa, Mexicana Airlines, SAS, Singapore Airlines, Thai Airways, United Airlines, Varig, formed May 1997.

starboard Right side of ship or **aircraft** when facing forward, with green navigation lights on the bridge or wings. See also **port**.

state codes See **country/state codes**

statute mile See **mile**

steam fog A type of fog formed when cold air

moves over relatively warm water or wet ground. See also **sea fog**.

steerage Term used to describe the part of a ship allotted to passengers travelling at the cheapest rate.

Sterling Of the several meanings of the word, probably most significant is its use to describe the **currency** of the **United Kingdom**, either on its own or as an epithet, as in **Pound Sterling**, to distinguish the UK currency from others, particularly other pound units.

stern Nautical term for back of ship or boat, also called **aft** or **abaft**, opposite end to **bow** or **forward**. See also **(a)midship(s)**; **astern**.

stopover Generally a **scheduled** break in a journey agreed in advance by the **carrier**. What constitutes a stopover for particular purposes may be officially defined, as, e.g., in air transport by the **International Air Transport Association (IATA)**. Also called **layover**.

strait(s) A narrow passage of water connecting two larger areas of water, such as the Straits of Gibraltar, linking the Mediterranean Sea and the Atlantic Ocean.

strategy Plan for reaching certain goals and objectives, commonly quantified and relatively long-term. Hence, *marketing strategy*, the plan identifying products, segments and actions required to achieve targets and to deliver **customer** satisfaction.

strath Scottish term for a wide valley or low-lying flat land bounded by hills or high ground, usually traversed by a river and cultivated. Hence, e.g., Strathspey, the place name for the strath of the river Spey. See also **glen**.

stratified sample See **sampling**

structure plans See **land use planning systems (UK)**

studio bed A bed approx. 36 × 75 in. (90 × 188 cm) without a headboard or footboard, serving as a sofa during the day. See also **sofa bed**.

studio room A **hotel** room with a **studio bed**.

Sub-Saharan Africa An area south of the Sahara, for some purposes excluding Namibia and the Republic of South Africa, with a landmass of more than 7 million square miles and more than 500 million population. Although endowed with significant tourism attractions, of the 46 countries only South Africa and Zimbabwe reached more than one million annual arrivals in the 1990s. Many countries in the **region** view tourism as a promising development tool but political instability, lack of resources and negative image are among the major impediments to growth.

subscribed circulation See **circulation**

subsidiary company A **company** which is controlled by another. See also **conglomerate**; **holding company**; **parent company**.

subsidy Direct or indirect financial support of a product, **establishment**, **firm** or **industry**, which may occur internally within a firm or from a government or other agency. *Cross-subsidy* refers to a shortfall of revenue compared with costs of a product or establishment being made good by an excess in respect of another product or establishment. There are frequent occurrences in travel, tourism and hospitality when, e.g., particular **services** or establishments are subsidized by others, and also when governments provide the subsidy.

subsonic transport See **aircraft types: speed**

subway
(a) In the **British Isles**, an underground passage, which enables pedestrians to pass below a road or railway.
(b) In North America, an underground railway.

suite Set of **connecting rooms** consisting of one or more bedrooms, bathrooms and living rooms and sometimes also additional rooms such as a dining room. Also used to describe a very large room with separate living and sleeping areas, called *junior suite*.

Sum Unit of **currency** of Uzbekistan.

summer home See **second home**

sunbake Australian expression for sunbathing, nowadays a less fashionable activity because of the relatively high incidence of skin cancer in Australia, a problem exacerbated by the intensity of the Australian sun, the prevalence of **beaches** and the paleness of skin of many Australians of European descent. Commonwealth and state governments have undertaken expensive promotional **campaigns** to encourage holiday makers to 'slip, slop, slap' (slip on a shirt, slop on the sunscreen and slap on a hat).

sunlust A **motivation** to pleasure travel described by economist H.P. Gray as generating tourism which depends on the existence elsewhere of better amenities for a specific purpose than are available at home. Much sunlust motivation may be satisfied in the country of residence without going abroad, except where that country is small or at a disadvantage climatically or in other ways. Sunlust travel normally calls for facilities for longer stay and for **recreation** and much of it is equated with **resort holidays (vacations)**. See also **wanderlust**.

sunrise/sunset The times at which the sun apparently rises in the morning above and sets in the evening below the horizon, which varies with **latitude** and with the time of year. In **meteorology**, sunrise is defined as the time at which the upper edge of the sun appears above the apparent horizon on a clear day, and sunset as the time at which the upper edge of the sun appears to sink below the apparent horizon on a clear day.

supersonic transport See **aircraft types: speed**

superstructure Physical facilities and services specific to particular types of development as, e.g., farms to agriculture, factories to manufacturing, **hotels** and other short-term **accommodation** to tourism and hospitality. (Particular facilities and services provided for the use of **tourists** are sometimes also referred to as tourism infrastructure, but see under **infrastructure** for the accepted meaning of that term.)

supper A late night meal or the evening meal when the midday meal is designated as dinner. See also **high tea**.

supplement Additional charge, also called **add-on**, e.g., single room supplement (an extra

charge for a person to have a room to himself/herself when charges are for two people sharing a room). See also **surcharge**.

supplementary tourist accommodation Term used by tourism organizations normally to include youth **hostels**, holiday centres and villages, rented rooms, houses and flats, **camping sites**. However, the exact meaning tends to differ between countries, and essentially reflects the designations given to **accommodation establishments** in each country. See also **hotels and similar establishments**.

surcharge Supplementary charge added to the air **fare** by the airline, **inclusive tour** price by the **tour operator,** or another travel purchase by the operator, usually to compensate for increases in costs between the time of booking and the time of travel. For example, a *currency surcharge* is levied to compensate for fluctuations in **exchange rates**, a *fuel surcharge* for increases in the cost of aviation fuel, a *security surcharge* for increased cost of security measures.

surfing Water sport of riding on breaking waves on a special board, also called *surf-riding*, particularly popular in Australia, Hawaii and on the Pacific coast of the USA.

Survey of Visits to Tourist Attractions Annual large-scale sample survey carried out by the **Department for Culture, Media and Sport**, sponsored by **British Tourist Authority** and **National Tourist Boards**, on number of visits, admission charges, revenue, employment and expenditure since 1976. Results are published in *Digest of Tourist Statistics* and in *Sightseeing in the UK*.

sustainable tourism Emerging from concepts of sustainable development, as defined in the 1987 report of the **United Nations** World Commission on Environment and Development, *Our Common Future* (the Brundtland Report), the term may be applied to all forms of tourism that are in harmony with their physical, social and cultural **environments** in the long term. Not confined to small-scale, as **alternative tourism**, sustainable tourism development may be viewed in terms of the Brundtland Report as development that meets the needs of the present without compromising the activity of the future generations to meet their own needs. The **World Tourism Organization (WTO)** defines sustainable tourism as a model form of economic development that is designed to: improve the quality of life of the host community, provide a high quality of experience for the **visitor**, and maintain the quality of the **environment**, on which both the host community and the visitor depend.

switch selling The practice of attracting **customers** by offer of low-priced, non-existent or non-available goods or **services**, in order to bring about a sale of an alternative. Called *bait and switch* in America, the practice is outlawed by legislation and/or a **code of conduct** in many countries.

SWOT An **acronym** for Strengths, Weaknesses, Opportunities and Threats, used as a framework for analysing information about an organization as part of developing its **marketing** strategy and tactics. Strengths and weaknesses include respectively present and future advantages and disadvantages of the organization *vis-à-vis* its competitors. Opportunities and threats are those identifiable in the present and future operating **environment** of the organization. The same framework may be used for analysing a project, site or area as part of an appraisal of its tourism potential. See also **situational analysis**.

syndicated survey Survey commissioned by or on behalf of a group of **clients** on a cost-sharing basis, in which all or some of the results are supplied to different clients, and in which individual clients may commonly include their own questions. This is significantly less expensive for the participants than each carrying out their own survey, and a cost effective approach especially for smaller businesses. **British National Travel Survey (BNTS)** is a major example of a syndicated survey in tourism.

synergy Term describing working together/cooperating when the combined action makes up a whole greater than the sum of the separate parts. See, e.g., **consortium**.

System One US **computer reservation systems (CRS)** owned by Texas Air (Eastern and Continental Airlines) as a **joint venture** with General Motors' Electronic Data Services.

table d'hôte menu A limited choice menu with a single price for any combination of items chosen or with a price determined by the choice of the main dish. See also **à la carte menu**.

table service
See **American service**
 English service
 family-style service
 French service
 Russian service

table tent Printed and folded card (also called *tent card*) placed on **restaurant** tables, bar counters and reception desks in **hotels** as internal **merchandising** to promote particular food and drink items and house services.

table wine Wine fermented to approx. 12–14 per cent alcohol and considered suitable for drinking with meals.

tachograph An instrument for recording the distance travelled and the speed of a **bus**, **coach** or truck.

TACIS *Technical Assistance to the Commonwealth of Independent States*, a programme of technical assistance of the **European Union** to help the countries of the **Commonwealth of Independent States (CIS)** build stable **market** economies.

tactics Methods and approaches employed in executing a **strategy**, usually relatively short-term. Hence, *tactical marketing*, which involves managing the **marketing mix**.

tail wind Wind blowing from behind a ship or **aircraft** and increasing its speed. See also **head wind**.

Taka (Tk) Unit of **currency** of Bangladesh.

Tala Unit of **currency** of Samoa.

Taoism Religious doctrine and philosophy of Lao-tsze, Chinese philosopher (c. 500 BC).

tapas Spanish term for small plates of snacks, such as fish, cheese and olives, usually served with beer or wine. Hence *tapas bar* which specializes in serving tapas.

target marketing Focusing the **marketing** effort on a clearly defined group or groups of potential **customers** chosen for specific marketing attention (target **market**), which is generally identified by **segmentation**. Also known as *niche marketing*. Target markets in travel, tourism and hospitality are commonly defined by reference to demographic, socio-economic and psychographic criteria.

tarmac See **macadam**

tarn A small lake among **mountains**, fed by rainwater from the surrounding steep slopes rather than by a distinct tributary.

tavern Term of mediaeval origin for an **inn** or **public house** serving food and drink.

tax(es)
See **Air Passenger Duty**
 airport maintenance tax
 bed tax
 departure tax
 entry tax
 exit tax
 hotel tax
 Passenger Movement
   Charge

resort tax
room tax
sales tax
security tax
tourist tax
value added tax
   (VAT)
visitor tax

technical economies See **economies of scale**

technical rights In civil aviation, the First and Second **freedoms of the air** as distinct from **traffic rights**. See also **Bermuda Agreement**; **Chicago Convention**.

teleconferencing Meeting in which three or more participants in different locations communicate with each other through telecommunications. In *audioconferencing*, as by telephone, they hear each other; *videoconferencing* provides a combined audio and visual link through a satellite or other network and they can both hear and see each other. The system enables people to hold meetings without the time and expense of travelling.

telemarketing/telephone marketing Any **marketing** activity in which the telephone is used to contact people and to seek information (*telephone marketing research*) or to solicit orders (*telephone selling*).

telephone marketing research See telemarketing/telephone marketing

telephone selling See **telemarketing/telephone marketing**

teletex An information transmission system similar to but faster than **telex**, which allows, i.a., for direct connection between word processors. To be distinguished from **teletext**.

teletext See **videotext**

teleworking People working from home using **information technology**, a growing practice in **developed countries**. E.g., in the 1990s more than 10 per cent of employers in **Great Britain** employed workers based at home and more were planning to do so.

telex Automated transmission system for sending printed messages nationally and internationally between subscribers to the system. The **rental** usually covers equipment and maintenance service; telex use is charged to subscribers on a tariff basis similar to that for telephones. See also **teletex**.

temperate zones Broad latitudinal temperature belts between the **Arctic** Circle and the Tropic of Cancer (Northern Temperate Zone) and between the **Antarctic** Circle and the Tropic of Capricorn (South Temperate Zone). The North Zone includes the bulk of Europe and all continental USA except Alaska, the South Zone much of Australia, the whole of New Zealand and the bulk of South Africa.

temporary visitor Any person, without distinction as to race, sex, language or religion, who **disembarks** and enters the territory of an **ICAO** contracting state other than that in which that person normally resides, and remains there for not more than three months for legitimate non-immigrant purposes [**International Civil Aviation Organization**]. See also **visitor**.

Tempus III The third phase of the **European Union** programme designed to support curricular development and structural reform in **higher education**. The programme is open to the non-associated countries of central and eastern Europe and 13 **TACIS** countries (12 **NIS** and Mongolia) in association with the 15 **EU** member states.

tender
(a) Boat used to convey passengers and crew, as well as stores, between ship and shore when the ship is anchored off shore.
(b) Formal offer in writing to execute work or supply goods and **services** at a stated price, usually made in response to an invitation to tender.
(c) **Currency**, as in *legal tender*, i.e., currency that cannot be legally refused in payment of a debt.

Tenge Unit of **currency** of Kazakhstan.

tent card See **table tent**

terminal
(a) Passenger and/or cargo area at the end of transport **routes** where passengers **embark** and **disembark** and cargo is loaded and unloaded. Air transport terminals in **city** centres are known as *air terminals* or *city terminals*.
(b) Computer equipment normally consisting of a keyboard and visual display unit (VDU) screen linked to the computer, which enables the operator to input data and instructions and obtain output.

terms of trade
(a) Terms and conditions under which business is conducted, usually set out by the seller and including the rights and

obligations of the buyer. Such terms cover, e.g., methods of payment, discounts, refunds and cancellation fees, as well as other respective rights and liabilities of the parties.

(b) In economics, ratio of index of export prices to index of import prices used as a measure of trading prospects of a country in international trade. The terms of trade are said to improve when export prices rise more quickly or fall more slowly than import prices and vice versa.

territorial waters Waters under the jurisdiction of a state, usually within three **miles** of the seashore, although some countries have claimed longer distances. Inter alia, fishing in such waters is reserved for the benefit of the subjects of the adjoining state.

tertiary industries See **services**

tetanus A disease of the muscles and nervous system, causing spasms of the neck and jaw; can be fatal. It is caused by the introduction of bacterial spores present in soil, manure and dust through a wound into the body. The risk is worldwide. **Immunization** is the only protection, especially when travelling to remote rural areas.

thalassotherapy Treatment offered in a number of centres on the Mediterranean and other resorts in southern Europe, using sea-water, sea mud and seaweed to revitalize and invigorate the body.

thanatourism Also known as 'dark tourism', **trips** and visits to destinations associated with death, e.g., sites of murder and atrocities, battlefields.

Thanksgiving American national **holiday** celebrating the first harvest of settlers, on the fourth Thursday in November.

theme park A site designated and operated to provide **recreation** and entertainment for **visitors** through a variety of attractions based on one or more historical or other themes, including such **services** as **catering** and shopping, and usually charging for admission. Well-known examples are Disney Parks in the USA, Japan and France, Europa Park in Germany, and Alton Towers in the UK.

thermal springs See **hot springs**

Third Age Term of relatively recent origin to describe the population group previously usually confined to the retired. Now often seen as one of three ages of the human life span, the first (under 25) being associated with learning, the second (25–50 years) with intense employment, the third (over 50) with gradual withdrawal from employment. Third Age is of particular importance in travel, tourism and hospitality because of the size and growth of the group, as well as its growing activity, affluence and available time in which to participate. See also **senior citizen**.

Third freedom See **freedoms of the air**

Third World For a time in the 1950s the term, 'invented' by French economist Alfred Savry, denoted non-aligned countries, i.e., those committed neither to the **market economy** bloc of **the West (First World)** nor to the centrally controlled economy bloc of Eastern Europe and the USSR **(Second World)**. Nowadays a synonym for **developing countries**.

threshold As an economic concept, term commonly applied to the lowest demand necessary to support an activity. Measured in terms of population or income, it is used, e.g., in selecting a location for a **man-made visitor attraction** or a retail outlet.

through As an adjective, (going) all the way, as in *through carriage, through fare, through passenger, through train*.

throwaway An item in an **inclusive tour**, which is rarely used by the **customer**, included mainly to qualify for a **tour-basing fare**. Thus, e.g., a person visiting friends or relatives and staying with them may find it less expensive to buy an inclusive tour and discard the **accommodation** element than paying any other fare.

tick-borne encephalitis A viral infection causing an inflammation of the brain, contracted from the bite of an infected tick. Occurs in forested parts of central, eastern and northern Europe, including **Scandinavia**, especially in late spring and early summer. Walkers and campers in the affected areas are advised to wear clothing which covers most of the skin, use insect repellents, and a vaccine is also recommended.

Ticket Point Mileage (TPM) Airline term denoting the total flown mileage of a journey, computed as the sum total of flown **miles** between all points **en route**.

ticket tout Colloquial term for a person offering tickets for admission to popular events at prices higher than published.

ticketing codes One-letter standard abbreviations of the **International Air Transport Association (IATA)** to show various characteristics of a flight on an airline ticket, such as class of service (e.g. F for first, C for business/club, Y for economy); timing (e.g., N for night, W for weekend, X for weekday); types of **fares** (e.g., E for excursion, P for family, Z for youth fares). See also **airline codes** and other **codes** entries.

ticketing deadlines See **ticketing time limits**

ticketing time limits Minimum time limits for ticketing agreed by the **International Air Transport Association (IATA)**: (a) for reservations made more than two months before travel, at least 30 days before departure date; (b) for reservations made between two months and 15 days before travel, at least seven days before departure; (c) for reservations made between 14 and three days before travel, at least 48 hours before departure; (d) for reservations made within three days of travel, as soon as possible.

ticketless travel See **electronic ticketing**

tidal range The difference in elevation between high and low water marks in coastal areas, affected by orientation and the nature of the coast and of the sea bed. Thus, the Mediterranean Sea is virtually tideless, presenting problems for keeping **beaches** clean but helpful for navigation, launching craft and using beaches at all times. In contrast, the funnel-like Bay of Fundy in eastern Canada has tidal range of up to 50 feet (16 m) at its head.

tied house Term most commonly applied to a **public house** in **Great Britain** owned by a brewery and let to a tenant who is in business on his own account but under certain obligations to the landlord, in particular to obtain supplies from the brewery and its nominated

suppliers. The system represents vertical forward **integration** and accounts for many public houses in England and Wales but is less common in Scotland. As an alternative to tenancy, the brewery-owned public houses may be operated under direct **management**, when the manager is a salaried employee with no financial stake in the business. See also **free house**.

time charter See **charter**

time series analysis A statistical approach using historical data development of a variable (e.g., past numbers of **tourist** arrivals at a destination) to forecast its future development. Various techniques are available to break down a time series into trend, cycle, seasonal and random elements. This is a widely used approach in travel, tourism and hospitality, as well as in other forecasting, of value in producing short-term forecasts, but the forecasts tend to become less accurate and reliable the longer the time scale.

Time Share Directive **European Union** Council **Directive** agreed by EC Consumer Affairs Ministers and adopted by the Council of Ministers in 1994, taking effect in April 1997 and laying down certain measures for the protection of buyers. *Inter alia*, buyers in the **EU** have a ten-day 'cooling off period' and do not have to pay a deposit before the end of this period. However, this is weaker than the UK Timeshare Act, which allows 14 days for contracts signed in the UK or under UK law. See also **timesharing**.

time slot Time allocated to **aircraft** at an **airport** for take-off and landing.

time zones Divisions of the world into **zones** based on the Greenwich **meridian**, in which local **standard time** is applied. As the earth makes a complete rotation on its axis through 360° of **longitude** every 24 hours, there are 24 time zones. The mean solar time in each zone is at its central meridian, generally 15° apart from the next, but actual zones correspond to political units rather than strictly following the meridians. Large countries with a wide east to west spread are divided into a number of time zones, e.g. the continental USA into five, Canada into six and the Russian Federation into 11. See also **International Date Line**.

timesharing Use of a furnished and serviced **holiday (vacation)** home by a number of parties, each of whom is entitled to occupy the property for one or more pre-determined periods each year. This is the most common meaning of the term and although a timeshare is said to be owned, there are important distinctions between mere timesharing, which gives no more than a right to use the property, and ownership, with such rights as to rent or sell, and variants of both. Also called *holiday (vacation) ownership, interval ownership* and *multi-ownership*, especially in Australia and the USA. It was estimated in 2000 that there were 4 million timeshare 'owners' worldwide, more than 1 million of them in Europe (the second largest number after the USA), of whom more than 300 000 were in the **British Isles**. See also **Time Share Directive**.

tip Term said to have originated in early English coffee-houses as an **acronym** formed from the first letters of 'To Insure Promptitude'. A synonym for **gratuity**. See also **service charge**; **tronc**.

toastmaster Person, often uniformed, employed at a formal banquet for such functions as announcing the names of arriving guests and calling for silence for speakers to speak.

Tolar Unit of **currency** of Slovenia (SIT).

toll Charge levied on users of certain roads, bridges, **canals** and other permanent ways and applied to pay for their building and/or maintenance. See also **turnpike road**.

toll-free number In North America a telephone number beginning with 1-800, in the UK with 0800, which enables the caller to make a call for free, at the expense of the subscriber called.

tollway An **expressway** with **tolls**. See also **turnpike road**.

ton (tonne) A measure of weight which has several different meanings:
(a) In **avoirdupois**, 1 *long ton* (lgt) equals 2240 lb (20 cwt of 112 lb) or 1.016 metric ton (tonne).
(b) A *metric ton* (tonne) equals 1000 kilogram(me)s or 2204.62 lb or 0.984 long ton or 1.1 short ton.

(c) A *short ton* (American ton) equals 2000 lb (20 cwt of 100 lb) or 0.907 tonne or 0.892 long ton.

tonnage (shipping) There are three principal measures of the size of a ship in tonnage terms:
(a) *Deadweight tonnage* measures the weight in long tons (2240 lb) a ship can legally carry, i.e., the total weight of cargo, fuel, stores, passengers and crew.
(b) *Gross tonnage* measures the capacity, i.e., with certain exceptions the total volume of all enclosed spaces of a vessel (within the hull and above the **deck** available for cargo, stores, passengers and crew), the unit of measurement being a ton of 100 cubic feet (100 cubic feet of capacity is equivalent to one gross ton).
(c) *Net tonnage* is derived from the gross tonnage by deducting spaces for crew accommodation, propelling machinery and fuel.

topography Description or representation on a map of permanent/semi-permanent natural and man-made/modified surface of an area, i.e., both landforms and other natural features as well as those produced by man.

tornado A violent storm usually of short duration, common in West Africa at the beginning and end of the rainy season and in the USA between April and July.

total quality management (TQM) An approach to improving the effectiveness and profitability of business involving the whole organization to ensure **customer** satisfaction through focusing on customer needs and the objectives of the organization. The systematic process consists of determining the customers' requirements; developing facilities and **services** which will meet those requirements; operating them in conformity with the established standards; monitoring the customer satisfaction. Several airlines, Disney and Holiday Inns have led the way towards TQM in travel, tourism and hospitality. See also **BS 5750**.

tour conductor Also known as *tour director, tour guide, tour leader, tour manager*. See **courier**

tour operator A person or organization buying individual travel **services** (such as transportation and **accommodation**) from their providers (such as **carriers** and **hotels**) and combining them into a **package** of travel; the tour is sold with a **mark-up** to the public directly, or through **intermediaries**. Although sometimes described as a *wholesaler* (*tour wholesaler* in USA), a tour operator is, in fact, a manufacturer of travel products, whose activities may be compared to those of others principally assembling product components, such as motor car manufacturers or, indeed, book publishers.

tour wholesaler See **tour operator**

tour-basing fare A reduced **round trip** air or sea **fare** available to **tour operators** for use in **inclusive tour** construction. See e.g., **inclusive tour fare (ITX)**

tourism See *Preface* p. vii.

tourism accommodation There is no universally accepted definition of 'tourism accommodation', but it may be regarded as any facility that regularly (or occasionally) provides overnight accommodation for **tourists**. Tourism accommodation is divided into two main groups: **collective tourism establishments** and private tourism accommodation [**World Tourism Organization**].

tourism activity index Measure of relative change in tourism activity over time, in which attendance data at given locations are used as a measure of tourism level. Also known as *tourism barometer* [Huan, T.C. and O'Leary, J.T. (1999) *Measuring Tourism Performance*, Champaign, IL: Sagamore Publishing].

tourism attractiveness index Measure of tourism potential of different **regions**, attributed to G.E. Gearing, W.W. Swart and T. Var. The approach involves asking a panel of experts to assign weights to a series of attributes to reflect their overall importance for tourism development and asking the experts to evaluate each region on these attributes [Smith, S.L.J. (1989) *Tourism Analysis: A Handbook*, London: Longman].

tourism balance Difference between **international tourism receipts** and **international tourism expenditures** of a country. Accordingly, countries may be divided into

those with a positive tourism balance (particularly Austria, France, Italy, Spain) and those with a negative tourism balance (particularly Germany, Japan, the Netherlands, United Kingdom). Usually regarded as a measure of the net impact of **international tourism** on a country's **balance of payments**, but it does not include such effects as **leakages**. See also **travel account**.

tourism barometer See **tourism activity index**

tourism concentration index Measure of tourism concentration as a ratio of nights spent in an area from particular areas of **origin** attributed to M. Jensen-Verbeke, which indicates the degree of dependence of the area or the regional concentration of the **market** [*Tourism Management*, Vol.16, No.1, February 1995].

tourism destinations Countries, regions, towns and other areas which attract **tourists**, are main locations of tourist activity, and tend to account for most of tourists' time and spending. They are the main concentrations of **tourist attractions**, **accommodation** and other tourist facilities and **services**, where the main impacts of tourism – economic, social, physical – occur. See also **resorts**.

Tourism Development Action Plans (TDAPs) A network of initiatives established in England by the **English Tourist Board (ETB)** in the 1980s to develop tourism in 'areas of potential and need'. TDAPs covered both rural and urban areas and were based on **partnerships** between the ETB, **local authorities**, other public agencies and the **private sector**, normally over three years, to establish in each case a local commitment, to be sustained and progressed in the longer term with local resources. The first initiative started in Bristol in 1984 was followed by such **cities** as Bradford, Portsmouth, Carlisle and Lancaster, by such rural areas as Exmoor and Kielder Water, and by seaside **resorts** such as Bridlington and Torbay.

tourism expenditure Defined for statistical purposes as the total consumption expenditure made by a **visitor** or on behalf of a visitor for and during his/her **trip** and stay at a destination. The recommended breakdown comprises seven main categories: **package** travel, package **holidays** and package tours; **accommodation**; food and drinks; transport; **recreation**, culture and sporting activities; shopping; other [**World Tourism Organization**].

tourism expenditure impacts Tourist spending has, first, a *direct* effect on the initial recipients (e.g., **hotels**, **restaurants**, shops) and on factors of production employed by them (land, labour, capital). An *indirect* effect is created by successive rounds of business trans-actions, as supplies are purchased within the economy. An *induced* effect results from increased **consumer expenditure** due to direct and indirect effects. Direct impacts are sometimes referred to as *primary*, indirect and induced impacts are combined as *secondary*. The direct, indirect and induced impacts of tourism expenditure on a national, regional or local economy may be measured in terms of transactions or sales, output, income, employ-ment and government revenue. See also **leakages**; **linkages**; **tourism multipliers**.

tourism generating areas Areas of origin of **tourists**, i.e., the areas of their permanent residence, which represent the source of demand and the location of the **market**, where the major **marketing** functions of the **tourism industry** – promotion, tour operation, travel retailing – are based. Large concentrations of population in **developed countries** are the main generating areas of **international** and **domestic tourism**.

tourism impact In general terms, the effect that **tourists** and tourism development have on a community or area. The impact is commonly categorized into economic, social and cultural, and environmental. See also **tourism expendi-ture impacts**.

tourism industry Term to describe **firms** and **establishments** providing attractions, facilities and **services** for **tourists**. Economic activities are normally grouped into **industries** accord-ing to their products. As tourists use a range of attractions, facilities and services, they are **customers** of a number of industries as conven-tionally defined. Those significantly dependent on tourists for their business, such as **hotels** and **tour operators**, are sometimes called **tourism-related industries**. To the extent to which they supply tourist rather than local and

neighbourhood **markets**, they make up a tourism industry, that part of the economy which has a common function of meeting tourist needs. See also **tourism sector**.

tourism intensity The relationship between the number of **tourists** or tourist nights and the number of **residents** of a destination area, sometimes expressed as a ratio by dividing the former by the latter and described as *tourist intensity index* [Lundberg, D.E. (1974) *The Tourist Business*, 2nd edition, Boston, MA: Cahners]. See also **tourist function index**.

tourism multipliers Numerical coefficients which measure the total effect (i.e., direct, indirect and induced) of initial **tourism expen-diture** in an area, as a result of its subsequent diffusion in the economy. Different types of multiplier measure the effect on business turnover, the level of output in the economy, total incomes, employment and government revenue. The multiplier values depend on propensities to consume and to import: the higher the proportion of income which is spent rather than saved and the lower the **import content of tourism expenditure**, the larger the multiplier and vice versa. See also **leakages**; **linkages**; **tourism expenditure impacts**.

tourism peaking index Measure summariz-ing data on temporal use levels, attributed to D.J. Stynes, with a minimum value 0.00. The greater the degree of concentration over a period, the greater the value of the index [Smith, S.L.J. (1989) *Tourism Analysis: A Handbook*, London: Longman].

tourism police Police appointed in some countries specifically to assist and protect **tourists**. Available to answer enquiries and help in emergencies, they also protect tourists from exploitation by local traders.

tourism ratio index A measure of the relationship between incoming and outgoing **tourist** flows in an area, which assesses the net gain or loss of tourism in the area, attributed to M. Jensen-Verbeke [*Tourism Management*, Vol.16, No.1, February 1995].

tourism satellite account See **satellite account**

tourism sector The part of the economy which has a common function of meeting tourist needs, consisting of **tourism-related industries** to the extent to which they supply tourist rather than local and neighbourhood **markets**. See also **tourism industry**.

Tourism Statistics Directive European Union Council **Directive** of 1995 on the collection of statistical information in the field of tourism to establish an information system on tourism statistics at Community level. The Directive lays down that member states shall carry out the collection, compilation, processing and transmission of harmonized Community statistical information on tourism supply and demand, and specifies the information to be produced annually, quarterly and monthly. With regard to annual data the Directive came into force on 1 January 1996, with regard to monthly and quarterly data, on 1 January 1997.

Tourism Statistics of the Republic of Ireland

(a) Statistics of overseas **visitors** to Ireland and Irish **residents** travelling abroad are derived from the *Country of Residence Survey (CRS)* and the *Passenger Card Inquiry (PCI)*, both conducted by the Central Statistical Office (CSO) at the main air and sea **ports**.

(b) Estimates of the numbers of overseas **tourists** and their expenditure are produced by the **Irish Tourist Board** from this information and from estimates of visitors arriving and departing via Northern Ireland and from/to Northern Ireland, supplied by the **Northern Ireland Tourist Board (NITB)**.

(c) A separate *Survey of Overseas Travellers (SOT)* conducted by the Irish Tourist Board collects information on characteristics of overseas visitors and their **trips**.

(d) The volume and value of **domestic tourism** are measured through the *Irish Travel Survey (ITS)* conducted on behalf of the Irish Tourist Board, which also collects information on trips taken by Irish residents to Northern Ireland and abroad.

tourism transport For statistical purposes, the means of transport refers to the means used by a **visitor** to travel from his/her place of usual residence to the places visited [**World Tourism Organization**]. A suggested classification consists of two levels; the first level (major groups) refers to the transport **route** (air, water-

way, land) and the second level (minor group) specifies each means of transport within the major group (such as **scheduled** flights, passenger lines and **ferries**, railways).

tourism-related industries Term sometimes used for industries serving **tourists** directly and to a greater or lesser extent dependent on tourism for their business. In terms of the **Standard Industrial Classification (SIC)** the main industries normally included are **hotel and catering services**, transport, retail distribution, recreational and cultural services; these correspond broadly to main categories of tourism expenditure, i.e., **accommodation**, food and drink; transport; shopping; entertainment and **recreation**. However, the correspondence is far from precise and, moreover, the SIC does not always identify separately such activities highly dependent on tourism as tour operations and travel agencies. See also **tourism industry**; **tourism sector**.

tourist For statistical purposes, 'a **visitor** whose visit is for at least one night and whose main **purpose of visit** may be classified under one of the following three groups: (a) **leisure** and **holidays**; (b) business and professional; (c) other tourism purposes' [**World Tourism Organization**]. See also **domestic tourist**; **international tourist**.

tourist board A national, regional or local organization variously concerned with the development, promotion and coordination of tourism in its area, which may be a government department, a statutory body or a voluntary association of tourism interests. To be distinguished from sectoral organizations, such as **trade associations** concerned with particular **industries** or **personnel associations** concerned with particular **occupations** engaged in tourism.

tourist card See **visa**

tourist enclave A more or less enclosed and separated **tourism destination** area, in which **tourists** are concentrated and isolated from contact with the **resident** population, sometimes by design in order to avoid conflict. See also **tourist ghetto**.

tourist function index A crude measure of the importance of tourism in a location, attributed to French geographer Pierre Defert, and expressed as a ratio of the number of available tourist beds and the **resident** population. See also **tourism intensity** [Smith, S.L.J. (1989) *Tourism Analysis: A Handbook*, London: Longman].

tourist ghetto Term to describe pejoratively a **tourist enclave**.

Tourist Information Centre (TIC) Office offering information about **tourist/visitor attractions**, facilities and **services**, and sometimes also offering such services as **accommodation** reservations. May be provided by government, **tourist boards** or another organization and have a local or wider scope. TICs form a highly developed and integrated network in a number of countries, including the UK.

tourist intensity index See **tourism intensity**

tourist product In a narrow sense, what **tourists** buy, e.g., transport or **accommodation**, separately or as a **package**. In a wider sense, an amalgam of what the tourist does and of the attractions, facilities and **services** he/she uses to make it possible. From the tourist's point of view, the total product covers the complete experience from leaving home to return. As distinct from an airline seat or a **hotel** room as individual products, the total tourist product – be it a **beach holiday (vacation)**, a **sightseeing** tour or a **conference trip** – is a composite product.

tourist tax Any duty, levy or **tax** collected by **central** or **local government**, their agencies or other authorities from **visitors,** in such forms as **bed tax**, **departure** or **entry tax**, **hotel** or **room tax**, **resort tax** or *visitor tax*.

tourist/visitor attractions Elements of the **tourist product** which attract **visitors** and determine the choice to visit one place rather than another. Basic distinctions are between *site* attractions (e.g., climatic, scenic, historical) when the place itself is the major inducement for a visit, and *event* attractions (e.g., **festivals**, sporting events, trade **fairs**) when the event staged is the larger factor in the tourist's choice than the site; often the site and the event together combine to determine the tourist's choice. Another distinction is between *natural*

and **man-made** or *built* **attractions**, as between **beaches** and **heritage** towns.

townhouse hotel Type of small, usually privately owned **hotel** offering luxury accommodation in a town centre in a reconstructed building.

trade association A voluntary non-profit making body of independent **firms** in a particular trade or **industry** which exists to protect and advance their common interests through representation and provision of **services** to members to assist in the conduct of their businesses. Principal trade associations with an interest in travel, tourism and hospitality are based on component industries, and include **hotel and catering**, transport, **tour operator** and **travel agent** associations. For examples see those listed under **Trade associations in hospitality industry (UK)**; **Trade associations of tour operators and travel agents (UK)**; **Trade associations of transport operators (UK)**.

trade cycle See **business cycle**

trade day The day on which attendance to an exhibition is restricted to professional or trade **visitors**.

trade mission A group visit by business and/or government representatives to one or more countries to promote new business for their product(s), **services** or destinations.

trade show See **fair**

trade union An association of employees in a particular trade or **industry**, or of particular employees in more than one industry, whose principal functions include regulation of relations between them and employers or employers' associations. The three main types are: the *industrial* union (covering one industry with little or no occupational distinction); the *craft* union (which organizes mainly skilled employees in a particular **occupation**, in whatever industry they may be found); the *general* union (which includes in its membership mostly unskilled and semi-skilled employees in more than one occupation). Principal trade unions with an interest in travel, tourism and hospitality reflect the three types in most countries. For examples see those listed under **Trade unions in travel, tourism and hospitality (UK)**.

trade wind Wind blowing continuously towards the **equator** between about 30° north and 30° south **latitude** in the Atlantic and Pacific and deflected westward by the earth's rotation.

trading down Selling at a lower price, usually accompanied by reduction of quality or level of service, to achieve higher volume by attracting more **customers**. Thus, e.g., a switch to **self-service** at lower prices in an existing **restaurant** may be seen as 'trading down', especially if accompanied by reduction of choice and/or availability of 'quality' dishes. See also **down-market**; **downgrade**.

trading up Selling at a higher price, usually accompanied by improved quality or level of service, with a view to achieving higher profit margins. Thus, e.g., a **hotel** refurbishment resulting in provision of **en suite** facilities at a higher tariff would represent trading up. See also **up-market**; **upgrade**.

traffic conference areas Divisions of the world by the **International Air Transport Association (IATA)** for **route**- and rate-making purposes:

Area 1 TC1 covers the western **hemisphere**, i.e., North, Central and South America and adjacent islands, including Greenland, Bermuda, **West Indies** and Caribbean Islands and the Hawaiian Islands.

Area 2 TC2 covers Europe, Africa, the **Middle East** west of and including Iran, and adjacent islands.

Area 3 TC3 covers Asia east of Iran and **Australasia** including the Pacific Islands west of the **International Date Line**, which separates Areas 1 and 3.

The above areas are subdivided further and there are also four traffic **conferences** which cover **routes** between the **conference** areas.

traffic rights

(a) Broadly speaking, rights negotiated by **bilateral air services agreements** between states regulating international air services between them. See also **Bermuda Agreement**; **Chicago Convention**; **freedoms of the air**.

(b) More specifically, **Third**, **Fourth** and **Fifth freedoms of the air**, as distinct from **First** and **Second** freedoms, known as **technical rights**.

trail In **recreation** and tourism, most commonly a designated **route** with signposting to guide walkers, cyclists, motorists or skiers along it. Although mainly developed for the benefit of **visitors**, trails are also increasingly used as a means for 'managing' visitor flows in high density areas. See also **long-distance footpath**; **nature trail**.

trailer That which trails, e.g., trailer **caravan** (towed caravan), trailer interview/question/ survey (that joined on as part of a larger inter-view/questionnaire/survey).

Train à Grande Vitesse (TGV) High-speed train of French Railways and the fastest train in the world, introduced in 1981. See also **Advanced Passenger Train**; **Bullet Train**.

tramping Term used in New Zealand when referring to **backpacking**, **hiking**, rambling and **trekking**.

Trans Tasman Term used to describe relation-ships between Australia and New Zealand, countries separated by the Tasman Sea. E.g., flights between the two countries are referred to as Trans Tasman flights; these are international flights but under the emerging single aviation **market** in **Australasia** have moved towards domestic status. (See **Australia New Zealand Closer Economic Relations Trade Agreement**)

Trans-Siberian Express The train operating across Asia, originally from Moscow to Vladivostok, along the world's longest railway line, which covers nearly a hundred degrees of **longitude**, seven **time zones** and 5900 **miles** (9500 **kilometres**).

transcontinental Extending over or going across a **continent**, e.g., *transcontinental railway*. See also **intercontinental**.

transfer Service for arriving and departing passengers to transport them between **airports** and **ports**, air, sea and rail **terminals** and **hotels**, or between transport terminals, provided by **carriers**, hotels or other operators, usually free between airport terminals, as hotel courtesy service or as part of an **inclusive tour**. See also **passenger designations**.

transit hotel A description sometimes used for a **hotel** catering to short-stay guests **en route** to other destinations.

transit traveller In broad terms, a **traveller** passing through a location, which is not his/her ultimate destination. In **international travel**, commonly defined for technical reasons as one who does not formally enter the country, such as an air passenger remaining in a designated area of the **air terminal** or ship passenger not permitted to **disembark**; this may but need not be the definition used in particular tourism statistics. For countries with extensive land frontiers such as Austria, the Czech and Slovak Republics and Switzerland, transit traffic by road often represents a high proportion of **visitors** with a significant expenditure in transit. See also **passenger designations**.

transnational corporation See **multinational company/corporation**

transport account A component part of the current account of a country's **balance of payments** made up of separate sea transport and civil aviation accounts. For example, in the UK transport account sea transport covers transactions of UK operators with overseas **residents** and of overseas operators with UK residents; civil aviation covers overseas transactions of UK airlines and the transactions of overseas airlines with UK residents. See also **invisibles**; **travel account**.

transport advertising See **outdoor advertising**

trattoria An Italian **restaurant**.

travel See *Preface*, p.vii.

travel account A component part of the current account of a country's **balance of payments** showing earnings from and expenditure on **international travel** excluding international transport, i.e., amounts spent in the country by **residents** of other countries and by the country's **residents** in the countries visited. Major **receiving countries** tend to have a positive balance, major **generating countries** a negative balance on travel account. See also **invisibles**; **tourism balance**; **transport account**.

travel advisory Advice, often a warning, issued by a government authority (e.g., the Foreign Office in the UK or the State Department in the USA) regarding travel to a country or area, in such cases as civil unrest or health hazard.

travel agent A person or organization selling travel **services** (such as transportation, **accommodation** and **inclusive tours**) on behalf of **principals** (such as **carriers**, **hotels** and **tour operators**) for a **commission**. Most travel agents also normally provide ancillary services, such as obtaining **passports** and **visas**, **traveller's cheques (traveler's checks)**, **currencies** and **travel insurance**. The principal functions of the travel agent are those of a retailer – to provide access for a principal to the **market** and to provide a location for the **customer** to buy travel services.

Travel Compensation Fund (TCF) A central fund to which all Australian licensed **travel agents** are required to contribute. The fund is used to compensate **travellers** in the event of travel agent insolvency but it does not cover losses incurred by the collapse of **principals**.

travel coupon A coupon of a **carrier's** ticket which is collected from the passenger when the journey is undertaken. See also **audit coupon**.

travel document
(a) **Passport**, **visa** and any other document required to enable a person to enter or leave a country or to claim the use of certain facilities and services **en route**.
(b) A document issued to stateless persons by the authorities of their country of residence to travel abroad, which has to include a **visa** for all countries to be entered. See also **Nansen Passport**.

travel fair An exhibition and meeting place for suppliers such as attractions and **accommodation** providers and **tour operators** and buyers such as **travel agents** or the general public. A distinction may be drawn accordingly between travel fairs from which the general public is or is not excluded; in some both are accommodated, usually by admitting them on different days. See also **International Tourism Exchange (ITB)**; **World Travel Market (WTM)**.

travel industry In a narrow sense, passenger transport **carriers** and **firms** and **establish-**

ments selling their **services** including **tour operators** and **travel agents**. In a wider sense, all firms and establishments serving the needs of travellers, also described as *travel trade*, sometimes used synonymously with **tourism industry**.

travel insurance Contract providing, in consideration of a premium, for payment of a sum of money in the event of certain travel-related happenings. A travel insurance policy normally covers as a minimum: (a) personal accident; (b) medical and related expenses; (c) cancellation and curtailment; (d) travel abandonment and delay; (e) belongings and money; (f) personal liability.

travel sickness See **motion sickness**

travel/tourism forms/terms/types
See **agritourism/agricultural tourism**
alternative tourism
Antarctic tourism
appropriate tourism
Arctic tourism
business travel/tourism
circuit tourism
city tourism
common interest travel/tourism
community tourism
cultural tourism
domestic travel/tourism
ecotourism
ethnic tourism
export tourism
factory tourism
farm stay tourism
farm tourism
green tourism
hard tourism
health tourism
heritage tourism
import tourism
inbound/travel tourism
incentive travel/tourism
indigenous tourism
industrial tourism
internal travel/tourism
international travel/tourism
Koori tourism
long haul/short haul travel/tourism
mass tourism
national travel/tourism
nature tourism
outbound travel/tourism

religious travel/tourism
responsible tourism
roots tourism
rural tourism
sex tourism
social tourism
soft tourism
space travel/tourism
sports tourism
sustainable tourism
thanatourism
urban tourism
vacation farm tourism
youth tourism
See also **holidays (vacations) forms/ terms/types**.

travel trade See **travel industry**

travel voucher An all-purpose voucher issued by a **tour operator** to another person or organization, such as **ground handling agent**, to cover prepaid elements of a **package** tour. The voucher may cover **admission** to **tourist/visitor attractions**, local transport, meals or other items. See also **Miscellaneous Charges Order (MCO)**.

travel warrant Voucher providing written authorization to a **carrier** to issue a ticket to its holder. Issued under an arrangement by an organization with the carrier, e.g., by a military unit for military personnel to obtain a ticket to travel by rail.

travel-related illnesses
See **AIDS**
altitude sickness
amoebiasis
bilharziasis
breakbone fever
cholera
Delhi belly
dengue
diphtheria
hepatitis A
hepatitis B
hepatitis C
Japanese encephalitis
Legionnaires Disease
leishmaniasis
malaria
meningitis
Montezuma's revenge
motion sickness
mountain sickness
polio(myelitis)
rabies
schistosomiasis
tetanus
tick-borne encephalitis
travel sickness
traveller's diarrhoea (traveler's diarrhea)
tuberculosis
typhoid
yellow fever
See also **immunization for travellers; notifiable disease; quarantine**.

traveller Any person on a **trip** between two or more countries or between two or more localities within his/her country of usual residence. A distinction is made for purposes of tourism statistics between two broad types of travellers: 'visitors' and 'other travellers'. All types of travellers engaged in tourism are described as **visitors**. Therefore, the term 'visitor' represents the basic concept for the whole system of tourism statistics [**World Tourism Organization**].

traveller's cheque (traveler's check) A form of **cheque** used by **travellers**, especially for travel abroad. Issued by banks, large travel **companies** and other institutions, in several **currencies** and in various denominations, traveller's cheques are normally convertible into currencies of the countries where they are encashed. Each cheque has to be signed by the purchaser at the time of issue, and countersigned when encashed. In the event of loss or theft, most issuing organizations undertake to make a refund to holders, provided simple precautions have been observed. Traveller's cheques are a common means of payment for travel, tourism and hospitality **services** worldwide. See also **cheque (check)**.

traveller's diarrhoea (traveler's diarrhea) Generic term for a wide range of bowel infections, caused by many different organisms, and spread by contaminated food and water. It covers most common travel-related illnesses with some degree of risk in most parts of the world, especially in **developing countries**. The main forms of prevention are strict hygiene and care with food and water.

Treaty of Amsterdam Outcome of the 1996 **European Union** inter-governmental conference convened to consider Treaty amendments, including integration of the **Social Chapter** into the Treaty, which entered into force in 1999.

Treaty on European Union See **Maastricht Treaty**

Treaty of Maastricht See **Maastricht Treaty**

Treaty of Rome Agreement signed in 1957 by the six founding countries of the **European Economic Community** creating a regional group with the primary aims of free movement of goods, **services**, capital and people between member countries (France, Germany, Italy, Belgium, Netherlands, Luxembourg).

treeline The *climatic* treeline represents the upper limit of tree growth under natural conditions and varies with orientation, size of the upland mass and the nature of the **climate**. It is much lower in the oceanic climate of the **United Kingdom**, reaching almost sea level in the Western Highlands and only 2800 feet (850 m) in the Cairngorms, than in the more massive size and continental climate of the Alps. The *commercial* treeline is much lower since it is determined by commercial considerations.

trekking Recreational walking in **open country** along **trails** usually over difficult terrain and long distances, popular, e.g., in Nepal. See also **tramping**.

trespass Unlawful entry to the property of another, important in a recreational context in relation to activities on rural land. The legal situation varies considerably from country to country and the significance of trespass as an issue depends largely on the amount of public land available, its location, the intensity of use of private land and the density of population. In England and Wales, where perhaps 10 per cent of the land is publicly owned/managed, trespass is a civil offence, although recent legislation has identified a category of *aggravated trespass*. Trespass is complicated by the network of **rights of way** across private land, which confer only rights of passage. Despite a widespread public opinion that there should be a right of access to **open country** in the uplands, this does not exist; access agreements can be negotiated by **local authorities** with private landowners, but few in fact have been made. In the USA, where there is much more public land for **recreation** and no network of rights of way across private land, attitudes to trespassers tend to be much harder. See also **Allemansrätt**.

TRINET *Tourism Research Information Network*, an international electronic network coordinated by the School of Travel Industry Management in conjunction with the Computing Center of the University of Hawaii. The network facilitates exchange of information among subscribers on research projects, references, conferences and their proceedings, theses, grant proposals and funding, and tourism education, utilizing telecommunication links in use in universities worldwide. See also **Internet**.

trip There is no generally accepted definition of a trip and the term tends to be defined for particular purposes by reference to such criteria as distance, duration and purpose. E.g., *Statistics Canada* and *Tourism Canada* use a minimum distance of 80 km (50 miles), *US Bureau of Census* and *US Travel Data Center* 160 km (100 miles); in UK surveys a stay of one or more nights away from home for most purposes tends to be the definition of a **tourist** trip, and **round trips** lasting at least 3 hours are used to define day trips and visits.

trip index A statistical technique attributed to D.G. Pearce and J.M. Elliott, to examine the extent to which places visited by **tourists** are major destinations or merely **stopovers**, and calculated by dividing nights spent at the destination by the total number of nights spent on a **trip** ($\times$ 100). An index value of 100 indicates that the entire **trip** was spent at one destination, a value of zero that no overnight stay was made on the trip [*Journal of Travel Research*, 32, 1: 6–9].

triple room **Hotel** room to accommodate three people.

trishaw A disappearing form of three-wheeled bicycle transportation for carrying people and an exotic form of transport for **tourists** used in Asia. See also **rickshaw**.

tronc A traditional method of pooling and sharing **gratuities** in **restaurants** whereby money received by employees from **customers** is paid into a common fund and distributed at regular intervals on a pre-arranged basis, commonly using a points system. The person in charge of the fund and its distribution is known as the *troncmaster*. See also **service charge**; **tip**.

tropics The zone of the earth's surface between the Tropic of Cancer and the Tropic of Capricorn, i.e., between 23° 30′ north (Tropic of Cancer) and south (Tropic of Capricorn) of the **equator**, in which the sun is overhead at midday for some time during the year. The term also refers to the **zone** outside the equa-

torial belt with its own distinctive types of **climate**, vegetation and other characteristics of importance for travel and tourism. These areas include some of the best known **international tourism destinations** as, e.g., the bulk of the Caribbean, Hawaii and other Pacific islands.

truckshop American term for transport **café**.

trunk roads Main roads; in the UK the national network of through **routes**, for which the Secretary of State for Transport is the highway authority. The network consists of all-purpose trunk roads, which are open for use by all classes of traffic, and special roads such as **motorways**, which are reserved for use by specified classes of traffic only. County councils are the highway authorities for public roads which are not trunk roads.

tuberculosis A disease once considered virtually eliminated but now increasing worldwide, especially in Eastern Europe, Asia, Africa, Central and South America. Those staying more than a month in those areas, should discuss the need for **immunization** with their doctor, preferably at least two months before travelling.

tug(boat) A small powerful vessel used for towing other larger vessels.

Tughrik Unit of **currency** of Mongolia.

tundra A treeless **region** between the **treeline** and **polar** ice in Eurasia and northern Canada, with long severe winters and permafrost, where even the mean monthly summer temperature is below 10 °C (50 °F).

turning down An early evening practice of some **hotels** preparing the bed for use by removing the bedspread and sometimes also including other tasks such as drawing curtains and replacing used bathroom linen.

turnkey Term used in combination with other words to denote something completed to the point when the user only has to 'turn a key' to make it operational. Thus, e.g., a turnkey computer system is set to perform a complete set of procedures as soon as it is activated; a turnkey construction contract leaves the contractor to see to all details and hand over an operational unit.

turnpike road A road on which barriers known as turnpikes are or were erected for the collections of **tolls** levied on users, hence a main road or highway currently or formerly maintained by tolls as a means of charging the cost to the actual users. In North America also called *tollway* in contrast to *freeway*.

twin Adjective used, i.a., with such nouns as *beds* (two **single** beds), and *room* (a room with two such beds); a *twin double room* denotes a room with two **double** beds.

twinning A term given to a social relationship formed by civic leaders between two towns or **cities** (referred to as sister towns or cities) in different countries to promote contacts and goodwill between their **residents**. This provides a basis for group visits and various forms of cooperation and thus a stimulus to travel and tourism.

two-income families See **dual career families**

typhoid An infection caused by a *salmonella* virus, which manifests itself in fever. It is caught through the consumption of contaminated food or water and the risk is highest in **developing countries** but is not confined to them. A vaccine is available; strict hygiene and care with food and water are advised.

typhoon A violent **hurricane** in the China Sea and adjoining **regions** occurring between July and October.

typology A scheme of classification of types grouped according to specific criteria. Thus a *tourist typology* reflects types of **tourists** according to such criteria as **motivations**, interests and styles. In addition to their academic interest, typologies are also of practical importance in describing **market** niches as a basis for promotion. See, e.g., **allocentric/psychocentric**

umiak An open flat-bottomed Eskimo boat, usually worked by women.

underdeveloped countries See **developing countries**

undertow A strong current near the bottom of the sea close to the shore flowing in the opposite direction to the surface current caused by the water thrown on the shore flowing back; it represents a danger to swimmers.

Uniform System of Accounts for Hotels A system of guidelines for the preparation and presentation of **hotel** accounts in a standard form. First published by the Hotel Association of New York City in 1926 and now in its ninth revised edition, the system is in wide use throughout the world and enables data based on it to be compared between hotels. Similar systems developed in several countries, including **United Kingdom**, have a more limited use.

uniformed staff Term used to describe collectively **hotel** employees providing **front-of-house** personal services for guests, including commonly a **head hall porter (bell captain)**, porters **(bell hops)** and page boys **(bell boys)** but also others in some hotels.

union contract See **collective agreement**

unique selling proposition (USP) An **advertising** concept attributed to Rosser Reeves, American advertising copywriter, describing a particular product characteristic, which distinguishes it from competing products, can be regarded as exclusive to it, and represents the main reason to buy the product. This may be used as an advertising theme, which may be retained over a long period or a new one may be developed from time to time. Prominent examples in travel, tourism and hospitality have included: 'We try harder' (Avis); 'World's favourite airline'

(British Airways); 'Only one hotel chain guarantees your room will be right' (Holiday Inns).

unitary authorities Local authorities in England and Wales which combine responsibilities elsewhere divided between county, borough and district councils.

United Kingdom (UK) Great Britain and Northern Ireland.

United Kingdom tourism statistics
(a) International tourism to and from the UK is recorded by the **International Passenger Survey (IPS)** and published by the Office for National Statistics.
(b) Domestic tourism by UK **residents** is recorded by the **United Kingdom Tourism Survey (UKTS)** and published by the **British Tourist Authority (BTA)** and the **English Tourism Council (ETC)**.
In addition to the publications shown in each entry, results of the surveys are also available on *StatBase*, the Government Statistical Service website (www.statistics.gov.uk), and *StarUK*, the national tourism statistics website (www.staruk.org.uk).

United Kingdom Tourism Survey (UKTS) A monthly sample inquiry by personal interviews as part of an **omnibus survey** to measure travel for all purposes by UK **residents**, commissioned jointly by the **national tourist boards** for England, Scotland, Wales and Northern Ireland since 1989, when it replaced the monthly **British Tourism Survey (BTS)**. Like its predecessor, it covers travel by adults and accompanying children of one or more nights away from home. A summary of the results is available in the *Digest of Tourist Statistics*, published by the **British Tourist Authority (BTA)** and in *The UK Tourist* published by the **English Tourism Council (ETC)**.

175

United Nations Conference on Environment and Development See **Earth Summit**

United Nations Development Decade Description applied to the 1960s when much attention of individual governments and of international organizations was focused on the preparation of development plans, in which tourism usually played a significant and often dominant role.

United States Dollar (US$) Unit of **currency** of American Samoa, British Virgin Islands, East Timor, Ecuador, El Salvador, Guam, Marshall Islands, Micronesia, Northern Mariana Islands, Palau, Puerto Rico, Turks and Caicos Islands, United States of America, United States Pacific Islands, United States Virgin Islands.

United States tourism statistics

(a) Movements and activities of **international visitors** to the USA by air are recorded by the *In-flight Survey of International Air Travellers* conducted among passengers on outbound airline flights from the US and published quarterly by **Tourism Industries**, International Trade Administration, US Department of Commerce. Surface **visitors** to the US from Canada are surveyed by *Statistics Canada* and published annually. Surface visitors to the US from Mexico and **cruise** visitors are not counted.

(b) Movements and activities of **domestic visitors** within the USA are recorded by TravelScope® from a mail survey of US **residents** and published annually by the **Travel Industry Association of America (TIA)**.

up-market Colloquial term denoting **market** with higher prices, expectations of quality and/or level of service. See also **trading up**; **upgrade**.

upgrade To change to a superior standard, as in moving a passenger or a **hotel** guest or their reservation to a superior seat or **accommodation**. See also **downgrade**.

urban planning See **physical planning**

urban renewal The restoration, renovation and improvement of obsolescent urban areas, in which **leisure** and tourism often play a significant role. Also described as *urban regeneration*.

urban tourism **Trips** and visits with a focus on town and **city** destinations, also known as *city tourism*. A fast growing form of tourism, stimulated by historical and cultural attractions, as well as shopping and **event attractions**, and by **business travel**, it offers much scope for urban regeneration. Well-known examples of city regeneration through tourism include Baltimore in the USA, Barcelona in Spain and Glasgow in Scotland.

urbanization The process of growth of urban areas so as to account for an increasing proportion of population living in them. Usually associated with **industrialization**, the increase in urban population comes about by **migration** from rural areas and from natural increases. Urbanization is of major relevance to tourism, as urban areas tend to have high **holiday (vacation) propensities**. See also **Industrial Revolution**.

user bodies 'Watchdog' organizations representing the interests of particular groups of **consumers**, especially where a supplier has a **monopoly** or near monopoly of a **public utility** such as transport. *Statutory* user bodies in transport in **United Kingdom** include the **Air Transport Users Committee**, Airport Consultative Committees, Central Transport Consultative Committee and Transport Users' Consultative Committees. *Voluntary* user bodies have been formed, usually on a local basis by pressure groups and some transport operators.

user-oriented resources Resources devoted to **recreation** and tourism, which depend for their attraction more on their **accessibility** than on their quality, are located in proximity to concentrations of population, and cater primarily for local or regional needs rather than attracting nationally. Examples include parks, sites for sports or **restaurants**. See also **resource-based resources**.

vacation US term for **holiday** but also used in **British Isles** for periods of formal suspension of normal activity, such as law courts and university vacations. See also separate entries under **holiday**.

vacation farm tourism US term for **farm tourism**.

vacation home See **second home**

vacation ownership See **timesharing**

vacationscape Term used to describe integrated design and development for tourism, coined by American academic C. Gunn in his book of the same title (published 1988 by Van Nostrand Reinhold, New York).

vaccination Inoculation with a substance called vaccine, which contains modified virus or germs, to give a person **immunization** against a particular disease. The vaccine may be also administered in tablet or liquid form.

valet Manservant; a **hotel** employee responsible for cleaning and pressing guests' clothes.

valet parking See **car hop**

validation Action of imprinting an airline ticket with a stamp to make it valid for travel. The mechanical device fitted with the **carrier's** or **travel agent's** die plate used to validate the ticket is called *the validator*.

value added An economic concept denoting the value added by a **firm** or **industry** to the cost of its inputs, giving the value of its output; therefore, value added equals the difference between the total sales of the firm or industry and the cost of goods and **services** bought in. See also **value added tax (VAT)**.

value added tax (VAT) A **tax** based on the **value added** at each stage of the production and distribution of goods and **services**. In practice the selling price is increased by the percentage of VAT, which has to be accounted for to the authorities, but against this may be set any VAT included in suppliers' invoices. VAT is used throughout the **European Union (EU)** and forms the basis for the countries' contributions to the Community budget but the rates of tax as well as items subject to it continue to vary between the countries. It is also by far the most important tax levied on **visitors** in EU countries. To be distinguished from **sales tax**.

Vatu Unit of **currency** of Vanuatu.

vegetarianism There are five main categories:
(a) Generally *vegetarians* abstain from using meat, fish and poultry as food for religious, ethical, ecological or health reasons.
(b) *'Demi-vegetarians'* usually exclude red meat from their diet but generally not white poultry or fish.
(c) *Lacto vegetarians* eat milk and cheese but not eggs or anything which has been produced from a slaughtered animal.
(d) *Ovo vegetarians* are similar to lacto vegetarians but eat eggs.
(e) *Vegans* do not eat any animal food or product.

veld/veldt An Afrikaans term for unenclosed uncultivated grassland area in South Africa suitable for pasture.

vernacular Language, idiom, word of one's native place or country, i.e., not of foreign origin or of learned formation.

vertical integration See **integration**

vertical take-off and landing (VTOL) See **aircraft types: take-off and landing**

Victorian Of the time of Queen Victoria (1837–1901), e.g., Victorian architecture, furniture, glassware.

videoconferencing See **teleconferencing**

videotex Electronic **services** which display transmitted information on a video screen. *Teletext* systems, such as the BBC Ceefax or the Independent Television Teletext, are broadcast systems capable of receiving and displaying data, and are usually free. *Viewdata* systems, such as the British Telecommunications Prestel or the French Minitel, are telephone-based, enable two-way communication and are charged on a per call basis. In recent years interactive videotex has revolutionized the distribution of travel, tourism and hospitality products, and a number of **principals** operate their own systems.

viewdata See **videotex**

virtual reality (VR) Relatively recent development in computer simulations and human-computer interfacing, which attempts to replace the user's experience of the physical world with synthesized three-dimensional material. This takes place through a combination of visual, audio and kinetic effects, which make participants believe that they are actually experiencing the real thing. Used for some time in flight simulators for training pilots on the ground, VR technology is seen to have a potential in such areas as the creation of virtual **theme parks**, as a promotional and sales tool, and in the creation of artificial tourism, possibly even providing eventually a substitute for travel and tourism itself.

visa Authorization by the government, normally entered in the **passport**, to allow an **alien** to enter the country (*entry visa*) or a **resident** to leave the country (*exit visa*), or in some cases a resident travelling abroad on an alien passport to re-enter (*resident return visa*). Entry visas may be of varying validity, single or multiple entry, and classified according to the purpose of entry, e.g., tourist, business, transit. Exit visas are less common and are normally issued for a single exit (and re-entry if applicable). Entry visas are also known in some countries, particularly in Central and South America, as a *tourist card*. See also **travel document**.

visibles Receipts and payments included in the current (as distinct from capital) **balance of payments** account, from goods (as distinct from **services**). See also **invisibles**.

visiting friends and relatives (VFR) Classification of main **purpose of trip**/visit or activity in common use in most countries in segmenting the **market**. See also **visiting relatives**.

visiting relatives (VR) On Australian migration forms, inbound **travellers** may select 'visiting relatives (VR)' as their primary **purpose of visit** rather than **visiting friends and relatives (VFR)**, which is the more commonly used category in other countries. The VR category is the second most important (after **holidays**) as a result of the large immigrant population with relatives overseas.

visitor For statistical purposes, any person travelling to a place other than that of his/her usual **environment**, for less than 12 months and whose main **purpose of visit** is other than the exercise of an activity remunerated from within the place visited. A distinction is drawn between **international** and **domestic visitors** and this definition covers two classes of visitors: **tourist** and **same-day visitor** [World Tourism Organization].

visitor attractions See **tourist/visitor attractions**

visitor management Public and private **sector** systems and procedures designed to influence visitor behaviour at **tourist/visitor** sites and destinations, through such means as capacity **management**, interpretation, pricing, signposting and zoning. See **interpretation centre**; **zone**.

visitor tax See **tourist tax**

Visitor(s) and Convention Bureau Term of American origin but increasingly also used elsewhere as a designation for a local or area **tourist board**, e.g., Greater Manchester Visitor and Convention Bureau.

voodoo Belief in and use of witchcraft and the like rites and superstitions, prevalent in the **West Indies** and among African Americans.

W

wadi/wady A valley or stream course in hot desert or semi-arid areas in **Middle East** and North Africa, usually dry but sometimes carrying a stream after heavy rain.

Wagon-Lits Sleeping **coaches** on trains, also name of the **company** operating these, on the Continent of Europe; the coaches comprise bedroom accommodation for one or two people. See also **couchette**; **parlor car**; **Pullman**; **roomette**.

waiting list/waitlist A list of passengers wishing to join a flight, sailing or tour, which is fully booked; sometimes also used by **hotels** when full. Those on the list may then be accommodated in case of cancellations or **no shows**. See also **standby**.

wanderlust According to economist H.P. Gray, **motivation** to pleasure travel; the term describes the desire to exchange the known for the unknown, to leave things familiar and to go and see different places, people and cultures, i.e., to be exposed to what is different from that which is obtainable at home. Wanderlust is often more likely to be satisfied through **international** rather than **domestic tourism** and to call for facilities geared to short rather than longer stay. **Climate** is of secondary importance and more than one country or more than one place is often visited. See also **sunlust**.

Warsaw Convention An international agreement made in 1929 and, as amended subsequently, limiting the liability of airlines for loss of or damage to **baggage (luggage)** and injury to or death of passengers on most international flights (including domestic portions of international flights). As a result of the Convention, airlines normally accept liability for accidents up to set limits and claimants do not have to prove negligence. See also **excess value**.

waste management Systems and processes used by **companies** and other organizations to reduce waste for cost or environmental reasons. Such approaches often revolve round the '3Rs' – Reduce, Re-use, Recycle – and are core components of cost control and environmental programmes in travel, tourism and hospitality operations.

water management Systems and processes used by **companies** and other organizations to reduce their use of water resources for cost or environmental reasons. Such approaches are core components of cost control and environmental programmes in travel, tourism and hospitality operations.

water park A **recreation** area providing water sports, other water-based activities and such visual attractions as waterfalls, usually for the general public and on payment of an **admission** charge. The Cotswold Water Park is a recent example in England.

water resources depletion and pollution In many countries fresh water resources are already scarce and are being further depleted by high agricultural, industrial and domestic consumption and by **pollution**. Most water pollution is caused by agricultural, industrial and domestic waste, including inadequate sewage provision, with serious effects on human health. Travel, tourism and hospitality activities are large **consumers** of water and large generators of waste; they are also directly affected by water depletion and pollution in many locations, especially in **developing countries**. See also **water management**; **waste management**.

water skiing A popular form of active **recreation** on lakes and coastal waters in which the participant, mounted on skis, is pulled by a power boat, required to generate a speed of around 25 mph (49 kph), sufficient to maintain the skier on the surface. It is sometimes a source of conflict with other forms of recreation on/in the water, including swimmers, anglers and those sailing yachts, and on the shore. On publicly owned or controlled water, strict regulations often apply governing where and when water skiing may take place.

water sports holidays (vacations) A specialized **activity holiday (vacation) segment**, including such activities as dinghy and yacht sailing, diving and windsurfing but excluding **beach** holidays (vacations). It is still a small proportion of all holidays (vacations) – around one million were taken in **Great Britain** annually in the 1990s – but estimated to grow faster than all holidays (vacations).

wayports Airports constructed in remote, sparsely populated areas, with little or no origin and destination traffic, and dedicated more or less exclusively to handling **transfer** traffic, with a view to minimizing environmental problems. Such airports may be also developed from military airfields due for closure or from civil airports whose role has diminished.

Wesak Major religious **holiday**, also called *Buddha Day*, celebrated in Thailand and other Buddhist countries in May each year.

The West Collective term for the countries of Western Europe and North America, as distinct from the countries of Eastern Europe and Asia.

West Country The area of England normally seen to comprise the counties of Somerset, Devon and Cornwall, although South West Tourism, one of ten English **Regional Tourist Boards**, covers also parts of Dorset, Gloucestershire, Wiltshire and the Isles of Scilly. This is the most popular **holiday (vacation) region** for British **residents**, which attracts annually a quarter of all holidays of four nights or more taken in **Great Britain** by British residents, with South of England, Wales and Scotland being the next most popular destinations.

West Indies (WI) Collective term for the islands of the Caribbean Sea between North and South America.

wet lease See **dry/wet lease**

wet rent The rent payable by the tenant to the landlord in the supply price, an arrangement used, e.g., in the **tied house** system, when the tenant pays a low fixed rent (also termed *dry rent*) for his premises, usually much below the **market** rate, and is charged a higher price by the brewery for the supplied beer than is charged to the 'free trade'; this difference in price is termed wet rent, rising or falling with the volume of trade done, intended to adjust the tenant's outgoings to the fluctuations of turnover of the **public house**.

wetlands A natural or artificial landscape where the soil is waterlogged *or* the land is occasionally, periodically or permanently covered by fresh or salt water. Different types of wetlands are described as bog, peat, marsh or swamp.

whale watching An emerging tourist activity of growing popularity in Australia and New Zealand. In Australia the term covers the observation of whales from boats (as in Queensland) and from shore locations (such as the coast of Victoria).

wharf A stone or wooden structure alongside water beside which ships are moored to **embark** and/or **disembark** passengers or to load and/or unload cargo. See also **quay**.

white man's grave A colloquial term formerly applied to West Africa, where before the introduction of inoculation, prophylactic drugs, pest control and improved sanitation, the hot humid **climate** was particularly unhealthy for Europeans, resulting in widespread disease and high mortality. Nowadays sometimes still used for areas with similarly inhospitable climate.

white-collar An American term used to describe non-manual workers, in particular clerical and secretarial employees, now also widely used elsewhere. See also **blue-collar**; **class**; **socio-economic groups**.

wholesaler Intermediary who usually buys goods from suppliers for resale in small quantities to retailers and others. In tourism the term is sometimes used as a synonym for **tour operator**.

wide body aircraft See **aircraft types: bodies**

DICTIONARY OF TRAVEL, TOURISM AND HOSPITALITY

wind chill The effect of wind at low temperatures on shaded dry human skin in making the effective temperature considerably lower. Often expressed as a temperature quotient: thus a temperature of 20 °F (–7 °C) and a wind speed of 45 mph (72 kph) produces a temperature of –20 °F (–30 °C). Of great significance for those climbing, **skiing** and **trekking** at low temperatures, who must ensure that their clothing is adequate for the effective temperatures.

window-dressing Any practice that attempts to make a situation look better than it really is. In business used particularly by accountants and **public relations** consultants.

windsurfing Water sport of riding on water on a special board with a sail.

windward A nautical term denoting the direction from which the wind is blowing, i.e., the least sheltered side of a ship. See also **leeward**.

Wings Airline alliance formed 1989 as a partnership between KLM and NorthWest Airlines, and including also Braathens, Eurowings and Kenya Airways, part-owned by KLM.

Winter Olympic Games A **quadrennial** international sport meeting held, until 1992, as a separate event from 'Summer' **Olympic Games** but in the same year: St Moritz (Switzerland) 1948, Oslo (Norway) 1952, Cortina d'Ampezzo (Italy) 1956, Squaw Valley (USA) 1960, Innsbruck (Austria) 1964, Grenoble (France) 1968, Sapporo (Japan) 1972, Innsbruck (Austria) 1976, Lake Placid (USA) 1980, Sarajevo (Yugoslavia) 1984, Calgary (Canada) 1988, Albertville (France) 1992. Subsequent Winter Games have alternated with the Summer Games at two-year intervals: Lillehammer (Norway) 1994 (Summer Games 1996), Nagano (Japan) 1998 (Summer Games 2000), Salt Lake City (USA) 2002 (Summer Games scheduled for Athens 2004), and the 2006 Winter Games are scheduled for Turin (Italy).

winter sun Holidays (vacations) designed to take advantage of tourism facilities outside the main summer season in areas which have an acceptable winter **climate**, such as the Mediterranean coasts of Spain and the Canaries in Europe and Florida in North America, particularly attractive to those who have retired. Provided variable costs are covered and some contribution is made to fixed costs, such use is likely to be worthwhile from the hoteliers' perspective as an alternative to closing premises during the off-season months.

wog A derogatory slang description for a native of a Middle Eastern country, especially Egypt.

Won Unit of **currency** of North and South Korea.

word-of-mouth advertising Advertising communicated by a satisfied **customer** to a relative, friend or acquaintance, as a prospective customer for the same product. Considered as the most influential source of information about **consumer** products, including travel, tourism and hospitality products.

work permit See **employment pass/permit/visa**

work study 'The systematic examination of activities in order to improve the effective use of human and other material resources.' Also known as *organization and methods (O&M)*, it consists of *method study*, defined as 'the systematic recording and critical examination of ways of doing things in order to make improvements' and *work measurement*, defined as 'the application of techniques designed to establish the time for a qualified worker to carry out a task at a defined rate of working' [*British Standard Glossary* BS 3138: 1979].

Working Time Regulations In the UK hours of work and related conditions of employment are normally negotiated between employers and employees collectively or individually. However, **European Union** Regulations which came into force in the UK in 1998 (earlier in other EU countries), which apply to **full-time**, **part-time** and temporary workers, make the following provisions (subject to exemption for workers in some **sectors**, including transport, although individual workers can choose to work longer):

• a maximum average working week of 48 hours

- a minimum of four weeks' annual paid leave
- minimum daily and weekly rest periods
- specific provisions for adolescent workers in respect of the above rights and entitlements.

World Heritage Sites Natural and cultural **conservation** sites of exceptional interest designated by the **United Nations Educational, Scientific and Cultural Organisation (UNESCO)**. Examples include Hadrian's Wall in England, the islands of St Kilda in Scotland, the castles and town walls of King Edward I in North Wales, and the Giant's Causeway in Northern Ireland. By the end of 2001 721 sites had been designated worldwide, 24 of them in the UK. See **country-side conservation designation schemes** for other schemes.

World Travel Market (WTM) An annual international travel and tourism trade **fair** held in London in November each year since 1980.

Worldchoice Brand name of agencies of members of the UK **Alliance of Retail Travel Agency Consortia (ARTAC)**.

Worldspan *Worldspan Travel Agency Information Services*, US **computer reservation system (CRS)** formed as a **joint venture** between **DATAS II** and **PARS** systems, which it replaced in 1990. Delta Airlines, Northwest Airlines and Trans World Airlines (TWA) are principal shareholders, with a small stake by **Abacus**.

xenophobia Contempt, dislike or fear of strangers or foreigners, or of strange or foreign places.

Xplorer Australian rail service linking Sydney and Canberra and also Sydney and several centres in New South Wales.

XPT Express Australian rail service linking Sydney and Melbourne, Sydney and Brisbane, as well as several New South Wales centres.

yard (yd) A measure of length used in English-speaking countries, equal to 0.9144 **metre**. A yard is divided into 3 feet (ft.) or 36 inches (in.). In measures of area 1 square yard equals 9 square feet (0.836 square metre) or 1296 square inches. In measures of volume 1 cubic yard (cu. yd = 0.765 cubic metre) equals 27 cubic feet (cu. ft).

yellow fever A viral infection causing fever, vomiting and liver failure; can be fatal. It is caught by the bite of an infected mosquito and occurs in parts of Africa and South America. A vaccine is an effective prevention for a period of ten years. Some countries require a **vaccination** certificate for entry.

Yellow Pages Business telephone directory **advertising** various products, published in most countries worldwide.

Yen Unit of **currency** of Japan.

yield
(a) Return on an investment in terms of income in relation to the current capital value of the investment.
(b) Profit or revenue attributable to a product, commonly expressed as average profit or revenue earned per unit of output, e.g., **passenger kilometre** in transport or room/night in **accommodation**. See also **yield management**.

yield management The concept and techniques concerned with the maximization of profit or revenue and the development of an optimum **business mix** to those ends. In recent years, yield management has received increasing attention and application in transport, especially in airline operations, and in hospitality **management**.

Young Persons Railcard See **British railcards**

Youth The **European Union** programme which, within the overall aim of allowing young people to acquire knowledge and skills and to exercise responsible citizenship, includes exchanges between groups, individual mobility, youth initiatives, joint actions and related support measures. The programme is open to 31 countries (15**EU**, 3**EFTA/EEA**, 13 EU candidate countries including Malta and Turkey).

youth hostel See **hostel**

youth tourism A segment of the tourism **market** variously seen to embrace those aged between 15–18 and 25–29 years. Whatever definition is adopted, available statistics suggest that youth tourism has been developing faster than tourism as a whole.

Yuan Unit of **currency** of China, also called Ren Min Bi Yuan or People's Bank Dollar.

Yukon Standard Time A Canadian **time zone** based on the standard of the 135th **meridian**. Time equals GMT –8.

Yuppie Term derived from *young urban professional* and denoting an ambitious and successful individual in their 30s with an upwardly mobile **lifestyle**.

'Z' bed A folding and movable bed; when folded, it can be moved on castors and stand as a piece of furniture with a headboard providing a horizontal surface.

Zionism The movement resulting in the establishment of a Jewish state in Palestine.

ZIP code Abbreviation for *Zone Improvement Plan code* established by the US Postal Service to identify numerically the destination of mail for sorting and dispatch.

Zloty Unit of **currency** of Poland.

zone Generally a more or less defined area of land, usually distinguished from others by a particular quality or condition indicated by a defining word as, e.g., building zone, tariff zone, **temperate zone**. In **land use planning** an area designated (zoned) for a particular purpose, e.g., industry, housing, **recreation**. Hence, *zoning*, i.e., designating areas for particular purposes. See also **development plans**; **land use planning**; **physical planning**; **time zones**.

zoo Colloquial abbreviation for *zoological garden*, site where wild animals are kept for the public to view.

Zulu time Synonym for **Greenwich Mean/ Standard Time (GMT/GST)**.

2

International Organizations

International Organizations

Africa Travel Association (ATA) Regional organization founded 1975 to promote and foster public interest in and the growth and development of travel and tourism to Africa. Members are government ministries of tourism, **National Tourism Organizations, industry** and allied **firms** and institutions. [www.africa.ata.org]

African Development Bank (ADB) Regional development bank established 1964 to contribute to the economic development and social progress of independent African countries. Since 1982 membership has been also open to non-African states. [www.afdb.org]

African Development Fund (ADF) An affiliate organization of the **African Development Bank (ADB)** established with an open membership 1972 to make loans to African member states at low rates of interest. Substantial loans have been made for projects in the transport **sector** with direct impact on tourism. [www.afdb.org]

Airports Council International (ACI) Sectoral organization created 1991 to succeed three existing bodies concerned with airport operations and combine their functions. Its membership includes several hundred **airports** and airport authorities in more than 100 countries and territories worldwide. [www.airports.org]

Alliance Internationale de Tourisme (AIT) *International Touring Alliance (ITA)* Worldwide organization founded 1898, present name adopted 1919, to represent **motoring organizations** and touring clubs, study and disseminate information, and render advice and assistance on touring and motoring. [www.aitgwa.ch]

Andean Group Regional **inter-governmental organization** of several South American countries established 1969 to accelerate the harmonious development of the member states through economic and social integration, including cooperation in transport, adoption of a common **passport**, and tourism promotion. [www.communidadandina.org]

ANTOR **Acronym** commonly denoting a body of **National Tourism Organization** representatives in a particular **city** or country as, e.g., *Assembly of National Tourist Office Representatives in New York* or *Association of National Tourist Office Representatives in Great Britain.*

Arab Fund for Economic and Social Development (AFESD) Regional **inter-governmental organization** established 1973 to participate in the financing of economic and social development projects in the Arab States. A significant proportion of the loans have been made to transport and other projects of relevance to travel and tourism. [www.arabfund.org]

Arab Tourism Organization (ATO) Regional **inter-governmental organization** established 1954, present name adopted 1969. Aims to promote tourism in the Arab area, coordinate efforts towards a unified Arab tourism policy, and provide **services** to members. Membership consists of governments and several tourism-related international Arab organizations.

ASEAN Tourism Association (ASEANTA) Regional association of South East Asian countries to promote cooperation and assistance in furthering and protecting the interests of members, as well as standards of facilities and **services** for **travellers** and **tourists** and the development of tourism into

and within the **region**. Members are national airlines, **hotel** associations and **travel agent** associations.
[www.aseanta.org]

ASEAN Tourism Information Centre (ATIC) Regional **inter-governmental organization** established 1988 to publicize the **tourist attractions** and investment potential in **ASEAN** countries.
[www.atic.org.ro]

Asia Travel Marketing Association (ATMA) Regional organization founded 1966, present name adopted 1999, to stimulate tourist traffic to East Asia by combining efforts of member organizations in promotional activities and by enhancing reception **services** and tourist facilities. Membership consists of government members representing **National Tourism Organizations; carrier, hotel** and **agent** associations in member countries; carriers providing services to, from and within those countries.
[www.asiatravel.org]

Asian Development Bank (ADB) Regional development bank established 1966 to foster economic growth and co-operation in Asia and the Pacific, with regional and non-regional membership.
[www.adb.org]

Asian Development Fund (ADF) An affiliate organization of the **Asian Development Bank (ADB)** established to make **soft loans** to the poorest countries in the **region**. A significant proportion of loans has accrued to transport and other tourism-related projects.
[www.adb.org]

Association of South East Asian Nations (ASEAN) Regional **inter-governmental organization** established 1967 to accelerate the economic growth, social progress and cultural development in the **region**, as well as promote collaboration and mutual assistance, including tourism-related activities. The ASEAN region includes some of the world's fastest-growing economies, as well as **tourism destinations**.
[www.aseansec.org]

CAB International (CABI) Inter-governmental organization providing an international information service, which acts as a clearing house for the collection, collation and dissemination of information, under the control of an executive council comprising representatives of the countries which contribute to its funds. *CABI Publishing* produces a growing number of books on travel, tourism and hospitality and also *Leisure, Recreation and Tourism Abstracts*, which provides a comprehensive listing of books and articles on tourism.
[www.cabi.org]

Caribbean Development Bank (CDB) Also known as *Caribank*, a regional development bank established 1970, to contribute to the economic growth and development of the member countries of the Caribbean and to promote economic cooperation and integration among members. Involvement includes regional integration projects in transport, loans to governments for tourism **infrastructure** and loans to **hotel** operators.
[www.caribank.org]

Caribbean Hotel Association (CHA) Regional sectoral organization founded 1959 to act as a **trade association** of the Caribbean **hotel industry.**
[www.caribbeanhotels.org]

Caribbean Tourism Organization (CTO) Regional **inter-governmental organization** established 1989 by merger of two existing organizations. Its main aims are increasing tourism flows to member states, creating greater awareness and understanding of tourism, developing skills and professionalism, and providing a tourism information system. The Caribbean represents the world's most tourism-dependent **region**.
[www.caribtourism.com]

Colombo Plan *The Colombo Plan for Co-operative Economic and Social Development in Asia and the Pacific*, initially agreed in 1950 to promote interest and support for such development and keep under review economic and social progress and the flow of development assistance in the **region**. Member countries include the USA, UK, Australia, Canada, New Zealand and Japan, as well as **developing countries** in Asia and the Pacific.
[www.colombo-plan.org]

Commonwealth Voluntary association of independent countries, which succeeded the

British Commonwealth of Nations (title discarded 1951), which in turn has grown out of the *British Empire*, to promote cooperation between them and to advance their common interests. There are 54 members who between them include one-third of the world's population (as of 2000). The *Commonwealth Fund for Technical Co-operation (CFTC)*, an integral part of the Commonwealth Secretariat, provides technical assistance to **developing countries** of the Commonwealth, with a significant involvement in tourism-related activities. [www.thecommonwealth.org]

Commonwealth of Independent States (CIS) Voluntary association of sovereign states established at the time of collapse of the Soviet Union in December 1991. Following the accession of Georgia in 1993, all the former Soviet republics except the three **Baltic States**, are now members (total 12). CIS acts as a coordinating mechanism for foreign, defence and economic policies and is a forum for addressing problems which have arisen from the break-up of the USSR. The 12 countries are also referred to collectively as the *Newly Independent States (NIS)*. [www.cis.minsk.by]

Confederation of National Hotel and Restaurant Associations in the European Community (HOTREC) Regional sectoral grouping founded 1982 to link employers' **hotel, restaurant** and **catering** organizations, promote cooperation, coordinate action and make representations on their behalf to EC institutions. [www.hotrec.org]

Conference of Regions of North West Europe (CRONWE) Regional body founded 1955 to coordinate studies and action with a view to planned development, including that of tourism, in the area which covers the **Benelux** countries, the western part of Germany, the north and north-west **regions** of France, and parts of south-east England. Members are individuals, government officials and institutions in the six countries.

Council of Europe (CE) Regional **inter-governmental organization** founded 1949 to achieve greater unity among its members with a view to safeguarding their European **heritage** and facilitating their economic and social progress. [www.coe.int]

Economic Community of Central African States (ECCAS) Regional **inter-governmental organization** established 1981 to promote cooperation and development in economic, social, cultural, scientific and technical activities. Specific objectives include, i.a., elimination of obstacles to free movement of people and travel and tourism promotion. [www.eccas.int]

Economic Community of West African States (ECOWAS) Regional **inter-governmental organization** established 1975 to promote economic, social and cultural cooperation and development with particular focus on agriculture and **industry** but it pursues also such tourism-related objectives as the abolition of obstacles to free movement of people and the development of a regional transport system. [www.ecowas.int]

European Bank for Reconstruction and Development (EBRD) Regional **inter-governmental** financial institution set up 1990 to assist the emerging democracies of Central and Eastern Europe in their transition towards **market** economies. The Bank provides technical assistance, training and investment, and its emphasis on promoting the **private sector** offers important scope for tourism development. [www.ebrd.com]

European Community (EC) Designation used for a number of years for the three institutions regarded in practice as a single entity and supervised by a single Commission since 1967: *European Coal and Steel Community (ECSC)* created 1951, **European Economic Community (EEC)** and *European Atomic Energy Community (Euratom),* created by two separate treaties 1957. This was formally recognized under the **Maastricht Treaty**, which changed the EEC to EC with effect from 1 November 1993. EC membership was extended by the accession of Austria, Finland and Sweden to a total of 15 states on 1 January 1995. See also **European Union (EU).**

European Economic Community (EEC) Regional group created by the **Treaty of Rome** (1957) with the primary aims of free movement of goods, **services**, capital and people between member countries. Initial membership of six (France, Germany, Italy, Belgium, Netherlands, Luxembourg) was extended by the accession of the UK, Ireland and Denmark in 1973, Greece in 1981, Portugal and Spain in 1986. In 1987 amendments to the Treaty of Rome came into effect in the *Single European Act* aimed to complete the **Single European Market** by the end of 1992. The **Maastricht Treaty** (1991) covers political and monetary union and adds new areas of formalized cooperation. It also changed the EEC formally to EC (**European Community**).

European Federation of Conference Towns (EFCT)

Regional organization founded 1964 to bring together European towns acting as venues for **conferences**; facilitate exchange of information and publication of studies; collaborate with institutions and organizations concerned with organization of conferences; promote Europe as a whole and individual member towns as conference destinations.
[www.fiec.org]

European Free Trade Association (EFTA)

Established in 1960, EFTA aimed to bring about free trade in industrial goods and to contribute to the liberalization and expansion of world trade. Now it serves as the structure through which the four remaining members (Iceland, Liechtenstein, Norway, Switzerland) participate in the European Economic Area (EEA) together with the 15 members of the **European Union**.
[www.efta.int]

European Fund

Term used in connection with three main **European Union** institutions of interest in the context of travel, tourism and hospitality: *European Development Fund (EDF)* to provide aid under the **Lomé Convention** and the **Cotonou Agreement**; *European Regional Development Fund (ERDF)* to make grants and loans for the development of less developed **regions** of the Union; *European Social Fund (ESF)* to assist the redeployment of workers who become unemployed, particularly by the creation and policies of the Community. Also relevant is the *European Agricultural Guarantee and Guidance Fund*, which has contributed, i.a., to the development of **farm** and **rural tourism.**

European Investment Bank (EIB)

A nonprofit bank based in Luxembourg set up under the **Treaty of Rome** in 1958 to finance capital projects in the **European Economic Community (EEC)** through long-term loans to private **companies** and public institutions, which further the aims of the Community.
[www.eib.org]

European Tourism Action Group (ETAG)

An international body founded in 1981 by the **European Travel Commission** as a technical liaison group with the aims of exchanging information and developing joint action between different **sectors** of European tourism.
[www.etag-euro.org]

European Travel Commission (ETC)

Regional body set up 1948 to promote travel to the European area represented by members, particularly from the USA, Canada, Japan, Australia and Latin America; to foster **international tourism** cooperation in Europe; to facilitate exchange of information; to undertake or commission research. Members are **National Tourism Organizations** in some 30 European countries (2000).
[www.etc-europe-travel.org]

European Union (EU)

Established by the *Treaty on European Union* (**Maastricht Treaty**) in 1993, the Union seeks to promote further European integration. The Treaty has three main elements, called 'the pillars': the **European Community (EC)**, foreign policy and interior policy. The EC is the main part of the European Union; technically foreign policy and interior policy are not part of the Community but part of the Union. Travel, tourism and hospitality are major activities in the Community, receiving increasing attention from its institutions.
[www.europa.eu.int]

European Union of Tourist Officers (EUTO)

Regional organization of national associations and individuals established 1975 to promote the exchange of experience and coordination, development and cooperation in matters relating to 'the profession'.
[www.euto.org]

Federation of ASEAN Travel Agents (FATA)

Regional sectoral organization of **tour operators** and **travel agents** in **ASEAN** countries.

Federation of International Youth Travel Organizations (FIYTO)

International **federation** founded 1951 to promote educational,

cultural and social travel among young people, assist the development of youth travel organizations, and further their interests with respect to other international organizations.
[www.fiyto.org]

Federation of Nordic Travel Agents' Associations Regional sectoral **federation** of national associations in the five **Nordic** countries.

Institute of Air Transport (IAT) International organization founded 1954, following from the French national association set up 1944, which studies economic, technical and policy aspects of air transport, as well as other means of transport, and tourism. [www.ita-paris.com]

Inter-American Development Bank (IDB) A regional development bank established 1959 to contribute to accelerating the process of economic and social development of the **developing countries** of **Latin America** and the Caribbean. The Bank provides finance for projects within the **region** both on commercial terms and as **soft loans**, for member states as well as private enterprise, and also technical assistance and advice, and has regional as well as non-regional membership.
[www.iadb.org]

Inter-American Hotel Association (IAHA) Regional sectoral organization founded 1941 with membership of national associations and individuals in the **Americas.**

Inter-American Travel Congresses (ITC) **Inter-governmental organization** founded 1939 as a specialist body of the **Organization of American States (OAS)** to aid and promote the development of tourism, meetings and **conferences** in the **Americas.**
[www.oas.org/tourism/tr_inte.htm]

International Air Transport Association (IATA) Voluntary international organization of **scheduled** airlines founded 1945 to promote safe, regular and economical air travel and provide means for collaboration among international **carriers.** All members are involved in **trade association** (non-tariff) activities, while participation in the coordination of international **fares** and rates is optional. An important aspect of the Association's work is accreditation of **agents** to allow them to sell **scheduled** airline tickets at published rates.
[www.iata.org]

International Association of Congress Centres International organization founded 1958 to bring together **conference** centres meeting certain criteria, to study the administration and technical problems of international conferences, to promote a common commercial policy, and to coordinate various aspects of conferences.
[www.aipc.org]

International Association of Convention and Visitor Bureaux (IACVB) International body founded 1914, present name adopted 1974. Aims to provide a forum for exchange of information and to promote professional practices; conducts research into the economic impact of **conventions** and of **visitors** on host communities. Members are **city** convention bureaux, mainly in North America.
[www.iacvb.org]

International Association of Scientific Experts in Tourism (AIEST) International body founded 1951 to promote scientific activity on the part of its members and to support the activity of centres of tourism research and education.
[www.aiest.org]

International Association of Tour Managers (IATM) Membership organization of individual **tour managers**, operators of transport, **accommodation** and other **travel industry services** worldwide. It promotes standards of competence and professionalism of its members, social contact and exchange of ideas between them, and represents them to the general public.
[www.iatm.org]

International Automobile Federation (FIA) International organization founded 1904, which aims to develop and organize motor touring, assist motorists, organize and promote motor sport, study problems related to motor vehicles and protect the interests of their users. Members are national automobile associations and clubs.
[www.fia.com]

International Bank for Reconstruction and Development (IBRD) See **World Bank Group**

DICTIONARY OF TRAVEL, TOURISM AND HOSPITALITY

International Bureau for Youth Tourism and Exchanges International federal organization founded 1961 to create conditions for, and to foster the development of **youth tourism** and exchanges.

International Bureau of Social Tourism (BITS) Founded in 1963, the Bureau aims to promote the development of **social tourism**, coordinate the activities of members, and inform members on economic, social and cultural aspects of social tourism. Membership consists of governmental and national associations.
[www.bits-int.org]

International Chamber of Shipping (ICS) Founded 1921 as *International Shipping Conference*, present name adopted 1948. Aims to promote internationally the interests of national associations of shipowners and operators and exchange of information on all aspects of shipping.
[www.marisec.org]

International Civil Aviation Organization (ICAO) Inter-governmental organization established 1947 as a specialized agency of the **United Nations**. Aims to develop the principles and techniques of international air navigation and foster the planning and development of international air transport. Major concerns are technical standards, practices and procedures, new technology and technical assistance to members.
[www.icao.int]

International Congress and Convention Association (ICCA) International organization founded 1964 to contribute to the development of all types of international meetings. It disseminates market information, initiates and organizes training, and facilitates the rendering of professional **services** by its members. *Multinational Meetings Information Services BV* is a related research organization of the Association.
[www.icca.nl]

International Council on Monuments and Sites (ICOMOS) International organization founded 1965, to further the **conservation**, protection, rehabilitation and enhancement of monuments, buildings and sites; to bring together individuals and bodies involved in conservation; to exchange information and promote interest in and protection of **cultural heritage**; has separate national committees in more than 100 countries.
[www.international.icomos.org]

International Council of Museums (ICOM) Voluntary association of individuals and institutions in more than 100 countries formed 1946 to further international cooperation among **museums** and to advance museum interests.
[ww.icom.org]

International Development Association (IDA) See **World Bank Group**

International Exhibitions Bureau Inter-governmental organization set up 1928 by International Convention to supervise the application of the Convention, which regulates the frequency of international exhibitions and establishes the guarantees and facilities the organizing country is required to offer to exhibitors.
[www.bie-paris.org]

International Federation of Camping and Caravanning International organization formed 1932, to link camping clubs and associations, collect and exchange information, and facilitate cooperation between members.
[www.ficc.be]

International Federation of Tour Operators (IFTO) Voluntary international organization formed 1970 to represent national associations of **tour operators.**

International Festival and Events Association (IFEA) An organization providing information, education and resources to its members who are **festival** and event managers and those who provide products and **services** to them.
[www.ifea.com]

International Finance Corporation (IFC) See **World Bank Group**

International Flight Catering Association (IFCA) Worldwide **trade association** established 1980 representing **catering** departments and subsidiaries of airlines, independent **in-flight** caterers, and suppliers.
[www.ifcanet.com]

International Forum of Travel and Tourism Advocates (IFTTA) Individual membership organization of travel attorneys and travel executives founded 1983 to promote international cooperation on legal issues as they relate to travel and tourism.
[www.tay.ac.uk/iftta]

International Hotel and Restaurant Association (IHRA) International sectoral organization founded 1946, replacing the *International Hotelmen's Association* and the *International Hotel Alliance*. Aims to act as the international organization of the **hotel** and **restaurant industry** and generally perform the functions of a **trade** association at international level. Members include national associations; hotel and restaurant chains and **establishments**; industry service and supply **firms**.
[www.ihra.com]

International Labour Organisation (ILO) **Inter-governmental organization** established as a UN specialized agency, which aims to improve working and living conditions, the spread of social security and the maintenance of social justice. ILO formulates international policies and programmes, creates labour standards and offers technical assistance to **developing countries** in education, training and research, including travel, tourism and hospitality.
[www.ilo.org]

International Maritime Organization (IMO) **Inter-governmental organization** established as a UN specialized agency 1948, present name adopted 1982, to provide machinery for cooperation among governments on technical matters affecting international merchant shipping, with special responsibility for safety of life at sea and efficient navigation, prevention of **pollution** by ships and other craft.
[www.imo.org]

International Monetary Fund (IMF) **Inter-governmental organization** established 1947 as a UN specialized agency to encourage international monetary cooperation and in particular to maintain **exchange rate** stability, assist countries with **balance of payments** difficulties, facilitate **multilateral** payments between countries and remove **foreign exchange** and foreign trade restrictions. It also provides recommendations for reporting travel receipts and payments as a basis for travel estimates in the balance of payments.
[www.imf.org]

International Organization for Standardization (ISO) World-wide **federation** founded 1947, of national standards bodies (ISO member countries) responsible for the preparation of International Standards, which include, i.a., the **country** and **currency codes.**
[www.iso.ch]

International Ho-Re-Ca International sectoral **federation** founded 1949 to bring together national organizations of **hotel, restaurant** and **café** proprietors in order to develop **services** in public interest.
[www.horeca.be]

International Road Transport Union (IRU) International sectoral organization founded 1947, present name adopted 1948. Aims to study questions in road transport, promote unification and simplification of regulations and practices; coordinate and support efforts made in different countries to develop transport of passengers and goods by road. Members are national organizations, vehicle manufacturers and international associations.
[www.iru.org]

International Shipping Federation (ISF) Founded 1909 as a body representing the interests of European shipowners as employers, scope extended 1919 to become a worldwide organization concerned with all matters relating to the employment and safety of merchant seamen.
[www.marisec.org]

International Special Events Society (ISES) An organization providing education, certification, information, resources and **networking** to its members who are professional event managers and those who provide products and services to them.
[www.ises.com]

International Union of Railways (IUR) International sectoral organization founded 1922. Aims to unify and improve conditions relating to construction and operation of railways engaged

in international traffic, coordinate, standardize and represent railway interests.
[www.uic.asso.fr]

International Youth Hostel Federation (IYHF) International organization founded 1932, present name adopted 1942. Coordinates activities of national associations, provides an exchange of information, and encourages the development of youth **hostels**.
[www.iyhf.org]

Islamic Development Bank (IDB) A regional financial institution established 1975 to encourage the economic development and social progress of member countries and of Islamic communities in non-member countries. Its major activities include the provision of interest-free loans and technical assistance.
[www.isdb.org]

Latin American Civil Aviation Commission (LACAC) Regional **inter-governmental organization** founded 1973 to provide a framework for cooperation and coordination of activities of civil aviation authorities of member states.

Latin American Confederation of Tourist Organizations (COTAL) Founded 1957 to group national associations of **travel agents** and **tour operators** of **Latin America** and promote their and their members' interests, as well as to assist in improving **tourist attractions**, facilities and **services**.
[www.world-tourism.org/cotal-e.htm]

Meeting Professionals International (MPI) Leading global **personnel association** with more than 19 000 members in 64 countries and more than 60 chapters (2001) providing education, research, professional development and **networking** opportunities.
[www.mpiweb.org]

Multilateral Investment Guarantee Agency (MIGA) See **World Bank Group**

Multinational Meetings Information Services BV See **International Congress and Convention Association (ICCA)**

Nordic Hotel and Restaurant Association Regional sectoral organization founded 1937, which aims to coordinate

cooperation between national **hotel** and **restaurant** associations in the five **Nordic Countries.**

Nordic Tourist Board Regional organization founded 1923 by Nordic **National Tourism Organizations**, which adopted present title 1980. It aims to work for and develop Nordic tourism, facilitate travel to and within the **Nordic countries**, and coordinate projects of common interest.

Organisation for Economic Co-operation and Development (OECD) Inter-governmental organization, which in 1961 replaced the *Organisation for European Economic Co-operation (OEEC)* set up 1948. It aims to achieve high economic growth and employment with financial stability in member countries; to contribute to economic development of less advanced countries; to contribute to the expansion of **multilateral** world trade. Its *Tourism Committee* has monitored for a number of years government tourism policies and trends in **international tourism** in the OECD area.
[www.oecd.org]

Organization of African Unity (OAU) Regional **inter-governmental organization** established 1963 to promote unity and solidarity of African states; coordinate and intensify their cooperation; defend their sovereignty, territorial integrity and independence; and harmonize members' policies. Main impact on tourism development is through OAU specialized agencies.
[www.oau.oua.org]

Organization of American States (OAS) Originally founded 1890 as regional **inter-governmental organization**. Major purposes include strengthening the peace and security of the **hemisphere** as well as providing economic, social and cultural development. Tourism is the concern of **Inter-American Travel Congresses,** a specialist body of the OAS founded 1939.
[www.oas.org]

Organization of Central American States (OCAS) Regional **inter-governmental organization** of five Central American countries formed 1951 to strengthen their unity, settle disputes, provide mutual assistance, and promote economic, social and cultural development through joint action.
[www.ocas.org]

Organization of the Petroleum Exporting Countries (OPEC) **Inter-governmental organization** set up 1960 by a number of oil-producing countries with a view to controlling the world price of oil. Of these only Indonesia ranks as a significant **international tourism destination**, but as a result of their oil-based wealth, most of the OPEC countries generate a significant volume of travel abroad by their **residents.**
[www.opec.org]

Pacific Asia Travel Association (PATA) Regional organization founded 1951, present name adopted 1986. Aims to encourage and assist in the development of travel **industries** throughout Pacific-Asia through research, education, training, product development, **heritage conservation**, promotion and related activities. Members are governments and **private sector** organizations worldwide. [www.pata.org]

South Pacific Tourism Organization (SPTO) Established 1983 as *Tourism Council of the South Pacific (TCSP)*, a **non-governmental organization** by National Tourism Organizations of twelve South Pacific island countries, the Council became a regional **inter-governmental organization** in 1988, to foster regional cooperation in tourism and to enhance the contribution of tourism to economic and social development of the member countries. It is assisted by the **European Union** within the framework of the Pacific Regional Tourism Development Programme under the **Cotonou Agreement** as well as by other **multilateral** and **bilateral** technical and development assistance agencies.
[www.tcsp.com]

Southern Africa Regional Tourism Council (SARTOC) Established 1973 as a regional **inter-governmental organization** to develop and promote tourism to and within member countries.

Third World Tourism European Ecumenical Network (TEN) Founded 1981 with the stated aim to reduce the damage caused by tourism in the **Third World** by education for tourists, **tour operators** and others, cooperation with others, and efforts to find alternatives within tourism and alternatives to tourism.

Union of International Associations (UIA) Founded 1907 as *Central Office of International Associations*, the Union undertakes and promotes study of and research into international organizations, and publishes, i.a., the *Yearbook of International Organizations*.
[www.uia.org]

Union of International Fairs (UIF) International non-profit organization founded 1925 with the principal aim of furthering international trade through its members who organize several hundred international events.
[www.ufinet.org]

United Nations (UN) Universal organization established 1945, to which almost all sovereign states belong. Its fundamental aims are to maintain international peace and security and to develop cooperation in economic, social, cultural and other aspects of relations between states. There have been several major UN resolutions on **international tourism** but the UN's main direct impact on tourism is through the activities of regional **commissions** and specialized agencies, in particular the **World Tourism Organization.**
[www.un.org]

United Nations Development Programme (UNDP) Specialized agency of the **United Nations** formed 1950, which assumed its current name and form 1965 with the merger of UN development assistance activities, to act as the central funding, planning and coordinating UN organization for technical cooperation. UNDP has the broadest coverage of any development organization and a significant involvement in tourism in **developing countries.**
[www.undp.org]

United Nations Educational, Scientific and Cultural Organization (UNESCO) **Inter-governmental organization** formed 1945. As a **United Nations** specialized agency UNESCO exists to promote international collaboration in education, science and culture. Involvement in tourism includes educational facilities, studies of social and cultural impacts, and **conferences**. See also **World Heritage Sites.**
[www.unesco.org]

United Nations Environment Programme (UNEP) Specialized agency of

United Nations formed 1972 to coordinate inter-governmental measures for the monitoring and protection of the **environment**. Functions extend to all issues of environmental concern and action leading to environmentally sound development, including tourism development, and funding, training and technical support to programmes of wildlife and **national park management**.
[www.unep.org]

Universal Federation of Travel Agents' Associations (UFTAA) An international organization founded 1966 by merger of two existing organizations. Aims to negotiate with **principals** and international bodies on behalf of the travel agency **industry** and profession, and provide for them standing, protection and assistance through national associations.
[www.uftaa.com]

West African Development Bank (WADB) Regional development bank established 1973 to promote balanced development and economic integration of West Africa, including the financing of projects.
[www.polisci.com/world/nation/70.htm]

World Association of Travel Agencies (WATA) An international sectoral organization founded 1949 with independent travel agencies as members (one per metropolitan area unit), which aims to contribute to the profits of member agencies and their protection by assisting in the development and organization of tourism, providing information to foster such development and by reducing risks through collective action.
[www.wata.net]

World Bank Group A group of **multilateral** UN development specialized agencies whose purpose is to help raise the **standard of living** in **developing countries** by lending funds, providing advice and technical assistance, and stimulating investment by others. *The International Bank for Reconstruction and Development (IBRD)* [www.worldbank.org] lends to governments and to other entities against guarantees by governments. *The International Development Association (IDA)* [www.worldbank.org.ida] makes concessional loans to the poorest countries. *The International Finance Corporation (IFC)* [www.ifc.org], an affiliate, promotes growth in the **private sector**.

Another affiliate, *the Multilateral Investment Guarantee Agency (MIGA)* [www.miga.org] protects investors from non-commercial risk. All the institutions are significantly involved in tourism development.

World Health Organization (WHO) Inter-governmental organization established 1946 as a specialized agency of the **United Nations**, it has particular responsibility for international health matters and public health and a wide range of functions, including world-wide monitoring of diseases and advising on recommended **vaccination** requirements for travellers.
[www.who.int]

World Industry Council on the Environment (WICE) International organization established 1993 by leading **companies** from 23 countries on the initiative of the *International Chamber of Commerce* to provide business leadership in the field of **environment** and sustainable development.

World Leisure and Recreation Association (WLRA) Founded 1956, present name adopted 1973. Aims to improve the quality of life through proper use of **leisure** and **recreation**; promote awareness of the significance of leisure and recreation; provide a forum for discussion and foster research in the field. Members are individuals, organizations and governments.
[http://www.worldleisure.org]

World Tourism Organization (WTO) **Inter-governmental organization** established 1975 as a UN specialized agency, when it replaced the **non-governmental** *International Union of Official Travel Organizations (IUOTO)*, founded 1925. In addition to continuing the technical work of its predecessor, WTO is concerned with tourism promotion and development worldwide. Among its main functions are monitoring trends, statistical analysis, provision of information and assistance to authorities in planning and managing tourism in their countries. Its members include 139 countries and territories as well as over 350 affiliate members from the **public** and **private sectors** (2001).
[www.world-tourism.org]

World Travel and Tourism Council (WTTC) Global coalition of chief executive officers of **companies** in various **sectors** of travel and tourism, including transportation, accommodation, **catering, recreation**, cultural and travel **services**. Created 1990, it aims to promote expansion of travel and tourism **markets** and encourage quality services to **customers.**

[www.wttc.org]

3

National
Organizations

National Organizations: Australia and New Zealand

Association of Australian Convention Bureaux (AACB) Organization of **convention and visitor bureaux**, Quantas Airways, and **Australian Tourist Commission**, concerned with fostering the development of the Australian meetings **industry**.
[http://www.aacb.org.au]

Australian Automobile Association (AAA) Coordinating body of State and Territory **motoring organizations.**
[http://www.aaa.asn.au]

Australian Bus and Coach Association (ABCA) Umbrella organization of **bus** and **coach** associations representing them to governments and other bodies and providing information on the **industry.**

Australian Council of Tour Wholesalers (ACTW) Trade association of **tour operators** and **travel agents** operating wholesaling programmes founded to represent and protect their interests.

Australian Federation of Travel Agents (AFTA) Trade association established 1957 to represent the interests of **retail travel agents**. Membership includes more than 1500 outlets and some 500 allied members in other **sectors** of travel and tourism.
[http://www.afta.com.au]

Australian Hotels Association (AHA) National **trade association** of **hotels** and **resorts** representing some 6000 **establishments.**
[http://www.aha.org.au]

Australian Institute of Tourism Officers (AITO) Professional body of members drawn mainly from regional and local tourism offices.
[http://www.aito.com.au]

Australian Institute of Travel and Tourism (AITT) Professional body of individuals employed in Australian travel and tourism with a national network of chapters.
[http://www.aitt.asn.au]

Australian State Government Organizations
Australian Capital Territory Tourism Commission (ACTTC/Canberra)
Northern Territory Tourist Commission (NTTC/Darwin)
[http://www.nttc.com.au]
Queensland Tourist and Travel Corporation (QTTC/Brisbane)
[http://www.qttc.com.au]
South Australian Tourism Commission (SATC/Adelaide)
[http://www.southaustralia.com]
Tourism New South Wales (TNSW/Sydney)
[http://www.tourism.nsw.gov.au]
Tourism Tasmania (Hobart)
[http://www.tourismtasmania.com.au]
Tourism Victoria (Melbourne)
[http://www.tourism.vic.gov.au]
Western Australian Tourism Commission (WATC/Perth)
[http://www.wa.gov.au/watc]

Australian Tourism Export Council (ATEC) Trade association founded 1972 to represent the interests of the **inbound sector** of the Australian **tourism industry**. In addition to a wide range of industry **firms** and organizations, its membership includes the **Australian Tourist Commission** and **State Government Organizations.** [http://www.atec.net.au]

Australian Tourism Portfolio The Federal Government involvement in tourism comprises three entities:
Office of National Tourism aims to maximize the contribution of tourism to the economy and develops, implements and delivers Federal Government policies and programmes.
[http://www.dist.gov.au/tourism/]

Bureau of Tourism Research is a national research body jointly funded by the Federal and State governments.
[http://www.btr.gov.au]

Australian Tourist Commission is a statutory authority responsible for the promotion of Australia overseas.
[http://www.atc.net.au]

Australian Tourist Commission (ATC)
See **Australian Tourism Portfolio**

Australian Transport Organizations
Airport Consultative Committees (ACCs)
Airport Facilitation Committees (AFCs)
Airservices Australia (ASA)
[http://www.airservices.gov.au]
Australian Bus and Coach Association (ABCA)
Australian Transport Council (ATC)
[http://www.dotrs.gov.au/atc/]
Aviation Industry Advisory Committee (AIAC)
Civil Aviation Safety Authority (CASA)
[http://www.casa.gov.au]
Federal Airports Corporation (FAC)
International Air Services Commission (IASC)
[http://www.dotrs.gov.iasc]
National Advisory Facilitation Committee (Australia) (NAFC)
National Passenger Processing Committee (NPPC)
Regional Airlines Association of Australia (RAAA)
[http://www.raaa.com.au]
Tourism Aviation Group (TAG)

Australian Youth Hostels Association (AYHA) Individual non-profit membership organization coordinating Australian State and Territory Youth Hostels Associations.
[http://www.yha.com.au]

Bureau of Tourism Research (BTR) See **Australian Tourism Portfolio**

Catering Institute of Australia (CIA) **Professional body** of individuals in the Australian food service **industry.**
[http://www.cateringinstitute.com.au]

Federal Airports Corporation (FAC) An Australian organization responsible for creating and enforcing civil aviation regulations.

Inbound Tour Operators Council New Zealand (ITOC) Trade association of inbound **tour operators** (full members) and their suppliers (allied members).
[http://www.itoc.org.nz]

National Restaurant and Catering Association (NRCA) Australian **trade association**, which represents members and promotes the **industry.**
[http://www.restaurantcater.asn.au]

New Zealand Convention Association (NZCA) Central organization of **convention and visitor bureaux, hotel** and transport operators and **conference management companies**, which markets New Zealand overseas as a **conference** destination.
[http://www.conventionsnz.co.nz]

New Zealand Hotel and Catering Industry Training Board (NZHCITB) Statutory body established as one of New Zealand training boards to assist the **industry** to provide systematic training and development.

New Zealand Institute of Travel and Tourism (NZITT) Professional **body** of individuals employed in New Zealand travel and tourism.
[http://www.nzitt.co.nz]

New Zealand Tourism Board (NZTB) Statutory body established 1991 with a responsibility for the development and **marketing** of New Zealand as a **tourist** destination.
[http://www.nztb.govt.nz/]

New Zealand Tourism Industry Association (NZTIA) A voluntary organization with membership drawn from national sectoral associations, regional tourism organizations, educational and training institutions, supply firms and tourism businesses, to promote the **industry**.
[http://www.tianz.org.nz]

New Zealand Trade Associations in Travel, Tourism and Hospitality
Bus and Coach Association of New Zealand (BCA)
[http://www.busandcoach.co.nz]
Camp and Cabin Association of New Zealand (CCA)

DICTIONARY OF TRAVEL, TOURISM AND HOSPITALITY

Food Services Association of New Zealand (FANZ)
Hotel Association of New Zealand (HANZ)
Motel Association of New Zealand (MANZ) [http://www.manz.co.nz]
Travel Agents Association of New Zealand (TAANZ)
[http://www.taanz.org.nz]

Office of National Tourism See **Australian Tourism Portfolio**

Tourism Council Australia (TCA) Successor body to *Australian Tourism Industry Association (ATIA)*, which provides a national umbrella body for travel, tourism, leisure and hospitality **industries** and promotes them.
[http://www.tourism.org.au]

Tourism Training Australia (TTA) Non-profit **company** of the **tourism industry** operating with financial assistance from the Federal Government, to identify the training needs of the industry and to take action to meet them.
[http://www.tourismtraining.com.au]

Youth Hostels Association of New Zealand (YHANZ) Individual non-profit membership organization providing low-cost **hostel** accommodation with a particular focus on young travellers.
[http://www.yha.org.nz]

National Organizations: North America

Air Transport Association of America (ATA) Oldest and largest US airline **trade association,** whose members account for the bulk of all passenger and cargo traffic of US **scheduled** airlines. [http://www.airlines.org]

Air Transport Association of Canada (ATAC) Organization of Canadian airlines, which sets standards and operational rules. [http://www.atac.ca/]

Airlines Reporting Corporation (ARC) Independent US **corporation** set up by **domestic airlines** concerned with **travel agent** appointments and operations. [http://www.arccorp.com]

American Automobile Association (AAA) Individual membership organization providing a wide range of **services** for motorists, founded 1902. [http://www.aaa.com]

American Bus Association (ABA) Trade association of intercity and **charter bus companies**, with a total membership of more than 3000, consisting of approx. 800 operators in the United States and Canada and 2300 other organizations in travel and tourism. [http://www.buses.org]

American Hotel & Lodging Association (AHLA) Leading North American hospitality **federation** of state lodging associations, with some 13 000 property members worldwide representing more than 1.7 million guest rooms (2001), with usual **trade association** functions. [http://www.ahla.com]

American Recreation Coalition (ARC) A Washington-based non-profit organization that seeks to encourage public–private **partnerships** to enhance and protect recreational opportunities and the resources on which such

experiences are based. It conducts research, organizes meetings and **conferences**, disseminates information, monitors legislative and regulatory proposals, and works with government agencies and the US Congress to study public policy issues that will shape future recreational opportunities. [http://www.funoutdoors.com]

American Resort Development Association (ARDA) US **trade association** representing the **vacation ownership** and **resort** development **industries**. [http://www.arda.org]

American Society of Travel Agents (ASTA) US **trade association** with some non-US membership of **travel agents,** and the **companies** whose products they sell, such as tours, **cruises, hotels** and **car rentals**, with 26 000 members (2001), established 1931 and mainly concerned with advancing the interests of members, as well as protecting the interests of the travelling public. [http://www.asta.net.org]

Association of American Railroads (AAR) Trade association of US passenger and freight railways. [http://www.aar.org]

Association of Canadian Travel Agents (ACTA) National **trade association** established 1977 to represent, support and assist in the conduct of their businesses. [http://www.acta.net]

Association of Travel Marketing Executives (ATME) Professional body of executives with responsibilities in the **marketing** of travel and tourism worldwide. Members come from airlines, **hotels, resorts, cruise** lines, **car rental companies, advertising** and **public relations firms**, research groups and tourist offices of domestic and foreign destinations. [http://www.atme.org]

Canadian Association of Caterers (CAC)
A professional association of caterers and their suppliers in Canada, conducting research, promoting education and training, and dealing with issues of common interest.
[http://www.enville.com/reg/associations/cac/html]

Canadian Hotel and Motel Association (CHMA) Trade association which represents its members and provides to them education, information and other **services.**
[http://www.chma.on.ca]

Canadian Tourism Commission (CTC)
One of the first public–private **sector partnerships** in tourism responsible for planning, directing, managing and implementing programmes for promoting tourism in Canada, between the Federal, provincial and territorial governments, and **tourism industry** businesses and associations.
[http://www.canadatourism.com]

Canadian Tourism Human Resource Council (CTHRC) Industry organization promoting and enhancing professionalism in Canadian tourism through setting industry standards, training and certification.
[http://www.cthrc.ca]

Convention Industry Council (CIC) US organization whose members represent most **convention industry** organizations; it conducts research, administers education and certification programmes, and discusses matters of common interest.
[http://www.c-i-c.org]

Cruise Lines International Association (CLIA) US-based internationally orientated **trade association** of **cruise** lines, which promotes cruises mainly through and with **travel agents** and performs such functions as the appointment of travel agents to sell cruises of its members.
[http://www.cruising.org]

Department of Transportation (DOT) US federal, provincial, state, county or local department concerned with developing and implementing policies for improving and regulating transportation facilities.
[http://www.dot.gov]

Environmental Protection Agency (EPA)
US federal government agency that enforces clean air and water legislation.
[http://www.epa.gov]

Federal Aviation Administration (FAA)
Government agency in the US **Department of Transportation**, responsible for the formulation of regulations and supervision or control of airline and **airport** operations.
[http://www.faa.gov]

Federal Maritime Commission (FMC)
Government agency in the US **Department of Transportation**, responsible for the formulation of regulations and supervision of the transportation of passengers and cargo at sea.
[http://www.fmc.gov]

Hospitality Sales and Marketing Association International (HSMAI) US-based international voluntary association with several thousand members and chapters in most parts of the world. Its stated aim is to provide members with 'educational opportunity to learn, develop and grow, so their professionalism in the **hotel** industry will be enhanced'. [http://www.hsmai.org]

Institute of Certified Travel Agents (ICTA) US **professional body** providing educational resources for the travel **industry** and administering the *Certified Travel Counselor (CTC)* programme. [http://www.icta.com]

International Association of Amusement Parks and Attractions (IAAPA) US-based **trade association** of the amusement **industry**, which exists to foster professionalism, to promote the **market** for its goods and **services**, and to represent it to government.
[http://www.iaapa.org]

(International) Council on Hotel, Restaurant and Institutional Education (CHRIE) North American non-profit organization with individual and organization membership drawn mainly from education, training and human resource development, established 1946 'to foster the advancement of teaching, training, learning, research and practice in the field of hospitality and tourism **management**, and to facilitate the professional development of its members'.
[http://www.chrie.org]

NATIONAL ORGANIZATIONS: NORTH AMERICA

National Amusement Park Historical Association (NAPHA) US national organization concerned with the **preservation** and enjoyment of the past, present and future of the amusement and **theme park industry**. [http://www.napha.org/]

National Association of RV Parks & Campgrounds (ARVC) US **trade association** of campground owners, with a membership of more than 3700 nationwide including **industry** suppliers and park developers (2001). [http://www.gocampinginamerica.com]

National Business Travel Association (NBTA) US **trade association** of firms specializing in business travel. [http://www.nbta.org]

National Passenger Traffic Association (NPTA) US **personnel association** of managers of **corporate** travel departments.

National Recreation and Park Association (NRPA) US national association formed 1965 by the merger of several organizations of long standing. It aims to promote the interests of the park and **recreation** movement through public information, political advocacy, research and professional development. [http://www.nrpa.org]

National Restaurant Association (NRA) Leading US **trade association** founded 1919 to represent, educate and promote the food service **sector**, comprised of 844 000 **restaurant** and food service outlets employing more than 11 million people (2001). [http://www.restaurant.org]

National Tour Association (NTA) Trade **association** of US **tour operators**. [http://www.ntaonline.com]

Society of Incentive Travel Executives (SITE) US **personnel association** of travel managers specializing in **incentive travel**. [http://www.site.intl.org]

State Tourism Offices (US) Government agencies responsible for travel development in each of the 50 states. See also **Visitor(s) and Convention Bureaux**, which perform similar functions in some of the states and major cities.

Tourism Industries (US) Office in the US *International Trade Administration* in the Department of Commerce, established 1996 following the abolition of the *United States Travel and Tourism Administration (USTTA)*, with a mission 'to foster an **environment** in which the travel and tourism **industry** can generate jobs through tourism exports', provide for tourism representation and policy coordination at federal level through the *Tourism Policy Council*. [http://www.tinet.ita.doc.gov]

Tourism Industry Association of Canada (TIAC) A voluntary organization with membership drawn from all **sectors** of the **tourism industry** promoting the interests of Canadian tourism. [http://www.tiac-aitc.ca]

Travel and Tourism Research Association (TTRA) North American body with both **corporate** and individual, and with some overseas, membership drawn from most parts of **travel** and **tourism industry**, as well as government, universities and consultancies, serving the needs of both producers and users of travel research, through meetings, publications and other means. [http://www.ttra.com]

Travel Industry Association of America (TIA) Originally founded 1941, a US voluntary non-profit organization with membership drawn from all **sectors** of the **travel industry** with a view to promoting and facilitating increased travel to and within the United States. The *US Travel Data Center*, which is now the research department of the TIA, seeks to meet the research needs of TIA members and the travel industry through economic and **marketing research**. [http://www.tia.org]

United Motorcoach Association (UMA) North American **trade association** founded 1971 as the *United Bus Owners of America* whose membership stands at more than 700 'active' operating member **companies** and close to 200 manufacturers, suppliers and related businesses as 'associate' members (2001). [http://www.uma.org]

United States Tour Operators Association (USTOA) Trade association of

US-based **tour operators** responsible for the majority of tours and vacation **packages** sold by **travel agents** in the USA.
[http://www.ustoa.com]

US Travel Data Center (USTDC) See **Travel Industry Association of America (TIA)**

ACE International *Association for Conferences and Events*, UK **personnel association** providing central source of information on various aspects of **conference**, exhibition and event organization. [www.martex.co.uk]

Air Transport Users Council Established in the UK first by the **Civil Aviation Authority (CAA)** under the terms of the Civil Aviation Act 1971 as the *Airline Users Committee*. Makes reports and recommendations to the CAA for furthering the interests of users of air transport and investigates complaints against airlines. [www.auc.org.uk]

Air Travel Trust Fund (ATTF) Part of the UK Civil Aviation Authority (CAA) ATOL **consumer** protection system. All **tour operators** offering **package holidays** by air must hold a licence from the CAA and provide a bond. If the operator fails, the CAA uses the bond to pay people abroad and reimburse anyone who has bought a holiday. The Air Travel Trust Fund makes up any shortfall. [www.caa.gov.uk]

Alliance of Retail Travel Agency Consortia (ARTAC) Voluntary British **consortium** of 770 independent **ABTA travel agents** (2001) formed 1975 to enable its members to compete with the **multiples**, all of which brand their agencies as **Worldchoice** agencies.

All-Party Tourism Committee A committee of Members of UK Parliament who have in common an interest in some aspect of tourism; many of them represent constituencies in which tourism is an important element in the economy. As an interest group rather than a pressure group, the Committee seeks, i.a., to monitor and evaluate the implications for tourism of changes in government policy and of changing economic conditions, keep Members of Parliament informed about tourism, and make representations to Ministers.

ARELS *Association of Recognised English Language Services*, a non-profit **trade association** with membership restricted to schools and organizations inspected and recognized by the **British Council**, which follow the Association's regulations and **code of conduct**. Overseas **visitors** coming to Britain primarily to learn English are an important **segment** of visitor traffic and English language schools thus an important part of the **tourism industry**. [www.arels.org.uk]

Arts Councils (UK) The Arts Council of **Great Britain** was originally an independent body as a principal channel for the Government's support of the arts. Following reorganization in the mid 1990s, there are four more or less autonomous Councils, which are also responsible for the distribution of the proceeds of the National Lottery allocated to the arts:
Arts Council of England (ACE)
[www.artscouncil.org.uk]
Scottish Arts Council (SAC)
[www.sac.org.uk]
Arts Council of Wales (ACW)
[www.ccc-acw.org.uk]
Arts Council of Northern Ireland (ACNI)
[www.artscouncil-ni.org]

Association of British Travel Agents (ABTA) UK **trade association** of **tour operators** and **travel agents** whose main purposes are to promote the interests of members, maintain standards of business practice, and represent members with government and other bodies. All members are bonded to ensure the travelling public is protected in the event of a member's financial failure. In 2001 membership comprised 2100 firms. See also **ABTA Bonding Scheme**. [www.abtanet.com/]

Association of Independent Museums (AIM) British voluntary organization of **museums** not administered directly by central government – a significant part of the **tourism industry** – founded 1977 to improve their standards and effectiveness.
[www.museums.org.uk/aim]

Association of Independent Tour Operators (AITO) UK alliance of fully bonded, mainly smaller and specialist, travel **companies** with the aim of providing alternatives to **mass market holidays (vacations)**, with a membership of more than 150 (2001). Set up *Campaign for Real Travel Agents (CARTA)*, which aims to offer **customers** unbiased advice about their **holidays (vacations)** and improve standards.
[www.aito.co.uk]

Association of Leading Visitor Attractions (ALVA) Trade association of Britain's biggest and best known attractions established in 1990, with membership drawn from **museums** and galleries; **heritage** organizations; cathedrals; **leisure** attractions; gardens, **zoos** and **conservation** sites, both in the **public** and **private sectors**. [www.alva.org.uk]. In Scotland there is the **Association of Scottish Visitor Attractions (ASVA).** [www.asva.co.uk]

Association of National Tourist Office Representatives (ANTOR) Personnel association founded in **Great Britain** 1953 to provide means for exchange of views among members and between them and the **tourism industry**, within the wider context of **international tourism** promotion.
[www.touristoffices.org.uk]

Association of Pleasure Craft Operators (APCO) British **trade association** of operators of inland waterway **holidays (vacations)** and boatyards in England and Wales.
[www.canals.com/orgs/apco.htm]

Association of Scottish Visitor Attractions (ASVA) Trade association of organizations directly involved in the provision or **management** of **visitor attractions** in Scotland, which meet certain minimum standards; founded 1988 to foster a greater degree of cooperation between them.
[www.asva.co.uk]

Association of Tourism Teachers and Trainers (ATTT) Personnel association formed 1975 as *Association of Teachers of Tourism (ATT)* with the aim of helping its members to be more effective teachers of tourism. Merged with the **Tourism Society** to form a specialist section of the Society 1981. Present name adopted 1988 to reflect widening interest and involvement in vocational training.
[tour.soc.@btinternet.com]

Automobile Association (AA) The largest of three UK membership organizations providing a wide range of **services** for motorists founded 1905. Leading publisher of atlases, maps and books on various aspects of travel and touring, the Association pioneered, with other **motoring organizations, hotel classification** and **grading** in **Great Britain**. [www.theaa.com]. *Royal Automobile Club (RAC)* was founded 1897 [www.rac.co.uk] and *Royal Scottish Automobile Club* in 1899.
[www.rsac.co.uk]

BAA Formerly the *British Airports Authority*, now the name of the privatized public limited **company** floated in 1987 on the London Stock Exchange to own and operate seven UK **airports** – Gatwick, Heathrow and Stansted, as well as Aberdeen, Edinburgh, Glasgow and Prestwick. It is responsible for their **infrastructure** and **management** and also has interests in eight overseas airports.
[www.baa.co.uk]

Bord Fáilte *Irish Tourist Board*, **national tourism organization** of the Republic of Ireland created under the Tourist Traffic Act, 1955. Following the establishment of **Tourism Ireland Limited**, the new North/South tourism **company**, Bord Fáilte now has responsibility for promoting the development of tourism products and regions, marketing on the island of Ireland, encouraging a sustainable approach to tourism development, and administration of funding under the National Development Plan, in conjunction with the **Department of Tourism, Sport and Recreation**.
[www.ireland.travel.ie]

British Activity Holiday Association (BAHA) Trade association of operators of activity **holidays (vacations)**, which provides, i.a., an advisory service to **consumers.**
[www.baha.org.uk]

NATIONAL ORGANIZATIONS: UNITED KINGDOM AND IRELAND

British Air Transport Association (BATA) Coordinating body which aims to assist by various means in the development of UK civil aviation.
[www.bata.uk.com]

British Arts Festivals Association (BAFA) Coordinating body founded 1970 to encourage greater interest in arts **festivals** in **Great Britain** and abroad through joint **marketing** activities and provision of information.

British Association of Conference Destinations (BACD) Voluntary **local government** organization with membership open to any **local authority** in **Great Britain**, the Channel Islands and the Isle of Man, concerned with the development of Britain as a venue for meetings, **conferences**, exhibitions and **incentive travel**, and promotion in Britain and internationally.
[www.bacd.org.uk]

British Association of Hospitality Accountants (BAHA) Personnel association founded 1969 to promote the interests of financial personnel in the **hotel, catering** and **leisure industries**.
[www.baha.uk.org]

British Association of Leisure Parks, Piers and Attractions (BALPPA) Trade association of owners and senior **management** of UK facilities and trade associate members.
[www.balppa.org]

British Beer and Pub Association Trade association of brewing firms and licensed premises, formerly called the *Brewers Society* and *Brewers & Licensed Retailers Association*, present name adopted 2001, which exercises an important influence through its members' ownership on tourism and hospitality development in **Great Britain.**
[www.beerandpubs.co.uk]

British Casino Association Trade association representing **casinos** in **Great Britain**, all operating as **clubs** under the Gaming Act 1968.
[www.1000casinos.com]

British Council (BC) Independent non-political organization which promotes **Britain** abroad. It provides access to British ideas, people and experience in education and training, books and periodicals, the English language, the arts, sciences and technology. In 2001 the Council was represented in more than 100 countries and well over 200 towns and **cities**. Although not directly concerned with tourism or hospitality, the activities of the Council, like those of the BBC, for example, contribute significantly to the promotion of Britain as a destination for **visitors** from other countries.
[www.britcoun.org]

British Holiday and Home Parks Association (BHHPA) Trade association of operators of chalet, **holiday (vacation)**, touring and tented sites, including residential home parks, and all types of **self-catering** holiday **accommodation**.
[www.ukparks.com]

British Hospitality Association (BHA) Leading British **trade association** of **hotel, restaurant** and **contract catering firms** formed 1972 by merger of two associations of long standing, present name adopted 1992.
[www.bha-online.org.uk]

British Incoming Tour Operators' Association (BITOA) Trade association of **companies** deriving a substantial part of their income from **inbound tourism** by providing tours and other **services** to overseas **visitors** in the UK.
[www.bitoa.co.uk]

British Institute of Facilities Management (BIFM) Professional body formed 1993 for individuals engaged in facilities **management**, defined as the integration of multidisciplinary activities within the built **environment** and the management of their impact on people and the workplace.
[www.bifm.org.uk]

British Institute of Innkeeping (BII) Professional body for the licensed trade whose mission is to promote high standards of professionalism throughout the licensed retail **sector** and to provide information, skills and qualifications to help members run successful businesses. The Institute has over 16 500 members (2001).

British Resorts Association (BRA) Voluntary **local government** organization of

inland and coastal **local authorities** with a tourism commitment and of **regional tourist boards**. The Association acts as a forum for the exchange of ideas and discussion of problems among its members and to protect and promote their interests.
[www.britishresorts.co.uk]

British Retail Consortium (BRC)
Coordinating body of retail **trade associations** formed to promote their common interests. Shopping accounts for a significant proportion of tourist spending in some countries, including Britain.
[www.brc.org.uk]

British Self-Catering Federation (BSCF)
Federation with membership consisting mainly of inspecting letting agencies, managing agencies, and associations letting, managing or representing self-catering **establishments**.

British Spas Federation (BSF) Voluntary association of **local authorities** and **tourist boards** representing principal **spa** towns. Main concerns are the utilization of natural mineral waters of British spas for health purposes and the promotion of spa towns and health centres.
[www.britishspas.co.uk]

British Standards Institution (BSI)
Independent national body incorporated by the Royal Charter and the recognized authority in the UK for the preparation and publication of national standards for industrial and **consumer** products; also source of definitions of such terms as **management** and **work study** in this volume. About 90 per cent of the standards are internationally linked through the **International Organization for Standardization (ISO)**.
[www.bsi.org.uk]

British Tourist Authority (BTA) Statutory body established under the Development of Tourism Act 1969, replacing the voluntary *British Travel Association*, with a specific responsibility for promoting tourism to **Great Britain** from overseas and a general responsibility for promotion and development of tourism and tourist facilities within **Great Britain** as a whole, as well as advising the government on tourism matters.
[http://www.visitbritain.com]

British Waterways Board (BWB) Statutory body with a responsibility as navigational authority for 3200 km (2000 miles) of **canals** and rivers in England, Scotland and Wales, and for their promotion and development for commercial and **leisure** use. More than one-half of the network, known as the *cruising waterways*, is being developed for boating, fishing and other leisure activities.
[www.britishwaterways.co.uk]

Campaign for Real Travel Agents (CARTA) See **Association of Independent Tour Operators (AITO)**

Camping and Caravanning Club
Individual membership association concerned with the promotion and servicing of camping and caravanning. In recent years camping and caravanning accounted for one in four of UK residents' domestic **holidays (vacations)**. [**United Kingdom Tourism Survey**].
[www.campingandcaravanningclub.co.uk]

The Caravan Club British membership organization for touring caravanners, motor caravanners and **trailer** tent campers providing a wide range of **services** and advice on all aspects of caravanning to its members.
[www.caravan.co.uk]

Chamber of Shipping Trade association of the UK shipping **industry**, which represents shipping **company** interests to Government, Parliament, international and other organizations.
[www.british-shipping.org]

Chartered Institute of Marketing (CIM)
UK **professional body** for those engaged in **marketing**. The *Hotel Marketing Association (HMA*, formerly *Hotel Industry Marketing Group, HIMG)* and the *Travel Industry Group (CIMtIG)* are special interest groups of the Institute concerned with hospitality, travel and tourism.
[www.cim.co.uk]

Chartered Institute of Transport (CIT)
UK **professional body** of men and women engaged in all forms of transport and grouped in branches in the UK and overseas.
[www.citrams.org.uk]

City and Guilds of London Institute (CGLI) Independent non-profit UK body

established to promote education and training, offering a wide range of educational and training schemes and awarding certificates, including many in travel and tourism, **hotel** and **catering**, and **leisure** subjects.
[www.city-and-guilds.co.uk]

Civil Aviation Authority (CAA) UK statutory body established under the Civil Aviation Act 1971 and responsible for the economic regulation of UK airlines by licensing **air routes** and **air travel organizers** as well as approving **fares**; for the safety regulation of UK civil aviation by the certification of airlines and aircraft, and by licensing **aerodromes**, flight crew and aircraft engineers; for the provision of **air traffic control** and telecommunications **services**. See also **ATOL Bonding Scheme**.
[www.caa.gov.uk]

Commonwealth Development Corporation (CDC) Statutory body established by the UK Government to channel overseas aid from the UK overseas aid budget, originally to the **developing countries** of the **Commonwealth**, but now also to other developing countries. It may invest alone or in association with others, indirectly through equities and debentures, or directly in projects administered by its own staff. Its involvement includes a wide range of enterprises, including **hotels** and other tourism-related projects.
[www.hmso.gov.uk]

Confederation of British Industry (CBI) An independent non-party political body representing business and **industry**, in particular to inform the government of their needs and problems. The CBI *Tourism Action Group (TAG)*, comprising leading **companies** and organizations in the tourism industry, focuses the industry's efforts on promoting and assisting it.
[www.cbi.org.uk] See also **Tourism Alliance.**

Confederation of Passenger Transport UK (CPT) Trade **association** of **public** and **private sector bus** and **coach** operators, which between them run the bulk of buses and most coaches in the UK. In recent years British residents made fewer than 10 per cent of their **holiday (vacation)** journeys in **Britain** by bus or coach.
[www.cpt-uk.org]

Confederation of Tourism, Hotel and Catering Management Independent UK non-profit examining body with a principal aim of setting and maintaining standards of education through the provision of course syllabuses and examinations for private colleges.
[www.cthcm.com]

Consumers' Association Ltd (CA) Trading subsidiary of the *Association for Consumer Research (ACR)*, a registered charity which exists to carry out research and comparative testing on behalf of **consumers**. Its publications as a membership organization include *Holiday Which?*, as well as books and guide books.
[www.which.net]

Council for Education, Recruitment and Training (CERT) State sponsored agency of the Republic of Ireland responsible for coordinating education, recruitment and training in tourism and hospitality.
[www.cert.ie]

Council for Hospitality Management Education (CHME) Voluntary non-profit organization of around 50 members representing universities and colleges offering courses in the **management** of the hospitality business, with the aim to add to the professional development and status of hospitality management education.
[www.chme.co.uk]

Council for Travel and Tourism (CTT) Coordinating body to provide a forum for travel and tourism organizations in the UK to identify and develop common interests and policies.

Countryside Agency British statutory body established from the merger of the *Rural Development Commission* and the *Countryside Commission* to conserve and enhance the natural beauty of the countryside in England and Wales; to promote social equity and economic opportunity for the people who live there; to help people, wherever they live, to enjoy the countryside.
[www.countryside.gov.uk]

Countryside Commission (CC) See **Countryside Agency**

Countrywide Holidays Association (CHA) British individual membership organization founded 1893 to organize walking and country **holidays (vacations)** in the UK and abroad, including own holiday centres. [www.pedt.demon.co.uk]

Customs and Excise Government Department responsible to the UK Treasury for collecting and administering customs and excise duties and **value added tax (VAT)**. [www.hmce.gov.uk]

Department for Culture, Media and Sport (DCMS) UK Government Department responsible for Government policy relating to the arts, public libraries, **museums** and galleries, tourism, sport and built **heritage** in England – in Scotland, Wales and Northern Ireland these are the responsibility of the devolved administrations. It has overall responsibility for the film **industry** and for alcohol and public entertainment **licensing** in England and Wales. It has also UK-wide responsibility for, i.a., broadcasting, gambling and the National Lottery. [www.culture.gov.uk]

Department for Environment, Food and Rural Affairs (DEFRA) UK Government Department responsible, i.a., for policies on sustainable development and the **environment**; agriculture, horticulture, fisheries and food; rural development and the countryside. [www.defra.gov.uk]

Department for Transport, Local Government and the Regions (DTLR) UK Government Department responsible, i.a., for policies for planning; local and regional government; roads; local transport (England), shipping (England), railways (GB); aviation including the **Civil Aviation Authority (CAA)**. In May 2002, following a Government reorganization, Transport became a separate Department.

Department of Tourism, Sport and Recreation Government Department of the Republic of Ireland responsible for the formulation of national policies for tourism, sport and **recreation**, which are implemented by the state-sponsored bodies and executive agencies under the aegis of the Department. As far as tourism is concerned, the Department is also responsible for funding and supervising roles. [www.irlgov.ie/tourism-sport]

English Heritage *Historic Buildings and Monuments Commission for England*, a statutory body established under the *National Heritage Act 1983* to secure the **preservation** of ancient monuments and historic buildings; to promote preservation and enhancement of **conservation areas**; to promote their public enjoyment. Most of the 400 properties in its care are significant **tourist/visitor attractions**. [www.english-heritage.org.uk] Similar separate bodies exist in Scotland (*Historic Scotland*) and Wales (*Cadw: Welsh Historic Monuments*).

English Nature *Nature Conservancy Council for England*, a statutory body established 1991. It promotes the **conservation** of wildlife and natural features; selects, establishes and manages **National Nature Reserves** and identifies and notifies **Sites of Special Scientific Interest (SSSI)**. Separate independent bodies responsible for promoting nature conservation exist in Scotland and Wales. [www.english-nature.org.uk]

English Tourism Council (ETC) Statutory body established under the Development of Tourism Act 1969 and incorporated under the Act as *English Tourist Board*, present name adopted 2000. Main responsibilities include tourism development in England and advising government on matters concerning tourism in England. [www.englishtourism.org.uk]

English Tourist Board (ETB) See English Tourism Council

Exhibition Industry Federation (EIF) UK coordinating body of associations of exhibition organizers, contractors, venue and hall owners set up by them to promote the growth of the UK exhibition **industry.**

Federation of Tour Operators (FTO) Formed 1967 by a group of established **tour operators** as the *Tour Operators Study Group (TOSG)* to promote cohesive development of the travel **market** from the UK for the benefit of tour operators, the **travel industry** and the general public. It has pioneered, i.a., the first **bonding** scheme to protect holiday makers (1970) and also taken a pro-active stance in promoting **sustainable tourism.** Now represents the 12 biggest UK operators (2001). [www.fto.co.uk]

Guild of Business Travel Agents (GBTA) The Guild provides a forum for UK **travel agents** (all of whom are members of the **Association of British Travel Agents**) concerned with the particular needs of business travellers. They have access to *Guildfares*, specially negotiated low **fares** for **corporate clients.**

Guild of Guide Lecturers (GGL) Founded as a voluntary British association to promote professionalism and act as a link between tourist guides trained and registered by **tourist boards**. *Scottish Tourist Guides Association (STGA)* performs a similar role in Scotland.

Highlands and Islands Enterprise A statutory core body of a network of the *Local Enterprise Companies (LECs)*, which encourage and deliver economic and social **development plans**, training and environmental renewal schemes at local level in the Highlands and Islands. [www.hient.co.uk]

Holiday Care Registered charity established to act as a UK central source of **holiday (vacation)** information for people whose age, disability or other personal or family circumstances affect their choice of holiday (vacation). [www.holidaycare.org.uk]

Hospitality Training Foundation (HtF) The hospitality **industry** *National Training Organization* which represents hospitality employers and is recognized by Government as their voice on all aspects of education, training, skills and qualifications. See also **IMPACT Network of NTOs**. [www.htf.org.uk]

Hotel and Catering International Management Association (HCIMA) UK based **professional body** for **management** in the **hotel and catering industry** formed 1971 by merger of two professional bodies of long standing, present name adopted 1995. [www.hcima.org.uk]

Hotel Marketing Association (HMA) See **Chartered Institute of Marketing (CIM)**

IMPACT Network of NTOs UK network of National Training Organizations (NTOs) formed in 1999 to support and promote education, skills, training and human resource development, to represent the following sectors:
Cultural Heritage (CHNTO)
[www.chnto.co.uk]
Hospitality Training Foundation (HtF)
[www.htf.org.uk]
Information Services (isNTO)
Métier (the arts)
[www.métier.org.uk]
Sport, Recreation and Allied Occupations (SPRITO)
[www.sprito.org.uk]
Travel, Tourism Services and Events (TTENTO)
[www.ttento.com]
The network was due to be abolished in 2002 and replaced by *Sector Skills Councils*.

Incoming Tour Operators Association (ITOA) Irish **trade association** of **companies** which package and promote elements of the Irish tourist product and provide land arrangements and other **services** for overseas traffic generators. [www.itoa-ireland.com]

Inland Waterways Association (IWA) Voluntary organization which campaigns for the **restoration**, retention and development of the navigable waterways in the **British Isles** and their fullest commercial and recreational use. There is also a separate *Scottish Inland Waterways Association (SIWA)*. [www.waterways.org.uk]

Institute of Leisure and Amenity Management (ILAM) UK **professional body** of **leisure** and amenity managers founded 1983 by amalgamation of four existing bodies. Members are drawn from sports centres, arts and entertainment **establishments**, parks, gardens, playgrounds, **museums**, other **tourist/visitor attractions**, and countryside **recreation**. [www.ilam.co.uk]

Institute of Sport and Recreation Management (ISRM) Professional body founded 1921 as *Institute of Baths and Recreation Management* with individual and **corporate** membership. [www.isrm.co.uk]

Institute of Travel and Tourism (ITT) UK **professional body** founded 1956 as *Institute of Travel Agents (ITA)*, present name adopted 1977 with a view to broadening membership base; most members are, however, still engaged in travel agencies.
[www.itt.co.uk]

Irish Hotel Federation National **trade association** of the **hotel** and **guest house industry** of Ireland with the primary function of promoting and defending the interests of its members.
[www.ihf.ie/]

Irish Tourist Industry Confederation (ITIC) Voluntary representative body of all **sectors** of Irish tourism as the voice of Irish tourism.
[www.itic.ie/who.htm]

Irish Travel Agents Association (ITAA) Trade association of 370 retail **travel agents** and 20 **tour operators** representing more than 80 per cent of all outlets in the Republic (2000), which are licensed and bonded with the Government.
[www.itaa.ie/]

Joint Hospitality Industry Congress (JHIC) UK forum of 14 hospitality associations, which sponsor research projects and organize national conferences.

Local Government Association (LGA) Voluntary coordinating organization of local government authorities in England and Wales, many of them with a significant involvement in tourism, formed by the merger of three existing bodies: *Association of County Councils (ACC), Association of District Councils (ADC)* and *Association of Metropolitan Authorities (AMA).*
[www.lga.gov.uk].

Meetings Industry Association (MIA) UK **trade association** providing education and training, a forum and a **corporate** voice on issues of common concern, together with a range of other benefits for members. Membership consists of **firms** concerned with planning, managing and supplying **services** to the meetings **market**.
[www.meetings.org]

National Association of Holiday Centres Limited (NAHC) UK **trade association** founded to promote the interests of **holiday (vacation)** centres.

National Association of Independent Travel Agents (NAITA) A **consortium** of UK **travel agents** formed to provide 'centralized coordination of its members' collective buying power to increase the profitability of members' businesses'. The 900 members (2001) brand their agencies *Advantage Travel Centres.*

National Trust (NT) *National Trust for Places of Historic Interest or Natural Beauty*, a charitable organization founded 1895 to preserve lands and buildings for the benefit of the nation. The main activity is the maintenance of properties and opening them to the public. Scope extends to England, Wales and Northern Ireland [www.nationaltrust.org.uk]. *National Trust for Scotland* is a separate organization.

Northern Ireland Hotels and Caterers Association (NIHCA) Leading sectoral **trade association** founded 1933, which represents most **accommodation** and **catering establishments** in the province registered with the **Northern Ireland Tourist Board.**

Northern Ireland Tourist Board (NITB) Statutory body established under the Development of Tourist Traffic Act (Northern Ireland) 1948, to promote the development of **tourist** traffic, to encourage the provision and improvement of tourist facilities and amenities, and to register certain **catering establishments** in the Province. Following the establishment of **Tourism Ireland Limited,** that company carries out strategic all-Ireland destination **marketing** outside the island of Ireland.
[www.discovernorthernireland.com]

Passenger Shipping Association (PSA) UK **trade association** of **cruise** and passenger **ferry** owners and operators, whose members are bonded to guarantee **consumer** protection from financial failure. The Association administers a cruise information service for the public.
[www.psa-psara.org]

Professional bodies in travel, tourism and hospitality (UK)
Chartered Institute of Transport (CIT)
[www.citrans.org.uk]
Guild of Guide Lecturers (GGL)

NATIONAL ORGANIZATIONS: UNITED KINGDOM AND IRELAND

217

Hotel and Catering International Management Association (HCIMA)
[www.hcima.org.uk]
Institute of Leisure and Amenity Management (ILAM)
[www.ilam.co.uk]
Institute of Sport and Recreation Management (ISRM)
[www.isrm.co.uk]
Institute of Travel and Tourism (ITT)
[www.itt.co.uk]
Institution of Environmental Health Officers (IEHO)
Museums Association
Scottish Tourist Guides Association (STGA)
[www.stga.co.uk]
Tourism Society (TS)
[www.toursoc.org.uk]

Ramblers' Association (RA) UK individual membership organization concerned with encouraging rambling and mountaineering and a greater knowledge and care of the countryside.
[www.ramblers.org.uk]

Restaurant Association (RA) Trade association of British restaurants founded 1967 to represent its members and provide services to assist them in the conduct of their businesses.
[www.ragb.co.uk]

Restaurants Association of Ireland National trade association of the Irish restaurant industry founded 1970, with the primary function of representing its members and providing for them certain services, including negotiating on pay and conditions for employees in the sector.
[www.adlib.ie/rai.asp]

Scottish Enterprise Statutory body with a remit to further the development of Scotland's economy, to enhance the skills of the Scottish workplace, to promote Scotland's international competitiveness, and to improve the environment. Many of its functions are contracted out to a network of Local Enterprise Companies (LECs), in which tourism and hospitality may be represented.
[www.scotent.co.uk]

Scottish Tourist Board See VisitScotland

Sports Councils (UK) UK Sports Council (UK Sport) [www.uksport.gov.uk] was established by Royal Charter 1997 to focus on high performance sport at UK level with the aim of achieving excellence in world competition, to promote the development of sport and foster the provision of sporting facilities, as well as being responsible for the distribution of the proceeds of the National Lottery allocated to sport. There are also separate Councils as follows:
Sport England
[www.sportengland.org]
Sport Scotland
[www.sportscotland.org.uk]
Sports Council for Wales
www.sports-council-wales.co.uk]
Sports Council for Northern Ireland
[www.sportni.com].

Timeshare Council UK trade association of timeshare developers and exchange companies founded to regulate, promote and represent the timeshare industry, improve standards and protect the public.
[www.timesharecouncil.com]

Tourism Alliance UK strategic alliance of seven leading trade associations in membership of the Confederation of British Industry (CBI) formed 2001 to coordinate the private sector response to the issues faced by the tourism industry and to create a united voice for tourism at national level.
[www.cbi.org.uk]

Tourism Concern Describing itself as a network with a subscribing membership of tourists and those variously concerned with tourism professionally and otherwise, it seeks to promote greater critical understanding of the impact of tourism.
[www.tourismconcern.org.uk]

Tourism Ireland Limited A company limited by guarantee established under the framework of the Belfast Agreement of Good Friday 1998 to promote increased tourism to the island of Ireland. Its principal functions are to carry out strategic all-Ireland destination marketing in all markets outside the island of Ireland and to undertake regional, product marketing and promotional activities for Bord Fáilte and the Northern Ireland Tourist Board overseas.
[www.ireland.ie/home]

Tourism Society (TS) Professional body established in the UK 1977 for those engaged in various **sectors** of tourism to enhance members' professionalism and develop opportunities for personal networking. The Society incorporates the **Association of Tourism Teachers and Trainers (ATTT)** and the *Consultants Group (TSCG)* as specialist sections, as well as the *Scottish Chapter*. [www.toursoc.org.uk]

Trade associations in hospitality industry (UK)
British Association of Leisure Parks, Piers and Attractions (BALPPA)
[www.balppa.org]
British Beer and Pub Association
[www.beerandpubs.co.uk]
British Federation of Hotel, Guest House and Self Catering Associations
British Holiday and Home Parks Association (BHHPA)
[www.ukparks.com]
British Hospitality Association (BHA)
[www.bha-online.org.uk]
British Self-Catering Federation (BSCF)
Mobile and Outside Caterers Association of Great Britain (MOCA)
[www.moca.org.uk]
National Association of Holiday Centres Limited (NAHC)
National Federation of Site Operators (NFSO)
Restaurant Association (RA)
[www.ragb.co.uk]

Trade associations of tour operators and travel agents (UK)
Alliance of Retail Travel Agency Consortia (ARTAC)
Association of British Travel Agents (ABTA)
[www.abtanet.com/]
Association of Independent Tour Operators (AITO)
[www.aito.co.uk]
Association of Multiple Travel Agents (AMTA)
British Incoming Tour Operators' Association (BITOA)
[www.bitoa.co.uk]
Federation of Tour Operators (FTO)
[www.fto.co.uk]
Guild of Business Travel Agents (GBTA)
National Association of Independent Travel Agents (NAITA)

Trade associations of transport operators (UK)
Association of Pleasure Craft Operators (APCO)
[www.canals.com]
British Hire Cruiser Federation
[www.yotting.com]
British Marine Industries Federation
[www.bmif.co.uk]
British Ports Federation
[www.britishports.org.uk]
Chamber of Shipping
[www.british-shipping.org]
Coach Tourism Council
[www.coachtourismcouncil.co.uk]
Confederation of Passenger Transport (CPT)
[www.cpt-uk.org]
Guild of British Coach Operators (GBCO)
[www.coach-tours.co.uk]
Passenger Shipping Association (PSA)
[www.psa-psara.org]

Trade unions in travel, tourism and hospitality (UK)
British Air Line Pilots Association (BALPA)
[www.balpa.org]
Hotel and Catering Union (HCU, part of General, Municipal, Boilermakers and Allied Trades Union, GMB)
[www.gmb.org.uk]
National Union of Marine, Aviation and Shipping Transport (NUMAST)
[www.numast.org]
National Union of Rail, Maritime and Transport Workers (RMT)
[www.rmt.org.uk]
Public and Civil Service Union (PCS)
Public and Commercial Services Union
[www.psc.org.uk]
Transport and General Workers' Union (TGWU)
[www.tgw.org.uk]
Transport Salaried Staffs' Association (TSSA)
[www.tssa.org.uk]
Union of Shop, Distributive and Allied Workers (USDAW)
[www.usdaw.org.uk]
Unison
[www.unison.org.uk]

The Travel and Tourism Programme (TTP) A registered charity launched nationwide 1988, founded and sponsored by *American Express* and supported by a number of organizations in the **tourism industry**. It has fostered the study of tourism in schools, developed qualifications available in schools and colleges, and provides curriculum development and support for teachers.

Travel Industry Marketing Group (CIMtIG) See **Chartered Institute of Marketing (CIM)**

Venuemasters A **consortium** of academic venues providing facilities for meetings and group events formed by merger of the *British Universities Accommodation Consortium (BUAC)* with *Connect Venues*.
[http://www.venuemasters.co.uk]

VisitScotland Statutory body established as *Scottish Tourist Board* under the Development of Tourism Act 1969, replacing a voluntary organization of the same name, present name adopted 2001. Main responsibilities are for tourism development in Scotland and for the promotion of Scotland as a **tourism destination** mainly within the UK, as well as advising government on matters concerning tourism in Scotland.
[www.visitscotland.com]

Wages Councils Statutory bodies which set minimum pay levels in British **industries** where no other adequate machinery existed for the regulation of wages. From the peak of 66 Councils covering some 3.5 million employees in the early 1950s, their number declined through abolitions and mergers to 26 Councils with around 2.5 million employees in the early 1990s. All Councils were abolished on 30 August 1993. The main travel-, tourism- and hospitality-related **sectors** covered by the Councils included licensed **hotels** and **restaurants, public houses** and **clubs,** unlicensed places of refreshment, and retailing.

Wales Tourist Board (WTB) Statutory body established under the Development of Tourism Act 1969, replacing a voluntary organization of the same name, with responsibilities for tourism development in Wales and for the promotion of Wales as a **tourism destination** mainly within the UK, as well as advising the government on matters concerning tourism in Wales.
[www.tourism.wales.gov.uk]

Welsh Development Agency (WDA) Statutory body set up 1976 to help regenerate the economy and improve the **environment** of Wales with powers to provide finance and advisory services.
[www.wda.co.uk]

Youth Hostels Associations There are three UK organizations providing low cost **hostel** accommodation and activity **holidays (vacations),** with a particular focus on youth travel: *Youth Hostels Association (England and Wales)* [www.yha.org.uk], *Scottish Youth Hostels Association* [www.syha.org.uk] and *Youth Hostel Association of Northern Ireland Ltd.*

Part 4

Biographical Dictionary

Agnelli, Giovanni (1866–1945) Italian industrialist and philanthropist who was the founder (1899) and chairman of *FIAT* (*Fabrica Italiana Automobili Torino*), the largest industrial enterprise and automobile manufacturer in Italy and the main arms supplier to Government during the two World Wars.

Alcock, Sir John William (1892–1919) British aviator who made, with his navigator A.W. Brown, the first non-stop transatlantic flight (1919) from St John's, Newfoundland, to Clifden, Ireland.

Amundsen, Roald (1872–1928) Norwegian explorer and navigator, and the first man to reach both Poles – the South Pole on skis and with a dog team in 1911 (35 days before Captain Scott) and the North Pole using an airship in 1926.

Anderson, Sir Donald Forsyth (1906–1973) British shipping executive and industry leader, successively director, managing director and chairman, *Peninsular & Oriental Steam Navigation Co (P&O)* and Chairman/President, *British Shipping Federation* and *International Shipping Federation*.

Ansett, Sir Reginald Myles (1909–1981) Australian businessman and aviation entrepreneur who became a pioneer of passenger flying before World War II. When he took over the rival *Australian National Airways (ANA)* in 1957, *Ansett Transport Industries* became the largest private transport system in the southern hemisphere, which was later given parity with the state-owned *Trans Australian Airlines (TAA)* by the Federal Government under its 'two airlines' policy.

Austin (of Longbridge), Baron Herbert (1866–1941) English car manufacturer who produced, when with the Wolseley Company, his first three-wheel car in 1895; his own works opened near Birmingham in 1905 and the output included in 1921 the popular 'Baby' Austin 7.

Baedeker, Karl (1801–1859) German publisher who started his own business in 1827 in Koblenz and became the best known nineteenth-century publisher of authoritative guidebooks, which still bear his name.

Baum, Vicki (originally Vicki Hedwig) (1888–1960) Novelist born in Vienna who, after writing several novels and short stories, made her name with *Grand Hotel* (1930), which became a best seller and a popular film. Emigrated to USA in 1931.

Beeching, Baron Richard (Life Peer) (1913–1985) English engineer and administrator who was chairman of the *British Railways Board* (1963–65) and deputy chairman of *ICI* (1966–68). Best known for the scheme devised and approved under his chairmanship (the Beeching Plan) for the substantial contraction of the UK rail network in the 1960s.

Bemelmans, Ludwig (1898–1962) Australian-born US writer and artist, author of numerous magazine pieces and of more than 30 wryly humorous books, including *On Board Noah's Ark*, a travel book and *Hotel Bemelmans*.

Bennett, Arnold (1867–1931) English novelist, author of *Great Hotel Babylon* (1902) and *Imperial Palace* (1930), the latter novel based on the Savoy Hotel in London.

Berni, Frank (1903–2000) Italian born British restaurateur, elder of the two brothers who created *Berni Inns*, the largest restaurant chain of steak houses outside America, which was sold to *Grand Metropolitan* with almost 150 outlets in 1970.

Blériot, Louis (1872–1936) Airman born in France who made the first flight across the

English Channel, from Baraques to Dover in 1909, in a small monoplane.

Boeing, William Edward (1881–1956) US aircraft manufacturer. Having learnt to fly, he formed his first company to build seaplanes, which became *Boeing Aeroplane Company*, eventually the largest manufacturer of military and civil aircraft in the world; in 1927 he formed the *Boeing Air Transport Company* which introduced many novelties in aviation. When he retired in 1934, the Company became *United Airlines*.

Boyd, Louise Arner (1887–1972) US explorer, who began organizing, financing and leading polar expeditions during the 1920s, participated in the search for missing explorer Roald Amundsen in 1928, and during the 1930s explored eastern Arctic Canada and Greenland. She was the first woman to fly over the North Pole (1955).

Bradshaw, George (1801–1853) English printer, mapmaker and publisher, best remembered for the series of railway guides (*Bradshaws*), which he originated in 1839.

Bridges, John Gourlay (1901–1985) Scottish administrator, businessman and consultant who served *The Overseas League* in Scotland and in Canada before World War II and between 1945 and 1963 was first Director General of Britain's voluntary National Tourism Organization, the forerunner of the British Tourist Authority. He was responsible for its management through a period of considerable growth and change: the staff of 29 at the time of his appointment approached 400 when he retired and the number of overseas offices exceeded 20.

Brittain, Sir Harry (1873–1974) British newspaper director, politician and businessman who was, inter alia, active head of *The Pilgrim's Club* for 17 years, prominent member of the *Royal Commonwealth Society*, founder member of the *British Travel Association*, as well as chairman and member of the committees of the two organizations.

Brunel, Isambard Kingdom (1806–1859) British engineer and inventor born in France who built steam-powered ships, railways and bridges and became known as the 'Father of

the Great Western Railway', having served as engineer to the Company.

Butlin, Sir William ('Billy') (1899–1980) South-African born entrepreneur who emigrated first to Canada and after World War I to England, where he set up his first large-scale holiday camp in 1937 which grew to a chain with 70 000 beds (as well as a number of hotels) by the time he retired in 1968.

Chandler, Henry (1913–1992) British travel industry leader who founded the *Travel Club* and *Chandler's Travel of Upminster*, was largely responsible for the development of the Portuguese Algarve for mass tourism in the 1960s, and a prime mover in the creation of financial protection for package holiday makers, serving as chairman and President of the *Association of British Travel Agents (ABTA)*. After his death, the business was continued by his wife and son.

Chaucer, Geoffrey (c.1345–1400) English poet and author, i.a., of *Canterbury Tales*, based on an early pilgrimage to Canterbury.

Chevrolet, Louis (1879–1941) Swiss-born US automobile racer and designer who designed and built in 1911, in collaboration with W.G. Durant, the first 'Chevrolet' that was produced to compete with Ford. However, Chevrolet lost confidence in the car and sold his interest to Durant who incorporated the *Chevrolet Motor Co.* into his *General Motors* organization. Chevrolet thus benefited little from the hugely successful car that bore his name.

Chib, Som Nath (1908–1985) Leading Indian tourism expert, for many years senior executive of *All India Radio*, first Director General of the Indian Tourist Department 1957–1966, and for more than six years Director of Tourism in the Bahamas. He has advised and conducted studies for, i.a., the UN, UNDP and World Bank. He also served as President of the *International Union of Official Travel Organizations (IUOTO)* and of the *Pacific Asia Travel Association (PATA)*. His extensive published work includes *Essays on Tourism* (1989), edited posthumously by one of his daughters.

Chichester, Sir Francis (1901–1972) Pioneer air navigator, adventurer and yachtsman born in England who made several pioneer flights before taking up ocean sailing. He won the first solo transatlantic yacht race (1960) in *Gipsy Moth III*, sailing from Plymouth to New York, made a successful circumnavigation of the world (1966–67) in *Gipsy Moth IV*, sailing from Plymouth to Sydney and from there back to Plymouth via Cape Horn.

Citroën, André Gustave (1878–1935) French engineer and industrialist who built his Citroën Automobile in 1919 and became known as the 'French Henry Ford' for introducing Ford's methods of production and marketing to the French automobile industry.

Columbus, Christopher (1451–1506) Genoese navigator, explorer and discoverer of the New World in the service of Spain.

Cook, Thomas (1808–1892) British tour operator, retail travel agent and publisher whose railway trip in 1841 was the first public excursion; in 1856 he organized a railway tour of Europe, and in the early 1860s started the travel firm *Thomas Cook and Son*, which grew into a worldwide organization.

Coppock, Terry (1921–2000) British geographer and administrator who made major contributions to agricultural geography, geographical information systems, planning, tourism and recreation. He was Ogilvie Professor of Geography at Edinburgh University (1965–86) and Director of the *Tourism and Recreation Research Unit (TRRU* 1966–80), from where 50 TRRU research reports had a major influence on the planned development of Scottish tourism.

Crowther (of Headingley), Baron Geoffrey (Life Peer) (1907–1972) British economist, journalist and businessman who became a director of *Trust Houses* relatively early in his career, eventually chairman and, following a merger with *Forte & Co*, chairman of *Trust House Forte*. He also made a major contribution to British education.

Cunard, Sir Samuel (1787–1865) Shipowner born in Canada who emigrated to England where he co-founded the *Cunard Line* and pioneered the first regular transatlantic steamship service between Liverpool and Halifax, Nova Scotia.

D'Erlanger, Sir Gerard (1906–1962) British businessman and aviation executive who served as director of *British Airways* (1935–40), and of *BOAC* (1940–6), managing director (1946–7) and chairman (1947–9) of *BEA*, and also chairman of *BOAC* (1956–60).

De Haan, Sidney (1919–2002) British entrepreneur who founded in 1951 *Saga Holidays*, the specialist tour operation for those of pensionable age, and pioneered direct marketing. The many successful spin-offs included the popular *Saga Magazine*, financial services and insurance. When the Company was floated on the Stock Exchange in 1978, it was one of the most oversubscribed issues of the year. At the time of De Haan's death, the Group was worth £185 million.

De Havilland, Sir Geoffrey (1882–1965) English aircraft designer who built his first plane in 1908 and became director of the firm bearing his name, which produced many famous models, including the *Tiger Moth* (1930), the *Mosquito* (1941) and the *Comet* jet airliner (1952). He also established a height record for light aircraft and won the King's Cup air race.

Disney, Walt (1901–1966) US artist and film producer who founded the organization which created the world's largest theme parks: he opened *Disneyland* in California in 1955, and his company opened *DisneyWorld* in Florida in 1971, the *Tokyo Park* in 1983 and *Euro Disney* on the outskirts of Paris in 1992.

Douglas (of Kirtleside), Baron William Sholto (1893–1969) British air force officer and airline executive who served in both World Wars, was military governor of the British zone of occupation in Germany, and after leaving the air force, chairman of *British European Airways* 1949–64.

Doyle, Paschal Vincent (1923–1988) Irish builder and hotelier who built and operated a number of Irish hotels, becoming the most successful hotelier in the history of the industry, employing 2000 people and owning hotels also in Britain and the United States. From 1973 he served as chairman of the Irish Tourist Board under successive Governments. In 1999 Doyle Hotels were acquired by Jurys and the new company became Jurys Doyle.

Edwards, Sir Ronald (1910–1976) British industrialist and promoter of management education; manufacturer of cars, trucks and buses; i.a., chairman of the *Committee of Inquiry into Civil Aviation Transport ('Edward's Committee')* whose report *British Air Transport in the Seventies* was published in 1969.

Eiffel, (Alexander) Gustave (1832–1923) French civil engineer who designed many notable bridges and viaducts before his most famous project, the *Eiffel Tower* in Paris, erected 1887–9, the highest building in the world until 1930 and the world's major visitor attraction. He also designed the framework of the *Statue of Liberty* in New York.

Escoffier, Auguste (c.1847–1935) A famous French chef at the Grand Hotel, Monte Carlo, before César Ritz persuaded him to come to the Savoy Hotel in London and finally to the Carlton; his publications included the *Guide Culinaire* (1903) and *Ma Cuisine* (1934).

Ford, Henry (1863–1947) American automobile designer and manufacturer who produced his first petrol-driven motor car in 1893 and in 1899 founded a company in Detroit designing his own car. In 1903 he started the *Ford Motor Company* pioneering modern assembly line mass production techniques for his famous model 'T' introduced to the market at a price which brought the motor car within the reach of the masses.

Fuchs, Sir Vivian (1908–1999) Explorer, Director of *British Antarctic Survey* 1958–73, first person to cross Antarctica.

Geddes, Baron (1897–1983) British businessman, i.a., director of *P&O Steamship Navigation Company* 1957–72 and President UK *Chamber of Shipping*, Deputy Chairman (1960–4) and Chairman (1964–9) of the *British Travel Association*, the official tourism organization.

Gluckstein, Montague (1854–1922) English caterer and food manufacturer who founded with brother Isidore and Joseph Lyons, a distant relative, J. Lyons & Co., registered 1894. The Company's operations extended from well-known teashops and London Corner Houses to outside catering and hotels, including the largest London hotels, as well as using mass food production methods, notably at its headquarters, Cadby Hall.

Gordon, Frederick (1835–1904) A solicitor, politician and founder and chairman of *Gordon Hotels*, leading figure of the Victorian hotel industry in Britain, described as 'the Napoleon of the hotel world'.

Guthrie, Sir Giles (1916–1979) British airline executive who served on the board of the nationalized *British European Airways (BEA)* and was chairman and chief executive of the *British Overseas Airways Corporation (BOAC)* as well as chairman of *BOAC–Cunard Ltd*.

Hacking, Baron Douglas Hewitt (1884–1950) British civil servant and politician, the effective founder of Britain's national tourism organization, first chairman of the *Travel Association of Great Britain and Ireland* and its successor bodies 1929–50.

Henderson, Ernest (1924–1994) 'Mr Sheraton'; leading US hotelier who did not enter the hotel business until he was 44 years old but by the time he died 26 years later, *Sheraton* was the largest hotel chain in the world.

Hilton, Conrad (1887–1979) US entrepreneur who bought his first hotel in Texas in 1919, bought/sold/operated hotels 1919–46, before founding the *Hilton Hotel Corporation* and *Hilton International* after World War II. Wrote *Be My Guest* (1957) and *Inspirations of an Innkeeper* (1963).

Hunziker, Walter (1899–1974) Leading Swiss tourism academic, administrator and entrepreneur, Professor of Tourism at the University of St Gallen, head of several national as well as co-founder and President of international organizations.

Jerome, Jerome Klapka (1859–1927) English humorous writer, novelist and playwright, author of classic *Three Men in a Boat* (1889, an account of a boat trip up the Thames from Kingston to Oxford) and of another travelogue, *Three Men on a Bummel* (1900).

Johnson, Amy (1903–1941) Pioneer English aviator who flew solo from England to Australia (1930), to Japan via Siberia (1931) and to Cape Town (1932), making new records in each case.

Johnson, Howard Deering (1896–1972) US entrepreneur and founder of the chain, which by the time he handed it over to his son in 1959, had 550 restaurants and 75 motor lodges, and the name Howard Johnson was becoming synonymous with highway travel.

Jones, Albert Henry (1907–1966) British hotel executive who, for some 30 years, ran London's *Grosvenor House* hotel, first as general manager and then managing director. A dynamic leader of the industry, he served as chairman of the *Hotel and Catering Institute*, the professional body, and promoted apprenticeship schemes as well as management education.

Joseph, Sir Maxwell (1910–1982) British entrepreneur, chairman of *Grand Metropolitan Hotels*, who had by 1973 built the largest hotel group in London, the second largest in Britain, and the 12th largest UK company from a base of one small hotel in 1947. In the early days of the Company, his partners included Henry Edwards and Fred Kobler, who should be also credited with its success.

Kroc, Ray (1902–1984) American entrepreneur born in the USA of Czech parents, whose name is forever connected with the firm *McDonald's*. Although he had not founded it, having bought all rights from brothers McDonald, he developed it to become the leading fast food corporation worldwide.

Lindbergh, Charles Augustus (1902–1974) American aviator who made the first solo transatlantic flight from New York City to Paris in the monoplane *Spirit of St Louis* in 1927.

London, Jack (1876–1916) A prolific American writer and political speaker who wrote more than 50 books between 1900 and his death in 1916, most based on his own travel experiences, ranging from searching for gold in the Klondike to riding freight trains as a hobo, many in Alaska and Canada. *White Fang* and *The Call of the Wild* are probably best known today.

Low, Erna (originally Erna Löwe) (1909–2002) Austrian born British pioneer tour operator and tourism consultant who from 1932 continued to run ski and summer trips almost uninterrupted for 60 years. After World War II she established *Erna Low Travel Services*, to which she added a small travel agency chain in the 1960s. In the 1970s she sold and bought the Company back twice. For a number of years she ceased to organize holidays and worked as a consultant for ski, golf and spa resorts. When the Company was restarted as a ski operator in the 1990s, she handed the business over to her co-director but her name lives on and the firm flourishes.

Lunn, Sir Arnold (1888–1974) British Alpine ski pioneer (son of Sir Henry Lunn), founder of the *Ski Club of Great Britain* and the *Alpine Ski Club*, who invented slalom gates, and obtained Olympic recognition for the modern Alpine slalom race and downhill races.

Lunn, Sir Henry (1859–1939) British travel bureau and skiing pioneer credited with introducing skiing to Switzerland (father of Sir Arnold Lunn).

Lyons, Sir Joseph Nathaniel (1847–1917) English caterer and food manufacturer who first studied art and invented a stereoscope before joining the Gluckstein and Salmon families to establish a restaurant company, and becoming head of J. Lyons and Co. Ltd, one of the largest catering businesses in Britain.

McAlpine, Sir Robert (1847–1934) Scottish building contractor who, having left school at the age of ten to work in the pits, after which he was apprenticed as a bricklayer, founded and built up a large company using new building techniques and labour-saving machinery, winning major contracts especially for roads and such projects as Wembley Stadium and the prestigious Dorchester Hotel in London, owned by the family for more than 40 years.

McCrindle, John Ronald (1894–1977) British airline executive whose early civil aviation career began in 1932. He was managing director of the original *British Airways* and, when it merged with *Imperial Airways* to become the *British Overseas Airways Corporation (BOAC)*, became Director-General of the airline. He also played a major role in international organizations.

Marriott, J. Willard (1900–1985) US hotelier and caterer, founder of *Marriott*

International, which by early 2001 operated 2200 properties with 400 000 rooms in 60 countries, as well as contract food services, theme parks and a cruise line.

Mabane, Baron William (1895–1969) British businessman, civil servant and politician, Chairman (1960–3) and President (1964–6) of the *British Travel Association*, the official tourism organization.

McDonnell, James Smith (1899–1980) US aircraft manufacturer and pioneer in space technology who had a varied career as test pilot and chief engineer to several US companies before setting up his own company in 1928, to become the *McDonnell Aircraft Corporation*, which built many successful military and naval aircraft and later constructed the Mercury and Gemini manned satellite capsules.

Maxwell, Sir Alexander (1880–1963) British civil servant and chairman of British Travel and Holidays Association, the official tourism organization, 1950–4.

Meek, Howard Bagnall (1893–1969) US educator who founded in 1922, at the age of 29, the Department that later became the Cornell University School of Hotel Administration and led the program for 39 years until his retirement in 1961, where he rose above the politics of an Ivy League university and of the industry. Between 1961 and 1969 he was executive director of the *Council on Hotel, Restaurant and Institutional Education (CHRIE)*.

Metcalf, John (1717–1810) Known as *Blind Jack of Knaresborough;* Scottish engineer and one of the great road-makers of the eighteenth century, who laid out hundreds of miles of roads, designed bridges and viaducts and supervised their building without being able to see since he was six years old.

Michelin, André (1853–1931) French industrialist who established with his younger brother the *Michelin Tyre Company*, the first to use demountable tyres on motor cars; also initiated the production of high-quality road maps and guide books to promote tourism by car, as well as the well-known system of restaurant grading.

Milward, Sir Anthony (1905–1981) British businessman and airline executive who served with BEA in various capacities between 1946 and 1970 and as chairman of BOAC (1964–70), as well as, after his retirement, as chairman (1971–6) and President (1976–80) of the *London Tourist Board*.

Morse, Sir Arthur (1892–1964) British banker and businessman, chairman of the *British Travel and Holidays Association*, the official tourism organization, 1954–60.

Nansen, Fridtjob (1861–1930) Norwegian explorer, oceanographer, statesman and humanitarian, awarded the Nobel Prize for Peace for Russian relief work after the Revolution and work for the League of Nations (a forerunner of the United Nations), including the creation of the *Nansen Passport*, an internationally recognized identification document for refugees.

Norval, Arthur Joseph (1896–1980) South African businessman and economist, director and chairman of various companies, Professor of Commerce and Industrial Economics, University of Pretoria, Founder Member of SA Tourist Corporation, author of *The Tourist Industry, A National and International Survey*, one of the earliest texts of its kind, published 1936.

O'Driscoll, Timothy Joseph (1908–1998) Irish public servant who made outstanding contributions to the development of the modern Irish state, Irish civil aviation, and Irish as well as international tourism. He served in several Government Departments, was director general of the *Irish Tourist Board* 1956–71, member of the board of directors of Aer Lingus, consultant on tourism under various United Nations programmes, and executive director of the *European Travel Commission* 1971–86.

Ogilvie, Sir Frederick Wolff (1893–1949) Scottish academic and administrator, Professor of Economics at Edinburgh University, second Director General of the BBC, Principal of Jesus College, Oxford. He was one of the first economists to see the significance of tourism and his *The Tourist Movement, An Economic Study* published in 1933 was one of the earliest texts of its kind.

Opel, Wilhelm von (1871–1948) German industrialist known as the 'Henry Ford of Germany' who built more than one million cars at the works he founded in 1887 at Rüsselsheim, before selling control of the company to *General Motors* in 1929.

Polo, Marco (1254–1324) Venetian merchant and explorer, probably the first well-known traveller, who visited, i.a., Persia, Tibet, Burma, India, Ceylon and Siberian Arctic.

Pontin, Sir Fred (1906–2000) British businessman and holiday camp pioneer who opened his first holiday village in Somerset in 1946 and developed the company in early years through conversion of former military and other camps. Later expanded into hotels and holiday camps in Europe through the *Pontinental* brand. Chairman and joint managing director *Pontin's* 1946–79 and of *Pontinental* 1972–9. Sold the company to *Coral Leisure Group* in 1979 with more than 20 camps and more than 30 000 beds in Britain alone.

Porsche, Ferdinand (1875–1951) German automobile designer who designed cars for Daimler and Auto Union before setting up his own studio and in 1934 producing plans for a revolutionary cheap car with the engine in the back, which the Nazis gave the name *Volkswagen* (people's car).

Pullman, George Mortimer (1831–1897) US inventor, designer and businessman who built the first modern sleeping and dining rail cars.

Ritz, César (1850–1918) Swiss-born hotelier described as 'Hotelkeeper to Kings and King of Hotelkeepers' who managed successively such luxury establishments as the Grand National Hotel in Lucerne, Switzerland, the Savoy Hotel in London, the Paris Ritz (the first hotel to bear his name), and the Carlton Hotel in London.

Salmon, Henry (1881–1950) Known as 'Harry'; English caterer and food manufacturer, who joined the family firm of Salmons and Glucksteins after leaving school, worked as a kitchen boy and waiter, became managing director of J. Lyons and Co. at the early age of 27, and chairman in 1941 as well as remaining managing director until 1949.

Scott, Robert Falcon (1868–1912) English naval officer and Antarctic explorer who, after various expeditions, reached the South Pole with four companions pulling their own sledges, to find Amundsen's Norwegian flag already flying there.

Shackleton, Sir Ernest Henry (1874–1922) English Antarctic explorer born in Ireland who made his first expeditions with Captain Scott, commanded the expedition that located the south magnetic pole, and later an expedition to cross the Antarctic which failed when his ship *Endurance* was crushed in the ice.

Smallpeice, Sir Basil (1906–1992) British transport executive whose long career in the industry began in 1948 with the *British Transport Commission*, then responsible for the nationalized inland transport system. Later he joined the *British Overseas Airways Corporation (BOAC)*, becoming managing director, and in 1964 the *Cunard Steamship Co* as director, soon becoming executive chairman.

Soyer, Alexis (1809–1858) Leading French chef who became chef in the Reform Club in London (1837–1850), went to Ireland during the famine (1847) and tried to reform the food supply in the Crimea by introducing the 'Soyer stove' (1855).

Stakis, Sir Reo (1913–2001) Greek Cypriot entrepreneur who arrived in Britain aged 15 and over the following 70 years built an empire of 54 four-star hotels, 22 casinos and 70 health clubs, which was sold to Ladbrokes for £1.2 billion in 1999.

Statler, Elsworth Milton (1863–1928) US hotelier who began work as a hotel bellboy, advanced to become restaurant owner, built his first hotel in 1901 and founded the Statler chain, which was acquired by *Hilton Hotels Corporation* in 1954. Known for his personal slogan 'The customer is always right'; to him is also attributed the saying that 'there are only three rules for success in the hotel business – location, location, location'.

Stephenson, George (1781–1848) English railway engineer whose reputation stemmed from both locomotive and rail construction, the former in 1814 when he constructed his first engine, the latter as engineer for the construction of the *Stockton & Darlington Railway*, opened in 1825, of the *Liverpool & Manchester Railway*, opened in 1830, and of several other railways in England, as well as consulting work about proposed lines in Belgium and Spain.

Stevenson, Robert Louis (1850–1894) Scottish lawyer, novelist, poet and essayist, whose *Inland Voyage* (1878) describes a canoe trip in Belgium and northern France, and *Travels with a Donkey* a tour undertaken in the same year in Southern France.

Tenzing, Norgay (1914–1986) Known as *Sherpa Tenzing*; Nepalese mountaineer who climbed many Himalayan peaks before, as member of the John Hunt expedition, he with Edmund Hilary reached the summit of Everest in 1953.

Thomas, David (1932–2002) American restaurateur who was the founder of Wendy's hamburger chain, having opened his first Wendy's restaurant in 1969, named after one of his daughters. He began franchising in 1972 and the company went public in 1976. At the time of his death he was senior chairman and there were more than 6000 restaurants worldwide.

Thomson, Sir Adam (1926–2000) British aviation entrepreneur, founder and between 1976 and 1988 chairman of *British Caledonian* (The Tartan Airline), the second largest UK airline, with around 50 daily flights from its London Gatwick base, before the merger with *British Airways* in 1988.

Towle, Sir Francis William (1876–1951) Leading British hotelier; managing director of Gordon Hotels (1921–36); founder in 1926 of the 'Come to Britain' movement, which was the forerunner of Britain's official tourism organization; first chairman and president of the *Hotel and Catering Institute*, the industry professional body, president *International Hotel Alliance* and *International Hotel Association*.

Twain, Mark (1835–1910) Pseudonym of Samuel Langhorne Clement, well-travelled novelist, journalist and lecturer, author of the classic *The Innocents Abroad* (1869), which sold 125 000 copies in the first three years after publication.

Wells, Henry (1805–1878) US shipper specializing in valuables and bullion who worked as an agent before joining with William Fargo and Daniel Dunning to found, *Wells & Co*, which later merged with other companies to become *American Express Company* in 1850.

Whittle, Sir Frank (1907–1996) English aviator, aeronautical engineer and inventor of the British jet engine as a replacement for the conventional internal combustion aero engine.

Zeppelin, Graf Ferdinand (1838–1917) German army officer who, between 1897 and 1900, constructed his first airship, setting up a factory for its construction in Friedrichshafen, which produced more than 100 Zeppelins for use in World War I.

Part 5

Abbreviations

A

a	acre	AC	Aero Club
A	letter followed by abbreviation of the name of a professional body denotes Associate (Member) of that body		Air Canada
			Alpine Club
			alternating current
			Arts Council
AA	Advertising Association	ACAC	Arab Civil Aviation Council
	American Airlines	ACC	Airport Consultative Committee (Australia)
	Automobile Association		
AAA	American Automobile Association	ACE	Association for Conferences and Events
	Australian Automobile Association		Arts Council of England
		ACI	Airports Council International
AACB	Association of Australian Convention Bureaux	ACNI	Arts Council of Northern Ireland
		ACORN	(acronym for) A Classification of Residential Neighbourhoods
AACC	Airport Associations Coordinating Council		
		ACP	African, Caribbean, Pacific (States)
AACO	Arab Air Carriers' Organization	ACR	Association for Consumer Research
AACVB	Asian Association of Convention and Visitor Bureaux		
		ACT	Australian Capital Territory
AADFI	Association of African Development Finance Institutions	ACTA	Association of Canadian Travel Agents
		ACTTC	Australian Capital Territory Tourism Commission
AAFRA	Association of African Airlines		
AAR	Association of American Railroads	ACTW	Australian Council of Tour Wholesalers
AB	Alberta, Canada	ACW	Arts Council of Wales
ABA	American Bus Association	ADB	African Development Bank
ABC	ABC Islands (Aruba, Bonaire, Curacao)		Asian Development Bank
		ADC	advise duration and charge
	Advance Booking Charter	ADF	African Development Fund
	Audit Bureau of Circulations		Asian Development Fund
ABCA	Australian Bus and Coach Association	ADFIAP	Association of Development Financing Institutions in Asia and the Pacific
ABCC	Association of British Chambers of Commerce		
		ADP	automatic data processing
ABPCO	Association of British Professional Conference Organisers	AE	(routing) via the Atlantic and Eastern Hemisphere
		AEA	Association of European Airlines
ABS	Australian Bureau of Statistics	AEO	Association of Exhibition Organisers
ABTA	Association of British Travel Agents		
		AER	Assembly of European Regions
ABTAC	ABTA Travel Agents' Certificate	Aeroflot	Russian Airlines
ABTOC	ABTA Tour Operators' Certificate	Af	Afghani (currency of Afghanistan)

AF	Air France (routing) via Africa
AFC	Airport Facilitation Committee (Australia)
AFCAC	African Civil Aviation Commission
AFESD	Arab Fund for Economic and Social Development
AFl	Aruban Guilder/Florin (currency)
AFRAA	African Airlines Association
AFTA	Australian Federation of Travel Agents
AGM	annual general meeting
AHA	Australian Hotel Association
AHLA	American Hotel & Lodging Association
AHRA	ASEAN Hotel and Restaurant Association
AI	Air India
AIAC	Aviation Industry Advisory Committee (Australia)
AIDA	(mnemonic for) Attention, Interest, Desire, Action
AIDS	(acronym for) Acquired Immune Deficiency Syndrome
AIEST	International Association of Scientific Experts in Tourism
AIM	Association of Independent Museums
AISC	International Association of Skal Clubs
AIT	Alliance Internationale de Tourisme
AITO	Association of Independent Tour Operators
	Australian Institute of Tourism Officers
AITT	Australian Institute of Travel and Tourism
AK	Alaska, USA
AL	Alabama, USA
A level	Advanced level examination of the General Certificate of Education (GCE) in the UK (excluding Scotland)
Alitalia	Italian international airline
ALM	Netherlands Antilles Airlines
Alta	Alberta, Canada
ALVA	Association of Leading Visitor Attractions
a.m.	*ante meridiem* (before noon)
Amex	American Express
AMS	Ancient Monuments Society
AMTA	Association of Multiple Travel Agents

ANTOR	Assembly/Association of National Tourist Office Representatives
ANZCERTA	Australia New Zealand Closer Economic Relations Trade Agreement
AOCI	Airport Operators Council International (US)
AONB	Area of Outstanding Natural Beauty
AP	American Plan (routing) via the Atlantic and Pacific
APCO	Association of Pleasure Craft Operators
APEX	Advance Purchase Excursion
approx.	approximately
Apr.	April
APRS	Association for the Protection of Rural Scotland
APT	Advanced Passenger Train
AR	Arkansas, USA
ARC	Airlines Reporting Corporation (US)
	American Recreation Coalition
ARDA	American Resort Development Association
ARELS	Association of Recognised English Language Services
arr.	arrival/arrives
ARR	average room rate
ARTAC	Alliance of Retail Travel Agency Consortia
ARTC	Air Route Traffic Control
ARVC	National Association of RV Parks and Campgrounds (US)
ASA	Airservices Australia
a.s.a.p.	as soon as possible
ASEAN	Association of South East Asia Nations
ASEANTA	ASEAN Tourism Association
ASEANTTA	ASEAN Tourism and Travel Association
ASHTAV	Association of Small Historic Towns and Villages of the United Kingdom
ASPA	Association of South Pacific Airlines
ASSI	Area of Special Scientific Interest
AST	Atlantic Standard Time (Canada)
ASTA	American Society of Travel Agents
ASVA	Association of Scottish Visitor Attractions
AT	(routing) via the Atlantic

ATA	Africa Travel Association
	Air Transport Association of America
ATAC	Air Transport Association of Canada
ATB	Area Tourist Board (Scotland)
ATB2	automatic ticket and boarding pass
ATC	Air Traffic Conference
	Alpine Tourist Commission
	Australian Tourist Commission
	Australian Transport Council
ATE	Australian Tourism Exchange
ATEC	Australian Tourism Export Council
ATIC	ASEAN Tourism Information Centre
ATM	automated teller machine
ATMA	Asia Travel Marketing Association

ATME	Association of Travel Marketing Executives
ATO	Arab Tourism Organization
ATOA	Air Transport Operators Association
ATOL	Air Travel Organiser's Licence
ATTC	Association of Travel Trades Clubs
ATTF	Air Travel Trust Fund (UK)
ATTT	Association of Tourism Teachers and Trainers
ATW	around the world
Aug.	August
AUKDA	Association of UK Domestic Airlines
AYHA	Australian Youth Hostels Association
AZ	Alitalia airline
	Arizona, USA

ABBREVIATIONS

B	Balboa (currency of Panama)
	Bolivar (currency of Venezuela)
	Boliviano (currency of Bolivia)
BA	British Airways
BAA	British Airports Authority
BACD	British Association of Conference Destinations
BAFA	British Arts Festivals Association
BAHA	British Activity Holiday Association
	British Association of Hospitality Accountants
BAHREP	British Association of Hotel Representatives
BALPA	British Air Line Pilots Association
BALPPA	British Association of Leisure Parks, Piers and Attractions
BARUK	Board of Airline Representatives United Kingdom
BATA	British Air Transport Association
BATO	British Association of Tourism Officers
B&B	bed and breakfast
BBQ	barbeque
BC	British Columbia, Canada

BC	British Council
BCA	Bus and Coach Association (of New Zealand)
BCC	British Caravanners Club
BCECEC	British Conference and Exhibition Centres Export Council
Bd	Boulevard
BD	Bahraini Dinar (currency)
B$	Bahamian Dollar (currency)
	Bermudian Dollar (currency)
	Brunei Dollar (currency)
Bds$	Barbados Dollar (currency)
BDST	British Double Summer Time
BEA	British European Airways (now British Airways)
BECA	British Exhibition Contractors Association
Beds.	Bedfordshire, England
BENELUX	Belgium, Netherlands, Luxembourg
Berks.	Berkshire, England
BES	Business Expansion Scheme
BEVA	British Exhibition Venues Association
BFA	British Franchise Association

BHA	British Hospitality Association	BOAC	British Overseas Airways Corporation (now British Airways)
B'ham	Birmingham		
BHHPA	British Holiday and Home Parks Association	BP	Bermuda Plan
BHRA	British Hotels and Restaurants Association (now BHA)	BPF	Best Practice Forum
		BRA	British Resorts Association
BHRCA	British Hotels, Restaurants and Caterers Association (now BHA)		British Retailers Association
		BRC	British Retail Consortium
		BRF	British Road Federation
BHTS	British Home Tourism Survey	BS	British Standard
BIFM	British Institute of Facilities Management	B/S	balance sheet
		BSCF	British Self-Catering Federation
BII	British Institute of Innkeeping	BSF	British Spas Federation
BIM	British Institute of Management (now CIM)	BSI	British Standards Institution
		BSP	Bank Settlement Plan
BIMCO	Baltic and International Maritime Council	BST	British Summer Time
		BTA	British Tourist Authority
BITOA	British Incoming Tour Operators' Association		British Travel Association
		BTR	Bureau of Tourism Research (Australia)
BITS	International Bureau of Social Tourism		
		BTS	British Tourism Survey
bkg	booking	Bucks.	Buckinghamshire, England
BLRA	Brewers & Licence Retailers Association	BVI	British Virgin Islands
		BVRLA	British Vehicle Rental Leasing Association
Blvd	Boulevard		
BMT	British Mean Time	BWB	British Waterways Board
bn	billion	BWI	British West Indies
BNTS	British National Travel Survey	BWIA	British West Indies Airways
		BYO	Bring Your Own
		BZ$	Belize Dollar (currency)

C	Cedi (currency of Ghana)	Cambs.	Cambridgeshire, England
	Celsius/centigrade	CAR	Central African Republic
	one hundred (Roman numeral)	Caribank	Caribbean Development Bank
¢	Colon (currency of Costa Rica)	CARICOM	Caribbean Community and Common Market
CA	California, USA		
	Consumers' Association	CARTA	Campaign for Real Travel Agents
CAA	Civil Aviation Authority		
cab	cabriolet	CASA	Civil Aviation Safety Authority (Australia)
CAB	Civil Aeronautics Board (USA, phased out 1985)		
		CATC	Commonwealth Air Transport Council
	Commonwealth Agricultural Bureaux		
		CBA	cost benefit analysis
CABEI	Central American Bank of Economic Integration	CBD	central business district
		CBEVE	Central Bureau for Educational Visits and Exchanges
CAC	Canadian Association of Caterers		
		CBI	Confederation of British Industry

CC	Countryside Commission (now Countryside Agency)	CIM	Chartered Institute of Management
CCA	Camp and Cabin Association (New Zealand)	CIMtIG	Chartered Institute of Marketing Travel Industry Group
CCTV	closed-circuit television	CIS	Commonwealth of Independent States
CCW	Countryside Council for Wales		
CDB	Caribbean Development Bank	CIT	Chartered Institute of Transport
CDC	Commonwealth Development Corporation	C£	Cyprus Pound (currency)
		CLIA	Cruise Lines International Association (US)
C$	Canadian Dollar (currency)		
	Cordoba (currency of Nicaragua)	CLOA	Chief Leisure Officers Association
CE	Council of Europe	Club Med	Club Mediterranée
CEEC	Central and Eastern European Countries	cm	centimetre
		CMAA	Club Managers Association of America
CEI	Centre for Environmental Interpretation		
		CMT	Common Market Travel Association
CER	Council of European Regions		
CERT	Council for Education, Recruitment and Training (Republic of Ireland)	c/o	care of
		Co.	company
		CO	Colorado, USA
cet. par.	*ceteris paribus* (other things being equal)	C.O.D.	cash on delivery
		COSLA	Convention of Scottish Local Authorities
cf.	*confer* (compare)		
CFA	*Communauté financière africaine*	COTAL	Latin American Confederation of Tourist Organizations
	Cookery & Food Association		
CFP	*Comptoirs français du Pacifique*	CP	Canadian Pacific (Air, Hotels, Railway, etc)
CFTC	Commonwealth Fund for Technical Co-operation		*case postale* (post box)
			Continental Plan
C&G	City and Guilds	CPA	critical path analysis
CGLI	City and Guilds of London Institute	CPRE	Council for the Protection of Rural England
CGOT	Canadian Government Office of Tourism (now Tourism Canada)	CPRW	Council for the Protection of Rural Wales
CHA	Caribbean Hotel Association	CPT	Confederation of Passenger Transport
	Countrywide Holidays Association		
		CRONWE	Conference of Regions of North West Europe
Ches.	Cheshire, England		
CHMA	Canadian Hotel and Motel Association	CRS	central reservation system(s) computer reservation system(s) Country of Residence Survey (Republic of Ireland)
CHME	Council for Hospitality Management Education		
CHNTO	Cultural Heritage National Training Organization	CSA	Czechoslovak Airlines
		CSQ	Customer Satisfaction Questionnaire
chq.	cheque		
CHRIE	(International) Council on Hotel, Restaurant and Institutional Education (US)	CST	Central Standard Time (USA)
		CT	Civic Trust
			Connecticut, USA
CI	Channel Islands	CTA	Caribbean Tourism/Tourist/Travel Association
CIA	Catering Institute of Australia		
CIC	Convention Industry Council (US)		
		CTC	Canadian Tourism Commission Cyclists' Touring Club
CI$	Cayman Islands Dollar (currency)		
c.i.f.	cost, insurance, freight	CTCC	Central Transport Consultative Committee
CIGA	*Compagnia Italiana dei Grandi Alberghi* (Italian hotel group)		

ABBREVIATIONS

237

CTHRC	Canadian Tourism Human Resource Council	CTT	Council for Travel and Tourism
CTO	Caribbean Tourism Organization	cu.	cubic
	Cyprus Tourism Organisation	c.v.	curriculum vitae
		cwt	hundredweight

D	Dalasi (currency of Gambia)	Derbys.	Derbyshire, England
	five hundred (Roman numeral)	DET	domestic escorted tour
	(train) Durchgehender Zug	D-G	Director General
DA	Algerian Dinar (currency)	Dh	UAE Dirham (currency of
DATAS II	Deltamatic Assisted Travel		United Arab Emirates)
	Agency System (Mark II)	DH	Moroccan Dirham (currency)
Db	Dobra (currency of São Tome	Dip.	Diploma
	and Principe)	DIT	domestic independent tour
DC	direct current	DMO	destination marketing organiza-
	District of Columbia, USA		tion
DCF	discounted cash flow	$A	Australian Dollar (currency)
dcm	decimetre	$NZ	New Zealand Dollar (currency)
DCMS	Department for Culture, Media	$T	Pa'anga (currency of Tonga)
	and Sport	DOT	Department of Transportation
D Day	Decimal Day (UK 15 February		(US)
	1971)	doz.	dozen
D-Day	first day of Allied invasion of	DR	Democratic Republic
	Continental Europe during	DST	daylight saving time
	WWII (6 June 1944)	DTI	Department of Trade and
DE	Delaware, USA		Industry
Dec.	December	DTLR	Department for Transport,
DEFRA	Department for Environment,		Local Government and the
	Food and Rural Affairs		Regions
deli	delicatessen (US and Australia)	DTM	Domestic Tourism Monitor
Den.	Denmark		(Australia)
dep.	departs/departure	DVS	day visits survey(s)

E	east(ern)	EB	Ethiopian Birr (currency of
	Lilangeni (currency of		Ethiopia)
	Swaziland)	EBRD	European Bank for
EADB	East African Development		Reconstruction and
	Bank		Development
EAL	Eastern Air Lines	EC	European Community/
EATA	East Asia Travel Association		Commission/Council

ECA	European Catering Association	EI	Aer Lingus
ECAC	European Civil Aviation Conference	EIA	Environmental Impact Assessment
ECCAS	Economic Community of Central African States	EIB	European Investment Bank
		EIF	Exhibition Industry Federation
ECD	early closing day	El Al	Israeli airline
	early completion day	ELRA	European Leisure and Recreation Association
EC$	Eastern Caribbean Dollar (currency)	e-mail	electronic mail
ECGD	Export Credits Guarantee Department	EMECA	European Major Exhibition Centres Association
ECMT	European Conference of Ministers of Transport	EMF	European Motel Federation
		EMS	Environmental Management System
ECOSOC	(United Nations) Economic and Social Council		European Monetary System
ECOWAS	Economic Community of West African States	EMU	Economic and Monetary Union
		EP	European Plan
ECSC	European Coal and Steel Community	EPA	Environmental Protection Agency (US)
ECTAA	Group of National Travel Agents' and Tour Operators' Associations within the EC	equiv.	equivalent
		ERA	European Regional Airlines Organisation
ECTWT	Ecumenical Coalition on Third World Tourism	ERDF	European Regional Development Fund
ECU	European Currency Unit	ERM	Exchange Rate Mechanism
ECY	European Conservation Year	ERP	European Recovery Programme
ed.	editor	ESA	Environmentally Sensitive Area
E/D (card)	embarkation/disembarkation (card)	ESF	European Social Fund
		est.	estimate
EDF	European Development Fund	EST	Eastern Standard Time (USA)
edn	edition	ETA	estimated time of arrival
EDP	electronic data processing	ETAG	European Tourism Action Group
EEA	European Economic Area	ETB	English Tourist Board (now ETC)
EEC	European Economic Community		
EFAH	European Foundation for the Accreditation of Hotel School Programmes	etc.	*et cetera* (and so on)
		ETC	English Tourism Council
			European Travel Commission
EFCT	European Federation of Conference Towns	ETD	estimated time of departure
		ETP	Excellence Through People
EFT	electronic funds transfer	EU	European Union
EFTA	European Free Trade Association	EUHOFA	European Association of Hotel School Directors
EFTPOS	electronic funds transfer at point of sale	Euratom	European Atomic Energy Community
e.g.	*exempli gratia* (for example)	Euro Chambers	Association of European Chambers of Commerce and Industry
EH	(routing) within the Eastern Hemisphere		
EHMA	European Hotel Managers Association	EUTO	European Union of Tourist Officers

F	Fahrenheit
F	letter followed by abbreviation of the name of a professional body denotes Fellow of that body
FAA	Federal Aviation Administration (US)
FAC	Federal Airports Corporation (Australia)
fam	familiarization (as, e.g., fam trip)
FANZ	Food Services Association of New Zealand
FATA	Federation of ASEAN Travel Agents
fax	facsimile
F&B	food and beverage
FC	Forestry Commission
FCSI	Foodservice Consultants Society International
FCU	Fare Construction Unit
F$	Fiji Dollar (currency)
FE	Far East
	Further Education
Feb.	February
fem.	feminine
FES	Family Expenditure Survey
FET	foreign escorted tour
FFCS	Food Facilities Consultants Society
FFP	frequent flyer programme
FG	Guinean Franc (currency)
fhld	freehold

fiche	microfiche
FIA	International Automobile Federation
FIFO	first in, first out
FI£	Falkland Islands Pound (currency)
Finnair	Finnish Airlines
FIT	foreign independent tour
FIYTO	Federation of International Youth Travel Organizations
Fl	Florin/Guilder (currency)
FL	Florida, USA
Flt	flight
FMC	Federal Maritime Commission (US)
f.o.b.	free on board
Fr	Franc (currency)
	France/French
Franc CFA	*Franc de la Communauté financière africaine* (African Franc)
Franc CFP	*Franc des Comptoirs français du Pacifique* (Pacific Franc)
FRG	Federal Republic of Germany
Fri.	Friday
ft.	feet (measurement)
FT	full-time
FTE	full-time equivalent
FTO	Federation of Tour Operators
fwd	forward
FZGB	Federation of Zoological Gardens of Great Britain and Ireland

g	gram(me)
G	Guarani (currency of Paraguay)
G7	Group of Seven (largest industrialized countries: Canada, France, Germany, Italy, Japan, UK, USA))
G8	Group of Eight (G7 plus Russia)

GA	Georgia, USA
gal.	gallon
GATS	General Agreement on Trade in Services
GATT	General Agreement on Tariffs and Trade
GB	Great Britain

GB and I	Great Britain and Ireland	Gk.	Greek
GBCO	Guild of British Coach Operators	Glam.	Glamorgan, Wales
GBTA	Guild of Business Travel Agents	GLC	Greater London Council (abolished 1986)
GCE	General Certificate of Education		
GCSE	General Certificate of Secondary Education	G£	Gibraltar Pound (currency)
		Glos.	Gloucestershire, England
G$	Guyana Dollar (currency)	GMB	General, Municipal, Boilermakers and Allied Trades Union
GDP	gross domestic product		
GDS	global distribution system		
GEBTA	Guild of European Business Travel Agents	GMT	Greenwich Mean/Meridian Time
Ger.	German(y)	GNP	gross national product
GFG	*Good Food Guide* (Consumers' Association, annual)	GNVQ	General National Vocational Qualification
GFR	German Federal Republic	GOETO	Grand Order of European Travel Organizers
GGL	Guild of Guide Lecturers		
GHS	General Household Survey	gov(t)	government
Gib.	Gibraltar	GRS	global reservation system
GIGO	(computing term for) garbage in, garbage out	GRT	gross registered ton
		GSA	General Sales Agent
GIT	group inclusive tour	GST	Greenwich Standard Time

ha	hectare	HHA	Historic Houses Association
HA	Hospitality Assured	HI	Hawaii, USA
HAG	Have-a-Go	HIDB	Highlands and Islands Development Board (now Highlands and Islands Enterprise)
Hants.	Hampshire, England		
HANZ	Hotel Association of New Zealand		
		HIMG	Hotel Industry Marketing Group (now HMA)
h.b.	hard back (publication)		
hbr	harbour	HIV	Human Immuno-Deficiency Virus
HCI	Hotel and Catering Institute (now HCIMA)		
		HK$	Hong Kong Dollar (currency)
HCIMA	Hotel and Catering International Management Association	hl	hectolitre
		HM	Harbour Master Her/His Majesty
HCITB	Hotel and Catering Industry Training Board (now HtF)		
		HMA	Hotel Marketing Association
HCPTA	Hotel and Catering Personnel and Training Association	HMS	Her/His Majesty's Ship
		HMSO	Her/His Majesty's Stationery Office (now The Stationery Office)
HCTB	Hotel and Catering Training Board (now HtF)		
HCTC	Hotel and Catering Training Company (now HtF)	HNC	Higher National Certificate
		HND	Higher National Diploma
HCU	Hotel and Catering Union	HO	Home Office
HE	Higher Education	hols	holidays
Herts.	Hertfordshire, England	HoReCa	International Organization of Hotel and Restaurant Associations
HFTP	Hospitality Financial and Technology Professionals		

HOTREC	Confederation of National Hotel and Restaurant Associations in the European Community	hr(s)	hour(s)
		HSMAI	Hospitality Sales and Marketing Association International
HQ	headquarters	HtF	Hospitality Training Foundation

I	one (Roman numeral)	IBTA	International Business Travel Association
i.a.	*inter alia* (among other things)		
IA	Iowa, USA	i/c	in charge/command
IAAPA	International Association of Amusement Parks and Attractions	ICA	International Co-operative Alliance
IACA	International Air Carrier Association	ICAA	International Civil Airports Association
IACVB	International Association of Convention and Visitor Bureaux	ICAO	International Civil Aviation Organization
IAFCT	International Association of French-Speaking Congress Towns	ICC	International Chamber of Commerce
IAFTAC	Inter-American Federation of Touring and Automobile Clubs	ICCA	International Congress and Convention Association
IAHA	Inter-American Hotel Association	ICM	Institute of Commercial Management
	International Association of Hospitality Accountants (now HFTP)	ICOM	International Council of Museums
		ICOMOS	International Council on Monuments and Sites
IAHMS	International Association of Hotel Management Schools	ICS	International Chamber of Shipping
IAPA	International Airline Passengers Association	ICTA	Institute of Certified Travel Agents (US)
IAPCO	International Association of Professional Congress Organizers	id.	*idem* (the same)
		ID	Idaho, USA
			identification (card etc.)
IASC	International Air Services Commission (Australia)		Iraqi Dinar (currency)
IASTWL	International Association for Social Tourism and Workers' Leisure	IDA	International Development Association
		IDB	Inter-American Development Bank
IAT	Institute of Air Transport		Islamic Development Bank
IATA	International Air Transport Association	IDD	International Direct Dialling
		i.e.	*id est* (that is)
IATM	International Association of Tour Managers	IEHO	Institution of Environmental Health Officers
IB	Iberia (Spanish airlines)	IFAPA	International Foundation of Airline Passengers Associations
ibid.	*ibidem* (in the same book, chapter, place)	IFC	International Finance Corporation
IBRD	International Bank for Reconstruction and Development	IFCA	International Flight Catering Association

IFCC	International Federation of Camping and Caravanning	Iran Air	Iran National Airlines
IFEA	International Festival and Events Association	IRU	International Road Transport Union
IFPTO	International Federation of Popular Travel Organizations	Is	Islands
		ISD	International Subscriber Dialling
IFTO	International Federation of Tour Operators	ISES	International Special Events Society
IFTTA	International Forum of Travel and Tourism Advocates	ISF	International Shipping Federation
IFWTO	International Federation of Women's Travel Organizations	ISFSC	International Society of Food Service Consultants
IGO	inter-governmental organization	ISIC	International Standard Industrial Classification
IHASA	International Hotel Association South Asia	isNTO	Information Services National Training Organization
IHEI	International Hotels Environment Initiative	ISO	International Organization for Standardization
IHRA	International Hotel and Restaurant Association	ISRM	Institute of Sport and Recreation Management
IIM	Institution of Industrial Managers (now CIM)	ISTC	International Student Travel Confederation
IIP	Investors in People	IT	inclusive tour
IL	Illinois, USA		information technology
ILAM	Institute of Leisure and Amenity Management	ITA	Institut du Transport Aérien
			Institute of Travel Agents (now ITT)
ILO	International Labour Organisation		
IM	Institute of Management (now CIM)	ITAA	Irish Travel Agents Association
		ital.	italic
IMA	Institutional Management Association (now HCIMA)	ITB	International Tourism Exchange (Börse)
IMCO	Inter-Governmental Maritime Consultative Organization		Industrial Training Board
IMF	International Monetary Fund	ITC	Inter-American Travel Congresses
IMO	International Maritime Organization		inclusive tour charter
impt	important	ITHA	International Tourist Health Association
in.	inch(es)		
IN	Indiana, USA	ITIC	Irish Tourist Industry Confederation
Inc.	Incorporated		
incl.	including/inclusive	ITM	Institute of Travel Management in Industry and Commerce
indiv.	individual		
INSPASS	(acronym for) Immigration and Naturalization Service Passenger Accelerated Service System		Institute of Travel Managers in Industry and Commerce
		ITMA	Incentive Travel and Meetings Association
inst.	instance/instant		
intro.	introduce/introduction/ introductory	ITOA	Incoming Tour Operators Association
IOC	Indian Ocean Commission	ITOC	Inbound Tour Operators Council (New Zealand)
IOM	Isle of Man		
IOW	Isle of Wight	ITT	Institute of Travel and Tourism
IPS	International Passenger Survey	ITV	Independent Television
IPU	Inter-Parliamentary Union	ITX	inclusive tour fare
IR	Iranian Rial (currency)	IUCAT	International Union of Co-operative and Associated Tourism
IRA	International Recreation Association		

IUOTO	International Union of Official Travel Organizations (now WTO)	IW	Isle of Wight
		IWA	Inland Waterways Association
IUR	International Union of Railways	IWTC	International World Travellers Club
IVS	International Visitor Survey (Australia)	IYHF	International Youth Hostel Federation

JAA	Joint Aviation Authorities	JHIC	Joint Hospitality Industry Congress
JAL	Japan Air Lines	JICNARS	Joint Industry Committee for National Readership Surveys
Jan.	January		
JAT	*Jugoslovenski Aerotransport* (Yugoslav Airlines)	Jnl	Journal
		jnr	junior
jct.	junction	jt	joint
JD	Jordanian Dinar (currency)	JTC	Joint Twinning Committee
J$	Jamaican Dollar (currency)	Jul.	July
		Jun.	June

K	Kina (currency of Papua New Guinea) Kip (currency of Lao, PDR) Kwacha (currency of Malawi and Zambia) Kyat (currency of Myanmar)	km	kilometre(s)
		KM	Konvertibilna Marka (currency of Bosnia and Hercegovina)
		kph	kilometres per hour
		Kr	Krona (Icelandic and Swedish currency)
k. & b.	kitchen and bathroom		Krone (Danish and Norwegian currency)
Kč	Koruna (currency of Czech Republic)		
		Ks	Kenyan Shilling (currency)
KD	Kuwaiti Dinar (currency)	KS	Kansas, USA
kg	kilogram(me)	KY	Kentucky, USA
KLM	Royal Dutch Airlines	KZ	Kwanza (Angolan currency)

L	fifty (Roman numeral)
£	*libra* (Pound Sterling; UK currency)
LA	Latin America
	Los Angeles, USA
	Louisiana, USA
LAADFI	Latin American Association of Development Financing Institutions
LACA	Local Authority Caterers Association
LACAC	Latin American Civil Aviation Commission
Lancs.	Lancashire, England
LAS	League of Arab States
lb	pound (measurement)
l.c.	lower case (i.e., not capitals)
LCB	London Convention Bureau
LD	Libyan Dinar (currency)
LDC	less developed country
Ldn	London
L$	Liberian Dollar (currency)
LDP	long-distance path
Le	Leone (currency of Sierra Leone)
£E	Egyptian Pound (currency)
LEA	Local Education Authority

LEC	Local Enterprise Company (Scotland)
Leics.	Leicestershire, England
LFS	Labour Force Survey
LGA	Local Government Association
LGMB	Local Government Management Board
lgt	long ton
LH	Lufthansa (German Airlines)
LIFO	last in, first out
LILO	last in, last out
Lincs.	Lincolnshire, England
Lk	Lek (currency of Albania)
£L	Lebanese Pound (currency)
LM	Maltese Lira (currency)
loc.cit.	*loco citato* (in the place cited)
locn	location
LOT	*Polskie Linie Lotnicze* (Polish Airlines)
L'pool	Liverpool
L/R	left to right
LRT	London Regional Transport
LRV	light refreshment voucher
£S	Syrian Pound (currency)
LSA	Leisure Studies Association
LTB	London Tourist Board
Ltd	Limited
LVL	Lats (Latvian currency)

m	metre/mile/million
M	one thousand (Roman numeral)
M	letter followed by abbreviation of the name of a professional body denotes Member of that body
MA	Massachusetts, USA
	(routing) via mid Atlantic
MAC	Museums Association of the Caribbean
MAE	Maritime Advisory Exchange

MAGLEV	magnetic levitation
Man.	Manitoba, Canada
MANZ	Motel Association of New Zealand
MAP	Modified American Plan
Mar.	March
Marit.	maritime
masc.	masculine
max.	maximum
MB	Manitoba, Canada
mbr	member

m/c	machine
M/C	Manchester
MC	master of ceremonies
MCO	Miscellaneous Charges Order
MCT	Minimum Connecting Time
MD	Managing Director
	Maryland, USA
M$	Ringgit (currency of Malaysia)
ME	Maine, USA
	Middle East
MEA	Middle East Airlines
med.	medium
Med(it).	Mediterranean
met(eor).	meteorological/meteorology
mgr	manager
MI	Michigan, USA
MIA	Meetings Industry Association
MICE	(acronym for) Meetings, Incentive Travel, Conventions and Exhibitions
Middx	Middlesex, England
MIGA	Multilateral Investment Guarantee Agency
min.	minimum
	minute
misc.	miscellaneous
mkt	market
mm	millimetre
MN	Minnesota, USA
MO	Missouri, USA
MOCA	Mobile and Outside Caterers Association of Great Britain
MOD	minor operated departments (in hotels)
mod. con.	modern convenience
Mon.	Monday
MOU	Memorandum of Understanding
mpg	miles per gallon
mph	miles per hour
MPI	Meeting Professionals International (US)
MPM	Maximum Permitted Mileage
mrt.	mass rapid transit
Ms	Miss/Mrs
MS	Mississippi, USA
	Motor Ship
MSC	Manpower Services Commission
MST	Mountain Standard Time (USA)
Mt	Mount(ain)
MT	Metical (currency of Mozambique)
	Montana, USA
mtg	meeting
mth	month
MV	Motor Vessel
Mx	Middlesex, England

N	north(ern)
N̶	Naira (currency of Nigeria)
n.a.	not available/applicable
NA	(routing) via North Atlantic
NABTA	National Association of Business Travel Agents (US)
NACE	Nomenclature Générale des Activités Économiques dans les Communautés Européennes
NAEH	National Association of Exhibition Halls
NA Fl	Netherlands Antilles Guilder/Florin (currency)
NAFC	National Advisory Facilitation Committee (Australia)
NAFTA	North American Free Trade Agreement
NAHC	National Association of Holiday Centres Limited
NAITA	National Association of Independent Travel Agents
NALGO	National Association of Local Government Officers
NALHM	National Association of Licensed House Managers
N. Am.	North America
nat(l).	national
NAPHA	National Amusement Park Historical Association
naut.	nautical
n.b.	*nota bene* (note well)
NB	New Brunswick, Canada
NBC	National Bus Company
NBTA	National Business Travel Association (US)

NC	no charge	NR	Nepalese Rupee (currency)
	Nordic Council	NRA	National Restaurant Association
	North Carolina, USA		(US)
NCC	National Caravan Council		National Rivers Authority
NCIT	National Council on Inland	NRCA	National Restaurant and
	Transport		Catering Association
N/cle	Newcastle		(Australia)
n.c.v.	no commercial value	NRPA	National Recreation and Park
NCVQ	National Council for Vocational		Association (US)
	Qualifications	NRPC	National Railroad Passenger
ND	National Diploma		Corporation (AMTRAK)
	North Dakota, USA	NS	Nova Scotia, Canada
N$	Namibian Dollar (currency)	NSW	New South Wales, Australia
NE	Nebraska, USA	NT	National Trust
	north-east		Northern Territory, Australia
NEDC	National Economic Development	NTA	National Tour Association (US)
	Council (abolished 1992)		National Tourism
NEDO	National Economic Development		Administration
	Office (abolished 1992)	NT$	New Taiwan Dollar (currency)
nem. con.	*nemine contradicente* (no one	NTO	National Tourism/Tourist
	opposing, unanimously)		Office/Organization
nem. dis.	*nemine dissentiente* (no one		National Training Organization
	dissenting)	NTS	National Trust for Scotland
n.e.s.	not elsewhere specified	NTTC	Northern Territory Tourist
Neth.	Netherlands		Commission (Australia)
NF	Newfoundland, Canada	Nu	Ngultrum (currency of Bhutan)
NFSO	National Federation of Site	NU	Nunavut, Canada
	Operators	NUC	Neutral Unit of Construction
NGO	non-governmental organization	NUCPS	National Union of Civil and
NH	New Hampshire, USA		Public Servants
N.I.	Northern Ireland	NUMAST	National Union of Marine,
NIHCA	Northern Ireland Hotels and		Aviation and Shipping
	Caterers Association		Transport
NIS	Newly Independent States	NUR	Neckermann Group (German
NITB	Northern Ireland Tourist Board		tour operator)
NJ	New Jersey, USA	NV	Nevada, USA
NM	New Mexico, USA	NVQ	National Vocational
	(routing) via North and Mid		Qualification
	Atlantic	NW	north-west
no.	number	NWT	Northwest Territories, Canada
Northants.	Northamptonshire, England	NY	New York, USA
Northumb.	Northumberland, England	NZ	New Zealand
Notts.	Nottinghamshire, England	NZCA	New Zealand Convention
Nov.	November		Association
NP	(routing) via North or Central	NZHCITB	New Zealand Hotel and
	Pacific		Catering Industry Training
NPPC	National Passenger Processing		Board
	Committee (Australia)	NZITT	New Zealand Institute of Travel
NPTA	National Passenger Traffic		and Tourism
	Association (US)	NZTB	New Zealand Tourist Board
nr	near	NZTIA	New Zealand Tourism Industry
	number		Association

ABBREVIATIONS

O

OAA	Orient Airlines Association	O level	Ordinary level examination of
OAG	Official Airline Guide		the General Certificate of
OAP	old age pension(er)		Education (GCE) in the UK
OAS	Organization of American		(excluding Scotland)
	States	O&M	organization and methods
OAU	Organization of African Unity	OMMSA	Organization of Museums,
OCAS	Organization of Central		Monuments and Sites of Africa
	American States	OND	Ordinary National Diploma
Oct.	October	Ont.	Ontario, Canada
ODA	Overseas Development	op. cit.	*opere citato* (in the work quoted)
	Administration	OPEC	Organization of the Petroleum
OECD	Organisation for Economic		Exporting Countries
	Co-operation and Development	OR	operational/operations research
OECS	Organization of Eastern		Oregon, USA
	Caribbean States	ORC	Organization of Railways
OFT	Office of Fair Trading		Cooperation
OH	Ohio, USA	orig.	original(ly)
OK	Okay, all correct/confirmed	OS	Ordnance Survey
	Oklahoma, USA	o'seas	overseas
		OT	overtime
		OW	one way
		Oxon.	Oxfordshire, England
		oz	ounce

P

p.	page	Pax	passenger
	pence	PAX	private automatic (telephone)
P	Pula (currency of Botswana)		exchange
p.a.	*per annum* (yearly)	p.b.	paper back (publication)
PA	Pennsylvania, USA	PBX	private branch (telephone)
	Personal Assistant		exchange
	(routing) via the Pacific	PC	personal computer
PABX	private automatic branch		postcard
	(telephone) exchange	PCI	Passenger Card Inquiry
Pan Am	Pan American Airways		(Republic of Ireland)
para	paragraph	PCS	Public and Civil Service Union
PARCA	Pan American Railway Congress	PDR	People's Democratic Republic
	Association	P/E	price-earnings (ratio)
PARS	Passenger Airline Reservation	PEI	Prince Edward Island, Canada
	System	PERT	Programme Evaluation and
PAS	public address system		Review Technique
PATA	Pacific Asia Travel Association	PEX	Public Excursion fare

DICTIONARY OF TRAVEL, TOURISM AND HOSPITALITY

PG	paying guest	POS	point of sale
PHARE	(acronym from French for) Poland and Hungary; Assistance for Economic Restructuring	pp.	pages
		p&p	post and packing
		PR	People's Republic
PIA	Pakistan International Airlines		public relations
PIN	personal identification number	prelim.	preliminary
PIR	Property Irregularity Report	prelims	preliminaries (book pages preceding main text)
pkt	packet		
P&L	profit and loss (account)	prepn	preparation
PLC	public limited company	priv.	private
p.m.	*post meridiem* (after noon)	pro tem	*pro tempore* (for the time being)
p.n.g.	*persona non grata* (undesirable person)	PS	*post scriptum* (postscript)
		PSA	Passenger Service Agent
PNG	Papua New Guinea		Passenger Shipping Association
PNR	Passenger Name Record		
PO	(routing) via Polar route between Europe and Japan or Korea	PSR	passenger space ratio
		PST	Pacific Standard Time (USA)
		PSV	Public Service Vehicle
P&O	Peninsular and Oriental Steam Navigation Company	pt	part
		PT	part-time
POB	Post Office Box	PTA	Prepaid Ticket Advice
POE	port of embarkation/entry	pub	public house
Port.	Portugal/Portuguese	p.w.	per week

Q	Quetzal (currency of Guatemala)	qr	quarter
QANTAS	Queensland and Northern Territory Aerial Service (Australian airline)	QR	Qatar Riyal (currency)
		QTTC	Queensland Tourist and Travel Corporation
Qbc	Quebec, Canada	quango	quasi-autonomous non-governmental organization
Qld	Queensland, Australia		

R	Rand (currency of South Africa)	RAC	Royal Automobile Club
	Rouble/Rubl/Ruble (currency of Belarus and Russian Federation)	RACV	Royal Automobile Club of Victoria (Australia)
RA	Ramblers' Association	RAeS	Royal Aeronautical Society
	Restaurant Association	R/D	refer to drawer (of a cheque)
RAA	Regional Airlines Association (US)	R&D	research and development
		R$	Brazilian Real (currency)
RAAA	Regional Airlines Association of Australia	RD$	Dominican Peso (currency of Dominican Republic)

recd	received	RPM	Resale Price Maintenance
ref.	refer(ence)		revenue passenger mile
reg.	regular	RRP	recommended retail price
regd	registered	Rs	Rupee (currency of India and
REKA	Swiss Travel Saving Fund		Pakistan)
Rep.	Republic	RSAC	Royal Scottish Automobile Club
revpar	revenue per available room	RSNC	Royal Society for Nature
RI	Rhode Island, USA		Conservation
Rio	Rio de Janeiro (Brazil)	RT	return trip
RM	Ringgit (currency of Malaysia)		round trip
RMA	Recreation Managers Association	RTA	Regional Tourism Authority
	of Great Britain		(Republic of Ireland)
RMT	National Union of Rail,		Regional Tourist Association
	Maritime and Transport		(Northern Ireland)
	Workers	RTB	Regional Tourist Board
RO	Omani Rial (currency of Oman)	RTC	Regional Tourism Company
ROC	return on capital		(Wales)
ROI	return on investment	RTK	revenue tonne kilometre
Rp	Rupiah (currency of Indonesia)	rte	route
RPI	Retail Price Index	RTW	round the world
RPK	revenue passenger kilometre	RV	recreation(al) vehicle (US)

S	south(ern)	SD	South Dakota, USA
SA	South Africa/America/Australia	SDA	Scottish Development Agency
	(routing) via South Atlantic		(now Scottish Enterprise)
SAC	Scottish Arts Council	S$	Singapore Dollar (currency)
SABENA	Belgian Airlines	SE	south-east
SADCC	Southern African Development	SED	Scottish Education Department
	Coordination Conference	Sep(t).	September
s.a.e.	stamped addressed envelope	Sf	Suriname Guilder/Florin
Salop.	Shropshire, England		(currency)
SARTOC	Southern Africa Regional	SF	Swiss Franc (currency)
	Tourism Council	sgd	signed
SAS	Scandinavian Airlines System	SGIT	Special Group Inclusive Tour
Sask.	Saskatchewan, Canada		(fare)
Sat.	Saturday	sgle	single
SATA	Student Air Travel Association	s/he	he/she
SATC	South Australian Tourism	SIA	Singapore International Airlines
	Commission	SIBH	Society for the Interpretation of
SC	South Carolina, USA		Britain's Heritage
SCHMC	Society of Catering and Hotel	SIC	Standard Industrial
	Management Consultants		Classification
SCOT	Scottish Confederation of Tourism	SICTA	Standard International
SCOVA	Standard Classification of Visitor		Classification of Tourism
	Accommodation (Australia)		Activities
scuba	(acronym for) self-contained	SI$	Solomon Islands Dollar
	underwater breathing apparatus		(currency)

SITE	Society of Incentive Travel Executives (US)
SIWA	Scottish Inland Waterways Association
Sk	Koruna (currency of Slovakia)
SK	Saskatchewan, Canada
S level	Scholarship level examination of the General Certificate of Education (GCE) in the UK (excluding Scotland)
SIT	Slovenian Tolar (currency)
SMA	Systems Managers Association
smog	smoke-laden fog
SNCB	Belgian National Railways
SNCF	French National Railways
SNH	Scottish National Heritage
snr	senior
SO	Scottish Office
SOC	Standard Occupational Classification
Som	Somerset, England
So. Sh.	Somalia Shilling (currency)
SOT	Survey of Overseas Travellers (Republic of Ireland)
Soton	Southampton
Sp.	Spain/Spanish
SP	(routing) via South Pacific
SPAB	Society for the Protection of Ancient Buildings
SPEC	South Pacific Bureau for Economic Co-operation
SPF	South Pacific Forum
SPRITO	Sport, Recreation and Allied

	Occupations National Training Organization
SPTO	South Pacific Tourism Organization
sq.	square (in measurements)
SR	Saudi Riyal (currency of Saudi Arabia)
	Seychelles Rupee (currency)
SS	Steamship
SSSI	Site of Special Scientific Interest
SST	supersonic transport
Staffs.	Staffordshire, England
STB	Scottish Tourist Board
stbd	starboard
std	standard
STD	Subscriber Trunk Dialling
stg	sterling
STGA	Scottish Tourist Guides Association
stn	station
STOL	short take-off and landing
STTE	Society of Travel and Tourism Educators (US)
STUC	Scottish Trades Union Congress
Sun.	Sunday
SVQ	Scottish Vocational Qualification
SW	south-west
Swissair	Swiss Air Transport
SWOT	(acronym for) Strengths, Weaknesses, Opportunities, Threats
SYHA	Scottish Youth Hostels Association

t	ton(ne)
TAANZ	Travel Agents Association of New Zealand
TAC	Tourism Aviation Group (Australia)
TACC	Travel Associations Consultative Council
TACIS	Technical Assistance to the Commonwealth of Independent States
TAP	Portuguese Air Lines
Tas.	Tasmania, Australia
t.b.a.	to be announced/advised

TC	Traffic Conference
	traveller's cheque (traveler's check)
TCA	Tourism Council Australia
TCF	Travel Compensation Fund (Australia)
TCSP	Tourism Council of the South Pacific (now SPTO)
TD	Tunisian Dinar (currency)
TDA	Timeshare Developers Association
TDAP	Tourism Development Action Plan

TEC	Training and Enterprise Council	TRINET	Tourism Research Information Network
TEE	Trans-Europe Express (now EuroCity)	TS	(routing) Trans Siberia
tel.	telephone		Tourism Society
TEN	Third World Tourism European Ecumenical Network	TSA	Tourism South Australia
TGV	*Train à Grande Vitesse* (high-speed train of French railways)	TSCG	Tourism Society Consultants Group
TGWU	Transport and General Workers' Union	tsp.	teaspoon(ful)
Thu.(r)	Thursday	TSSA	Transport Salaried Staffs' Association
TIA	Travel Industry Association of America	TTA	Tourism Training Australia
		TT$	Trinidad and Tobago Dollar (currency)
TIAC	Tourism Industry Association of Canada	TTENTO	Travel, Tourism Services and Events National Training Organization
TIC	Tourist Information Centre		
TICA	Tourism International Cooperative and Associated	TTP	Travel and Tourism Programme
tip	(acronym for) To Insure Promptitude	TTRA	Travel and Tourism Research Association (US)
Tk	Taka (currency of Bangladesh)	TU	trade union
tkt	ticket	TUC	Trades Union Congress
TL	Turkish Lira (currency)	TUCC	Transport Users Consultative Committee
TN	Tennessee, USA	Tue(s).	Tuesday
TNSW	Tourism New South Wales (Australia)	TUI	Touristik Union International (German tour operator)
TOSG	Tour Operators Study Group (now FTO)	turboprop	turbine propelled
		TWA	TransWorld Airlines
tpk.	turnpike	TX	Texas, USA
TPM	Ticket Point Mileage	TTGAC	Travel and Tourism Government Affairs Council (US)
TQM	total quality management		

UA	United Airlines	UKHA	United Kingdom Housekeepers Association
UAA	United Arab Airlines		
UAE	United Arab Emirates	UKTS	United Kingdom Tourism Survey
UAR	United Arab Republic	UM	Ouguiya (currency of Mauritania)
UDC	Urban Development Corporation		
UEHHA	Union of European Historic Houses Associations	UMA	United Motorcoach Association (US)
UFTAA	Universal Federation of Travel Agents' Associations	UN	United Nations
		UNCTAD	United Nations Conference on Trade and Development
u/g	underground		
UIA	Union of International Associations	UNDP	United Nations Development Programme
UIF	Union of International Fairs	UNEP	United Nations Environment Programme
UK	United Kingdom		

UNESCO	United Nations Educational, Scientific and Cultural Organization	USSR	(former) Union of Soviet Socialist Republics
UPC	Universal Producer Code	USTDC	United States Travel Data Center
US	United States	USTOA	United States Tour Operators Association
USA	United States of America		
USAID	United States Agency for International Development	USTTA	United States Travel and Tourism Administration (abolished 1996)
USDAW	Union of Shop, Distributive and Allied Workers	USVI	United States Virgin Islands
		UT	Utah, USA
US$	United States Dollar (currency)	Utd	United
		UTDA	Ulster Tourist Development Association
USP	unique selling proposition		

V	five (Roman numeral)	VIP	Very Important Person
VA	Virginia, USA	VJ Day	15 August 1945 (day of Japanese surrender in Asia in WWII)
vac.	vacancy/vacant		
var.	variable	VR	virtual reality
VARIG	Brazilian airline		visiting relatives
VAT	value added tax	vs.	*versus* (against)
V Day	Victory Day	VT	Vermont, USA
VDU	visual display unit	VTO	vertical take-off
VE Day	8 May 1945 (Victory in Europe in WWII)	VTOL	vertical take-off and landing
		VTOHL	vertical take-off and horizontal landing
VFR	visiting friends and relatives		
VIASA	Venezuelan airline	v.v.	*vice versa* (the other way round)
Vic.	Victoria, Australia		

W	west(ern)	WATC	Western Australian Tourism Commission
WA	Washington (state), USA		
	West Africa	WDA	Welsh Development Agency
	Western Australia	WEAA	Western European Airports Association
WADB	West African Development Bank		
WAPTT	World Association for Professional Training in Tourism	Wed.	Wednesday
		WF	Wells Fargo and Company
		WFTU	World Federation of Trade Unions
Warwicks.	Warwickshire, England		
WATA	World Association of Travel Agencies	WH	(routing) within the Western Hemisphere

WHO	World Health Organization	WTB	Wales Tourist Board
WI	West Indies	WTM	World Travel Market
	Wisconsin, USA	WTO	World Tourism Organization
WICE	World Industry Council on the		World Trade Organization
	Environment	WTTC	World Travel and Tourism
Wilts.	Wiltshire, England		Council
wk(ly)	week(ly)	WTTERC	World Travel and Tourism
WL	waiting list/waitlist		Environment Research Centre
WLRA	World Leisure and Recreation	WV	West Virginia, USA
	Association	WWI	World War I (1914–1918)
Worcs.	Worcestershire, England	WWII	World War II (1939–1945)
w.p.m.	words per minute	WWF	World Wide Fund for Nature
WS$	Tala (currency of Samoa)	WY	Wyoming, USA

X	ten (Roman numeral)

yd	yard (measurement)	YMCA	Young Men's Christian
YD	Yemeni Dinar (currency)		Association
YH	youth hostel	Yorks.	Yorkshire, England
YHA	Youth Hostels Association	yr	year
	(England and Wales)	YT	Yukon Territory, Canada
YHANI	Youth Hostel Association of	YWCA	Young Women's Christian
	Northern Ireland Ltd		Association
YHANZ	Youth Hostels Association of		
	New Zealand		

Z$	Zimbabwe Dollar (currency)	ZIP (code)	Zone Improvement Plan (US numerical postcode)

DICTIONARY OF TRAVEL, TOURISM AND HOSPITALITY

Part 6

Countries of the World

Countries of the World

English name	ISO code	Area (sq. m)	Area (sq. km)	Population[a] (000)	Capital	Currency	ISO/ IATA code	Political status[b]
Afghanistan	AF	251 773	652 225	25 869	Kabul	Afghani (Af) = 100 Puls	AFA	A
Albania	AL	11 100	28 748	3 375	Tirana	Lek (Lk) = 100 Quindarka	ALL	A
Algeria	DZ	919 595	2 381 741	29 950	Algiers	A. Dinar (DA) = 100 Centimes	DZD	A
American Samoa	AS	78	201	64	Pago Pago	US Dollar (US$) = 100 Cents	USD	C (US)
Andorra	AD	181	468	66	Andorra La Vella	Euro = 100 Cents	EUR	B (Fr/Sp)
Angola	AO	481 354	1 246 700	12 357	Luanda	Kwanza (KZ) = 100 Lwei	AOR	A
Anguilla	AI	37	96	11	The Valley	EC Dollar (EC$) = 100 Cents	XCD	B (UK)
Antigua and Barbuda	AG	171	442	67	St Johns	EC Dollar (EC$) = 100 Cents	XCD	A
Argentina	AR	1 075 518	2 780 400	36 580	Buenos Aires	A. Peso = 100 Centavos	ARS	A
Armenia	AM	11 484	29 743	3 809	Yerevan	Dram = 100 Luma	AMD	CIS
Aruba	AW	75	193	98	Oranjestad	A. Guilder (AFl) = 100 Cents	AWG	B (Neth)
Australia	AU	2 969 909	7 692 030	18 967	Canberra	Aus Dollar ($A) = 100 Cents	AUD	A
Austria	AT	32 378	83 859	8 092	Vienna	Euro = 100 Cents	EUR	A
Azerbaijan	AZ	33 400	86 600	7 983	Baku	A. Manat = 100 Gopik	AZM	CIS
Bahamas	BS	5 382	13 939	298	Nassau	B. Dollar (B$) = 100 Cents	BSD	A
Bahrain	BH	274	710	666	Al-Manamah	B. Dinar (BD) = 1000 Fils	BHD	A
Bangladesh	BD	56 977	147 570	127 669	Dhaka	Taka (Tk) = 100 Poisha	BDT	A
Barbados	BB	166	430	267	Bridgetown	B. Dollar (Bds$) = 100 Cents	BBD	A
Belarus	BY	80 153	207 595	10 032	Minsk	B. Rouble (R) = 100 Kopeks	BYB	CIS
Belgium	BE	11 787	30 528	10 226	Brussels	Euro = 100 Cents	EUR	A

DICTIONARY OF TRAVEL, TOURISM AND HOSPITALITY

English name	ISO code	Area (sq. m)	Area (sq. km)	Population[a] (000)	Capital	Currency	ISO/ IATA code	Political status[b]
Belize	BZ	8 867	22 965	247	Belmopan	B. Dollar (BZ$) = 100 Cents	BZD	A
Benin	BJ	43 484	112 622	6 114	Porto-Novo	Franc CFA = 100 Centimes	XOF	A
Bermuda	BM	21	53	64	Hamilton	B. Dollar (B$) = 100 Cents	BMD	C (UK)
Bhutan	BT	17 954	46 500	782	Thimphu	Ngultrum (Nu) = 100 Chetrum	BTN	A
Bolivia	BO	424 164	1 098 581	8 138	La Paz and Sucre	Boliviano (B$) = 100 Centavos	BOB	A
Bosnia and Hercegovina	BA	19 740	51 129	3 881	Sarajevo	Konvertibilna Marka (KM) = 100 Pfenings	BAM	A
Botswana	BW	224 607	581 730	1 588	Gaborone	Pula (P) = 100 Thebe	BWP	A
Brazil	BR	3 300 171	8 547 404	167 967	Brasilia	Real (R$) = 100 Centavos	BRL	A
Brunei	BN	2 226	5 765	322	Bandar Seri Begawan	B. Dollar (B$) = 100 Cents	BND	A
Bulgaria	BG	42 855	110 994	8 208	Sofia	Lev = 100 Stotinki	BGL	A
Burkina Faso	BF	105 870	274 200	10 996	Ouagadougou	Franc CFA = 100 Centimes	XOF	A
Burundi	BI	10 747	27 834	6 678	Bujumbura	B. Franc = 100 Centimes	BIF	A
Cambodia	KH	69 898	181 035	11 757	Phnom-Penh	New Riel = 100 Sen	KHR	A
Cameroon	CM	183 569	475 442	14 691	Yaounde	Franc CFA = 100 Centimes	XAF	A
Canada	CA	3 844 928	9 958 319	30 491	Ottawa	C. Dollar (C$) = 100 Cents	CAD	A
Cape Verde	CV	1 557	4 033	428	Praia	C.V. Escudo = 100 Centavos	CVE	A
Cayman Islands	KY	100	259	39	George Town	C.I. Dollar (CI$) = 100 Cents	KYD	C (UK)
Central African Republic	CF	240 535	622 984	3 540	Bangui	Franc CFA = 100 Centimes	XAF	A
Chad	TD	495 755	1 284 000	7 486	N'Djamena	Franc CFA = 100 Centimes	XAF	A
Chile	CL	291 930	756 096	15 018	Santiago	Chilean Peso = 10 Centavos	CLP	A
China	CN	3 695 500	9 571 300	1 253 595	Beijing	Ren Min Bi Yuan = 10 Jiao = 100 Fen	CNY	A
Colombia	CO	440 831	1 141 748	41 539	Bogota	Colombian Peso = 100 Centavos	COP	A
Comoros	KM	719	1 862	544	Moroni	Comoro Franc = 100 Centimes	KMF	A
Congo, Dem. Rep.	CD	905 365	2 344 885	49 776	Kinshasa	Congolese Franc = 100 Centimes	CDF	A
Congo, Rep.	CG	132 047	342 000	2 859	Brazzaville	Franc CFA = 100 Centimes	XAF	A
Cook Islands	CK	92	237	14	Avarua	NZ Dollar ($NZ) = 100 Cents	NZD	B (NZ)
Costa Rica	CR	19 730	51 100	3 589	San Jose	C.R. Colon (¢) = 100 Centimos	CRC	A
Côte d'Ivoire	CI	124 503	322 462	15 545	Abidjan	Franc CFA = 100 Centimes	XOF	A
Croatia	HR	21 831	56 542	4 464	Zagreb	Kuna = 100 Lipa	HRK	A
Cuba	CU	42 803	110 860	11 178	Havana	Cuban Peso = 100 Centavos	CUP	A

English name	ISO code	Area (sq. m)	Area (sq. km)	Population[a] (000)	Capital	Currency	ISO/ IATA code	Political status[b]
Cyprus	CY	3 572	9 251	760	Nicosia	Cyprus Pound (C£) = 100 Cents	CYP	A
Czech Republic	CZ	30 450	78 866	10 278	Prague	Czech Koruna (Kč) = 100 Hellers	CZK	A
Denmark	DK	16 640	43 096	5 326	Copenhagen	Danish Krone (Kr) = 100 Øre	DKK	A
Djibouti	DJ	8 958	23 200	648	Djibouti	Djibouti Franc = 100 Centimes	DJF	A
Dominica	DM	290	751	73	Roseau	EC Dollar (EC$) = 100 Cents	XCD	A
Dominican Republic	DO	18 696	48 422	8 404	Santo Domingo	Dominican Peso (RD$) = 100 Centavos	DOP	A
East Timor	TP	5 641	14 609	750	Dili	US Dollar (US$) = 100 Cents	USD	A
Ecuador	EC	105 037	272 045	12 412	Quito	US Dollar (US$) = 100 Cents	USD	A
Egypt	EG	386 174	1 002 000	62 655	Cairo	Egyptian Pound (£E) = 100 Piastres	EGP	A
El Salvador	SV	8 124	21 041	6 154	San Salvador	US Dollar (US$) = 100 Cents	USD	A
Equatorial Guinea	GQ	10 831	28 051	443	Malabo	Franc CFA = 100 Centimes	XAF	A
Eritrea	ER	46 774	121 144	3 991	Asmara	Nakfa = 100 Cents	ERN	A
Estonia	EE	17 462	45 227	1 442	Tallinn	Kroon = 100 Cents	EEK	A
Ethiopia	ET	437 600	1 133 380	62 782	Addis Ababa	Ethopian Birr (EB) = 100 Cents	ETB	A
Falkland Islands	FK	4 700	12 173	3	Stanley	F. Pound (FI£) = 100 Pence	FKP	C (UK)
Faroe Islands	FO	540	1 399	44	Torshavn	Danish Krone (Kr) = 100 Øre	DKK	B (Den)
Fiji	FJ	7 095	18 333	801	Suva	F. Dollar (F$) = 100 Cents	FJD	A
Finland	FI	130 559	338 145	5 166	Helsinki	Euro = 100 Cents	EUR	A
France	FR	210 026	543 965	58 620	Paris	Euro = 100 Cents	EUR	A
French Guiana	GF	32 253	83 534	157	Cayenne	Euro = 100 Cents	EUR	C (Fr)
French Polynesia	PF	1 609	4 167	231	Papeete	Franc CFP = 100 Centimes	XPF	C (Fr)
Gabon	GA	103 347	267 667	1 208	Libreville	Franc CFA = 100 Centimes	XAF	A
Gambia, The	GM	4 361	11 295	1 251	Banjul	Dalasi (D) = 100 Butut	GMD	A
Georgia	GE	26 911	69 700	5 452	Tbilisi	Lari = 100 Tetri	GEL	CIS
Germany	DE	137 846	357 022	82 100	Berlin	Euro = 100 Cents	EUR	A
Ghana	GH	92 100	238 537	18 785	Accra	Cedi = 100 Pesewas	GHC	A
Gibraltar	GI	2	6	27	Gibraltar	G. Pound (G£) = 100 Pence	GIP	C (UK)
Greece	GR	50 949	131 957	10 538	Athens	Euro = 100 Cents	EUR	A
Greenland	GL	836 330	2 166 086	56	Nuuk	Danish Krone (Kr) = 100 Øre	DKK	B (Den)
Grenada	GD	133	344	97	St George's	EC Dollar (EC$) = 100 Cents	XCD	A

COUNTRIES OF THE WORLD

DICTIONARY OF TRAVEL, TOURISM AND HOSPITALITY

English name	ISO code	Area (sq. m)	Area (sq. km)	Population[a] (000)	Capital	Currency	ISO/IATA code	Political status[b]
Guadeloupe	GP	658	1 705	422	Basse-Terre	Euro = 100 Cents	EUR	C (Fr)
Guam	GU	212	549	152	Hagatha	US Dollar (US$) = 100 Cents	USD	C (US)
Guatemala	GT	42 042	108 889	11 088	Guatemala City	Quetzal (Q) = 100 Centavos	GTQ	A
Guinea	GN	94 926	245 857	7 251	Conakry	G. Franc (FG) = 100 Centimes	GNF	A
Guinea-Bissau	GW	13 948	36 125	1 185	Bissau	Franc CFA = 100 Centimes	XOF	A
Guyana	GY	83 000	214 969	856	Georgetown	G. Dollar (G$) = 100 Cents	GYD	A
Haiti	HT	10 714	27 750	7 803	Port-au-Prince	Gourde = 100 Centimes	HTG	A
Honduras	HN	43 433	112 492	6 318	Tegucigalpa	Lempira = 100 Centavos	HNL	A
Hong Kong S.A.R.	HK	424	1 098	67	Victoria	HK Dollar (HK$) = 100 Cents	HKD	C (China)
Hungary	HU	35 919	93 030	10 068	Budapest	Forint = 100 Fillers	HUF	A
Iceland	IS	39 769	103 000	278	Reykjavik	Icelandic Krona (Kr) = 100 Aurar	ISK	A
India	IN	1 269 219	3 287 263	997 515	New Delhi	Indian Rupee (Rs) – 100 Paise	INR	A
Indonesia	ID	742 308	1 922 570	207 022	Jakarta	Rupiah (Rp) = 100 Sen	IDR	A
Iran	IR	636 296	1 648 000	62 977	Tehran	Iranian Rial (IR) = 100 Sen	IRR	A
Iraq	IQ	169 235	438 317	22 797	Baghdad	Iraqi Dinar (ID) = 20 Dirhams	IQD	A
Ireland, Republic of	IE	27 133	70 273	3 752	Dublin	Euro = 100 Cents	EUR	A
Israel	IL	8 550	22 145	6 105	Jerusalem	New Shekel = 100 Agorot	ILS	A
Italy	IT	116 346	301 338	57 646	Rome	Euro = 100 Cents	EUR	A
Jamaica	JM	4 244	10 991	2 598	Kingston	Jamaican Dollar (J$) = 100 Cents	JMD	A
Japan	JP	145 891	377 855	126 750	Tokyo	Yen = 100 Sen	JPY	A
Jordan	JO	37 738	97 740	4 740	Amman	Jordanian Dinar (JD) = 1000 Fils	JOD	A
Kazakhstan	KZ	1 049 150	2 717 300	14 927	Astana	Tenge = 100 Tein	KZT	CIS
Kenya	KE	224 081	580 367	29 410	Nairobi	Kenyan Shilling (Ks) = 100 Cents	KES	A
Kiribati	KI	313	811	88	Bairiki	Aus. Dollar ($A) = 100 Cents	AUD	A
Korea, PDR (North)	KP	47 399	122 762	23 414	Pyongyang	Won = 100 Chon	KPW	A
Korea, Rep. (South)	KR	38 345	99 313	46 858	Seoul	Won = 100 Chun	KRW	A
Kuwait	KW	6 880	17 818	1 924	Kuwait City	Kuwaiti Dinar (KD) = 1000 Fils	KWD	A
Kyrgyzstan	KG	76 600	198 500	4 865	Bishkek	Som = 100 Tyiyns	KGS	CIS
Lao, PDR	LA	91 400	236 800	5 097	Vientiane	New Kip (K) = 100 Cents	LAK	A
Latvia	LV	24 938	64 589	2 431	Riga	Lats (LVL) = 100 Santimi	LVL	A

English name	ISO code	Area (sq. m)	Area (sq. km)	Population[a] (000)	Capital	Currency	ISO/ IATA code	Political status[b]
Lebanon	LB	4 036	10 452	4 271	Beirut	Lebanese Pound (£L) = 100 Piastres	LBP	A
Lesotho	LS	11 720	30 355	2 105	Maseru	Loti = 100 Lisente	LSL	A
Liberia	LR	37 743	97 754	3 044	Monrovia	Liberian Dollar (L$) = 100 Cents	LRD	A
Libya	LY	685 524	1 775 500	5 419	Tripoli	Libyan Dinar (LD) = 1000 Dirhams	LYD	A
Liechtenstein	LI	62	160	32	Vaduz	Swiss Franc (SF) = 100 Rappen	CHF	A
Lithuania	LT	25 213	65 301	3 699	Vilnius	Litas = 100 Centas	LTL	A
Luxembourg	LU	999	2 586	432	Luxembourg-Ville	Euro = 100 Cents	EUR	A
Macau S.A.R.	MO	9	24	434	Macau	Pataca = 100 Avos	MOP	C (China)
Macedonia	MK	9 928	25 713	2 021	Skopje	Denar = 100 Deni	MKD	A
Madagascar	MG	226 658	587 041	15 051	Antananarivo	Malagasy Franc = 100 Centimes	MGF	A
Malawi	MW	45 747	118 484	10 788	Lilongwe	Kwacha (K) = 100 Tambala	MWK	A
Malaysia	MY	127 311	329 733	22 710	Kuala Lumpur	Ringgit (M$) = 100 Sen	MYR	A
Maldives	MV	115	298	269	Male	M.Rufiyaa = 100 Laari	MVR	A
Mali	ML	478 841	1 240 192	10 584	Bamako	Franc CFA = 100 Centimes	XOF	A
Malta	MT	122	316	379	Valetta	Maltese Lira (LM) = 100 Cents	MTL	A
Marshall Islands	MH	70	180	51	Majuro	US Dollar (US$) = 100 Cents	USD	A
Martinique	MQ	425	1 100	381	Fort-de-France	Euro = 100 Cents	EUR	C (Fr)
Mauritania	MR	397 950	1 030 700	2 598	Nouakchott	Ouguiya (UM) = 5 Khoums	MRO	A
Mauritius	MU	788	2 040	1 174	Port Louis	Mauritius Rupee = 100 Cents	MUR	A
Mayotte	YT	144	374	140	Dzaoudzi	Euro = 100 Cents	EUR	C (Fr)
Mexico	MX	754 120	1 953 162	96 586	Mexico City	M. Peso = 100 Centavos	MXN	A
Micronesia	FM	270	700	116	Pohnpei	US Dollar (US$) = 100 Cents	USD	A
Moldova	MD	13 050	33 800	4 281	Kishinev	Leu = 100 Bani	MDL	CIS
Monaco	MC	1	2	32	Monte Carlo	Euro = 100 Cents	EUR	A
Mongolia	MN	603 909	1 564 116	2 378	Ulan Bator	Tughrik = 100 Möngö	MNT	A
Montserrat	MS	40	102	5 000	Plymouth	EC Dollar (EC$) = 100 Cents	XCD	C (UK)
Morocco	MA	274 461	710 850	28 238	Rabat	M. Dirham (DH) = 100 Centimes	MAD	A
Mozambique	MZ	308 641	799 380	17 299	Maputo	Metical (MT) = 100 Centavos	MZM	A
Myanmar	MM	261 218	676 552	45 029	Yangon (Rangoon)	Kyat (K) = 100 Pyas	MMK	A
Namibia	NA	318 261	824 292	1 701	Windhoek	N. Dollar (N$) = 100 Cents also Rand (R) = 100 Cents	NAD ZAR	A

COUNTRIES OF THE WORLD

DICTIONARY OF TRAVEL, TOURISM AND HOSPITALITY

English name	ISO code	Area (sq. m)	Area (sq. km)	Population[a] (000)	Capital	Currency	ISO/ IATA code	Political status[b]
Nauru	NR	8	21	12	Yaren	Aus. Dollar ($A) = 100 Cents	AUD	A
Nepal	NP	56 827	147 181	23 384	Kathmandu	Nepalese Rupee (NR) = 100 Paisa	NPR	A
Netherlands	NL	16 034	41 528	15 805	Amsterdam and The Hague	Euro = 100 Cents	EUR	A
Netherlands Antilles	AN	309	800	215	Willemstad	NA Guilder (NA Fl) = 100 Cents	ANG	B (Neth)
New Caledonia	NC	7 172	16 575	209	Noumea	Franc CFP = 100 Centimes	XPF	C (Fr)
New Zealand	NZ	104 454	270 534	3 811	Wellington	NZ Dollar ($NZ) = 100 Cents	NZD	A
Nicaragua	NI	46 430	120 254	4 919	Managua	Cordoba (C$) = 100 Centavos	NIO	A
Niger	NE	489 191	1 267 000	10 496	Niamey	Franc CFA = 100 Centimes	XOF	A
Nigeria	NG	356 669	923 768	123 897	Abuja	Naira (N) = 100 Kobos	NGN	A
Niue	NU	101	263	2	Alofi	NZ Dollar (N) = 100 Cents	NZD	B (NZ)
Norfolk Island	NF	13	35	2	Kingston	Aus. Dollar ($A) = 100 Cents	AUD	C (Aus)
Northern Mariana Islands	MP	177	457	69	Saipan	US Dollar (US$) = 100 Cents	USD	B (US)
Norway	NO	125 004	323 759	4 460	Oslo	Norwegian Krone (Kr) = 100 Ore	NOK	A
Oman	OM	119 500	309 500	2 348	Muscat	Omani Rial (RO) = 1000 Baizas	OMR	A
Pakistan	PK	307 374	796 095	134 790	Islamabad	P. Rupee (RB) = 100 Paisa	PKR	A
Palau	PW	196	508	19	Koror	US Dollar (US$) = 100 Cents	USD	B (US)
Panama	PA	29 157	75 517	2 811	Panama City	Balboa (B) = 100 Cents	PAB	A
Papua New Guinea	PG	178 704	462 840	4 705	Port Moresby	Kina (K) = 100 Toea	PGK	A
Paraguay	PY	157 048	406 752	5 359	Asunción	Guarani (G) = 100 Centimos	PYG	A
Peru	PE	496 225	1 285 216	25 230	Lima	Nuevo Sol = 100 Centimos	PES	A
Philippines, The	PH	115 831	300 000	74 259	Manila	P. Peso = 100 Centavos	PHP	A
Poland	PL	120 728	312 685	38 654	Warsaw	Zloty = 100 Groszy	PLN	A
Portugal	PT	35 655	92 345	9 989	Lisbon	Euro = 100 Cents	EUR	A
Puerto Rico	PR	3 459	8 959	3 890	San Juan	US Dollar (US$) = 100 Cents	USD	B (US)
Qatar	QA	4 416	11 437	565	Doha	Q. Riyal (QR) = 100 Dirhams	QAR	A
Réunion	RE	968	2 507	706	Saint-Denis	Euro = 100 Cents	EUR	C (Fr)
Romania	RO	92 043	238 391	22 458	Bucharest	Leu = 100 Bani	ROL	A
Russian Federation	RU	6 592 850	17 075 400	146 200	Moscow	Rouble (R) = 100 Kopeks	RUR	CIS
Rwanda	RW	10 169	26 338	8 310	Kigali	Rwanda Franc = 100 Centimes	RWF	A
Samoa	WS	1 093	2 831	169	Apia	Tala = 100 Sene	WST	A

English name	ISO code	Area (sq. m)	Area (sq. km)	Population[a] (000)	Capital	Currency	ISO/ IATA code	Political status[b]
St Helena	SH	47	122	7	Jamestown	St Helena Pound (£) = 100 Pence	SHP	C (UK)
St Kitts and Nevis	KN	101	262	43	Basseterre	EC Dollar (EC$) = 100 Cents	XCD	A
St Lucia	LC	238	616	154	Castries	EC Dollar (EC$) = 100 Cents	XCD	A
St Pierre and Miquelon	PM	93	242	6	Saint Pierre	Euro = 100 Cents	EUR	C (Fr)
St Vincent and Grenadines	VC	150	389	111	Kingstown	EC Dollar (EC$) = 100 Cents	XCD	A
San Marino	SM	24	61	26	San Marino	Euro = 100 Cents	EUR	A
São Tome and Principe	ST	387	1 101	145	São Tome	Dobra (DB) = 100 Centimos	STD	A
Saudi Arabia	SA	864 869	2 240 000	20 198	Riyadh	Saudi Riyal (SR) = 100 Halalah	SAR	A
Senegal	SN	75 955	196 722	9 285	Dakar	Franc CFA = 100 Centimes	XOF	A
Seychelles	SC	176	455	80	Victoria	S. Rupee (SR) = 100 Cents	SCR	A
Sierra Leone	SL	27 699	71 740	4 949	Freetown	Leone (Le) = 100 Cents	SLL	A
Singapore	SG	255	660	3 952	Singapore City	S. Dollar (S$) = 100 Cents	SGD	A
Slovakia	SK	18 932	49 034	5 396	Bratislava	Slovak Koruna (Sk) = 100 Hallers	SKK	A
Slovenia	SI	7 820	20 253	1 986	Ljubljana	Tolar (SIt) = 100 Stotins	SIT	A
Solomon Islands	SB	10 639	27 556	429	Honiara	SI Dollar (SI$) = 100 Cents	SBD	A
Somalia	SO	246 201	637 657	9 388	Mogadishu	S. Shilling (So. Sh) = 100 Cents	SOS	A
South Africa	ZA	470 689	1 219 080	42 106	Pretoria et al.	Rand (R) = 100 Cents	ZAR	A
Spain	ES	194 897	504 782	39 410	Madrid	Euro = 100 Cents	EUR	A
Spanish North Africa	ES	12	32	130	Ceuta and Melilla	Euro = 100 Cents	EUR	C (Sp)
Sri Lanka	LK	25 299	65 525	18 985	Colombo	SL Rupee = 100 Cents	LKR	A
Sudan	SD	967 500	2 505 813	28 993	Khartoum	S. Dinar (SD) = 100 Piastres	SDD	A
Suriname	SR	63 037	163 265	413	Paramaribo	S. Guilder (Sf) = 100 Cents	SRG	A
Swaziland	SZ	6 704	17 363	1 019	Mbabane	Lilangeni (E) = 100 Cents	SZL	A
Sweden	SE	173 732	449 964	8 857	Stockholm	S. Krona (Kr) = 100 Ore	SEK	A
Switzerland	CH	15 940	41 284	7 136	Berne	Swiss Franc (SF) = 100 Centimes	CHF	A
Syrian Arab Republic	SY	71 498	185 180	15 711	Damascus	Syrian Pound (£S) = 100 Piastres	SYP	A
Taiwan	TW	13 900	36 000	22 034	T'aipei	New Taiwan Dollar (NT$) = 100 Cents	TWD	A
Tajikistan	TJ	55 251	143 100	6 237	Dushanbe	Somoni = 100 Diram	TJS	CIS
Tanzania	TZ	364 900	945 087	32 923	Dar es Salaam/Dodoma	Tanzanian Shilling = 100 Cents	TZS	A
Thailand	TH	198 115	513 115	60 246	Bangkok	Baht = 100 Satangs	THB	A

COUNTRIES OF THE WORLD

DICTIONARY OF TRAVEL, TOURISM AND HOSPITALITY

English name	ISO code	Area (sq. m)	Area (sq. km)	Population[a] (000)	Capital	Currency	ISO/ IATA code	Political status[b]
Togo	TG	21 925	56 785	4 567	Lomé	Franc CFA = 100 Centimes	XOF	A
Tokelau	TK	5	12	2	(No capital)	NZ Dollar ($NZ) = 100 Cents	NZD	B (NZ)
Tonga	TO	289	748	100	Nukualofa	Pa'anga ($T) = 100 Cents	TOP	A
Trinidad and Tobago	TT	1 980	5 128	1 293	Port of Spain	T & T Dollar (TT$) = 100 Cents	TTD	A
Tunisia	TN	63 170	163 610	9 457	Tunis	T. Dinar (TD) = 1000 Milliemes	TND	A
Turkey	TR	300 948	779 452	64 385	Ankara	Turkish Lira (TL) = 100 Kurus	TRL	A
Turkmenistan	TM	188 456	488 100	4 779	Askhabad	Manat = 100 Tenge	TMM	CIS
Turks and Caicos Islands	TC	166	430	17	Grand Turk	US Dollar (US$) = 100 Cents	USD	C (UK)
Tuvalu	TV	10	26	11	Funafuti	Aus. Dollar ($A) = 100 Cents	AUD	A
Uganda	UG	93 104	241 139	21 479	Kampala	U. Shilling = 100 Cents	UGS	A
Ukraine	UA	233 090	603 700	49 950	Kiev	Hryvna = 100 Kopiykas	UAH	CIS
United Arab Emirates	AE	30 000	77 700	2 815	Abu Dhabi	Dirham (Dh) = 100 Fils	AED	A
United Kingdom	GB	93 788	242 910	59 501	London	Pound Sterling (£) = 100 Pence	GBP	A
United States of America	US	3 787 319	9 809 155	278 230	Washington, DC	US Dollar (US$) = 100 Cents	USD	A
Uruguay	UY	68 037	176 215	3 313	Montevideo	U. Peso = 100 Centesimos	UYU	A
Uzbekistan	UZ	172 740	447 400	24 406	Tashkent	Sum = 100 Teen	UZS	CIS
Vanuatu	VU	4 707	12 190	193	Port Vila	Vatu	VUV	A
Venezuela	VE	352 144	912 050	23 707	Caracas	Bolivar (B) = 100 Centimos	VEB	A
Vietnam	VN	127 844	331 114	77 515	Hanoi	Dong = 100 Xu	VND	A
Virgin Islands (British)	VG	59	153	20	Road Town	US Dollar (US$) = 100 Cents	USD	C (UK)
Virgin Islands (US)	VI	134	347	120	Charlotte Amalie	US Dollar (US$) = 100 Cents	USD	C (US)
Wallis and Futuna	WF	62	161	14	Mata-Utu	Franc CFP = 100 Centimes	XPF	C (Fr)
Yemen	YE	207 286	536 869	17 048	San'a	Y. Riyal = 100 Fils	YER	A
Yugoslavia[c]	YU	39 449	102 173	10 616	Belgrade	New Dinar = 100 Para	YUM	A
Zambia	ZM	290 586	752 614	9 881	Lusaka	Kwacha (K) = 100 Ngwee	ZMK	A
Zimbabwe	ZW	150 872	390 757	11 904	Harare	Z. Dollar (Z$) = 100 Cents	ZWD	A

Abbreviations:
Aus. Dollar = Australian Dollar ($A).
EC Dollar = Eastern Caribbean Dollar (EC$).
Franc CFA = Franc de la Communauté financière africaine (African Franc).
Franc CFP = Franc des Comptoirs français du Pacifique (Pacific Franc).

Notes:
(a) Population figures refer to 1999.
(b) Political status is indicated in the last column as follows:

    A = independent countries.
    B = self-governing countries which are under protection of another country for defence and foreign affairs purposes.
    C = colonies and dependencies of other countries and Special Administrative Regions of China.

    Former republics of the USSR, which form the Commonwealth of Independent States, are labelled CIS.
(c) Yugoslavia: Following declarations of independence by Bosnia and Hercegovina, Croatia, Macedonia and Slovenia in 1991, Yugoslavia comprises Serbia and Montenegro.

Sources:
OAG Flight Atlas, December 2001, for country codes.
OAG Flight Guide Supplement, September 2001, for currencies and currency codes.
The Europa World Year Book 2001 for areas, capitals, currencies, political status and populations.
World Bank Atlas 2001 for populations.

COUNTRIES OF THE WORLD

Part 7

Bibliography

Dictionaries

Abercrombie, N., Hill, S. and Turner, B.S. (2000) *The Penguin Dictionary of Sociology*, 4th edn, London: Penguin Books

Baker, M.J. (ed.) (1990) *Macmillan Dictionary of Marketing and Advertising*, 2nd edn, London: The Macmillan Press

Beaver, A. (1993) *Mind Your Own Travel Business, A Manual of Retail Travel Practice.* Volume 3: *Cyclopaedia of Travel & Tourism Terminology*, Sponsored by Barclays Merchant Services

Clark, A.N. (1990) *The New Penguin Dictionary of Geography*, London: Penguin Books

Collin, P.H. (1994) *Dictionary of Hotels, Tourism and Catering Management*, Teddington: Peter Collin Publishing

Crystal, D. (ed.) (1994) *The Cambridge Biographical Encyclopaedia*, Cambridge: Cambridge University Press

Dervaes, C. (1994) *The Travel Dictionary*, 7th edn, Tampa, FL: Solitaire Publishing

Goldblatt, J. and Nelson, K.S. (eds) (2001) *The International Dictionary of Event Management*, New York: Wiley

Hall, R.J. and Campbell, R.D. (1991) *Dictionary of Aviation*, Oxford: BSP Professional Books

Harris, R. and Howard, J. (1996) *Dictionary of Travel, Tourism and Hospitality Terms*, Melbourne: Hospitality Press

Hart, N.A. (1996) *The CIM Marketing Dictionary*, 5th edn, Oxford: Butterworth–Heinemann

Metelka, C.J. (1990) *The Dictionary of Hospitality, Travel and Tourism*, 3rd edn, Albany, NY: Delmar Publishers

Pallister, J. and Isaacs, A. (1996) *Oxford Dictionary of Business*, 2nd edn, Oxford: Oxford University Press

Parry, M. (1997) *Chambers Biographical Dictionary*, Edinburgh: Chambers Harrap Publishers

Pass, C., Lowes, B. and Davies, L. (2000) *Collins Dictionary of Economics*, 3rd edn, Glasgow: Harper Collins Publishers

Reber, A.S. (1995) *Penguin Dictionary of Psychology*, 2nd edn, London: Penguin Books

Small, J. and Witherick, M. (1989) *A Modern Dictionary of Geography*, 2nd edn, London: Edward Arnold

Sullivan, E. (1992) *The Marine Encyclopaedic Dictionary*, 3rd edn, London: Lloyds of London Press

Torkildsen, G. (1994) *Leisure Management A to Z: A Dictionary of Terms*, Harlow: Longman

Vernoff, E. and Shore, R. (1987) *The International Dictionary of 20th Century*, London: Sidgwick & Jackson

Youell, R. (1996) *Complete A–Z Leisure Travel and Tourism Handbook*, London: Hodder & Stoughton

Directories and Yearbooks

Bord Fáilte, *Tourism Directory & Diary* (annual)

Columbus Press, *World Travel Atlas* (annual)

Europa Publications, *The Europa World Year Book* (annual)

OAG Worldwide, *OAG Flight Atlas* (biannual)

OAG Worldwide, *OAG Flight Guide* (quarterly)

OAG Worldwide, *OAG Guide to International Travel* (quarterly)

Office for National Statistics, *UK 2002: Official Yearbook of Great Britain and Northern Ireland* (annual)

Travel Trade Gazette, *Travel Trade Directory* (annual)

Union of International Organizations, *Yearbook of International Organizations* (annual)

J Whitaker and Sons, *Whitaker's Almanac* (annual)

Manuals

Buglear, J. (2000) *Stats to Go: A Guide to Statistics for Hospitality, Leisure and Tourism Studies*, Oxford: Butterworth–Heinemann

Eurostat (1990) *General Industrial Classification of Economic Activities within the European Communities (NACE)*, Luxembourg: Office for Official Publications of the European Community

Frechtling, D.C. (2001) *Forecasting Tourism Demand: Methods and Strategies*, Oxford: Butterworth–Heinemann

Huan, T.C. and O'Leary, J.T. (1999) *Measuring Tourism Performance*, Champaign, IL: Sagamore Publishing

International Association of Hospitality Accountants (1996) *A Uniform System of Accounts*, 9th rev. edn, New York: Hotel Association of New York City Inc.

International Labour Organisation (1993) *International Standard Classification of Occupations*, Geneva: ILO

Office for National Statistics (1992) *Standard Industrial Classification of Economic Activities 1992*, London: The Stationery Office

Office for National Statistics (2000) *Standard Occupational Classification*, London: The Stationery Office

Scarrott, M. (ed.) (1999) *Sport, Leisure and Tourism Information Services, A Guide for Researchers*, Oxford: Butterworth–Heinemann

Smith, S.L.J. (1989) *Tourism Analysis: A Handbook*, Harlow/New York: Longman/Wiley

Statistical Office of the United Nations (1990) *International Standard Industrial Classification of All Economic Activities (ISIC)*, 3rd revision, New York: United Nations

Syratt, G. (1995) *Manual of Travel Agency Practice*, 2nd edn, Oxford: Butterworth–Heinemann

Theobald, W. and Dunsmore, H.E. (2000) *Internet Resources for Leisure and Tourism*, Oxford: Butterworth–Heinemann

United Nations/World Tourism Organization (1994) *Recommendations on Tourism Statistics*, New York: United Nations

Veal, A.J. (1997) *Research Methods for Leisure and Tourism*, 2nd edn, London: Pitman

Sources of International Statistics

American Express, *World Tourism Overview* (annual)

Caribbean Tourism Organization, *Caribbean Tourism Statistical Report* (annual)

Eurostat, *Distributive Trade, Services and Transport* (monthly)

Eurostat, *Statistics in Focus: Distributive Trade, Services and Transport* (quarterly)

Eurostat, *Tourism: Annual Statistics* (annual)

Horwath International, *Worldwide Hotel Industry* (annual)

Pacific Asia Travel Association, *Annual Statistical Report* (annual)

Pannell Kerr Forster, *EuroCity Survey* (annual)

Pannell Kerr Forster, *Europe, Middle East and Africa Trends* (annual)

Pannell Kerr Forster, *Middle East and Africa City Survey* (annual)

World Bank, *World Bank Atlas* (annual)

World Tourism Organization, *Compendium of Tourism Statistics* (annual)

World Tourism Organization, *Yearbook of Tourism Statistics* (annual)

Sources of UK Statistics

British Tourist Authority, *Digest of Tourist Statistics* (annual)

British Tourist Authority, *Tourism Intelligence Quarterly* (quarterly)

British Tourist Authority, *Visits to Tourist Attractions* (annual)

English Tourism Council, *English Heritage Monitor* (annual)

English Tourism Council, *Sightseeing in the UK* (annual)

Office for National Statistics, *First Release – Overseas Travel and Tourism* (monthly)

Office for National Statistics, *Overseas Travel and Tourism MQ6* (quarterly)

Office for National Statistics, *Travel Trends* (annual)

Office for National Statistics, *Labour Market Trends* (monthly)

Office for National Statistics, *Social Trends* (annual)

TRI Hospitality Consulting, *United Kingdom Hotel Industry* (annual)

UK National Tourist Boards, *The UK Tourist* (annual)

Other Books

Boniface, B.G. and Cooper, C.P. (2001) *Worldwide Destinations: The Geography of Travel and Tourism*, 3rd edn, Oxford: Butterworth–Heinemann

Brown, F. (2000) *Tourism Reassessed: Blight or Blessing?* Oxford: Butterworth–Heinemann

Cooper, C., Fletcher, J., Gilbert, D. and Wanhill, S. (1993) *Tourism: Principles and Practice*, London: Pitman

Davis, B., Lockwood, A. and Stone, S. (1998) *Food and Beverage Management*, 3rd edn, Oxford: Butterworth–Heinemann

Gee, C., Makens, J. and Choy, D. (eds) (1997) *The Travel Industry*, 3rd edn, New York: Van Nostrand Reinhold

Goeldner, C.R., Brent Ritchie, J.R. and McIntosh, R.W. (2000) *Tourism: Principles, Practices, Philosophies*, 8th edn, New York: Wiley

Graham, A. (2001) *Managing Airports: An International Perspective*, Oxford: Butterworth–Heinemann

Hanlon, P. (1999) *Global Airlines: Competition in a Transnational Industry*, 2nd edn, Oxford: Butterworth–Heinemann

Holloway, J.C. (1998) *The Business of Tourism*, 5th edn, Harlow: Addison Wesley Longman

Jafari, J. (ed.) (2000) *Encyclopedia of Tourism*, London: Routledge

Jeffries, D. (2001) *Governments and Tourism*, Oxford: Butterworth–Heinemann

Khan, M., Olsen, M. and Var, Turgut (1993) *VNR's Encyclopaedia of Hospitality and Tourism*, New York: Van Nostrand Reinhold

Lockwood, A. and Medlik, S. (eds) (2001) *Tourism and Hospitality in the 21st Century*, Oxford: Butterworth–Heinemann

Mathieson, A. and Wall, G. (1982) *Tourism: Economic, Physical and Social Impacts*, Harlow: Longman

Medlik, S. (1997) *Understanding Tourism*, Oxford: Butterworth–Heinemann

Medlik, S. and Ingram, H. (2000) *The Business of Hotels*, 4th edn, Oxford: Butterworth–Heinemann

Middleton, V.T.C. and Clarke, J.R. (2001) *Marketing in Travel and Tourism*, 3rd edn, Oxford: Butterworth–Heinemann

Page, S.J. (1994) *Transport for Tourism*, London: Routledge

Swarbrooke, J. (2001) *The Development and Management of Visitor Attractions*, 2nd edn, Oxford: Butterworth–Heinemann

Swarbrooke, J. and Horner, S. (1999) *Consumer Behaviour in Tourism*, Oxford: Butterworth–Heinemann

DICTIONARY OF TRAVEL, TOURISM AND HOSPITALITY

International Journals

Annals of Tourism Research
quarterly from Elsevier Science Ltd (UK)
[http://www.elsevier.nl:80/inca/
publications/store/6/8/9/]

Current Issues in Tourism
bimonthly from Channel View Publications
(UK)
[www.channelviewpublications.com]

*International Journal of Contemporary Hospitality
Management*
7 issues p.a. from MCB University Press Ltd
(UK)
[http://www.mcb.co.uk/cgi-bin/journal/
ijchm]

International Journal of Hospitality Management
quarterly from Elsevier Science Ltd (UK)
[http://www.elsevier.nl:/inca/publications/
store/6/5/9/]

Journal of Ecotourism
quarterly from Channel View Publications
(UK)
[www.channelviewpublications.com]

Journal of Hospitality and Leisure Marketing
quarterly from Haworth Press Ltd (USA)
[http://web.spectra.net/cgi-bin/SoftCart.exe/
cgi-bin/haworth/jtitle_search?U+haworth+]

*Journal of International Hospitality, Leisure and
Tourism Management*
quarterly from Haworth Press Ltd (USA)
[http://web.spectra.net/cgi-bin/SoftCart.exe/
cgi-bin/haworth/jtitle_search?U+haworth+ojq
3050+]

Journal of Sustainable Tourism
quarterly from Channel View Publications (UK)
/www.channelviewpublications.com/

Journal of Travel and Tourism Marketing
quarterly from Haworth Press Ltd (USA)
[http://web.spectra.net/cgi-bin/SoftCart.exe/
cgi-bin/haworth/jtittle_search?U+haworth+]

Journal of Travel Research
quarterly from Sage Publications (UK)
[http://bus.colorado.edu/BRD/JTR.htm]

Journal of Vacation Marketing
quarterly from Henry Stewart Publications
(UK)
[www.henrystewart.com]

Tourism and Hospitality Research
quarterly from Henry Stewart Publications
(UK)
[www.henrystewart.com]

Tourism Economics
quarterly from In Print Publishing Ltd (UK)
[www.ippublishing.com]

Tourism Management
bimonthly from Elsevier Science Ltd (UK)
[http://www.elsevier.nl:80/inca/
publications/store/3/0/4/7/2/]

*Tourist Review/Revue de Tourisme/Zeitschrift für
Fremdenverkehr*
quarterly from International Association of
Scientific Experts in Tourism (Switzerland)
[www.aiest.org]

Travel and Tourism Analyst
bimonthly from Mintel International (UK)
/http://www.t-ti.com/

TTI Country Reports
quarterly from Mintel International (UK)
/http://www.t-ti.com/

International Time Zones

The Earth rotates through 360° in 24 hours, and so moves 15° every hour. The World is divided into 24 standard time zones, each centred on lines of longitude at 15° intervals.

The Greenwich meridian lies on the centre of the first zone. All places to the west of Greenwich are one hour behind for every 15° of longitude; places to the east are ahead by one hour for every 15°.

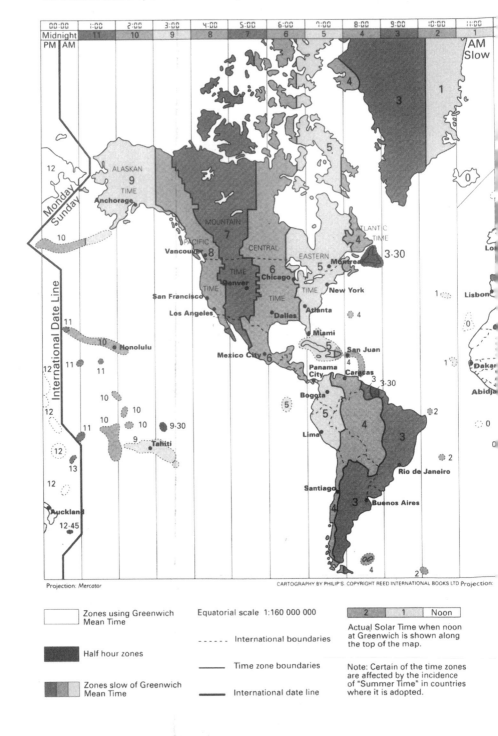

00:00	1:00	2:00	3:00	4:00	5:00	6:00	7:00	8:00	9:00	10:00	11:00
Midnight	11	10	9	8	7	6	5	4	3	2	1

PM | AM

AM Slow

Projection: Mercator

CARTOGRAPHY BY PHILIP'S. COPYRIGHT REED INTERNATIONAL BOOKS LTD Projection:

	Zones using Greenwich Mean Time	Equatorial scale 1:160 000 000		2	1	Noon

Actual Solar Time when noon at Greenwich is shown along the top of the map.

----- International boundaries

■ Half hour zones

Zones slow of Greenwich Mean Time

——— Time zone boundaries

——— International date line

Note: Certain of the time zones are affected by the incidence of "Summer Time" in countries where it is adopted.